D0506087

UNIVERSITY OF WALES

Explaining Labour's Second Landslide

Explaining Labour's Second Landslide

Robert Worcester
and
Roger Mortimore

First published in Great Britain 2001
Politico's Publishing
8 Artillery Row
Westminster
London
SW1P 1RZ

www.politicos.co.uk/publishing

A catalogue record for this book is available from the British Library.

ISBN 1 902301 84 6

Printed and bound by Creative Print and Design, Wales

Contents

List of tables   v
List of figures and graphs   ix

Foreword xi

Introduction...I
    What decides an election?   6

1. Blair's First Term: the 1997-2001 Parliament 17
    Labour tries to lose   17
      Teflon Tony   18
      Prudence Brown   23
      Labour's failure to deliver   31
      "Don't Panic, Don't Panic"   35
      "When in a hole, stop digging"   45
      The Petrol 'Crisis'   51
      Sleaze failed to impact   57
    Conservatives unfit to win   61
      Central Office   62
      Success at subsidiary elections   64
      Personal public recognition   67
      Re-uniting the Party behind its leader   68
      Hague's image as potential Prime Minister   71
      Credibility as an alternative government   76
      Identifying issues on which to fight the general election   81

2. Not just apathy: why two in five didn't vote.......................... 107
    Why was the turnout so low?   107
    Why people vote   111
    'Elections aren't important'   114
      Lack of interest is not the 'problem'   122
      Party Values   126
    'This election wasn't important'   135
    The lacklustre campaign   142

Interest in the campaign   142
The public's thirst for information   145
Media coverage of the election campaign   149
The party campaigns   166
Election advertising   170
The election and the Internet   173
'My vote doesn't count'   179
A foregone conclusion?   179
The electoral system   180
Labour's stay-at-homes in the safe seats   181
'I wanted to vote but I couldn't'   187
Voting by post   187
Other means of voting   190
Non-registration   193

3. The Result **195**
Middle ground, Middle England   195
The gender gap   199
The "grey" vote   205
Rural constituencies and rural voters   209
Foot & Mouth   214
Delaying the election   215
Religion and voting   218
How the Lib Dems won the campaign   221
Tactical voting   224
The Lib Dem appeal   226
The first devolved election   228

4. Pundits and Pollsters **233**
Predicting the result   233
The polls in the 2001 election   239
The pollsters   239
Non-national polls   244
Accuracy of the polls   246
Methodology   249
Exit polls   280
Private polls   286

Reporting the polls   289
   Seat projections and the ICM/*Guardian* 'Variometer'   290
   Constituency polls – how not to do it   295
   Headline News?   297
   Reporting focus groups   298
   Voodoo polls   300

5. The Second Term **305**
   Public hopes and expectations of government   305
   The referendum on the Euro   308
   Tory leadership   317

Conclusions **321**

Appendices **322**
   Appendix I: An Almost Infallible Forecasting Model   322
   Appendix II: Reflections on the Attacks by our Critics   325

Index **331**

List of tables

Table 1: 2001 British General Election - results 3
Table 2: How Britain voted, 2001 5
Table 3: The Political Triangle 1987-2001 10
Table 4: Relative importance of influences on vote 11
Table 5: Leo Blair and Voting Intention.. 11
Table 6: Leo Blair and Satisfaction with Tony Blair............................ 12
Table 7: Switching and Churning, 2001.. 13
Table 8: Switching and Churning, 1979-2001...................................... 14
Table 9: Politicians as strength or weakness to party 18
Table 10: Like or dislike Tony Blair and his policies 21
Table 11: Tony Blair: Leader Image 22
Table 12: Leader Image – Importance of attributes 23
Table 13: Public reaction to Budgets, 1976-2001................................ 27
Table 14: Best Party on Key Issues.. 30
Table 15: Has Labour kept its promises? 32
Table 16: Importance to the public of Labour's key promises............. 33
Table 17: Most capable Prime Minister 41
Table 18: Swing in Labour's marginal seats, Autumn 2000................. 55
Table 19: The Impression of Sleaze 58
Table 20: Blair's government more or less sleazy than Major's?........... 59
Table 21: Satisfaction with government pre- and post- Mandelson...... 60
Table 22: Most clear and united party 69
Table 23: Like or dislike William Hague and his policies.................... 73
Table 24: William Hague: Leader Image.. 74
Table 25: MORI Index of popular leadership 74
Table 26: Expectations in Government... 76
Table 27: Party with best team of leaders.. 78
Table 28: Party with best policies 78
Table 29: Party Image 79
Table 30: Rating the parties 81
Table 31: Most Important Issues facing Britain 83
Table 32: Effect of UKIP votes 88
Table 33: Tax and Spend 97
Table 34: Issues important in deciding vote 101
Table 35: Reasons for voting... 112
Table 36: The importance of voting 115

Table 37: The 'Michigan' Question 117
Table 38: Socio-Political Activism 118
Table 39: Trust in people to tell the truth 120
Table 40: Interest in politics 123
Table 41: Turnout projections from MORI's polls 125
Table 42: Political identification by vote 127
Table 43: Political identity and issues for the second term 129
Table 44: Political identity by demographics 132
Table 45: Political identity by readership 133
Table 46: Importance of who wins 136
Table 47: MORI Excellence Model – "Word of mouth" 137
Table 48: Leaders' average scores on positive and negative attributes. 139
Table 49: Parties' average scores on positive and negative attributes .. 139
Table 50: Public attitudes to manifestos 140
Table 51: Interest in election coverage 1992-2001 145
Table 52: Why undecided 146
Table 53: Trusted sources of political information 147
Table 54: Trust in the media 148
Table 55: Degree of media coverage – public attitudes 150
Table 56: Satisfaction with level of election information 151
Table 57: Summary of Newspaper Bias 153
Table 58: Scale of election coverage in national daily newspapers 153
Table 59: Stance of articles in national daily newspapers 155
Table 60: The Poison Index and Con-Lab bias Index 157
Table 61: Voting by national newspaper readership 159
Table 62: Readers' perceptions of newspaper bias, 1992-2001 161
Table 63: Stance and negativity of articles, by journalist 164
Table 64: Campaign penetration 1979-2001 166
Table 65: Effect of Labour's poll lead on voting intention 179
Table 66: Average change in percentage turnout by type of seat 183
Table 67: Certainty to vote by marginality, January-April 2001 185
Table 68: Average change in Conservative share by type of seat 185
Table 69: MORI final pre-campaign poll and result, 1997 and 2001 . 186
Table 70: Voting by social class 196
Table 71: Middle-class (ABC₁) voting 1974-2001 197
Table 72: The Gender Gap 1974-97 199
Table 73: Voting by sex, age and class 200

Table 74: Gender Gap by Age, 1983-2001 201

Table 76: Gender Gap by Age and Social Class, 2001 201

Table 77: "Grey Power": voting by electors aged 55+ 206

Table 78: Change in vote share 1997-2001 by rurality..................... 212

Table 79: Voting by religion... 220

Table 80: Change in party support during the campaign 221

Table 81: Definitely decided or may change mind............................. 223

Table 82: Issues important to vote in Scotland, Wales and London ... 228

Table 83: Pundits' predictions in the *Observer*, 13 May 2001........... 237

Table 84: The campaign polls, 2001... 241

Table 85: Polls on delaying the election, March 2001 243

Table 87: Non-national polls... 244

Table 88: The Final Polls, 2001... 246

Table 89: Accuracy of the polls, 1945-2001.................................... 247

Table 90: Error in the "Poll of Polls", 1945-2001 248

Table 91: Calculation of Voting Intention Figures 252

Table 92: Poll averages (monthly series), 2000................................ 259

Table 93: MORI Face to Face and Telephone Polls, 2000
                   – average findings 260

Table 94: MORI Face to Face and Telephone Polls, 2000
                   – comparison 261

Table 95: ICM, Gallup and MORI results, end of May 2001 264

Table 96: Recall of past vote in MORI's polls 1997-2001 272

Table 97: Likelihood of voting questions, 2001 276

Table 98: MORI, Gallup and ICM final polls 2001,
                   not re-percentaged.. 277

Table 99: Exit polls, 2001 280

Table 100: Scottish constituency polls, 2001 296

Table 101: Priorities for the next Government.................................. 305

Table 102: Support for possible government policies 306

Table 103: Expectations of Labour in its second term 307

Table 104: Attitudes to the Euro 312

Table 105: Trust in politicians on Europe... 315

Table 106: Best Tory leader after Hague 317

Table 107: Voting under alternative Tory leaders 318

Table 108: The Political Football 322

List of figures and graphs

Figure 1: Labour's Landslides 4
Figure 2: The Political Triangle 8
Figure 3: Tony Blair's Honeymoon 1997-9 19
Figure 4: Satisfaction with Mr Blair and the Government 1997-2001 .. 20
Figure 5: Labour lead and economic optimism 25
Figure 6: Best party on key issues 29
Figure 7: Labour's Slides and Recoveries in the polls, 2000-2001 42
Figure 8: The 'Mandelson effect' - nil 60
Figure 9: Satisfaction with William Hague 70
Figure 10: Leader Image 2001 (Perceptual map) 75
Figure 11: Party Image 2001 (Perceptual Map) 80
Figure 12: Leaving the EU 86
Figure 13: Nationalism and Europeanism 91
Figure 14: Public Services and Tax under a Tory government 100
Figure 15: Interest in politics over time 123
Figure 16: The Political Pie 127
Figure 17: Was the election interesting? 143
Figure 18: The e-MORI Technology tracker, May 2001 174
Figure 19: Use of the Internet 175
Figure 20: The campaign did matter! 224
Figure 21: The Euro – if the government were to urge... 314

Foreword

When Iain Dale, publisher, political junkie and book store proprietor *extraordinaire* approached us some time before the election to write a sequel to "Explaining Labour's Landslide", he asked what we planned to call it. "Explaining Labour's *Second* Landslide", I said cheerfully, having for four years irritated Tory Central Office by my confident pronouncement that the election would be on 3 May 2001 and that Labour would win by a second landslide. Early in the life of the last Parliament I began my steady forecast of a Labour majority of between 100 and 120 seats and held constant to that throughout the four years, even during that brief period when hit by the double whammy of first the deficit of the Dome and then the so-called 'petrol crisis', the Tories actually gained a lead over Labour in our poll for the News of the World, but never in our monthly polls for *The Times*.

I also irritated the Liberal Democrats by forecasting they would do badly when the election came, losing about 15 seats from their 1997 triumph of 46, to end with about 32 seats. They said they would win over 50. They did. I had put my money where my mouth was, betting with my friends Stuart Wheeler and Patrick Jay at IG Index selling LibDems at 40 at £100 a seat, figuring to make about £800.

Little did I know then that the Tories would have learned nothing from their 1997 hiding, and that, Bourbon-like, they would make all the mistakes they'd made in 1997 all over again. So in the third week of the 2001 election I cut my losses, losing £750, and instead bought LibDem seats at 46.5 for £150 a seat, hoping to break even. In the end, the Lib Dems' 52 seats enabled me to enough to chalk up a net loss of just £75, a close run thing. Wish they'd won one more seat!

Still, it's exciting if you are political junkies like Iain and me to be a part of the big game of politics, if only bit players. When you consider that political opinion polling is but 2% of the turnover of MORI, and less than that for NOP and Gallup (I don't know about ICM), it's an interesting diversion, certainly gets the name mentioned, and if you get it right, or close enough, it must be good for the image of MORI and of market research, although some of my partners and no doubt some of the industry would disagree. This is especially true in the case of focus groups, and the media's fascination with them, with those who do them, and what they find, which is just about anything they wish to find, or so it would seem from the leaks given out by the political parties during the campaign about the results of their focus groups.

There are many myths which arise from general elections, some deliberately planted and others arising out of commonly assumed 'fact', which sound and consistent research proves 'just ain't so', but the myths feed upon themselves, are repeated endlessly by pundits and commentators, and believed by those whose own prejudices support them. The myth that plagued me for five years following the 1992 election was that 'the public may tell pollsters that they are willing to pay higher taxes, but they don't vote that way in the polling booth!' I must have had that thrown into my teeth by over a hundred BBC interviewers during the five years between 1992 and 1997, and it was still being brought out after the 1997 election, despite my standard response in dozens of interviews on radio and television that in our poll for *The Times* on 29 April 1997, just before polling day, we found that despite their promise not to, 63% of the British public said they expected Labour to increase income tax, and that notwithstanding, gave them the biggest landslide of half a century. Now that myth can finally be laid to rest. Of course there are some who vote specifically against higher taxes, but there are some who vote against, or for, nearly anything you care to name. It's not a black and white thing; nothing in politics ever is.

Another continuing myth is the one of 'Shy Tories', who are waiting in their homes refusing to talk to pollsters or even lying to them saying they will be supporting Labour when really they are all along planning to vote for the Conservatives. These voters may exist in very small quantity, but they are nothing like Central Office would like us to believe, and that the exit polls in 1997 underestimated Labour's seats and overestimated the Tories was forgotten by the apologists in the media for the Tories and certainly by Central Office spin doctors. In fact, our 1997 exit poll for ITN from some 15,000 interviews taken in polling stations throughout the country on 1 May forecast 180 Conservative seats, 15 more than they got, and 410 seats for Labour, nine fewer than the 419 they won on the day.

In 2001, with NOP's exit poll for the BBC forecasting a Tory seat capture of 177 and MORI 154, we neatly bracketed the 166 the Conservatives actually got, so it's hard to see how Central Office and its apologists can get away with the 'shy Tory' argument yet again. But they and their sympathisers in the media and pundits who see what they want to see will, and already are, claiming that the polls are underestimating the Tory share of the vote, and steps will have to be taken if they are not to get egg on their face again (sic). Even ICM's Martin Boon has now recognised that their cherished 'shy Tories' are few and far between, quoted on the BBC's web site on 8 August 2001 as saying "The idea that there is a hidden army of Tory voters ... has simply been put to bed."

Which brings me to the biggest myth. That polls can be expected to do better than the laws of sampling and the reality of politics will let them. Much is made of 'which came closest', ignoring my avowal back in 1983 when MORI got it spot on that 95% of the pollsters' work is skill, and 5% luck[1], but if you are not lucky it's not a good business to be in. As I've so often said, if I were to send 100 interviewers out to a carefully selected sample of constituencies across the country on the day before the election, and armed them with precisely calibrated thermometers, instructed them to go to the highest point in the constituency, and at precisely 12 noon read the temperature and phone their reading back to our office where we would average the readings, which we would then publish as our 'forecast' of the temperature the following day, who would expect it to be precisely accurate? And as we have proven over and over again, public opinion is more mercurial than the weather.

Once again we have conducted a post-election recall survey, this time for the Electoral Commission, and among many other things asked when the voters made up their mind for whom they would vote. In 1992, as we reported in the June 2001 issue of *British Public Opinion* newsletter, we

---

[1] Later used as the title of a paper: Robert Worcester, 'Political opinion polling – 95 percent expertise and 5 percent luck', *Journal of the Royal Statistical Society Series A 159*, pp 5-20.

found from a similar survey that 8% of voters said they'd decided who to vote for in the final 24 hours of the election, after the pollsters had finished their fieldwork for forecasts published on the day. In 1997, when we didn't ask the question, NOP found 11% of voters in their exit poll saying that they had made up their minds on election day. And in 2001 the figure in MORI's post-election poll was 7%. This means that unless these 'shifters' exactly cancel each other out, the final result is bound to be a point or two different that the final published polls, yet our academic critics castigate us for our 'failures', as if we had some sort of magic ability to foretell the future. We don't, only the tools of our trade, which time and time again have proved to be more accurate than any 'expert' in assessing what is likely to happen on the day as was certainly the case in 2001.

Another myth is that little happened during the campaign, that voters didn't budge much apart from a rise in the Liberal Democrat's share. Since the calculation of share is a zero-sum game, it's surprising to see people who regard themselves as psephologists and political pundits saying that the polls recorded the rise for the LibDems but found no change in the voting intentions for the two main parties or the other parties. They've got to come from somewhere, folks!

Just for the record, this was not the most boring election in living memory, 1987 was. In fact, when we asked the public 'How interested would you say you are in news about the election?', six percent more people this time said they were interested than in 1997, and six percent more were also interested in politicians' speeches. Why then is there the impression that it was so boring? Because the media get bored, and in every election since I came here, bored news editors have sent bored reporters out to find bored people who will vox pop to say it is the most boring election they can recall. Boring.

* * * * * * *

Our own experience with the internet was of an important and interesting addition to the election process. I wrote a daily essay of c. 1,000 words on www.epolitix.com which was also added to their daily

Bulletin, which goes out to more than 3,500 subscribers to their email service. Roger wrote a daily article on the MORI web site, which again was sent out to the thousand-odd who have asked for an emailed download, which we provided free daily during the election and provide weekly in 'peacetime'.

Our own web site had c. 50,000 hits a day during the election, topping 100,000 on the 17 May, 22 May and on 6 June, and hitting an all-time high of just over 250,000 hits on election day itself. The spread of unique visitors was interesting: most, several thousand, of course, from the UK and the US, but 219 from Germany, 107 from Australia, 86 from Canada, 84 from Japan, 65 Dutch, 47 French, 43 each from Belgium and Italy, 31 from Ireland, and so on. There were four from Taiwan, Thailand, Indonesia and Colombia, five from Estonia and Malaysia and three from Iceland. Some of the singles are fun too: Guatemala, Bolivia, Mauritius, China, Bulgaria, Namibia and Uruguay. And there were some appreciative fan letters too. Robert Waller emailed in to say "I just thought I'd like to let you know how absolutely splendid I find the political commentaries on the MORI site, usually (but I know not always!) under Roger's name. These are informative, clear, well chosen and provide a body of fascinating and valuable electoral analysis of the highest quality. I at least appreciate them enormously and have been informing as many people as I can."

Let me then in conclusion pay tribute to the co-author of this second volume in what may turn out to be a trilogy of explaining Labour's landslides, Dr Roger Mortimore, without whose questioning eye and statistical brain there would have been even more errors than may have crept in as we go to press. We stand by our judgments; we apologise for any errors that have not been caught in the interactions that have passed between us both during and since the 2001 British General Election. I could have started this book without Roger; I certainly wouldn't have finished it, much less polished and refined it as he has done.

And to the political team at MORI, who put up with the long days and sometimes nights, the pressure of over 100 radio and television interviews between us, the incessant enquiries by mail, telephone, fax and now e-mail that arise daily from journalists, researchers, the parties and the public, which we try to the best of our ability to respond to, even when they are clearly party inspired, and threaten us with exposure for the biases that they are convinced we harbour since we don't agree with their view of the political scene.

To MORI's CEO Brian Gosschalk, the head of the political unit in earlier elections, to Simon Braunholtz, who led the team in 1997, now head of MORI Scotland, to Simon Atkinson, another former head of the Unit and of tremendous help in this election, to Jessica Elgood, current Political Unit head, who kept her cool, appeared on many radio and especially TV shows showing herself on top of the job, knowledgeable about not only polls but politics, and who proved a hit with BBC 24, who kept asking for her when they needed a pollster's comment.

Also to the other stalwarts on the team: Ben Marshall, Gideon Skinner, Roger Mortimore of course, Kully Kaur-Ballagan, Nick Gilby, Gregor Jackson, Amy Kirby and Suzanne Walton; to Dave Evans, James Edwards and Ian Goodspeed on the www.mori.com team, who ensured that our findings were up on the site as soon as our clients published them. And to Suzie Faulkner and the Field and Tab team and their interviewers, Rosemary Murrey and the gang at MORI Telephone Surveys, Barbara Lee and her troops at FACTS, and Kevin Wilks and his people at Numbers and Martyn Mayor at Infocorp; to Scott Phillips and Melanie Bye and the Systems team who made sure the computers didn't let us down during the crucial minutes between getting in the data and delivering it over to our media clients; to the other MORI executives who though not part of the core political team worked on some of the surveys we report in this book; to the research assistants and other staff, both permanent and temporary, who have helped us in various ways assemble some of the data we report, including Jan Thompson, Salli Barnard, Henry Mackintosh, Nicholas Ingrassia and Hans Noel; and to the rest of the c. 300 staff at MORI who watched us do what we had to do to 'get it right on the night'. Also thanks to Craig Hoy and his team at epolitix.com, who gave me access to the World Wide Web to comment on the election daily as it unfurled. I'm not sure who read my daily outpourings in total, but from their comments our competitors certainly did! And certainly to the team at ITN for making the Election Night Programme such fun to be part of, to ITN's consultant on the Exit Poll, Colin Rallings, and to our consultant, Robert Waller.

And finally, to our clients, without whose support and confidence we would not be publishing this book, for without witness from the electorate, we couldn't with certainty say what the voters, and non-voters, thought about it all. Foremost to that Dean of Political Journalists and Political Pundits Peter Riddell of *The Times* and to Brian MacArthur, Philip Webster, Peter Stothard and George Brock at *The Times*; to Chris Long, Nigel Dacre and Richard Tait at ITN, to Joe Murphy, Con Coughlin and Matthew D'Ancona on the *Sunday Telegraph*, Emma Duncan, Peter David and Bill Emmott on the *Economist*, Sam Younger and Nicole Smith at the Electoral Commission, and to the other clients and friends who in the long campaign took interest in what the public thinks about issuess of the day, Russell Twisk of the *Reader's Digest*, Peter Dobbie and Simon Walters of the *Mail on Sunday*, Trevor Kavanagh of the *Sun*, Stuart Kuttner, Robert Warren and Ian Kirby of the *News of the World*, John Pickett of *Saga Magazine*, to Michael Saunders at Schroder Salomon Smith Barney and all the many others.

Also thanks tongue-in-cheek to Stuart Millar in the *Guardian*, who has awarded me a much-deserved knighthood in his Campaign Diary on 14 May. To paraphrase General (Sir) Colin Powell, I can understand why an American like me can't have a knighthood, but I have a terrible time explaining it to Lady Worcester! Thanks anyway Stuart. Sir Bob it is (but don't tell President Bush; he wouldn't understand).

Robert M. Worcester
August 2001

Introduction

The British General Election of 2001 delivered the Labour Party's first ever working majority for a second full term – and what a majority! Not only a second victory, but a second landslide.

Yet though unprecedented it was no surprise. Nobody – not even the most hardened Conservative Central Office sceptics, trying to make themselves disbelieve the opinion polls by self-hypnosis – really doubted which party would win the 2001 election, and that was true long before the date was announced and the campaign underway. This was true, no matter what they said for public consumption, their continuing attacks on the polls and their expressions of confidence in the face of evidence to the contrary notwithstanding (in the case of both the Labour 'poor mouthing' and the Tories' slagging off the polls, adding to the public's cynicism towards politicians). The exception was the pronouncements early on by the Liberal Democrats who admitted cheerfully they were not expecting to form the next government, but expected to better their 1997 record – which they did.

What was always less certain – perhaps to the last minute, if you believed it possible that the polls were badly wrong – was whether Tony Blair would secure another landslide on the same scale as his 1997 victory, or whether the Tories could make up at least some ground and cut Labour's Commons majority to a less daunting size. For there were moments in the previous four years when Tony Blair looked far from an effortlessly all-conquering hero, when his surefootedness and his government's grasp of the public's affections looked severely shaken. Fortunately for Mr Blair, to echo one of his predecessors, there was no alternative.

It was an election that under other circumstances the Government might have lost, yet which the Opposition was not fit to win. Labour's vote fell by millions, but so did the Opposition's. Disillusionment with the choice they were being offered, with the whole political system which could reduce them to such a choice, and a lacklustre campaign by all parties persuaded many to stay at home altogether. So too, no doubt, did a

I

foregone conclusion with which few were so strongly dissatisfied as to be motivated to try and prevent it. Labour was the unenthusiastic yet clear choice of enough of the public to merit a second term, and enough of those voted to deliver it.

The mismanagement of Scotland, worse in Wales, and a disaster in London (poor Frank), the Gould memos, the slow hand-claps of the Women's Institute, the Dome, the Petrol Crisis, all dented the Prime Minister's image ratings and, momentarily, his party share. But none of these affected the voting intention for long, for when the electorate turned to alternatives, they did not see one that they thought viable, which is why I coined the phrase 'Black Thursday', 19 June 1997, when the Conservative Party chose William Hague to be their leader instead of Kenneth Clarke.

Ken Clarke wouldn't have won this election, but he might at least have climbed the foothills, to put the Conservatives in with an outside chance at the election after this one. As it is, no progress has been made, the Tory Party is still split on Europe, and divided parties don't win elections.

We said for the last four years that there was too big a mountain to climb for the Conservatives to get back in a single parliament. A year before the election I thought they'd make some headway, as the Prime Minister began to lose the Teflon coating he'd enjoyed the previous three years. From 2 May 1997 I was saying, in publications as diverse as *The Times* and *Red Pepper,* that it was likely that the next election would be fought in 2001, and that Labour would win by another landslide, expecting the magnitude of that margin to be of the order of an 100-120 seat majority.

As the election itself began, our dismay at the way the Conservatives were managing their campaign caused us to slide the estimate upwards (as did, to be fair, Peter Kellner) first in my case to '140-150', then to 'perhaps 180-200', and then to 'over 200', but in the final few days, as a result of watching the turnout estimates stay low and the Liberal Democrats' campaign take off, we reduced it back to under 200, and at the KPMG non-executive directors' breakfast meeting of some 80 guests on 5 June, as the speaker of the day I announced that my best guess would be a majority of 166, thus hedging my bet between an overall majority of between 165 and 167. Two days later, it was determined to be 167.

Table 1: 2001 British General Election - results

	SEATS (n)			SHARE OF VOTE (% - GB only)			VOTES (millions – GB only)		
	1997	2001	Change	1997	2001	Change	1997	2001	Change
Conservative	165	166	+1	31.4	32.7	+1.3	9.59	8.36	-1.24
Labour	419*	413*	-6	44.4	42.0	-2.4	13.52	10.72	-2.80
Lib Dems	46	52	+6	17.2	18.8	+1.6	5.24	4.81	-0.43
SNP	6	5	-1	1.9	1.8	-0.1	0.78	0.66	-0.12
PC	4	4	0	0.5	0.8	+0.3	0.81	0.00	-0.81
Others	19	19	0	4.6	3.9	-0.7	0.55	1.01	+0.46
TOTAL	659	659		100.0	100.0		30.49	25.56	-4.93
Majority	179	167	-12	13.0	9.3	-3.7			
Swing						1.85			

*Including the Speaker

3

Figure 1: Labour's Landslides

1997: Labour's First Landslide

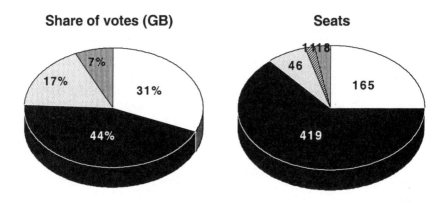

Share of votes (GB)

Seats

2001: Labour's Second Landslide

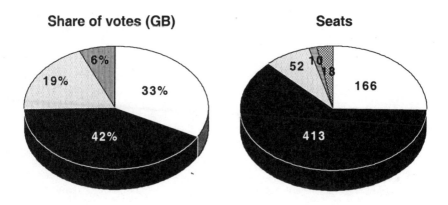

Share of votes (GB)

Seats

Table 2: How Britain voted, 2001

	Vote share 2001				Lead	Change since 1997			Swing	Turn-out
	Con	Lab	LD	Other		Con	Lab	LD		
	%	%	%	%	%	%	%	%		%
All	33	42	19	6	-9	+2	-2	+2	+2.0	59
Gender										
Men	32	42	18	8	-10	+1	-3	+1	+2.0	61
Women	33	42	19	6	-9	+1	-2	+1	+1.5	58
Age										
18-24	27	41	24	8	-14	0	-8	+8	+4.0	39
25-34	24	51	19	6	-27	-4	+2	+3	-3.0	46
35-44	28	45	19	8	-17	0	-3	+2	+1.5	59
45-54	32	41	20	7	-9	+1	0	0	+0.5	65
55-64	39	37	17	7	+2	+3	-2	0	+2.5	69
65+	40	39	17	4	+1	+4	-2	0	+3.0	70
Social Class										
AB	39	30	25	6	+9	-2	-1	+3	-0.5	68
C₁	36	38	20	6	-2	-1	+1	+2	-1.0	60
C₂	29	49	15	7	-20	+2	-1	-1	+1.5	56
DE	24	55	13	8	-31	+3	-4	0	+3.5	53
Work Status										
Full time	30	43	20	7	-13	-1	-1	+2	0.0	57
Part time	29	43	21	7	-14	-3	-2	+5	-0.5	56
Not working	36	41	18	5	-5	+5	-3	+1	+4.0	63
Unemployed	23	54	11	12	-31	+8	-10	-1	+9.0	44
Male Full-Time	30	43	19	8	-13	-1	-1	+2	0.0	57
Female Full-Time	29	44	21	6	-15	-2	0	+2	-1.0	55
Self-employed	39	32	18	11	+7	-1	0	-1	-0.5	60
Private sector†	33	42	18	7	-9	0	-4	+3	+2.0	52
Public sector†	24	46	23	7	-22	+1	-4	+4	+2.5	60
Housing Tenure										
Owner	43	32	19	6	+11	+2	0	-1	+1.0	68
Mortgage	31	42	20	7	-11	-2	-1	+2	-0.5	59
Own/mortgage ABC₁	40	33	22	5	+7	-1	+1	+2	-1.0	66
Own/mortgage C₂DE	31	47	15	7	-16	+2	-2	-1	+2.0	57
Council/HA	18	60	14	8	-42	+3	-4	+2	+3.5	52
Private rent	28	40	25	7	-12	+2	-8	+5	+5.0	46
Ethnicity†										
White	33	41	19	7	-8	+1	-1	0	+1.0	60
Non-white	12	73	13	2	-61	-6	+3	+4	-4.5	47
Trade Union†										
Member	21	50	19	10	-29	+3	-7	+1	+5.0	63
Non-member	36	40	19	5	-4	+2	-2	+2	+2.0	58

Source: MORI election aggregate, 2001

Base: 18,657 adults aged 18+, interviewed 8 May-6 Jun 2001

These estimates of the British electorate's voting behaviour are based on the aggregate of all MORI's surveys during the election, involving interviews with 18,657 British adults aged 18+. The data is weighted at regional level to the final result and turnout of the election (taking those who said they were "certain to vote" as having voted in line with their voting intentions, and the remainder as having not voted). Comparisons are with MORI's final election aggregate for 1997.

†: Variables not measured on all surveys; figures from surveys for *The Times*, total sample 6,231.

What decides an election?

What decides an election? In the final analysis, of course, it is the voters. That is why this book is being written. There will be a dozen or more books published on the 2001 election, from instant books by journalists to dense academic tomes. Some will concentrate on the politicians, the decision makers and the spin doctors – how and why the campaign was fought. Some will concentrate on the media and the coverage, or the party foot-soldiers at the grass-roots or other aspects of the parties' attempts to deliver their message. Some, of course, will discuss the turnout and wonder what can be done to improve it. Many will analyse the statistics of the results, and derive conclusions from the constituency variations or regional trends. Some will be collections of essays covering most of these topics.

But, if past experience is any guide, none apart from this one will concentrate on viewing the election, its participants and the circumstances surrounding it, from the point of view of the voters themselves – and, let it not be forgotten, of the non-voters. Our aim is to draw on the evidence of the opinion polls, whose sole function is to measure and report what the public (or rather a representative sample of it) thinks and believes. It is their election; and this, as far as we can make it, is their book.

What decides an election? What the members of the public think, and what they believe, and what they want. And this is what opinion polls are for: they can provide understanding, analysis and tracking of the behaviour, knowledge, opinions, attitudes and values of the public. By measuring this, within the limits of the science of sampling and the art of asking questions, surveys can determine what people do and what they think. Their beliefs may be wrong, their motivations misguided or the way in which they use their vote to sustain their values naïve, but it is their perceptions that matter. As we have said many times, quoting the first century slave-philosopher Epictetus, 'Perceptions are truth, because people believe them'.

What do the public think, and why? Is an election worth taking an interest in at all? Is this election, in particular? If so, which party would suit them best? Which is the most competent, has the most trustworthy or able leader, which has the most desirable or realistic policies on the issues that each voter cares about? Can that party win the election? Can it win this constituency? Is its candidate a fit and proper person to be a member of Parliament? And, when all is weighed and measured, is it worth the trouble of voting at all? Indeed, for an elector in ill-health or with heavy commitments, is it actually practical to vote?

Our hope is to explore how the public answer some or all of these questions, and why the answers put Tony Blair back in 10 Downing Street in June 2001 with such a commanding majority, in spite of the failings of his first Labour government.

More than thirty years ago, when first working as the Labour Party's private pollster, I developed a basic model[2] of the electorate's decision making that gave a framework to the polling. At its centre was what I later called the political triangle, the three interacting aspects of overwhelming importance by which voters choose between competing governments in Britain – their attitudes to the parties themselves, their leaders (as candidates for the premiership) and their policies on the issues facing the country. Later I developed it to incorporate values, not so much as a fourth dimension but as a deeper understanding of how the other three were viewed and the rock upon which they rested. The model also incorporated the question of whether to vote at all, though never before the 2001 election did this ever become of more than marginal importance.

---

[2] The development of the model is described in more detail in Robert M Worcester, *British Public Opinion* (Basil Blackwell, 1991) and in Robert M Worcester and Roger Mortimore, *Explaining Labour's Landslide* (Politico's Publishing, 1999), pp 43-8.

Figure 2

The Political Triangle©, 2001

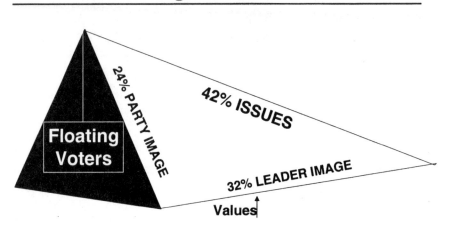

Base: 1,018 British adults 18+, 29 May 2001. Source: MORI/*The Times*

What decides an election? It is image above all, the electors' image of the personalities of the leaders and the leadership of the parties, the image of the parties fighting the campaign, and the consonance and dissonance of the image the elector has of his or her view of the issues and how they relate to what the parties have put on offer, all viewed in the light of electors' own values. And it's do you care at all.

Few voters like to admit that they are moved by 'image', and no sensible politician would admit he values image over substance (though, admit it or not, he will find it easier to be re-elected if he does). So issues, rather than leader image or party image, tends to be the 'respectable' face of the triangle. Politicians and pundits alike declaim that 'this election should be about the issues'. Yet personalities intrude. In the four-sided tetrahedron that drives this model of voting behaviour, 'values' count for most, as roughly 80% of the public have their mind made up before any election is called, and most of them don't change the habits of a lifetime.

That is not to say that individuals don't switch their allegiance from one party to another over the course of a number of elections. Nevertheless

8

the 'core' vote for the Tories is about 30%, tested nearly to destruction in 1997, and again in 2001; the 'core' vote for Labour is about 30%, tested beyond destruction in 1983, and the 'core' vote for the collective others, Lib Dems, Nationalists, etc., is about 20% or a bit more, as proven in the European Parliamentary elections in 1989 when the Greens soared to 15% as the Liberals and the Social Democrats were falling out of bed. That leaves 20% who determine not only the outcome, but also the magnitude of every general election result.

But this 20% are not of equal importance in every constituency. Only in the marginal constituencies, which might conceivably change hands – usually around one constituency in five but in this past election one in four – do votes matter. So only 20% of the voters in 25% of the constituencies, about one voter in twenty in total, 5% of those who vote, determine the result of this, and every other one of the nine elections since I've been here closely monitoring British general elections. On a turnout of 59%, this means 3% of the adult population. Just three people in a hundred helped determine the outcome of the 2001 British general election. That's what the election campaign was about: finding these three people in a hundred, identifying what it is that would make them shift from one party to another, and convincing them that they should or should not. Just three people in a hundred.

Issues don't count for as much as perhaps they should in an election, for four very good reasons:

- **Salience:** If people don't care about an issue, one party or another's argument is not going to sway that voter to move his or her allegiance.
- **Discernment:** If people don't discern differences between the parties on the issues they care about, then they are not going to change their allegiance either to support the party which they think has a sound policy on the issue they care about, or reject a party which they don't think has the best policy on that issue.
- **Ability:** If people don't think the party that has the best policy on the issue they care about has the ability (power) to do something about it, they won't be moved; and

- **Will**: If people don't think the party that has the best policy on the issue they care about has the will to something about it, they won't be moved.

There are precious few issues that can jump those four hurdles. Consistently, more than 40% of the determinants of the 'floating voters' are issues (42% according to our survey to test it during the 2001 election[3]), and the remaining 60% image, generally these days more leader image than party.

Table 3: The Political Triangle 1987-2001

Q (To all giving a voting intention) I want you to think about what it is that most attracted you to the …. party. Some people are attracted mainly by the policies of the party, some by the leaders of the party and some because they identify with the party as a whole. If you had a total of ten points to allocate according to how important each of these was to you, how many points would you allocate to the leaders of the party you intend voting for, how many to its policies, and how many to the party as a whole? Please bear in mind that the total of all your points should add up to ten. (Mean scores out of ten are converted into percentages)

	1987	1992	1997	2001
	%	%	%	%
Policies	44	47	41	42
Leaders	35	33	34	32
Parties	21	20	23	24

Source: MORI

A separate series of questions, devised in collaboration with Dr Paul Baines of Middlesex University for a joint paper due out next year, found similar preference for policies though with the differences less marked. (Table 4.) Interestingly, parties were given more prominence when the question was about "the values that each party stands for" than in the trend question that mentions simply identifying with the party as a whole[4].

One point to remember is that the public is always fickle, and this is especially true today. Essentially trivial factors can swing the polls, and perhaps indeed affect the results of elections.

---

[3] MORI survey for *The Times*, published on 31 May. MORI interviewed 1,013 British aged 18+ on 29 May 2001.

[4] MORI interviewed 1,928 British aged 18+ on 24-30 May 2001.

Table 4: Relative importance of influences on vote

Q. *From this card, how important, if at all, would you say the things I am going to read out will be in helping you decide how to vote in the general election?*

		Very important	Fairly important	Not very important	Not at all important	Don't know
The parties' policies on national issues	%	58	30	5	4	3
The parties' policies on issues that affect your local area	%	52	32	9	4	3
The values that each party stands for	%	51	31	9	5	4
The parties' leaders	%	46	33	12	6	3
The quality of your local candidates	%	38	34	15	6	7

Source: MORI
Base: 1,928 British aged 18+, 24-30 May 2001

Take as a case in point the birth of a fourth child to the Prime Minister a year before the election. MORI's monthly poll for *The Times* in May 2000 was conducted, as it happened, over the weekend when Leo Blair was born: almost half the interviews were completed by Friday night, before the birth was announced, and the remainder in the next couple of days. By weighting each half of the sample separately to the national profile, to ensure that the two sub-samples are entirely comparable, we can see exactly what effect the arrival of Leo Blair had on the state of public opinion.

As Table 5 shows, the effect was dramatic; in voting intention, there was a 3% swing to Labour from the Conservatives, and Mr Blair's personal satisfaction score rose six points, from 45% to 51%.

Table 5: Leo Blair and Voting Intention

	Interviewing	Con %	Lab %	LD %	Other %	Lead
MORI/*Times* (1st half) (Leo Blair born)	18-19 May 2000	34	46	14	6	-12
MORI/*Times* (2nd half)	20-23 May 2000	31	49	14	6	-16

Source: MORI/*The Times*
Base: c. 2,000 British aged 18+, 18-23 May 2000

Table 6: Leo Blair and Satisfaction with Tony Blair

Q. *Are you satisfied or dissatisfied with the way Mr Blair is doing his job as Prime Minister?*

	Interviewing	Satisfied %	Dissatisfied %	Don't know %	Net
MORI/ *Times* (1st half)	18-19 May 2000	45	42	13	+3
(Leo Blair born)					
MORI/ *Times* (2nd half)	20-23 May 2000	51	40	9	+11

Source: MORI/ *The Times*
Base: c. 1,000 British aged 18+, 18-23 May 2000

To understand the scale of the impact a little better, we might convert the percentages into numbers. Tony Blair's satisfaction score rose by 6%: in other words, two-and-a-half million people went to bed on Saturday night dissatisfied with his performance as Prime Minister, and changed their minds the following morning.

Who was it who swung? Almost exclusively those who live in households with no children – apparently the sight of Tony and Cherie cuddling Leo was less impressive to those who have kids of their own – and working class Britons (C_2DEs) rather than the middle class (ABC_1s) – probably because they are less likely to take a deep interest in politics, and therefore more susceptible to changing impressions, image or mood. Regular readers of broadsheet newspapers showed no Leo effect at all; indeed, Labour's share of their vote fractionally fell over the weekend – perhaps they see through the spin? But tabloid readers swung, and those reading no daily title regularly swung even more. In understanding why the public has become more fickle over the years, it may not be entirely irrelevant that the same period has seen an increase in the number who do not read a national daily paper regularly (though of course that may be as much symptom as cause of political disengagement).

People often criticise opinion polls because they seem to fluctuate wildly over time. (Others of course criticise them because they don't!) But if a single event, so apparently irrelevant, can have this much effect on public opinion then it would hardly be surprising if events of real political moment can produce swings over days and weeks. Election panel studies, which interview the same people more than once, bear out this impression of volatility.

During the 1997 election we interviewed a panel of voters twice for the *Evening Standard*, once towards the start of the campaign and again the day before polling, and found that a quarter of them had changed their answers. In 2001, with the second wave of interviewing after polling day, it was more than a third, although the number switching between the main parties had fallen.

Table 7: Switching and Churning, 2001

A sample of c. 1,000 electors in Great Britain who had been asked their voting intention during the first week of the campaign were re-interviewed after the election and asked whether they had voted and, if so, for which party. The table shows the percentages giving each answer on each wave. As the final column shows, the reported vote was close to the final result although - as is usually the case with panels - it under-represented abstainers.

	Voting intention (1st week)								
%	Con	Lab	LD	SNP/ PC	Green	Other	DK†	Total %	Reper- centaged %
Reported vote:									
Conservative	18.0	1	0.5	0.2	0	0.2	3.3	23.2	31
Labour	0.9	26.1	0.5	0.7	0	0.2	3.0	31.4	42
Liberal Democrat	1.2	2.6	7.1	0	0.1	0.2	3.0	14.3	19
SNP	0	0	0	0.8	0	0	0.2	1	1
Plaid Cymru	0	0	0	0.6	0	0.1	0	0.7	1
Green Party	0.1	*	0.1	0	0.1	0	0	0.3	*
UKIP	0.2	0	0.1	0	0	0	0.1	0.4	1
Other	0.2	0.6	0.2	0	0.2	0.1	2	3.2	4
Refused	0.2	0.8	0.7	0	0	0.1	4.4	6.2	
Did not vote	2.8	4.8	1	0.8	0.7	0.3	9.2	19.6	
Total	23.5	35.9	10.2	3.1	1.1	1.1	25.2		

†DK = "Would not vote", "undecided" or "refused"
*= Less than 0.05% but greater than zero
Source: MORI

The 'churn' (those switching between parties, don't knows who voted and those who gave a voting intention but didn't vote or refused to say) in the sample was 33.7%, more than we have ever found before. Switching between parties alone, though, accounted for 9.9%, of which

6.7% was switching between the three major parties; this suggests there was less switching between the parties in 2001 than in any of the previous five elections. But even 6.7% represents two-and-a-half million adults.

Table 8 gives figures from previous elections.

Table 8: Switching and Churning, 1979-2001

	Switching between three major parties %	Switching (all parties) %	Total 'churn' %
1979	8.2	10.1	24.7
1983 *	7.8	n/a	14.9
1987 *	8.4	9.0	18.5
1992	9.5	12.2	26.7
1997 *	7.3	11.1	27.2
2001	6.7	9.9	33.7

*Figures in 1983, 1987 and 1997 are not directly comparable to 2001, as the re-interviews were pre-election.

Source: MORI

Furthermore, in the last two elections far more people have been keeping an open mind and said that they had not definitely decided, right up to polling day, than has been the case in the past. At the start of the 1987 campaign, 25% of the public said they might change their mind before they voted, but this had fallen to only 11% in our final poll a month later. In 1992 the waverers started at 32% and fell to 16%. But in 1997, it started at 25% and had only fallen to 21% by the end of the campaign. In 2001 we found 32% saying they might change their mind in the first poll after the election was called, but there were still 21% wavering on the Tuesday before polling day. With an electorate this volatile, it is plain that a campaign, or even a single incident, has the power to materially alter the result of an election. Nor does it help the opinion polls' job of predicting the outcome in their final polls!

Because the floating voters are predominantly less interested in politics and less well informed about it, the floating vote can be easily swung in the right circumstances. On the other hand, once the floating voters have made up their mind about an issue or a person, that decision may be very resilient and not easily altered – especially if it is a negative or dismissive one. This is the problem the Liberal Democrats always have (floating voters tend not to consider them as a viable alternative) and was the problem the Tories had in 2001 (floating voters still adhered to the negative image of the party that they had acquired during the last years of the Major government, and embellished it with a dismissively negative image of William Hague). Wise political leaders bear this in mind, which is why 'spin doctors' have become so important in modern elections: the superficially trivial can swing millions of minds and millions of votes, a single gaffe or story can brand a politician for life. There are many who would consider spin doctors and their 'black art' to be an abomination in any democratic political system, but they earn their place in a politician's team because what they do works.

Is all this just a sign of the degenerate state of British politics as we enter the 21st Century? Well, maybe. But a degree of fickleness in the electorate is nothing new. When the date of the 2001 election was finally announced, much comment was made to the effect that Mr Blair was tempting fate because England were due to play a World Cup football match in Greece the evening before polling day. Why did this concern them? They were harking back thirty years, as it happens to the first election in which MORI polled – there are many Labour supporters of a certain age who are still convinced in their heart of hearts that Harold Wilson would have defeated Ted Heath in 1970 if only West Germany hadn't knocked England out of the World Cup a couple of days earlier. Substantive issues have their place, of course, but mood is too important to be neglected. It's still the voters who decide an election.

1. Blair's First Term: the 1997-2001 Parliament

Labour tries to lose

How did the record of the government and Prime Minister over four years contribute to their entering the election as certain winners?

In other circumstances, it might have been a negative. It was a much-touted maxim in the past that oppositions don't win elections, governments lose them. This time Labour might be said to have tried, and failed. Labour in government did almost everything wrong, especially in the latter part of the Parliament: they were caught spinning, putting appearances before substance, they became smeared with the suspicion of sleaze and the undeniable fact of 'cronyism', they were seen to have failed to deliver on most of their key promises. They alienated Old Labour with a Thatcherised, non-socialist agenda, then disappointed the voters New Labour attracted by failing to deliver on it.

That they were able to survive none the less and return for a second landslide victory owes a great deal to the weakness of the Opposition, but also to two assets – the strength of the economy and Gordon Brown's reassuring stewardship of it, and to Tony Blair's own image as leader.

On the eve of the election campaign, we asked the public[5] about each of a list of twelve leading figures – whether they had heard of them and, if so, whether they were a strength or weakness to their party. Though a number on the list came out with positive scores, it was Brown and Blair who easily led the way. Sadly for the Tory Party, their leader took the wooden spoon.

---

[5] MORI survey for the *Sun*, published on 2 May. MORI Telephone Surveys interviewed 1,008 British aged 18+ on 30 April-1 May 2001.

Table 9: Politicians as strength or weakness to party

Q. I am going to read out a list of politicians. For each one you know would you say they are a strength or a weakness to their party?

	Strength	Weakness	Don't know him/her	No opinion	Net
	%	%	%	%	±%
Gordon Brown	63	18	10	9	+45
Tony Blair	66	24	3	7	+42
David Blunkett	49	20	19	11	+29
Charles Kennedy	39	19	28	14	+20
Ann Widdecombe	47	30	14	9	+17
Jack Straw	44	29	13	14	+15
Ken Clarke	39	26	20	15	+13
David Davis	6	9	77	8	-3
John Prescott	36	44	10	10	-8
Michael Portillo	35	45	11	9	-10
Robin Cook	25	52	12	12	-27
William Hague	23	64	5	8	-41

Source: MORI/*Sun*
Base: 1,008 British adults 18+, 30 April-1 May 2001.

Teflon Tony

Although it slipped in a number of respects during the last year-and-a-half of the Parliament, and had not fully recovered by the general election, Tony Blair's image was generally highly beneficial for Labour. Of course, any government to some extent stands or falls by the reputation of the Prime Minister. But Tony Blair persistently for his first two years in office achieved personal levels of public approval unprecedented in the history of opinion polling in Britain, and even after he slipped from those levels was always an asset, with his standing higher than that of his party or government.

Figure 3:

Tony Blair's Honeymoon 1997-9

% satisfied with PM

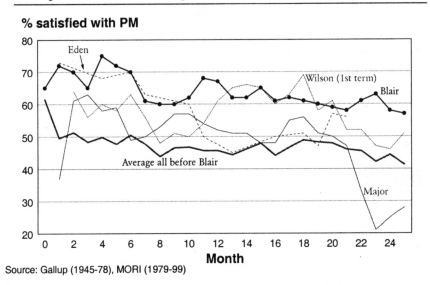

Source: Gallup (1945-78), MORI (1979-99)

The graph showing Prime Ministers' satisfaction figures for the first two years in office of every Prime Minister since the War illustrates how unprecedented the Blair honeymoon period was. (The graph uses Gallup data[6] for the period before MORI was conducting monthly polls, up to and including the Callaghan premiership, and MORI data from 1979.) The heavy black line marked with circles is Tony Blair's ratings. Only two previous premierships, those of Anthony Eden (the black dashed line) and Harold Wilson's first ministry (the thinner line) came close to Blair's ratings for any period of time, and neither sustained such ratings for a whole two years. Blair's ratings were consistently ten points or more better than the average ratings for all Prime Ministers from Attlee to Major at the same point in their first term.

Probably Blair's finest moment was the week after Diana, Princess of Wales, was killed in a car crash in the Autumn of 1997. Here he palpably read the mood of the nation and showed himself in tune with it when

---

[6] See Anthony King (ed.) and Robert Wybrow, *British Political Opinion 1937-2000* (Politico's Publishing, 2001), pp 185-91.

both the new Opposition leader, William Hague, and the Royal Family from the Queen downwards, largely failed to do so. His reward was a 75% satisfaction score (with 13% dissatisfied a net +62), a record for a British Prime Minister in MORI's polls. His sure grasp of the public mood was later to desert him – in September 2000, during the petrol crisis, 72% thought he was "out of touch with what ordinary people think" – yet much of the buoyancy he imparted to his government's image remained, even when temporarily ducked beneath the waterline.

Figure 4

Satisfaction with Blair/Government

Q Are you satisfied or dissatisfied with the way...
... the Government is running the country?
... Mr Blair is doing his job as Prime Minister?

Net satisfaction

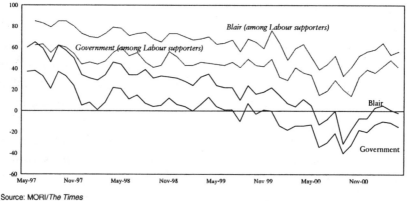

Source: MORI/*The Times*
Base: c. 1,000/2,000 British 18+ each month

An alternative means of gauging a leader's popularity is the like him/like his policies measure, which among its other merits offers a safety valve by which his political opponents can register regard for him while still expressing their political opposition (or, in the case of a really poor leader, vice versa). Mr Blair's personal net rating has always been a positive one.

Table 10: Like or dislike Tony Blair and his policies

Q. *Which of these statements come closest to your views of Mr Blair?*

	1994	Jan 1996	Jun 1996	Jan 1997	Jun 1997	1998	Jan 2001	May-Jun 2001
	%	%	%	%	%	%	%	%
I like him and I like his policies	31	35	33	35	47	42	34	41
I like him but I dislike his policies	18	18	19	18	22	22	23	20
I dislike him but I like his policies	10	12	12	13	7	9	9	11
I dislike him and I dislike his policies	14	17	19	22	14	15	25	18
No opinion	28	19	17	13	10	12	10	10
Like Mr Blair	49	53	52	53	69	64	57	61
Dislike Mr Blair	24	29	31	35	21	24	34	29
Net like Mr Blair	+25	+24	+21	+18	+48	+40	+23	+32
Like his policies	41	47	45	48	54	51	43	52
Dislike his policies	32	35	38	40	36	37	48	38
Net like his policies	+9	+12	+7	+8	+18	+14	-5	+14
Net like Blair/ policies	+34	+36	+28	+26	+66	+56	+18	+46

Source: MORI

But to disentangle the elements of the public's perceptions of Tony Blair, we turn to the more detailed leader image question, which uses 14 possible descriptions of politicians, of which 9 are positive and five negative. (In Table 11 for ease of reference the negative attributes are italicised.)

In the 2001 election we carried out a separate survey asking the public to rate the importance of the 14 measures which we include in the leader image battery; the image attributes in the table are as a result ranked in order of the importance the public assigns them; the results are shown in Table 12.

Table 11: Tony Blair: Leader Image

Q. *Here is a list of things both favourable and unfavourable that have been said about various politicians. I would like you to pick out all those statements that you feel fit Mr Blair.*

	Oct 1997 %	Apr 1998 %	Oct 1998 %	Apr 1999 %	Oct 1999 %	Apr 2000 %	Sep 2000 %	Apr 2001 %
Understands the problems facing Britain	48	44	40	37	34	31	22	25
A capable leader	58	53	47	51	44	43	29	33
Good in a crisis	18	25	21	33	23	20	12	15
Has sound judgement	27	24	20	26	15	17	12	13
Out of touch with ordinary people	*6*	*13*	*18*	*16*	*24*	*27*	*54*	*36*
Understands world problems	31	37	37	38	28	28	19	22
Tends to talk down to people	*9*	*13*	*12*	*18*	*23*	*23*	*37*	*25*
More honest than most politicians	36	29	26	27	21	20	16	17
Rather narrow minded	*3*	*5*	*6*	*6*	*10*	*11*	*21*	*15*
Down to earth	37	29	28	24	19	20	13	18
Patriotic	26	26	24	29	17	20	17	15
Rather inexperienced	*19*	*20*	*17*	*12*	*8*	*9*	*12*	*11*
Too inflexible	*6*	*7*	*10*	*10*	*11*	*16*	*29*	*16*
Has got a lot of personality	50	42	40	37	32	32	21	24
Average positive	36.8	34.3	31.4	33.6	25.9	25.7	17.9	20.2
Average negative	8.6	11.6	12.6	12.4	15.2	17.2	30.6	20.6
Net (positive minus negative)	+28.2	+22.7	+18.8	+21.2	+10.7	+8.5	-12.7	-0.4

Source: MORI/*The Times*
Base: c. 1,000 - 2,000 British adults 18+

The leader image data underlines how far Blair fell at the time of the fuel crisis: on every one of the 14 measures his score was worse in September than six months before, and the number thinking he was "out of touch" had doubled.

Table 12: Leader Image – Importance of attributes

Q. *From this card, how important, if at all, would you say the things I am going to read out will be in helping you decide whether to vote for a particular party?*

		Very important	Fairly important	Not very important	Not at all important	Don't know
That the party's leader...						
... understands the problems facing Britain	%	77	17	2	2	2
... is capable	%	75	19	2	2	2
... is good in a crisis	%	74	19	2	2	3
... has sound judgement	%	71	22	2	3	2
... is in touch with ordinary people	%	68	25	3	3	1
... understands world problems	%	67	25	3	2	3
... does not talk down to people	%	64	25	5	3	3
... is more honest than most politicians	%	62	27	5	3	3
... is not narrow minded	%	60	30	5	3	2
... is down to earth	%	50	37	8	3	2
... is patriotic	%	47	34	12	5	2
... is not inexperienced	%	47	35	12	4	2
... is not too inflexible	%	42	46	6	3	3
... has got a lot of personality	%	31	43	18	5	3

Source: MORI
Base: 1,928 British aged 18+, 24-30 May 2001

Prudence Brown

The Chancellor, Gordon Brown, throughout the Parliament laid emphasis on "prudence" to the extent that it became a running joke in the press, restricting spending and holding income tax down, as Labour had promised before 1997.

Superficially the government entered the election worse placed in terms of the public's economic confidence than any government since Callaghan's. At the end of March, when Tony Blair was deciding whether to call the election for its apparently pre-destined and universally assumed date of 3 May, or to delay because of the outbreak of Foot and Mouth Disease, the MORI Economic Optimism Index (EOI: the balance of those who expect the state of the economy to get better over the next year minus those who expect it to get worse) had fallen sharply, from –2 (2% more people thinking that the British economy would get worse in the following 12 months than thinking it would improve) in February to –29. This was probably a reaction to falling share prices rather than the impact of Foot and Mouth on the agricultural and tourist industries; the fall in the Index was sharpest among those owning shares[7]. By the end of April the EOI had risen only marginally, to –22, although there was a much sharper improvement after the election began, with surveys on 10-14 May[8] and on 24-30 May[9] both finding the index at –4. Yet despite this improvement, the 2001 general election was the first in which MORI has polled where the EOI was not positive before polling day.

Yet even when there had been earlier economic wobbles, Labour's overall poll ratings had remained high. Month after month, our polls found that the public mood was becalmed. In May 1998, the MORI EOI stood at +1. In June it fell to -19. By October it had fallen to -46. Yet in May 55% of the electorate said that if there had been an election just then they would have voted Labour. In June, 56%. In October, 53%. It dipped below 50% just once (to 49% in August 1999) before May 2000. Given sampling tolerances, a steady state. The opposition had allowed the biggest one-month fall in the Economic Optimism Index to pass without making any effect on the Labour lead in the polls.

Interestingly, as the graph shows, while there was considerable fluctuation in the public's view of how the economy would fare in the coming twelve months, the MORI Financial Services survey which measured how the public thought they themselves and their families

---

[7] As further evidence, the European Commission's consumer confidence index, a composite measure based on a survey by GfK, published at the same time but with fieldwork conducted before the fall in share prices though well after the start of the Foot and Mouth epidemic, found no fall in confidence. (Christopher Adams, "Consumers shrug off farm and share price woes, *Financial Times*, 30 March 2001.)

[8] MORI survey for the *Economist*, published on 18 May. MORI interviewed 1,846 British aged 18+ on 10-14 May 2001.

[9] Unpublished MORI Omnibus survey, 24-30 May, reported in *British Public Opinion* newsletter, June 2001.

would fare remained steady and positive. No doubt this weakened the effect of the economic pessimism.

Figure 5

Party support and economic optimism

Net optimism/lead

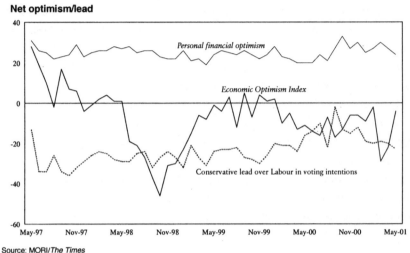

Source: MORI/*The Times*
Base: c. 2,000 British 18+ each month

It is a moot point how much economic confidence really affects voting in modern elections. In the 1980s, there was a very clear correlation between MORI's EOI and voting intention figures, and the academic David Sanders was able to produce models using economic data which were powerfully predictive of the general election results. Since then, the relationship has been much weaker – especially since 'Black Wednesday', when sterling fell out of the Exchange Rate Mechanism. This humiliation for John Major's government presumably made it clear to voters that international economic forces are often too strong to be within the control of national governments, and to be less likely to apportion blame or give credit to the party in power for the state of the economy. Between the 1997 election and March 2001, the relationship between EOI and voting intention in our polls was only weak: the r^2 co-efficient, which measures how closely two variables are correlated, was 0.071, meaning that only 7.1% of the variation in Labour's lead can be attributed to changes in economic optimism.

Nor were economic issues very high in the public's list of worries and priorities, either in the election run-up or, as it transpired, during the election itself. In April 2001, only 12% named unemployment as one of the most important issues facing the country, and 10% named the economy in general or the economic situation; by contrast, 41% mentioned the Foot and Mouth outbreak, and 41% the National Health Service. Asked immediately before polling day[10] which of a list of 17 issues would be "very important" in helping them decide which way to vote, 31% picked "managing the economy", putting the issue only in equal sixth place, and 30% picked unemployment – by contrast, 73% said health care would be very important, 62% education and 50% law and order. The contrast with, for example, the 1987 election, when both our monthly surveys for *The Times* nationwide, and a survey of Conservative-Labour marginals, found unemployment much the most frequently-selected issue, is a striking one.

Partly, no doubt, this simply reflected that other issues seemed more pressing in 2001. Unemployment was at its lowest level for years and the economy generally seen to be in good shape, despite the sudden rise in pessimism about the future, so perhaps it is natural that the public were more concerned about issues where they were dissatisfied with government performance than where they were not. It is an unfortunate fact of politics that a government can rarely hope to get as much credit for what it does well as it will get blame for what it does badly. Governments cannot necessarily afford to be complacent about the electoral effects of an economic downturn, but while the economy remains apparently healthy it will perhaps not be an election issue.

Contributing, surely, to the low priority of economic issues by the time of the election was the success of Gordon Brown's pre-election budget and, indeed, its predecessors.

---

[10] MORI survey for *The Times*, published on 7 June. MORI interviewed 1,967 British aged 18+ and registered to vote on 5 June 2001.

As Table 13 shows, every one of the Chancellor's five budgets were seen by a plurality of the public as being good for the country as a whole, an achievement which had only occasionally been achieved by his Conservative predecessors; and, indeed, the final budget convinced considerably more of the public that they would personally benefit from his proposals than that they would suffer – the classic aim of a pre-election budget achieved, with ease (and prudence). Combining the two measures, it was the best received pre-election budget since MORI first used these questions in 1976.

Table 13: Public reaction to Budgets, 1976-2001

Q. **Do you think the Budget proposals are a good thing or a bad thing (a) for you personally? (b) for the country as a whole?**

	(a) for you personally			(b) for the country		
	Good	Bad	Net Good	Good	Bad	Net Good
	%	%	%	%	%	%
March 1976	34	52	-18	47	38	+9
March 1977	68	18	+50	69	17	+52
April 1978	26	50	-24	39	39	0
July 1980	41	40	+1	47	36	+11
March 1982	36	48	-12	48	37	+11
June 1983	42	41	+1	46	38	+8
March 1985	32	47	+15	35	49	-14
March 1986	42	40	+2	37	48	-11
March 1987	49	36	+13	45	43	+2
March 1988	40	43	-3	40	49	-9
March 1989	36	35	+1	42	40	+2
March 1990	27	40	-13	28	50	-22
March 1991	36	46	-10	32	46	-14
March 1992	35	36	-1	34	42	-8
March 1993	11	64	-53	23	59	-36
December 1993	16	62	-46	29	54	-25
December 1994	15	67	-52	20	65	-45
December 1995	25	47	-22	23	55	-32
December 1996	20	54	-34	27	50	-23
July 1997	29	37	-8	56	20	+36
March 1998	33	39	-6	57	22	+35
March 1999	36	42	-6	46	33	+13
March 2000	26	49	-23	48	27	+21
March 2001	42	30	+12	52	25	+27

Source: MORI

Yet even Brown's success could be turned against the government when other things were going badly. The press took every opportunity to look for signs of a power struggle between the senior ministers, especially any indications that Gordon Brown was positioning himself for a future bid for the leadership. At times it was very reminiscent of Harold Wilson's paranoia about the 'July Plot' during his first term of office. In terms of public opinion, Blair had little to worry about; in July 2000, a MORI poll for the *Mail on Sunday*[11] found that, even though Gordon Brown's satisfaction ratings (for the way he was doing his job as Chancellor) were marginally higher than Blair's, only 18% of the public agreed that "Gordon Brown would make a better Prime Minister than Tony Blair", while a convincing 62% disagreed.

The considerable importance of the contribution to the government's standing made by Mr Brown's stewardship of the economy is plainly shown by comparing the government's poll performance in different policy areas. MORI's bank of "best party on key issues" questions offers the chance to compare credibility of government and opposition in 16 distinct fields[12]; in each case respondents are asked which party has the best policy on the issues they themselves say will be important to their vote – in other words, the parties' strength is measured where it is most salient. By the time of the 2001 election[13], Labour's standing relative to the Conservatives was as good as or better than in 1997 on almost every issue, though its lead on public transport had fallen from 37 points to 21, an 8% swing, and on housing from 37 to 29 (4% swing). Yet if these were weak areas for the government, why weren't the Tories exploiting it, chipping away at Labour's record? Who was the Tory transport spokesman, anyway? And Housing? These were potential winners for them, yet not a peep out of them so far as we noticed. But, as we shall see, one of the handicaps with which the Tories had to contend was an inability to make capital from Labour's weaknesses.

---

[11] MORI Telephone Surveys interviewed a representative quota sample of 610 British adults aged 18+ on 20-22 July 2000.

[12] A seventeenth issue, asylum and immigration, was added for our polls in the 2001 election, but earlier comparisons are not available.

[13] MORI survey for the *Economist*, published on 18 May. MORI interviewed 1,846 British aged 18+ on 10-14 May 2001.

Figure 6

Issues Important to Decide Vote:
Which Party Best (based on those choosing)

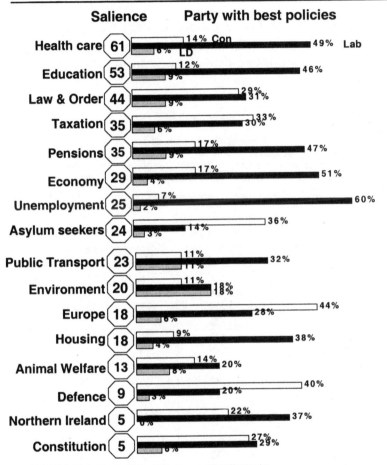

Base: 1,846 British Adults 18+, 10-14 May,2001. Source: MORI/*Economist*

The issues that concerned the voters most were, as so often in the past, the health service and education. At the start of the election campaign, health care was in primary position, and among the 73% of the electorate who named it, not the rest, Labour had a more-than-three-to-one lead, 49% to 14%. On education, in second place, Labour also led by nearly four to one, 46% to 12%.

But to understand Gordon Brown's importance, it is more revealing to look at the figures for July 2000, a month when things looked less rosy for Labour, when the Tories overall had reached their highest ratings since the election and might conceivably have felt themselves on the verge of being taken seriously as an alternative government. Table 14 shows the Conservative lead over Labour (a negative figure of course indicating a Labour lead) on each issue at the two elections and in July 2000, together with the saliency of the issues during the 2001 election campaign.

Table 14: Best Party on Key Issues

Q . *At this General Election, which, if any, of these issues do you think will be very important to you in helping you decide which party to vote for?*
Q. *Thinking of those issues you think are important please tell me if you think that the Conservatives, Labour, Liberal Democrats or some other party has the best policy on each.*

	"Very important in helping you decide which party to vote for"	Conservative lead over Labour as party with best policy *among all naming issue as important*		
	10-14 May 2001 %	8 Apr 1997	July 2000	10-14 May 2001
Health care	73	-38	-26	-35
Education	62	-23	-26	-34
Law and order	50	+2	+14	-2
Pensions	40	-25	+1	-30
Taxation	37	+15	+14	+3
Managing the economy	31	+22	-2	-34
Public transport	31	-37	-30	-21
Unemployment	30	-38	-38	-53
Asylum seekers/immigration	27	n/a	n/a	+22
Europe	26	+19	+10	+16
Protecting the natural environment	26	+1	-6	-7
Housing	21	-37	-18	-29
Animal welfare	11	-13	-26	-6
Defence	11	+30	+15	+20
Constitution/devolution	8	+21	+3	-2
Northern Ireland	7	+9	-17	-15
Trade Unions	6	-35	-23	-42

Source: MORI/ *The Times/Economist*

In July 2000, Labour had improved its standing on several issues, but almost all were issues of low saliency – Animal welfare, defence, the constitution/ devolution and Northern Ireland. Of the key issues at the top of the list it had lost ground since the election on almost all: a 7% swing to the Tories on health care, 6% on law and order, 13% on pensions. On education, true, there had been a slight improvement. But in Mr Brown's department, not only had he held the line on taxation, but there had been a 12% swing to Labour as party with the best policies for managing the economy. Furthermore, as the table also shows, this latter trend was continued further so that by the time of the election, in place of the 22-point lead the Tories had in 1997, Labour had built a 34-point lead as trusted stewards of the economy among those who felt this issue was important to their vote.

But except on the economy, it is clear that the opposition were scoring hits on the government. However, the Tories were less well-placed than these figures might suggest. On many of the issues where Labour's lead fell between 1997 and 2000, the real swing was not to the Conservatives but to "don't know", or "no party has the best policy". Those who were losing faith in Labour were not gaining it in the Tories. Labour's perceived failure to deliver on its promises had the potential to be a major vote-loser ... if only the Tories were a credible alternative.

Labour's failure to deliver

The best spin of modern politics was the breathtaking audacity of the Labour Party's launch of 'The Road to the Manifesto' which a few months before the 1997 election set the issues agenda for the election, health care, education, law and order, and jobs, stealing the momentum on issues from the government of the day. Issues don't count so much as image in winning over votes in general elections, but they play off each other in the public's mind, and issues impact on leader ratings, and the image of the party as capable of governing. But the trouble with promissory notes is that, eventually, they fall due.

A government as convincingly elected as was Tony Blair's in 1997, especially one which shortly afterwards reinforced the public's confidence in it through its sure-footed handling of the aftermath of Diana's death, can rely on a 'honeymoon period' during which the public is inclined to be well-disposed towards it and will tend to give ministers the benefit of the doubt. Voters realise perfectly well that governments cannot perform miracles and that major improvements inevitably take time. But, eventually, the shine wears off; by the halfway point in a Parliament, the public starts to feel it should be able to see some results. To meet its critics, the government needed 1999 to be the Year of Delivery on its manifesto pledges. It wasn't. Nor, for that matter, was 2000.

At the start of 2001, the *Sunday Telegraph* commissioned MORI to examine how far the public thought Blair and his government had delivered on their pledges.

Table 15: Has Labour kept its promises?

Q. *Before it was elected, the Labour Party made 5 key promises. For each one, please tell me whether you think the Labour Government has or has not kept the promise?*

		Has	Has not	No opinion	Net
Cut NHS waiting lists	%	30	59	11	-29
Get 250,000 under-25 year olds off benefit and into work	%	34	38	28	-4
Not increase income tax, cut VAT on heating to 5% and keep inflation and interest rates as low as possible	%	51	39	11	+12
Introduce fast-track punishment for persistent young offenders	%	17	62	21	-45
Cut class sizes to 30 or under for 5,6,7 year olds	%	32	34	34	-2

Source: MORI/*Sunday Telegraph*
Base: 1,007 British 18+, 11-13 January 2001

On four of the five original promises from the Road to the Manifesto pledge cards, more of the public thought Labour had failed than had succeeded; only on having kept taxes down was the balance of opinion in their favour, and the public ranked that pledge only third in importance of the five. Worse, on those remaining four pledges Labour's best percentage in favour was 34%. (In fact, with the derisory turnout that ensued, Labour was able to win a landslide with the votes of only 25% of the electorate – but we didn't know that in January.)

Table 16: Importance to the public of Labour's key promises

Q. *How important would you say it is to you that the government has or has not kept its promise to …?*

		Very important	Fairly important	Not very important	Not at all important	Don't know
Cut NHS waiting lists	%	81	15	2	1	1
Get 250,000 under-25 year olds off benefit and into work	%	70	24	3	1	2
Not increase income tax, cut VAT on heating to 5% and keep inflation and interest rates as low as possible	%	62	29	5	2	2
Introduce fast-track punishment for persistent young offenders	%	66	24	5	2	3
Cut class sizes to 30 or under for 5,6,7 year olds	%	59	25	8	4	4

Source: MORI/*Sunday Telegraph*
Base: 1,007 British 18+, 11-13 January 2001

Much the most significant of the services on which the public looked for improvement was the National Health Service, which has a deeply ingrained place in the British people's affections. At the end of 1999, the foundation of the NHS was a clear winner in a MORI/*Times* poll which asked the public to name achievements by governments in the 20th century which have contributed most to British life. In November 2000[14], although 58% were satisfied with the NHS and 28% dissatisfied, this represented a sharp deterioration over even the previous two years – in 1998, 72% had said they were satisfied, and only 18% dissatisfied; by January 2001- partly in the wake of an outcry over poor hygiene in hospitals – just 46% were satisfied. In November, 47% thought the NHS in need of much improvement, and many blamed the government. Nor was there much confidence in the future: more than half the public

---

[14] MORI poll for the BMA. MORI interviewed 2,033 British aged 15+ on 23-28 November 2000.

thought that most or all people in Britain will rely on private health provision by 2050[15].

Initially, memories of the previous government, and correspondingly low expectations for the new one, helped the government hold the fort. But the mere knowledge of money being spent, without a visible recovery in the state of the health service, could not suffice in the long run. In a poll reported in January 2000, 80% of doctors said they no longer believed in a sustainable free NHS service[16]. The government had to prove them wrong – given such a free hand to spend (and the public did believe its taxes had increased, even if Labour had kept its specific pledge on income tax), if the NHS continued in its long-term decline then ultimately the credibility of the Labour Party would be under threat. "You paid the taxes, so where are the nurses?", as the Tories pertinently asked.

Crime was equally a problem. At the start of 2001, the public thought the overall level of crime in their area had got worse rather than better by 36% to 17%, that standards of policing generally had deteriorated by 33% to 16%, and that the number of police on the beat had got worse by 49% to 9%.

The one bright spot for the government was education. Even though the public was unconvinced that the class size pledge had been met, surveys persistently rated the performance on education better than those on the other public services. Indeed, the poll in January for the *Sunday Telegraph* found almost two to one, 33% to 17%, in favour of the proposition that "the standard of education that children receive" had been improved.

An NOP survey for Channel 4's *Powerhouse* programme, released just as the election was called, had very similar findings.[17] Transport was the service deemed to have worsened most, 47% saying it has got worse

---

[15] MORI poll for the Adam Smith Institute, published in Madsen Pirie & Robert Worcester, *Facing the Future* (Adam Smith Institute, 2000). MORI interviewed 1,025 British aged 15+ on 20-24 July 2000.

[16] *Daily Telegraph*, 27 January 2000

[17] *Evening Standard*, 9 May 2001. NOP interviewed 1,000 electors on 4-7 May 2001.

compared, 36% that health services had deteriorated, and 28% thinking the same of police services. Of the four services tested, only schools were perceived as having improved, with 31% citing an improvement, compared to the 28% who felt school education had worsened. Even among Labour supporters, over two-fifths (44 per cent) believed transport services have worsened, and a quarter thought health services have got worse.

Yet the overall impression was not impossibly bad. Again comparison with the Tories saved the day. Only 16% thought that if the Conservatives were to win the election, public services would improve; 32% thought they would get worse.[18] With so low a view of the government's achievements, and yet a widespread conviction that a Tory government would be worse still, is it really surprising that turnout was low?

"Don't Panic, Don't Panic"

Public Opinion is like an 800lb gorilla. It sleeps a lot and much of the rest of the time sits happily chewing on leaves. However, if you poke it with a stick, it gets angry. During the year 2000, and especially in September, the Labour government found a series of sticks and poked the gorilla with them one after another.[19]

By the end of 1999, the government had failed to deliver but still maintained its solid lead in the polls. Then suddenly many things started to go wrong at once. The first days of the year 2000 brought a series of embarrassments that for the first time seemed to threaten the government's grip. The crisis in the health service over Christmas, the rise in the crime rate figures and the Lords' rebellion over trial by jury, questions about Labour's 'ethical foreign policy', the unravelling of devolution as Millbank tried to dominate Holyrood and Cardiff Bay, the developing fiasco of the election of the London mayor, the neutering of

---

[18] MORI survey for the *Sunday Telegraph*. MORI interviewed 1,007 British aged 18+ on 11-13 January 2001.

[19] I first used this analogy in an article for *Parliamentary Monitor* in November 2000.

the Freedom of Information Act, and daily from its disastrous opening, the lamentable Dome.

'Peers wreck Bill to curb trial by jury' was one headline in *The Times*. 'Poll reveals Livingstone's massive lead' splashed the *Independent*. 'Labour in retreat over ethical foreign policy' – *Guardian*. 'Robinson knew of hitch' – *FT*. 'The press coverage has been an absolute deluge that fell upon our heads', said Lord Falconer, talking about the failure of the Dome to attract visitors. And more damaging, uproar among teachers in many papers, and most damaging, all the press hammering away at the crisis in the health service.

Yet the MORI/*Times* survey in January 2000, carried out after a month of appalling coverage, showed little change in voting intentions. Labour had fallen from 54% to 50%, down four points, while the Tories gained two, from 28% to 30%, a 3% swing to the Tories. Why didn't a 29-point jump in concern over the health service and a eight-point drop in the government's satisfaction rating make more impact on voting intentions? No effective opposition.

It's easy to register dissatisfaction on how satisfied or dissatisfied you are with the job the government or a leader is doing in an opinion poll, but the crunch comes with the zero-sum game of choosing which party you'd vote for in an election or saying which of the party leaders would be the best PM. Even with a four-point drop in his personal satisfaction level, Teflon Tony was still deemed a satisfactory Prime Minister by 53% of potential voters, almost three times as many as the 19% who professed satisfaction with the job William Hague was making of being Leader of the Opposition. Labour was getting away with it.

But it quickly became clear that Mr Blair, among others, was becoming jumpy, though it was some weeks before the details were revealed. Over the spring, Philip Gould, the Prime Minister's political consultant, wrote a series of bleakly pessimistic memos. In June and July these found their way into the press, as did a note from the Prime Minister himself revealing similar concerns.

The memos caused a considerable stir at the time of their publication, partly because the timing was brilliantly contrived. However, there is no evidence that they were 'leaked' in the conventional sense (it was suggested that copies may have been stolen from somebody's dustbin). In a sense, beyond the embarrassment of the leaks themselves it is hard to see what much of the fuss was about. They told us little we didn't know or guess already. It was already plain that Labour had been on the verge of panic for weeks. It is public knowledge that Philip Gould conducts regular focus groups and polling to test public opinion for the Labour Party and reports on the results to the party leadership. It hardly needs Sherlock Holmes to suspect a link between the two. Their real significance is in the insight they give into Labour's thinking a year before the election was called.

The consensus opinion of many of the commentators after the second leak seemed to be "Sack Gould". Why? Two, to some extent contrasting, reasons – either because his conclusions were negative ("Mr Gould should never have committed this bleak view to paper, still less circulated it. His memo contains … enough pessimism to suck the life out of a demoralised cabinet", the *Sun* argued[20]), or because the critics oppose the idea of the governing party monitoring public opinion altogether. The first of these, the 'shoot the messenger' argument, is plainly misconceived. Are we really expected to prefer the Prime Minister to be entirely surrounded by fawning yes men? If there is bad news (of whatever sort) to be delivered, somebody should deliver it. Members of the Cabinet would end up a great deal more than demoralised if they were allowed to continue in blissful ignorance of their failures until unexpectedly ejected from office by the electorate. The job of any party's private pollster or political consultant is to make objective assessment of the state of public opinion and its political implications, and ensure that it is delivered to the party leader or other relevant officials without being distorted or diverted by his own or anybody else's political agenda.

---

[20] "The *Sun* Says: Testing times for Tony Blair", *Sun*, 19 July 2000.

Part of the problem is that the government let the media confuse Philip Gould's role. He's the first of the American-style political consultants in British politics, not a pollster. He's very good at what he does, certainly he makes use of polls and focus groups, and he is very committed to Tony Blair and to Labour, but the role of a private pollster is different and distinct: he (and/or she) should stand back from any personal commitment and give the leader the plain unvarnished view of what the public thinks, not concentrate on what he thinks the party should be doing to turn them. The consultant is his client's advocate; the pollster is not. Because Mr Gould in effect has to combine both roles, he must be sometimes in a difficult position.

But granted that Mr Gould in writing the memos was simply doing his job, was he right? As some commentators argued at the time, focus groups are not a reliable means of measurement, only a means of exploring the thought processes of small groups of selected electors in depth, which can throw up hypotheses that should then be tested quantitatively by conventional opinion polls. Sure, we use focus groups all the time both for media and other clients, private and public sector, and I conducted focus groups for the Labour Party both for Mr Wilson and Mr Callaghan, more than a decade before Philip Gould ever came onto the scene. But what we use them for is what they should be used for.

Polls are 'surveys of the views of a representative sample of a defined population', and are very good at finding out what people do, know and think. Focus groups, 'qualitative research', are very good at finding out *why* people think what they do, to develop hypotheses for testing, and to keep in touch with the semantics of the day so as to frame better questions, couched in the right language, for quantitative use. To use them to 'track' public opinion or to 'assess the national mood' is nonsense, in our view, and incompatible with the usual selection of people to attend such focus groups, e.g. Labour voters last time who are thinking of defecting now.

However, it is not clear from the leaked documents whether Philip Gould's conclusions were based entirely on focus group work or had also been tested with representative samples, or indeed were influenced by his reading of the published opinion polls in the newspapers. So let us consider some hard data, from polls taken in May and early June, just after those memos were written, from samples of c. 1,000 British public: "We are outflanked on patriotism and crime", Mr Gould wrote in early May. MORI's leader image poll for *The Times* in April found, as had the previous one in October 1999, that more people chose "patriotic" as a description of William Hague than Tony Blair – the only one of 14 measures on which Hague beat or at that point had ever beaten Blair.

On crime, the position was less clear cut. A MORI survey for the *Mail on Sunday* at the end of April, just after the Tony Martin case and when the Tories were making crime a particular issue for targeting the government, found that in England Labour led the Conservatives by 34% to 23% as the party with the best policies on law and order; but Mr Gould's concern was perhaps justified by the 37% who thought no party had a good policy on law and order or didn't know which party was best. But the panic measures, such as the notorious proposal that the Police should frogmarch drunken yobboes to the nearest cashpoint and levy on-the-spot fines, didn't help. It was only after this period that Tony Blair's personal ratings so deteriorated that, by the time of the election, more of the public thought he was "out of touch with ordinary people" and that he "tends to talk down to people" than thought so of William Hague.)

"We have been assailed for broken promises" wrote Mr Gould. True: at the start of June, only 25% thought the government had kept its promises, while 60% thought it had not. "We quickly seem to have grown out of touch"; 51% of the public thought Mr Blair was out of touch, and 44% that he was in touch. [21]

So, perhaps there was reasonable cause for concern. By the end of April, satisfaction with the government had dropped 7 points in four months (from 45% to 38%) and with Mr Blair personally 5 points (57% to 52%); certainly the honeymoon period when 57% were satisfied with

---

[21] MORI poll for the *Mail on Sunday*. MORI Telephone Surveys interviewed 1,008 British aged 18+ on 8-9 June 2000.

the government and 75% with the Prime Minister was well and truly over. [22]

Surely, though, to trace the spring flap to its true roots we need to look not at Mr Gould's memos but at the real election results. The previous year Labour had lost the European Parliamentary elections. On a 23% turnout? So what! The bottom line is that only 8% of the electorate voted for the Tories, and 6% for Labour.

The local government elections in 2000, similarly, produced dramatic Conservative gains but also on a low turnout, and predictive of nothing. It was easy to play up its importance: BBC News Online's political correspondent Nick Assinder wrote: "Tony Blair's worst fears have been realised with a devastating defeat in the English local elections. Millions of voters delivered their verdict on New Labour just days after the third anniversary of its historic 1997 general election landslide. And the message was clear – Labour is deeply unpopular, suffering its worst performance for around 20 years." [23] Fat lot of good it did the Tories a year later!

What did it mean politically? It was obviously a dreadful night of results for Labour – nearly six hundred council seats lost across England, beaten by the Tories in the London Assembly constituencies and humiliated with third place (almost fourth) for Mayor and a lost deposit at Romsey. Yet disappointing though their performance was, if repeated it would probably still have left them with a narrow majority in a general election. Furthermore, Labour rarely does as well in local elections as in Westminster elections, since part of their support switches to the Liberal Democrats at council level. The biggest danger, perhaps, was the boost that the good result gave to the Tories.

But what should the government have done as a result?

---

[22] MORI monthly polls for *The Times*.
[23] http://news.bbc.co.uk/hi/english/in_depth/uk_politics/2000/
local_elections/newsid_736000/736845.stm

For a start, they should have looked at the good news as well as the bad. When asked if they agreed or disagreed that 'The Conservatives are ready to form the next Government', only 23% of the public said they agreed, 60% disagreed. When asked if they agreed or disagreed that 'William Hague is ready to be Prime Minister', only 18% said they agreed, 64% disagreed. When asked whether they thought Blair or Hague was most in tune with the British public, Blair led Hague by 38 points on education, 36 points on the NHS, 22 points on jobs, 13 points on Europe, and by 6 points on law and order. On who they thought would make the more capable Prime Minister, Blair led Hague by more than two to one.[24]

Table 17: Most capable Prime Minister

Q. *Who do you think would be the most capable Prime Minister, Mr Blair, Mr Hague or Mr Kennedy?*

	29 Mar -3 Apr 2001 %	8 May 2001 %	8-14 May 2001 %	10-12 May 2001 %	15 May 2001 %	22 May 2001 %	29 May 2001 %	31 May -2 Jun 2001 %	5 Jun 2001 %
Tony Blair	49	52	52	51	52	51	50	49	51
William Hague	14	13	13	15	12	14	16	16	14
Charles Kennedy	8	9	9	8	9	10	11	12	14
Don't know/none	30	26	26	26	27	25	23	23	21

Source: MORI/ *Times/Economist/Sunday Telegraph*

Even in June, when Labour's disastrously counter-productive knee-jerk measures had dented its ratings still further, this merely restored the political scene in Britain to what we generally assume to be its normal state, after more than three years when it seemed as if the laws of gravity had been suspended. For most of the half-century in which opinion polls have been measuring the state of the parties and ratings of the governments and their leaders, it has been a constant that governments are unpopular; for the first time, Mr Blair's ratings were beginning to be comparable to those of his predecessors.

---

[24] MORI polls for *The Times* (MORI interviewed 979 British aged 18+ on 18-23 May 2000), and for the *Mail on Sunday* (MORI interviewed 1,008 British aged 18+ on 8-9 June 2000).

Let's look at the figures in their historical context. In June, 28% were satisfied with how the government was running the country, while 62% were dissatisfied, a worse than two-to-one negative ratio. If we look back a few years, though, we see that John Major was achieving very similar government satisfaction ratings in the last few months before the 1992 election – for example, in January 1992, 28% were satisfied with the government and 63% dissatisfied; ten weeks later, Mr Major was returned to office with a narrow majority. Even the further fall that came after the petrol crisis, to 26% satisfied and 66% dissatisfied, was hardly unprecedented – how many other past British governments would have been happy with that as their lowest point.

Figure 7

Labour's Slides and Recoveries in the Polls

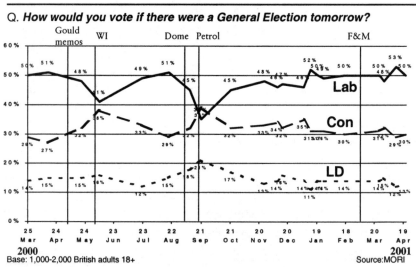

Q. *How would you vote if there were a General Election tomorrow?*

Base: 1,000-2,000 British adults 18+   Source:MORI

Similarly, in June 2000 39% were satisfied with the way Mr Blair was doing his job whereas 52% were dissatisfied – Mr Blair's first negative rating in our monthly polls; yet Margaret Thatcher consistently scored worse than this throughout 1986, yet won the 1987 election comfortably.

Sure, the polls were fluctuating a bit, but with the election coming closer, and the sharks of Fleet Street smelling blood in the water, you'd expect that. Remember, the 'natural core vote' for Labour is around 30%, for the Tories 30% and for the Liberal Democrats, Greens, Nationalists and others around 20%, adding up to 80%, leaving 20% to decide the outcome of every general election. To expect to soak up the whole 20% to add to your 'natural core' of 30% and get 50% at the election had never been realistic, despite the steady state of a 20-point lead, 50% Labour, 30% Tory, that held steady for more than two years. The upshot of all that happened over the first half of 2000 was to restore some degree of reality to the figures so they temporarily steadied at around 46%±3% Labour, 34%±3% Conservative, 15%±3% LibDems.

There was nothing that the government needed to be seriously alarmed about, so long as it learned its lessons. Even the worst of the polls at this stage, the 3% Labour lead that MORI reported in the *Mail on Sunday* at the start of June[25] was hardly disastrous: a uniform swing would give, even at a 3% lead, a 61-seat Labour majority. Why, our old clients Harold Wilson and Jim Callaghan, never mind Michael Foot and Neil Kinnock, would have sold their sisters for that size majority in the House of Commons! And this in a poll taken on the two days after Blair's less-than-well-received speech to the Women's Institute, exactly a year before the eventual election date, when the entire force 10 gale out of what we used to call Fleet Street was swirling around the country, and your look of 'who-got-me-into-this-mess' crossing Blair's face was being televised over and over.

Indeed, so strongly was the relationship between seats and votes tilted in the Labour's favour even at the 1997 election (it has now tilted further still) that assuming uniform swing, Labour would still have had an overall majority if the votes were to be level; for the Tories to gain an overall majority, they needed to lead by more than 10% of the vote, which meant securing a swing of 11.5%. Even an eight-point Tory lead, the high tide mark of the polls following the petrol crisis (in NOP's poll

---

[25] MORI interviewed 1,008 British adults aged 18+ on 8-9 June 2000.

for Channel 4) would easily leave Tony Blair in Downing Street with Charles Kennedy's help.

So why the panic? What on earth are the number-crunchers in the Prime Minister's office doing while he is listening every Monday morning to the results of the latest focus groups? Was nobody giving him solid figures instead of alarming but imprecise impressions? It is all very well to worry about one's own weaknesses, but is much safer to do so by viewing them in context with the countervailing strengths in the position. All this I pointed out in articles at the time.[26] The government's best way of re-stabilising its position was concentrating on making solid achievements in carrying out its promised programme, however long that took.

But the leaked note by Tony Blair shows that panic had indeed set in. This confirms what everybody had already assumed, that the government's reaction to the situation outlined in Mr Gould's memos had been fatally concerned with a quick fix of appearance rather than substance, and especially centred on maintaining a special aura of popularity round Mr Blair himself. Ironically, this was precisely what Philip Gould had been warning against: "TB [Blair] is not believed to be real. He lacks conviction; he is all spin and presentation, he says things to please people, not because he believes them."[27] The outcome, a disastrous series of initiatives and statements, more sharply undermined the government's position than anything that had gone before. In April, the poll figures on almost every front were still at a level most previous Prime Ministers could only have dreamed of. But between April and June, satisfaction with the government dropped by a further 10 points (to just 28%), with Mr Blair by 13 points (so that for the first time he was scoring negative net ratings), and the voting intentions though still showing a Labour lead had also taken a perceptible knock.

On individual issues the same was true. Look at the deterioration on law and order, a particular focus of the policy panic. At the end of April,

---

[26] Robert M Worcester, "Vox Pop: Memo to the Prime Minister", *The Parliamentary Monitor*, August 2000; reprinted in *British Public Opinion* newsletter, August 2000.
[27] Philip Webster, "No 10 told to cut the spin as poll lead dwindles", *The Times*, 12 June 2000.

34% thought Labour were the best party on law and order, and they led the Tories comfortably. (That poll was only in England, which should slightly disadvantage Labour). By July MORI found only 20% picking Labour[28], while ICM in the *Guardian*[29] put it at 22%; both polls found the Tories almost neck and neck.

In other words, everything Labour in general and Mr Blair in particular did in the weeks after those memos were written had been counter-productive. A leader should be reading and responding to the poll data, but also acting with judgment, not simply allowing himself to blown about by the winds of transient public opinion. It had always been an accusation of New Labour's opponents that this is one of Mr Blair's faults, but the impression over the spring and summer of 2000 – backed up by the Blair memo – was much stronger.

"When in a hole, stop digging"

The danger of the government being seen to flounder around trying to improve its image was that it would highlight the issue of 'spin', allowing the public to get the impression that it was more concerned with appearances than substance, to silence the critics rather than meet their criticisms. In July 2000, a MORI poll for the *Mail on Sunday*[30] found that 60% of the public agreed that "Tony Blair is more concerned with image than with dealing with the real issues", while only 33% disagreed.

It seems clear that the electoral blips that sparked the panic were in themselves caused, or at least magnified, by the obsession with spin and controlling the party's image. Millbank's problem was its inability to learn from experience. The pattern was all too familiar. In the Scottish Parliament, Millbank wanted to stop the left-wing MP Dennis Canavan from being nominated as MSP for his Westminster seat; he left the party,

---

[28] MORI survey for the *Mail on Sunday,* published on 16 July 2000. MORI Telephone Surveys interviewed 1,003 British aged 18+ on 12-14 July 2000).
[29] Alan Travis & Michael White, "Poll slide adds to Blair gloom", 18 July 2000. ICM interviewed 1,056 British aged 18+ by telephone on 14-15 July 2000.
[30] MORI Telephone Surveys interviewed a representative quota sample of 610 British adults aged 18+ on 20-22 July 2000.

ran as an independent against its official candidate, and won with embarrassing ease. In Wales, after the original plan was thrown into confusion by the forced resignation of Ron Davies, Millbank secured the election of Alun Michael as party leader, and eventual First Secretary, against the strength of local opinion which preferred Rhodri Morgan. This almost certainly severely dented the Labour vote (unbelievably, they lost Rhondda and Islwyn to Plaid Cymru). And even having got their way, at such cost, the party apparatchiks' triumph was short-lived, for eventually Michael was forced out by his colleagues and Morgan installed in his place. (An ICM poll[31] found only 24% of the Welsh satisfied with the job Alun Michael had been doing as First Secretary.)

At around the same time, the European elections were being contested, on a newly introduced 'closed list' system of proportional representation that gave maximum control over candidate selection to party headquarters and minimum degree of choice to the voters. There was, inevitably, party controversy that seemed to put Labour in the wrong, and even cast the unelected and unreformed Lords as defenders of democracy. Labour had its way. What impact the fuss really had on the election, and its 23% turnout, we shall never know, but Labour lost and the Tories had their first victory in a national election for seven years. Certainly the experience of crass list manipulation did a disservice to the reputation of PR in the minds of at least some of the public, and the media.

But, come the Autumn, they were at it again. Millbank's determination to prevent Ken Livingstone winning the party's candidacy for London Mayor was all too public, and it was unsurprising that having narrowly won the nomination, and having disowned the more dubious tactics alleged against his supporters, Frank Dobson was none the less tainted as well. Labour's electoral system was altered from the promised one-member-one-vote to an electoral college, where a third of the votes were reserved for Labour MPs, MEPs and assembly candidates (who were denied the privilege of a secret ballot), and where affiliated organisations (trade unions and co-operative societies) could cast block votes and

---

[31] ICM poll for the *Scotsman*, February 2000.

could do so without balloting their members, a past practice now outlawed in the Labour leadership elections upon which the electoral college was supposedly based. [32]

Of course the manipulation ultimately rebounded. How could it not? An ICM poll for the *Evening Standard*[33], taken immediately after the Labour selection result was announced, found only 15% thought that Mr Dobson's victory was "fair", and more than half of those who expressed a voting intention supported Mr Livingstone, even before he had formally confirmed that he would run as an independent. Even by the time of the election, 6% of Livingstone voters in a MORI poll for London News Network[34] said their reason for supporting him was that the selection had been unfair, and a further 3% that they didn't like Labour or the way Labour had treated Livingstone.

It was not Frank Dobson that was the problem, as such. A leaked private poll for the Labour Party[35] indicated that even were Mo Mowlam (then considered to be the most popular minister) to replace Frank Dobson as Labour's candidate, Ken Livingstone would still win. When we asked (for London News Network) all those voters who intended voting for other candidates why they were not supporting Dobson, the most frequent reason was that "he is a puppet/controlled by the government".

Suspicion was perhaps compounded by the government's decision to make no provision for a free mailshot to be allowed for each candidate to deliver campaigning material to the voters. This free delivery is routine in Parliamentary and European elections, and was also allowed in the elections to the Scottish Parliament and Welsh Assembly, but does not apply to local authority elections. What would have been the effects

---

[32] In any case, the high weight given to MPs' votes in the party leadership elections can be justified since the leader of the party is also leader of the Parliamentary Party, and his position would be impossible if he did not have their confidence; but a Labour Mayor of London would not be leader of the Labour group in the Assembly, let alone of London's Labour MPs or MEPs, so the analogy seems somewhat spurious.

[33] *Evening Standard*, 22 February 2000. ICM interviewed 1,003 Londoners by telephone on 20-21 February 2000.

[34] MORI interviewed 1,001 London adults aged 18+ and registered to vote by telephone on 2-3 May 2000.

[35] *Independent*, 25 February 2000.

of preventing the free mailshot? Surely, at the very least, a lower turnout, and one which could only be expected to harm the prospects of an independent candidate fighting the party machines. Even if the initial decision was made with the best will in the world, with no consideration but the cost in mind, it could only tarnish the electoral process.

The government argued that the cost would be unjustified, and that this was only a local election. In the end, a combination of Conservative, Liberal Democrat and crossbench peers in the Lords forced the government to reconsider. The government spin doctors then tried to spread disquiet that the unelected House of Lords was acting disgracefully in interfering with the arrangements for an election. But that is partly what they are there to do: almost the only power of uninhibited veto left to the Lords under the Parliament Acts allows them to prevent the Commons postponing general elections beyond the existing legal time limits. There was a precedent, too: it was the Lords who blocked James Callaghan in 1969 when they thought he, as Home Secretary, was trying to gerrymander constituency boundaries by selective implementation of the Boundary Commission recommendations. Again, the government merely looked worse rather than better by rubbishing the legitimate restrictions on elective dictatorship.

The London turnout was derisory, a further harbinger of things to come. In the 1998 London borough elections (which were run in tandem with the referendum on setting up the Mayor and Assembly in the first place), 35% voted, the lowest figure in 35 years; yet in the Mayoral election of 2000 the turnout was still only 36%. So much for directly-elected Mayors as a re-invigoration of local government in England; if the electorate could not be made to take more of an interest in the new forms of local government than in the old, then it must have failed. Subsequent referendums in a series of local authorities were to reject a switch to directly-elected mayors in other towns and cities.

That 36% turnout was after the government conceded a free mailshot (in the end, a single combined communication from all the Mayoral candidates), after the 'early voting' innovation, directly aimed at improving turnout, and after an expensive publicly-funded advertising campaign to emphasise the elections' importance. What would the turnout have been otherwise? (As we shall see, there are grounds for supposing that one of the contributory factors in the pitiful turnout at the 2001 election may have been a sharp fall in the number of leaflets delivered by candidates to electors.)

Perhaps the government took the low turnout as a mandate to ignore the new Mayor and continue pursuing its own policy; more likely it was simply, as with devolution to Scotland and Wales, a failure to accept that devolution involves the dispersal of power, and is a sham if not accompanied by a weakening of central control. Reform of the House of Lords was treated in the same way, with the all-out reform and introduction of an elected second chamber, for which there was considerable public support, pushed to one side in favour of an interim compromise that shows every sign of achieving permanence. Nothing achieved for which the government could claim a principled case, with not even the whole of the hereditary peerage removed; the sole achievement a pragmatic one, to destroy the House's Conservative majority and so ease the passage of government legislation. It is not an edifying tale.

In almost every policy area the government was acquiring a reputation, even in those parts of the press that are a Labour government's natural friends, for being more concerned by the symptoms than the causes of criticism, and being prepared to meet them by fair means or foul. Even if much of this passed over the head of the man-in-the-street, its effect was corrosive of good relations with the media. The incipient paranoia that already seemed to be driving Millbank's management of the party into an orgy of control freakery, got worse. People started to flap. And, as is so often the case in such circumstances, the cure was worse than the disease.

In fact this exemplifies the reason why the accusations against Mr Gould, and the rest of us in the polling industry, that our work brings an undemocratic threat of permanent 'government by opinion poll', is misplaced. Except in the very short term, government by opinion poll doesn't work. The public is not stupid, and you can only fool all of the people some of the time. Eventually it is substantive achievements (or failures) that will matter.

There are some who would argue that the Prime Minister shouldn't be taking any notice of public opinion at all. Stated in these bald terms it sounds, and is, ridiculous. We certainly don't believe in 'government by opinion poll'. The arguments of former Clinton pollster Dick Morris, mentioned by Mr Gould, that endorsement by opinion poll confers some sort of democratic legitimacy on a policy, is one with which most of us would disagree. Democratic legitimacy is conferred by popular election to office, sometimes by referendum, arguably perhaps even by 'citizen's jury', depending on how that is construed. But governments have always tried to take public opinion into account, even long before there were scientifically-conducted polls to use as measurements, and have sometimes let it dictate their governmental or electoral strategy. (One thinks of in particular Stanley Baldwin's "appalling frankness" in explaining how he refused to advocate rearmament in the 1930s because it would have lost him the election.) In exercising the decision-making power that is democratically his by reason of his general election victory, a Prime Minister is perfectly entitled to consider public opinion as one of the factors he ought to take into account. The real point is that Prime Ministers should not be isolated from public opinion, but that they should be capable of putting it in its proper place, weighing the thoughts of the electorate against the demands of good government.

Labour's embarrassing campaign launch in a Southwark school was a classic example of how counter-productive poor spin can be. Matthew Parris, in *The Times*[36], outspun the spin doctors in rewriting history to rewrite the script for the Prime Minister's announcement of the start of the election, contriving for him to arrive at an assembly at the school, his talk to the children about the future of the country, not to the press corps; cutting the length in half, and speaking entirely to the children, leaving the "drivel" (his word) to be released by others; explaining to the children his political philosophy, cutting out the acronyms and "slick, dreary names of programmes"; urging the children to listen to other

---

[36] Matthew Parris, "Tony, if only you'd let me write your script", *The Times*, 12 May 2001.

politicians' views, and lauding them as "good men and women who wanted the best for our country", and would have advised Tony to exit "swiftly", without goodbyes and handshakes, leaving the children to sing their hymn. Tony, if Matthew can be persuaded to join your spin staff at No. 10, you'd do worse than to employ him for your second term of office!

And still it goes on. Labour seems not to have learned the lesson yet. Since the election have come attempts to replace independently-minded Select Committee chairmen with ex-ministers (rejected by the Commons), and the forcing out of the respected heads of several public watchdogs.

New Labour was built on spin. But it was only able to achieve power because there was substance behind the façade. When spin is used to distract attention from a lack of substance, it runs the danger of becoming the centre of attention itself. Labour doesn't realise how close it came, given other circumstances, to bringing the whole edifice crashing down.

The Petrol 'Crisis'

For a few weeks after bottoming out in June, Labour recovered its equanimity and its poll ratings. Then in quick succession at the start of September came two events: first the Dome fiasco which erupted in early September, followed by the second blow of Labour's double whammy, the fuel boycott.

MORI's poll[37] for the *News of the World* published on 17 September put the Conservatives ahead of Labour, the first poll by any polling company to do so since sterling crashed out of the Exchange Rate Mechanism eight years before. NOP's poll, published on the same day in the *Sunday Times*[38], had very similar figures (varying by only 1% on the both Conservative and Labour shares). There seems no doubt that what the

---

[37] MORI interviewed 1,006 British adults on 14-15 September 2000.
[38] *Sunday Times*, 17 September 2000.

two polls measured was real, a very sharp swing against the government – and, furthermore, a swing that took place almost entirely over a couple of days, for Gallup's poll in the *Daily Telegraph* the previous week, which had been interviewing up to Tuesday, found almost no sign of it.

The reason, of course, was obvious – the petrol 'crisis' and what the media made of it, and the political situation it caused. Some of the news of that week – and the media coverage of it – had been highly evocative of the 'Winter of Discontent', which not only brought down the last Labour government but was a potent image for Conservatives to argue against electing another one for years afterwards. Speculation that the fuel shortages might disrupt refuse collection and even funerals must have brought back to many older voters' memories of the rubbish piled uncollected and the dead unburied in 1978-9. Gordon Brown, almost unbelievably (what were his spin doctors thinking of?) was even so foolish as to revive memories of a famous headline by quibbling over the use of the term "crisis". ("CRISIS, WHAT CRISIS?", as Jim Callaghan never said but the *Sun* said for him.)

The public made no bones about blaming the government. In the MORI/*News of the World* poll, 85% blamed the government a great deal or a fair amount, 85% said the government should reduce the current level of petrol tax, and 82% thought that the protesters who blockaded the oil refineries were right to take direct action in this way. Overall, only 19% were satisfied with the way Mr Blair handled the issue while 79% were dissatisfied, a four-to-one margin.

But it was always clear that the swing in voting intention was anti-government rather than pro-Conservative. That could be seen partly in the voting intention figures themselves, for a substantial part of the fall in Labour's support has switched not to the Tories but the Lib Dems, who were at 18% in MORI's poll and 21% in NOP's (this despite the fact that the Lib Dems were the party most unequivocally in favour of high fuel taxes). But the same conclusion came equally clearly from the continuing poor rating of William Hague: only 29% were satisfied with the way he was doing his job as Conservative leader and 49% dissatisfied; he gained nothing from being on the popular side in the petrol dispute, implying that any support his party had gained was in spite of rather than because of his leadership. The public's rejection of the Tory reaction to the petrol crisis suggests that the government caricature of the Opposition leader as "Billy Bandwagon" might have been playing well with its intended audience of voters. Even though 56% of the public when asked a fortnight later thought the government had handled the issue "very badly", 59% also thought the Tories were wrong to promise a 3p in the litre tax reduction.

Meanwhile, though, the Prime Minister's ratings dropped precipitately: 32% satisfied with the way Mr Blair was doing his job as Prime Minister and 63% dissatisfied – much his worst ever rating – while 55% were dissatisfied with the job Gordon Brown was doing as Chancellor, giving him a net rating of –21 (negative for the first time ever and down from +14 in July.)

But again, on a deeper look at the figures, they were more reassuring for Labour. To deprive Labour of its overall majority, the Conservatives needed to gain 89 of Labour's seats; to win a majority of their own, they need a further 75 gains. (It may have been obvious by the time of the election that analysing the latter category was pretty academic, but there were a few days in September when it didn't necessarily feel like that.) When we analysed the results from these two groups of seats separately, the swing over the Dome and petrol crisis period was much smaller. Although the figures had to be treated with a little caution, as the sample size within those key seats in any single survey was relatively small (around 250 in each of the two categories), we could get at least a rough approximation of what was happening.

In the period between the three MORI Omnibus polls carried out over 3 August–4 September and the MORI political poll for *The Times* carried out on 21-26 September, there was a swing from Labour to the Conservatives across the country of 7%. Before this period, which included the announcement of further funding to bale out the Millennium Dome and then the petrol crisis, taking the aggregate of the three polls, the Conservatives had 32% of voting intentions and Labour had 48%, a lead of 16%; afterwards, the lead had been cut to just two points, with the Tories up 3 on 35% and Labour down 11 on 37%.

But this gain was not taking place in the key constituencies which the Tories needed to win. In fact, not only did Labour support fall less in these constituencies than in the rest of the country, but Tory support fell here too! The entire collapse in the Labour vote in the marginals went to the Liberal Democrats and to other parties. Furthermore, when the general election finally came the Tories did worse still in these key marginal seats. For all the Conservative complaints about 'shy Tories' and Conservative strength being under-represented in the polls (shades of Barry Goldwater and the 'hidden majority' of America's 1964 presidential election), their MORI poll ratings in the key seats at the start of September – even before the petrol crisis and the ensuing brief flurry that gave them a narrow national lead – were higher than the share of the vote they finally secured. (See Table 18.)

But what did this mean for the political significance of the petrol crisis? Up to the start of September, although the Conservatives were well behind in the polls, at least the pattern of swings was in their favour: there had been a 3.5% swing to them since the election in the most vulnerable seats, and a 3% swing in the pivotal seats, even though the country as a whole had swung against them. The vote shares were an under-indication of the number of seats they could expect to win. Not in September! All that gain of support had been concentrated where it couldn't do them any good, as Roger Mortimore explained on the MORI website[39]; and that pattern deepened as the election approached, with the eventual swing in the most vulnerable marginals 2% less than the national swing.

Was the petrol crisis just a 'blip' in public opinion, or did it have a lasting effect? Gordon Brown made some attempt to defuse the issue with his spending announcements in November, which took the two-fold tack of making some concessions to appease protesters while emphasising the greater priority that the government gave to health

---

[39] Roger Mortimore, "Commentary Column: Swing Low, Sweet William" (13 October 2000), http://www.mori.com/digest/2000/c001013.shtml

spending, hoping perhaps to shame or isolate its more intransigent opponents.

Table 18: Swing in Labour's marginal seats, Autumn 2000

Great Britain	General election 1997 %	3 Aug-4 Sep 2000 %	21-26 Sep 2000 %	General election 2001 %
Conservative	31	32	35	33
Labour	44	48	37	42
Liberal Democrat	17	14	21	19
Other	7	6	7	6
Conservative lead over Labour	-13	-16	-2	-9
Lab-Con Swing from 1997		-1.5	+5.5	+2.0

Source: MORI/ The Times

89 Labour seats most vulnerable to Tories	General election 1997 %	3 Aug-4 Sep 2000 %	21-26 Sep 2000 %	General election 2001 %
Conservative	37	41	39	38
Labour	45	42	37	46
Liberal Democrat	13	12	18	12
Other	5	5	6	4
Conservative lead over Labour	-8	-1	+2	-8
Lab-Con Swing from 1997		+3.5	+5.0	0.0

Source: MORI/ The Times

75 'pivotal seats'	General election 1997 %	3 Aug-4 Sep 2000 %	21-26 Sep 2000 %	General election 2001 %
Conservative	32	35	33	32
Labour	52	49	39	51
Liberal Democrat	11	12	20	13
Other	5	4	8	4
Conservative lead over Labour	-20	-14	-6	-19
Lab-Con Swing from 1997		+3.0	+7.0	+0.5

Source: MORI/ The Times

The government's real problem was that the public didn't believe that it needed the revenue from the petrol tax: in a MORI/*Mail on Sunday* poll at the start of November, after Mr Brown had announced minor concessions, 73% said they thought that "The Government can afford to cut petrol taxes as it has enough money in reserve to maintain spending on public services, such as schools and hospitals", while only 19% took the contrary view that "The Government cannot afford to cut petrol taxes as this would mean reducing the amount of money that goes into public services, such as schools and hospitals". Consequently, the vast majority (82%) still believed that the government should reduce the level of taxes on petrol.

Nevertheless, it became quickly obvious that the petrol blip was going to be short-lived. The issue gradually faded away without ever again reaching the top of the political agenda: in September 31% had named petrol prices as one of the most important issues facing the country in our monthly (unprompted) poll question; this fell to 22% in October, 17% in November, 11% in December, and into single figures by the new year.

The party impact was similarly short-lived. Though all the pollsters put the Tories ahead in at least one poll during September (the highest lead being eight points in an NOP poll for Channel 4), by the last week of the month all the polls agreed that Labour was back on top, and did not slip from the lead again. Nevertheless, the government should have been sobered by the knowledge that this sort of sudden swing, however short-lived, was possible. Of course, it is 'only a poll'; but it would be taking a big gamble to assume that under similar circumstances voters might not do the same thing in the privacy of the polling booths – or, which could be almost as bad, decide it is not worth voting at all. This was a crisis which apparently came out of the blue, and the government was plainly not ready for it, and didn't know how to handle it when it did come.

There was a potential for more lasting damage. A week after the fuel crisis had eased[40], when public tempers had had a chance to cool, the

---

[40] MORI poll for the *Mail on Sunday*, published on 24 September 2000. MORI Telephone Surveys interviewed 1,011 British adults aged 18+ on 21-22 September 2000.

majority of the public expressed doubts about the trustworthiness of the government and its leading ministers: 56% said they did not find Tony Blair trustworthy, 62% said the same of Gordon Brown, and only 27% thought that the government is more trustworthy than was John Major's – a damning indictment when the electorate's lack of trust of the Major government was one reason for its landslide defeat. Trust can be lost precipitately, but it can be regained only glacially; the government had forfeited a very important aspect of its image.

Fortunately for Mr Blair in terms of domestic politics however, William Hague's trust ratings were still not significantly better. Nor, although 49% thought the government was "divided" rather than "united", another key voting indicator, did the Tories score over Labour here either. So the immediate electoral consequences were muted. But in the longer term, the loss of the public's trust had another serious consequence for Mr Blair, for his ability to win a referendum on joining the Euro will depend on his ability to convince a basically hostile electorate that he knows what is best for the country. If the voters don't trust him more than they trust the Euro-sceptic leaders, he is highly unlikely win the referendum, regardless of his ability to win the general election. It was at this stage that I concluded that, contrary to my earlier beliefs, the Euro referendum could not now be won in the 2001 Parliament.

Sleaze failed to impact

The perception of sleaze was one of the factors that destroyed John Major's government. Yet when similar allegations began to be attached to the Blair administration, it had little bite.

In September 2000, the public could hardly have been less complimentary about the Blair government. While 27% thought that Tony Blair's government was more trustworthy than John Major's had been, 26% thought it was less trustworthy[41].

---

[41] MORI poll for the *Mail on Sunday*, published on 24 September 2000. MORI interviewed 1,011 British adults aged 18+ on 21-22 September 2000.

Nearly three in five of the public, 59%, said they thought Gordon Brown had lied about the Bernie Ecclestone affair; but only 39% thought he should resign while 51% thought he should not.

Only one supposed incident of sleaze, the Hinduja affair which seemed to implicate Peter Mandelson and Keith Vaz, was still an issue in the run-up to the election. Yet there is little sign that it did the government any electoral damage at all.

Mandelson's resignation was an embarrassment to the government, and naturally led to much speculation that the government was acquiring a sleazy image that might damage it at the election. Two polls conducted after the resignation explored this. Three-quarters of the public thought[42] the affair had damaged the government's reputation, and three in five that it has damaged the Prime Minister's. But on this matter, as on so much else, the government was insulated from real damage because even more of the public thought badly of the Tories than did so of Labour.

This was slightly blurred at the time by the mis-reporting of an NOP poll for the C4 programme *Powerhouse*. NOP repeated a question that Gallup asked just before the 1997 election. (Table 19.) Labour's image on 'sleaze', unquestionably, had deteriorated since 1997, while that of the Tories had improved somewhat. As many people thought that Labour gave the impression of being very sleazy and disreputable as thought it of the Tories.

It was unfortunate that almost every broadsheet paper misreported the finding as being that that the public thought that Labour was "more sleazy" than the Tories. Not only had the question been about the impression that the parties give, rather than the reality, but such reporting of the poll made a further – and very common – error, by confusing the prevalence of opinions with their intensity: more people thought that Labour was (giving the impression of being) sleazy; nobody

---

[42] MORI poll for the *Mail on Sunday*, published on 28 January 2001. MORI Telephone Surveys interviewed 1,001 British adults aged 18+ on 25-26 January 2001.

was asked whether they were *more* sleazy. The difference may be the distinction between switching votes to the less sleazy Tories, and not voting at all.

Table 19: The Impression of Sleaze

Q. *Do you agree or disagree with the following statements?*
    "The Conservatives these days give the impression of being very sleazy and disreputable."
    "Labour these days give the impression of being very sleazy and disreputable."

	Conservatives			Labour		
	Mar 1997	Jan 2001	Change	Mar 1997	Jan 2001	Change
	%	%		%	%	
Agree	63	47	+16	19	49	-30
Disagree	32	45	-13	73	43	+30
Don't know	5	8	-3	7	8	-1
Net agree	+31	+2	+29	-54	+6	-60
Swing			*+14.5%*			*-30.0%*

Source: Gallup/NOP/C4 *Powerhouse*

Table 20: Blair's government more or less sleazy than Major's?

Q. *The previous Conservative Government under John Major was accused of sleaze. Do you think the current Labour Government is more or less sleazy than the previous Conservative Government, or is there no difference between the two?*

	Jan 2001	15 May 2001
	%	%
More sleazy	12	10
Less sleazy	30	27
No difference between the two Governments	54	56
Neither is/was sleazy	1	1
Don't know	2	6

Source: MORI/*Mail on Sunday/The Times*
Base: c. 1,000 British 18+ in each poll

In fact, as two MORI polls demonstrated, the majority found the two governments as sleazy as each other. More than half thought that there was no difference in rectitude between the Blair government and the Major government, and only one in eight that the Blair government was more sleazy than was the Major government.

Whatever the impression of relative sleaziness, there was no shift of voting loyalties following Mandelson's resignation on 24 January. Similarly, just as the voting intention ratings were not moved by the Mandelson resignation, nor were the government's satisfaction rating or Mr Blair's personal rating.

Figure 8

The 'Mandelson effect'

Q   How would you vote if there were a General Election tomorrow?

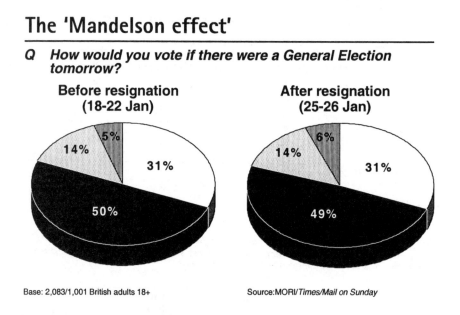

Before resignation (18-22 Jan): 5%, 14%, 31%, 50%

After resignation (25-26 Jan): 6%, 14%, 31%, 49%

Base: 2,083/1,001 British adults 18+   Source:MORI/*Times/Mail on Sunday*

Table 21: Satisfaction with government pre- and post- Mandelson

Q. Are you satisfied or dissatisfied with the way the Government is running the country?
Q. Are you satisfied or dissatisfied with the way Mr Blair is doing his job as Prime Minister?

	Government		Blair	
	18-22 Jan	25-26 Jan	18-22 Jan	25-26 Jan
	%	%	%	%
Satisfied	37	38	47	48
Dissatisfied	50	51	44	45
Don't know	13	11	9	7

Source: MORI/ *The Times/Mail on Sunday*

Conservatives unfit to win

As the public began to lose faith in Tony Blair and his government, probably only one factor saved them from a sharp collapse in support. Though disappointed with Mr Blair's performance, the public was even more disappointed in the Conservative Leader, the Conservative Front Bench, the Conservative Party's policies, and in the lack of any effective Conservative Party organisation. Mr Hague more than once called for a fresh start, in which he urged his party to stop apologising for the past and "focus on the new values agenda". That might have been fine, but the public felt they must have missed the apologies, half-hearted as they had been, and he had missed their values.

The Tories have no one to blame but themselves. It is our suspicion that this election was lost big when the leadership election chose William Hague over Ken Clarke to lead their party. Neither Ken Clarke nor anybody else could have won this election, but it might not have been 'poll meltdown'. The Conservative task in recovering from the party's defeat in 1997 was clearly a huge one, and inevitably most of the burden would fall upon the new leader. The Conservatives surely made the wrong choice when they elected William Hague as leader in 1997 (although there was not necessarily a right choice): he was young and inexperienced, and lacked the dominating personality to put himself across to the public and transform their opinions of the Conservative Party. There was never any point during the parliament at which it seemed that the electorate was taking Hague or his party seriously as an alternative government, and so eventually Blair's re-election, whatever his failings, was sure to occur by default.

Writing in 1999, Simon Atkinson and Roger Mortimore identified[43] seven distinct tasks that they believed a Tory leader would have to complete to restore the party to serious contention for government: to restore the morale and functionality of Central Office; to achieve concrete success at local and other subsidiary elections; to achieve

---

[43] Simon Atkinson & Roger Mortimore, "Hague's Progress", paper given at the Conference of the Elections, Public Opinion and Parties Group (EPOP) of the Political Studies Association, held at University College Northampton on 17-19 September 1999.

personal public recognition; to re-unite the Party behind him as leader; to develop his image with the public as leader and potential prime minister; to re-establish the credibility of the Party as an alternative government; and to identify issues on which to fight the general election campaign. A glance at the record shows how far he fell short of achieving most of these.

Central Office

There was a need to restore firm financial footing, establish Mr Hague's authority as leader and improve candidate selection procedures, and more generally to ensure that the party bureaucracy were all dedicated to fighting their Labour and Liberal Democrat opponents rather than each other. While this is a function not measurable by opinion polls, it seems fairly clear that despite apparent initial success the party machine was in little better state in 2001 than in 1997.

Admittedly, the finances were rather healthier, thanks to a few large donations from supporters such as Stuart Wheeler, John Paul Getty jr, and the treasurer, Lord Ashcroft. Reports after the election indicated that the Tories had had their most successful year ever for fundraising[44], and unprecedentedly had a £5m surplus[45] after the election rather than the perpetual overdraft. Indeed, they apparently raised twice as much during election year as the Labour Party.

But there was certainly no impression that the backbiting internal factionalism at Central Office had lessened in any way. One focal point was clearly Michael Portillo, not necessarily because he himself was disloyal or over-ambitious, but because his acolytes were ambitious on his behalf. There have been clear post-election indications, not least Amanda Platell's notorious video diary, that the atmosphere in Central Office may at times have been fairly poisonous.

---

[44] According to *The Times*, they raised £30.6m in the financial year – Andrew Pierce, "Eurosceptic peer bankrolls Clarke battle for Tory party leadership", *The Times*, 2 August 2001.
[45] Kevin Maguire, "Cash-strapped Labour steps up overdraft", *Guardian*, 1 August 2001.

The internal disunity surely damaged the party, allowing the public to hold a view of the Tories as riven by division, disloyal and backbiting. As one focus group member commented to us in 1998, "If they didn't trust each other, how is anybody else supposed to trust them?" Six in ten voters believed that Michael Portillo was plotting to replace William Hague as leader of the Conservative Party after the General Election, whilst only 12% believe he is really loyal to Mr Hague, according to an NOP/*Daily Express* survey.[46]

The party constitution, including the leadership election rules, was rewritten. The new rules gave the leadership greater direct power, but in reality they were better suited to bolstering up a weak leader – making him virtually invulnerable to a leadership challenge in ordinary circumstances – rather than identifying a strong leader or allow him to exercise leadership. Furthermore, they put the ultimate selection of a leader in the hands of the national party membership – in keeping with the spirit of the age but certainly not with the spirit of the history of the party, and which looked rather less advisable after the experience of giving the London members a free rein (the catastrophic selection of Jeffrey Archer as candidate for Mayor of London).

When it transpired after the election, during the farcical saga of the battle to elect Hague's successor, that the new rules had been so shoddily drafted that they made no provision for ties, it seemed to confirm all suspicions of the amateurishness of the once-professional Tory machinery during the Hague leadership. Key posts had been given to supporters trusted for their personal loyalty rather than their skill at the task in hand. It was reported that Sebastian Coe had to be relieved of responsibility for planning Hague's election campaign itinerary when it emerged, with but a few weeks to go, that plans for his nationwide tour had not gone beyond a vague outline on paper[47].

After the failure of Jonathan Holborow to cut the mustard as the Tories' head of communications, the party turned to another former Sunday

---

[46] *Daily Express*, 10 May 2001. NOP interviewed a representative sample of 1,000 voters between 4-7 May 2001.
[47] Roland Watson, "Hague's election tour plan misses bus", *The Times*, 1 February 2001.

tabloid editor. Amanda Platell was a dedicated but inadequate spin doctor. The incident when she bought a £ sign pendant for Hague to give to his wife Ffion, and the bill went unpaid so that her involvement in the transaction became embarrassingly public, should have been warning enough that the team was not up to the job. Hague was persuaded to court popularity through interviews with magazines such as GQ, yet nobody restrained him from claiming to have once drunk 14 pints of beer in a day, which brought nothing but ridicule. The incident which eventually derailed the Tory campaign at a promising moment, the Oliver Letwin fiasco which neutralised a key part of the Tory campaign, showed dismal lack of decisiveness, control or co-ordination. Letwin, a shadow Treasury spokesman, unguardedly admitted that he hoped a Conservative government would be able to achieve £20bn cuts rather than the carefully-costed £8bn promised in the manifesto; he then dropped from sight, refusing further interviews, without having made a convincing retraction. Alastair Campbell faced with a similar situation could probably have killed the story in hours; instead, days later Labour was still attracting minor headlines by dressing actors as Sherlock Holmes in their search for the 'missing' shadow minister.

Success at subsidiary elections

There were several justifications for the search for electoral success at sub-Parliamentary level, not least that the purpose of the party's existence is as much the promotion of Conservative ideals and where possible the exercise of political power by Conservatives at local and European level as at Westminster. But from the point of view of maximising prospects for the general election, three functions at least could be achieved by winning local elections, the European elections and the elections to the Scottish Parliament and Welsh Assembly: first and foremost the simple but vital task of raising the party's morale, both at Smith Square and in constituency and ward associations across the land, and as a consequence of this enabling the rebuilding of an efficient electoral machine on the ground; second, by winning control of councils and exercising power at local level, there was the opportunity to rehabilitate the party's reputation for competence with the voters; third, and not to be forgotten, was simply getting the party's former supporters back into the habit of voting Conservative.

Here at least the Tories had some substantial successes. It would certainly be wrong to minimise the effect on party morale of their first electoral victories since 1992. In the local government elections of 1999, they made net gains of over 1,400 seats at district level and, perhaps more importantly, took overall control of an extra 48 councils, which is the real beginning of rebuilding the Party. The following month they won the Euro-elections. In May 2000 again they managed substantial gains in the district council elections, with a net gain of just under 600 seats and 16 councils. In London they won 8 of the 14 constituency seats for the London Assembly as well as second place – ahead of Labour's Frank Dobson – for their mayoral candidate, Steven Norris (and the sight of the *Daily Mirror* front page instructing its readers to "Vote Tory" for the first time since 1929!). [48]

Yet the Romsey by-election, on the same night, with its warning that tactical voting for the Liberal Democrats in the South was still alive and well, was a much more negative message for Mr Hague, and one that fully justified itself in the subsequent general election. This was the first time an opposition party has lost one of its own seats in a by-election since Greenwich in 1987, an unenviable precedent given that Labour lost the following election by more than 100 seats. It was the first Tory loss in opposition since Roxburgh, Selkirk & Peebles in 1965, and that seat has been Liberal ever since.

The Romsey result also confirmed the message of the previous two by-elections with reasonable turnouts (Eddisbury and Ayr) that when turnout was respectable, the Tory share of the vote is static or worse. The opinion polls had already been suggesting that the Tories were moving nowhere, but Central Office preferred to decry their evidence; yet in the real elections most comparable to a future general election, they were winning or losing seats only through shifts in votes between the other parties.

---

[48] The *Mirror* did it again on 28 May 2001, with somewhat less pro-Tory intent: "Vote Tory ... and see what will happen to Britain if you do – Pages 2, 3, 4, 5, 6 and 7".

It is too easy to exaggerate the significance of the Tories' limited electoral success, and it may almost have been counter-productive for the national party. The 1999 local elections were fought against a very low baseline (the Conservatives' disastrous local elections of 1995). Turnout also was low, meaning that the votes the party had won were only a drop in the ocean of what would be needed for general election recovery: in the 1999 local elections the Tories won only 27.6% of the votes[49], or 3.4 million in total.

The local elections of 2000 were an equally illusory victory, even ignoring the Romsey by-election on the same day. Although the Tories made gains, the real danger sign was the highest-ever Liberal Democrat local election support. As Peter Kellner interpreted the outcome : "One overall message shines through. It is that millions of electors wanted to blow a raspberry at the government by every possible means – except voting Conservative."[50]

Nor were the European Elections quite the Tory victory that the spin doctors would have liked us to believe, even if it was a genuinely humiliating defeat for Labour. The overall turnout was only 23%. In fact, this was the worst performance by the Conservatives – in terms of the number of electors who actually turned out to vote for them – in any national election since women got the vote. This 'great triumph' may have secured the benefits of victory for party morale, but hadn't re-established among the public the habit of voting Conservative. Worse, dangerously, victories of any sort encouraged complacency, bolstering the obstinacy of those who wanted to disbelieve the opinion polls and believed it was possible to sweep Tony Blair out of office on a tide of hard-line Euro-scepticism and little else. The policy wonks carried on explaining away the 1997 defeat on sleaze and divisions, and while these played their part, they were by no means paramount. Their pollster reportedly presented evidence at a much derided 'dress-down Away Day' to suggest that some 40% of the defeat was the fault of the troops on the

---

[49] Colin Rallings and Michael Thrasher, *Local Elections Handbook 1999* (LGC Communications, 1999), p vi.
[50] Peter Kellner, "Labour still on course for elusive second term", *The House Magazine*, 15 May 2000.

ground. With three in four Tory councillors having lost their seats in Shire County Councils over the previous decade, this facile explanation did nothing except rile those who remained, and perhaps discourage prospective recruits from becoming candidates.

Finally, there was effectively no progress in the devolved elections in Scotland and Wales, with only a single constituency seat won in Wales and none in Scotland – and, worse, the establishment of these new legislatures providing a platform for the nationalist parties as the official Opposition could only help further to marginalise the Tories in both these countries. The Tories were there in both Parliaments, courtesy of the proportional representation 'top-up' seats, but it merely emphasised their role as a minor party. Following the mid-term elections, if we can call them that, the Tories were even more than they had seemed in 1997 an English rather than a British party.

Personal public recognition

Hague's primary personal task was, as a leader with a very low profile at the time of his election, to make a positive mark so that the voters knew who he was.

That, in one sense, was achieved. As we have seen (p 18), Hague was widely recognised – only 5% just before the election[51] said they didn't know who he was when read his name in a list of politicians, little worse than the Prime Minister (not recognised by 3%), and twice as good as the Chancellor of the Exchequer and the Deputy Prime Minister, who each went unrecognised by 10%. But, unfortunately, the public's opinion of his value to his party was a low one: 64% thought he represented a weakness and only 23% a strength, giving him a net score of –41. In 1997 using a similar question, John Major's net score had been +13. On the other evidence of Hague's image and its effect on the public, it is not a verdict with which we would wish to disagree.

---

[51] MORI survey for the *Sun*, published on 2 May. MORI Telephone Surveys interviewed 1,008 British aged 18+ on 30 April-1 May 2001.

It seems fairly evident that part of the reason for this was that the little the public 'knew' about Hague was full of inaccuracies and stereotypes. Focus groups revealed in the early months of his leadership that many of the public assumed that he had had a privileged public school education (he is the product of a state comprehensive), and, despite his Yorkshire accent that he was a Southerner – in both cases, presumably, they were simply projecting their preconceptions about the Conservatives onto the party's leader. But he missed the opportunity to dislodge this image with a more positive one, making some breathtakingly misjudged public appearances, riding a fairground water slide wearing a baseball cap, and drinking from a coconut at the Notting Hill Carnival. He came across as the worst sort of young fogey, desperately trying to look trendy.

Other comments from a MORI focus group in 1998 included: "William Hague ... I don't know enough about him... He doesn't project an image of a leader"; "It is all about someone you can relate to, and this person is abnormal"; and most discouragingly, this early, "I think the first feature is to get rid of William Hague".

Part of this, of course, came from the hostile caricatures of the cartoonists, who delighted in portraying him as still the schoolboy he had been when he famously first addressed a party conference. One strange consequence of this was that he was generally assumed to be considerably shorter than he actually is. A Gallup poll for the *Daily Telegraph*[52] found 40% of the public, and 60% of Tory supporters, thought Mr Hague's height was less than 5'9"; in fact he is 5'11" tall. Only 6% correctly named his height.

Re-uniting the Party behind its leader

The Conservative party between 1997 and 2001 remained as split as it ever had been and Hague showed no sign of having the leadership qualities necessary to deal with it. Europe has been, since before the fall of Mrs Thatcher, the great fault-line running through Conservative

---

[52] Roger Highfield, "Party leaders fall short in public's perception of political standing", *Daily Telegraph*, 21 March 2001.

politics. Few Tory MPs feel able to be neutral about it, and there is no realistic prospect of reaching agreement on one side or the other while the issue remains an active one.

Hague hoped to settle the issue with a members' 'referendum' on policy on the Euro, and indeed won handsome endorsement for his policy. But this was a back-me-or-sack-me ultimatum in all but name, worthy of John Major, and at best could only push dissent underground. If it had created the illusion of a strengthened and united party, perhaps it would be worthwhile in bolstering the morale of those supporting the leader; but a party whose support had already fallen so far could ill afford to marginalise any of its constituency.

It is true that the party remained surprisingly cohesive at the time of the European elections in 1999, when dissident MEPs split away to form the Pro-Euro Conservative party but failed to take any well-known names or a significant proportion of the votes with them, and also that divisions played slightly less of a part in the public image of the party in 2001 than four years before. (At the 1997 election, 44% of the public picked "divided" as a description fitting their ideas or impressions of the Conservative Party in our party image test; in 2001 it was 30%.)

But the illusion was not a very strong one.

Table 22: Most clear and united party

Q. *Which political party do you think is most clear and united about what its policies should be?*

	March 1992 %	1 Apr 1997 %	22 Apr 1997 %	15 May 2001 %
Conservative	35	13	11	9
Labour	28	37	34	40
Liberal Democrat	13	14	22	16
Other	1	2	3	2
None	9	16	14	15
Don't know	13	18	17	18

Source: MORI/ *The Times*

Although it almost beggars belief that any party could give a worse impression of not being clear and united on its policies than were John Major's Tories in 1997, the Conservatives' rating relative to the other parties had fallen, not risen. There can be little doubt that the government's failure to hold a referendum on the Euro contributed to this. If Britain were to join the Euro – or even, perhaps, if it were to vote against joining by so convincing a margin as to scotch the prospect for the foreseeable future – perhaps the rift could be healed. But while the issue remains active, every time the Tories bring it up it reminds people that their party is perceived as divided. Divided parties don't win general elections.

Figure 9

Satisfaction with William Hague

Q   Are you satisfied or dissatisfied with the way...
    ... Mr Hague is doing his job as leader of the Conservative Party?

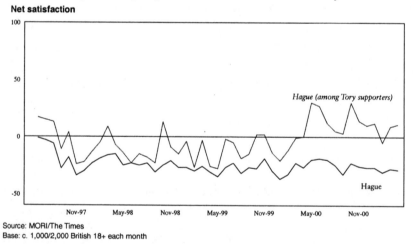

Source: MORI/The Times
Base: c. 1,000/2,000 British 18+ each month

Though apparently inspiring intense loyalty in those who knew him well, Hague was not very effective as a standard bearer to rally Conservatives throughout the country. It was not only the floating voters and 'lost Tories' who had little confidence in him. William Hague had a persistently negative leadership rating, and for much of the parliament this was true even among his own party's supporters, although there was a sharp improvement in the final year, as he and the party geared up for

70

the election campaign and attacked the government's weaknesses. This he did overwhelmingly by playing on themes dear to his party's core vote – Europe, law and order, asylum – yet which went little way towards winning back the middle ground. The increase in satisfaction among Conservative supporters, while his ratings among the country as a whole remained stubbornly negative, show the predictable outcome of such tactic.

But there was no likelihood of a leadership challenge, regardless of any ambitions of the 'Portillistas'. Even had the Hague disloyalists had the courage of their convictions, the newly introduced leadership election system meant Hague was glued in place until after the election. (Indeed, had Hague not voluntarily resigned it is at least questionable whether, even after a humiliation of the proportions of the 2001 election, it would have proved possible for his rivals to force him out.) On one occasion in mid-Parliament I was speaking to a former Tory Cabinet Minister who despaired of his Party's current leader.

"There's only three ways I know you can get rid of Hague," I told him. "Push him under a bus, he goes of his own accord, or the 'men in grey suits' call on him – but there aren't any men in grey suits anymore."

"I know", he replied. "I'm one of them."

Hague's image as potential Prime Minister

William Hague's satisfaction ratings with the general public were highly negative, he performed badly in 'most capable Prime Minister' polls (Charles Kennedy after about three weeks as a party leader was scoring almost as well as Hague after more than two years, chosen as most capable by 12% against 13% for Hague and 50% for Tony Blair), and his leader image profile if anything worsened rather than improved – he was most strongly associated with being 'inexperienced', 'out of touch' and 'narrow minded'.

Business leaders, too, who ought to be any Tory leader's natural constituency, rated Blair far higher than Hague: 65% of London business executives considered Tony Blair "competent" compared to the 25% who said the same of William Hague in a poll reported in the *Evening Standard*. Gordon Brown had a similar lead over the Shadow Chancellor, 83% considering the Chancellor's performance competent, compared to 46% who did so for Michael Portillo.[53]

An NOP poll for the *Sunday Times* found that less than a third of the electorate (28%) thought that the Conservatives could win an election with William Hague as leader; 60% believed that a victory at the polls could only be achieved with someone else in charge.[54]

His loyalists declaimed Hague's mastery of the despatch box, which most politicians recognised. But the despatch box no longer has much impression on even the chattering class, much less the masses, who are aware of it only through snippets in the broadcast news. This adversarial point-scoring may go over well in the Chamber, but is ridiculed in the focus groups. Playing to the electorate, little he did seemed to score at all.

But then the Tories are not the only politicians who don't fully realise how poorly what they consider the skills of their trade are viewed by the voters on whom they depend. A Gallup poll in the *Telegraph* during the election[55] managed to get to the heart of the issue: three people in four, 77%, agreed that "All politicians quote statistics and figures that are meaningless to most people". Not so good for those of us whose job is generating the statistics and figures, either!

By the time of the election, Mr Hague's ratings were still not good. Only 14% thought that of the three party leaders he would make the best

---

[53] *Evening Standard*, 9 May 2001. IDA interviewed 365 London executives of companies employing more than 250,000 workers across London for the IDA London Monitor on behalf of the London Chamber of Commerce and Industry in conjunction with the *Evening Standard*.
[54] *Sunday Times*, 13 May 2001. NOP interviewed 1,003 adults by telephone on 10-11 May 2001.
[55] *Daily Telegraph*, 24 May 2001. Gallup interviewed 1,439 British aged 18+ on 21-23 May 2001.

Prime Minister (see Table 17); indeed barely half (52%) of those who intended to vote for his party thought so[56].

In our "like him/like his policies" test, he achieved much the best personal score of his leadership, having won over some of the don't knows, but still only 35% said they liked him; by contrast, 51% said they liked John Major before the last election.

Table 23: Like or dislike William Hague and his policies

Q. *Which of these statements come closest to your views of Mr Hague/Major?*

	John Major	William Hague					
							31 May-2
	Jan 1997	Jun 1997	Dec 1997	Dec 1998	Feb 2000	Jan 2001	Jun 2001
	%	%	%	%	%	%	%
I like him and I like his policies	19	10	10	10	12	15	17
I like him but I dislike his policies	32	8	14	14	17	15	18
I dislike him but I like his policies	8	4	12	13	14	16	13
I dislike him and I dislike his policies	32	16	38	36	36	37	40
No opinion	9	62	26	27	21	17	12
Total like Mr Hague/Major	51	18	24	24	29	30	35
Total dislike Mr Hague/Major	40	20	50	49	50	53	53
Net like Mr Hague/Major	+11	-2	-26	-25	-21	-23	-18
Total like his policies	27	14	22	23	26	31	30
Total dislike his policies	64	24	52	50	53	52	58
Net like his policies	-37	-10	-30	-27	-27	-21	-28
Net like Hague/Major/policies	-26	-12	-56	-52	-48	-44	-46

Source: MORI/ *Times/Sunday Telegraph*

The more detailed leader image ratings tell the same story. His highest scoring image attributes were the negative ones, and his net rating (subtracting his average negative from his average positive score) was always well in the red.

---

[56] MORI survey for *The Times*, published on 7 June. MORI interviewed 1,967 British aged 18+ and registered to vote on 5 June 2001.

Table 24: William Hague: Leader Image

Q. *Here is a list of things both favourable and unfavourable that have been said about various politicians. I would like you to pick out all those statements that you feel fit Mr Hague.*

	Oct 1997 %	Apr 1998 %	Oct 1998 %	Apr 1999 %	Oct 1999 %	Apr 2000 %	Sep 2000 %	Apr 2001 %
Understands the problems facing Britain	10	14	12	11	16	14	14	17
A capable leader	9	11	10	10	12	11	11	12
Good in a crisis	3	3	3	3	4	4	3	6
Has sound judgement	5	8	5	6	6	7	8	5
Out of touch with ordinary people	29	30	36	34	35	32	28	28
Understands world problems	6	9	9	9	9	9	9	10
Tends to talk down to people	21	20	23	20	21	23	23	23
More honest than most politicians	9	11	11	12	11	11	9	11
Rather narrow minded	16	15	20	18	21	21	23	24
Down to earth	8	10	7	8	11	10	9	12
Patriotic	18	22	23	21	25	25	20	21
Rather inexperienced	52	46	47	46	38	35	39	33
Too inflexible	9	9	13	12	14	16	13	13
Has got a lot of personality	5	5	4	5	6	5	5	5
Average positive	8.1	10.3	9.3	9.4	11.1	10.7	9.8	11.0
Average negative	25.4	24.0	27.8	26.0	25.8	25.4	25.2	24.2
Net (positive minus negative)	-17.3	-13.7	-18.5	-16.6	-14.7	-14.7	-15.4	-13.2

Source: MORI/ *The Times*
Base: c. 1,000 - 2,000 British adults 18+

It is when the net scores of Blair and Hague are put in contrast that it is clear that there was no hope for the Tory Party at the last election.

Table 25: MORI Index of popular leadership

	Jun 1997 %	Dec 1997 %	Dec 1998 %	Jan 2001 %	31 May- 2 Jun 2001 %
Net like Blair/policies	+26	+66	+56	+18	+46
Net like Hague/policies	-12	-56	-52	-44	-46
Hague deficit	-36	-122	-108	-62	-92

Source: MORI/ *Times/Sunday Telegraph*

Combining the 'Like him/dislike him; like his policies/dislike his policies' election ratings of Blair and Hague into a single Index figure, Blair's dominance is confirmed. Then Blair's MORI Index was +14 and Hague's was -23. By the time of the election, Blair has moved his up to +23, mostly improving his policy image, while Hague was -22, effectively no change.

As a former Tory voter in hyper-marginal Torbay expressed it to the *Guardian*, "William Hague has no experience and about as much charisma as a bag of cold chips".[57]

Figure 10

Leader Image – April 2001

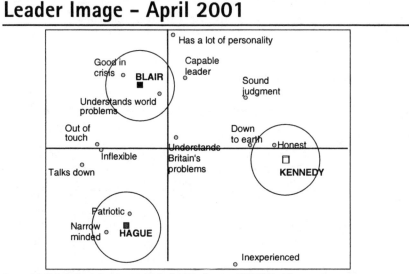

Base: 1,043 British adults 18+, 19-24 April 2001. Source: MORI/*The Times*

The perceptual map of leader image uses the statistical technique of correspondence analysis to summarise the relative positioning of the three leaders with regard to the 14 attributes in the public mind.[58]

---

[57] Nicholas Watt, "Flower power boosts Tories", *Guardian*, 2 May 2000.
[58] The perceptual maps are discussed in more detail in Robert M Worcester & Roger Mortimore, *Explaining Labour's Landslide* (Politico's Publishing, 1999), p 50-2.

Credibility as an alternative government

It is not very many years since it was possible to refer to the Conservatives as the "natural party of government" without giggling. Nor has the public respect in which the party was once held entirely disappeared. When we asked, in a poll for *The Times* at the end of December 1999, "Looking back over the twentieth century, which party – Conservative, Labour or Liberals – do you think has contributed most to Britain while in Government?", we half expected that attitudes to the past would be so coloured by present preferences that Labour would win hands down, but in fact the Conservatives were the winners by 45% to 32%, and even 33% of those intending to vote Labour said they thought that Conservative achievements in the previous century had been the greater.[59]

Table 26: Expectations in Government

Q. *If they were in power how good or bad would they be at doing what is best for Britain?*

	Conservative			Labour			Lib Dem		
	1997	1999	2001	1997	1999	2001	1997	1999	2001
	%	%	%	%	%	%	%	%	%
Very good	7	4	4	15	8	10	5	3	2
Fairly good	28	29	28	37	44	43	30	30	25
Neither good nor poor	22	24	26	26	24	25	33	31	37
Fairly poor	18	20	21	10	14	13	12	12	15
Very poor	18	14	15	5	4	6	7	5	7
Don't know/no opinion	6	9	6	7	6	4	15	19	14
Good	35	33	32	52	52	53	35	33	27
Poor	36	34	36	15	18	19	19	17	22
Net good	-1	-1	-4	+37	+34	+34	+16	+16	+5

Source: MORI/ *The Times*

So perhaps the public were prepared to be convinced that the Tories were a credible opposition; but the Tories were anything but convincing. Again, we can best gauge the failure by what the public told us they thought of the parties in the early days of the election campaign itself, using a question from the MORI Excellence Model, which we first used

---

[59] MORI interviewed 1,007 British adults aged 18+ on 10-14 December 1999.

in 1997 and which tends to find a more sympathetic assessment of the parties than any of our other regular measures. Not only did the Tories score negatively on this, more of the public thinking that in government they would be poor at doing what is best for Britain than thought they would be good at it – surely the minimum qualification for election – but the figures had actually deteriorated slightly since the end of the Major premiership.

On comparative questions the Tories fared even worse, despite the public's doubts about the government's performance. As we did during the 1992 and 1997 campaigns, we asked the public (in our second campaign poll for *The Times*) which of the three main parties they thought had the best team of leaders and which had the best policies. (Also, as already mentioned, which was most clear and united about its policies – see Table 22.)

The Tories had slipped a bit on policies, but the shift even since 1997 on best team of leaders was dramatic. Of course, this partly reflects the advantage of being in government – it is easier for cabinet ministers than members of the shadow cabinet to convince the public of their merits. But the Conservative shadow cabinet, with the exceptions of Mr Hague himself, Mr Portillo and Miss Widdecombe, had had an unusually low profile, and the ratio of Labour's lead doubled between 1997 and 2001. Further, even fewer of the public thought that Tory policies would be best for the country than thought so four years before.

Less than half even of those who intended to vote Tory, 46%, thought the Tories had the best team of leaders; only 2% of Labour supporters and 4% of Lib Dems agreed. It is clear, also, that the leadership question was related to the softness of the Tory vote: while 58% of those who said they had definitely decided to vote Conservative thought the party had the best team of leaders, among those who said they intended to vote Conservative but might change their minds, only 21% backed Mr Hague and his team while 23% preferred Tony Blair & co. Compare this with 1997, when 76% of those who definitely intended to vote Conservative, and 48% of those who thought they might change their mind, thought that the Conservatives had the best team of leaders.

Table 27: Party with best team of leaders

Q. *Which political party do you think has the best team of leaders to deal with the country's problems?*

	March 1992 %	I Apr 1997 %	22 Apr 1997 %	I5 May 2001 %
Conservative	40	20	21	13
Labour	30	40	34	47
Liberal Democrat	8	6	8	5
Other	1	1	1	1
None	10	14	16	13
Don't know	11	19	19	20
Labour lead	-10	+20	+13	+34

Source: MORI/ *The Times*
Base: c. 1,000 British 18+ in each survey

Table 28: Party with best policies

Q. *Which political party do you think has the best policies for the country as a whole?*

	March 1992 %	I Apr 1997 %	22 Apr 1997 %	I5 May 2001 %
Conservative	31	18	20	17
Labour	33	40	36	42
Liberal Democrat	13	8	13	11
Other	2	2	2	2
None	7	9	8	9
Don't know	14	23	20	18
Labour lead	+2	+22	+16	+25

Source: MORI/ *The Times*
Base: c. 1,000 British 18+ in each survey

Pretty strong stuff.

The more detailed party image measure told a similar story. In October 2000, Labour had just hit rock bottom, and was struggling to retrieve its reputation after the petrol crisis. Although Labour's image was, even then, superior to that of the Tories on many of the aspects tested, it was by no means strong. Indeed, with an average of almost 30% saying that they thought each of the negative descriptions fitted Labour (as bad a score as the Tories), while an average of only 15% picked the positive statements, the public was strongly critical.

Table 29: Party Image

Q. Here is a list of things both favourable and unfavourable that have been said about various political parties. Read through the list slowly keeping the ... party in mind.. Every time you come to a statement that fits your ideas or impressions of the .... party just tell me the letter next to it. You may pick as many or as few as you like. You don't have to be certain, just pick the letters next to the statements you feel fit the ... party.

	Conservative			Labour			Liberal Democrats		
	Oct	May		Oct	May		Oct	May	
	2000	2001	Ch.	2000	2001	Ch.	2000	2001	Ch.
	%	%	%	%	%	%	%	%	+%
Positive									
Keeps its promises	2	5	+3	6	9	+3	4	6	+2
Understands the problems facing Britain	19	18	-1	23	28	+5	19	22	+3
Represents all classes	10	8	-2	18	24	+6	23	21	-2
Looks after the interests of people like us	10	11	+1	11	21	+10	9	11	+2
Moderate	11	12	+1	17	20	+3	23	25	+2
Concerned about the people in real need in Britain	12	9	-3	19	21	+2	20	19	-1
Has a good team of leaders	7	7	0	13	25	+12	11	8	-3
Has sensible policies	14	15	+1	17	27	+10	24	27	+3
Professional in its approach	11	13	+2	11	19	+8	11	14	+3
Average positive	10.7	10.9	+0.2	15.0	21.6	+6.6	16.0	17.0	+1.0
Negative									
Extreme	14	12	-2	6	3	-3	2	2	0
Will promise anything to win votes	48	46	-2	42	35	-7	14	16	+2
Out of touch with ordinary people	40	36	-4	43	24	-19	8	9	+1
Too dominated by its leader	12	13	+1	33	26	-7	3	4	+1
Divided	31	30	-1	25	11	-14	5	6	+1
Average negative	29.0	27.4	-1.6	29.8	19.8	-10.0	6.4	7.4	+1.0
No opinion	13	10	-3	8	7	-1	38	30	-8
Net score (Average positive minus average negative)	-18.3	-16.5		-14.8	+1.8		9.6	9.6	

Source: MORI/ *Times*

But consider the changes over seven months. Not only did Labour's averages improve, but on every single one of the fourteen criteria the party's image moved in the right direction – more people picked each of the nine positives, fewer picked each of the five negatives. Overall, the party had a positive score. So did the Liberal Democrats, though this is based on far fewer of the electors having an opinion either way. But the Tories although getting some of the figures to move in the right direction, had barely made a dent in their negative rating.

Figure 11

Party Image – May 2001

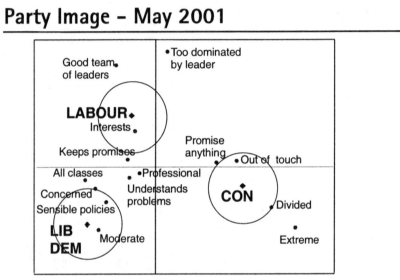

Base: 1,066 British adults 18+, 22 May 2001. Source: MORI/*The Times*

The party image perceptual map (Figure 11) similarly shows how the public most strongly associated the Conservatives with negative descriptions while the other two parties were seen more positively.

MORI research during the election suggests that it was the leadership of the party, above all else, that prevented its being taken seriously. The ratings also rather weaken the impression that the public's endorsement of Labour was grudging. Midway through the campaign[60], more than half of the public thought that Labour's policies nationally, the values

---

[60] MORI interviewed 1,928 British aged 18+ on 24-30 May 2001. The survey will be reported in more detail in a forthcoming paper by Robert Worcester and Paul Baines of Middlesex University.

that the party stood for and the quality of its leaders were good rather than poor.

Table 30: Rating the parties

Q. *From this card, how would you rate each of the following?*

	Conservative			Labour			Lab advan-tage %
	Good %	Poor %	Net %	Good %	Poor %	Net %	
The ... party's policies on national issues	34	32	+2	54	18	+36	+34
The ... party's policies on issues that affect your local area	25	28	-3	38	21	+17	+20
The values that the ... party stands for	33	32	+1	56	17	+39	+38
The quality of your local ... candidate	22	17	+5	36	13	+23	+18
The ... party's leaders	27	41	-14	55	22	+33	+47

Source: MORI
Base: 1,928 British aged 18+, 24-30 May 2001

Yet even the Conservatives managed net positive ratings on three of the five aspects of the party tested. Only on the quality of the party's leaders was there a clear thumbs down – 19% rated the Tory leaders as "very poor", just 5% as "very good".

Identifying issues on which to fight the general election

In the year or so before the election, the Tories cast around for suitable campaigning themes on which they could damage the government. Europe, or "saving the pound", was a constant. The government's failure to deliver on its promises was also an obvious theme, diligently pursued, but probably blunted by tying it in with the question of tax, which left it open whether the Tory solution to Labour's failures in public services was to spend the money more efficiently or not to spend it at all.

Other issues eventually emerged as news events prompted them, only to slip off the visible agenda again when they no longer seemed topical. Tory success in the local elections of 2000 was widely attributed, probably wrongly, to a new-found ability to tap into public concerns, not only on Europe and the Euro but on asylum-seekers and crime (and the case of the Norfolk farmer Tony Martin). Our poll for the *Mail on Sunday* across England just before the local elections investigated, and found that the Tories were indeed making limited progress on both issues.

But the problem for Mr Hague was that these issues were less the pre-occupation of the public as a whole than they were of 'core' Tory supporters (and the Tory media), and while they might achieve worthwhile council gains on low turnouts in the party heartlands they were far from being general election vote-winning issues. MORI's monthly polls for *The Times* throughout this period, as always, measured the salience of political issues with an unprompted question on the most important issues facing the country. In the February 2001 poll, race relations/immigration, at 18%, reached its highest level for twenty years but still ranked fifth behind the NHS and education on 48% and 37% respectively; by the end of April, after much of the pre-campaign news had revolved around the controversy over the refusal of some Conservatives to sign a Commission for Racial Equality pledge against racist campaigning and Hague's failure to remove the Tory whip from the retiring MP John Townend after a reportedly racist speech, the issue had far from becoming more prominent in public concern slipped slightly, to 16%. Crime and Europe were also secondary issues at 19% and 14%, and mentioned by fewer of the public than had been the case in February. (This was partly, of course, because the issues question is a zero-sum game: the sudden arrival on the public agenda of the Foot and Mouth outbreak limited the ability to get other issues prominent in the public mind; but, whatever the reason, the key Tory issues were not what most of the public were worrying about as the election approached.)

But among Conservative supporters, race relations/immigration was mentioned by 24%, Europe by 22% and crime by 26% – not far behind education (29%), though even among Hague's core supporters the NHS as well as Foot and Mouth disease were well out ahead. This may explain why Hague was able to consolidate an improving personal rating among party supporters while his public rating remains heavily negative.

Table 31: Most Important Issues facing Britain

Q. What would you say is the most important issue facing Britain today?
Q. What do you see as other important issues facing Britain today?
Most plus other important combined - all responses unprompted and spontaneous

	May 2000 %	Jun 2000 %	Jul 2000 %	Aug 2000 %	Sep 2000 %	Oct 2000 %	Nov 2000 %	Dec 2000 %	Jan 2001 %	Feb 2001 %	Mar 2001 %	Apr 2001 %
Foot & mouth disease	n/a	n/a	n/a	n/a	n/a	n/a	n/a	n/a	n/a	n/a	49	41
NHS/Hospitals	45	55	51	49	46	44	46	45	50	48	37	41
Education/schools	30	32	34	32	30	25	27	29	32	37	29	32
Crime/Law & Order	34	23	34	26	13	19	13	26	30	25	16	19
Race/immigration	16	17	11	11	6	10	6	8	11	18	10	16
Common market/EU	19	24	19	24	21	24	27	26	21	23	17	14
Unemployment	23	17	17	16	10	10	10	7	12	12	10	12
Economy	11	9	12	11	10	9	12	10	11	11	9	10
Pensions/social sec'y	15	12	14	15	23	19	14	9	8	11	8	8
Petrol prices/fuel	n/a	n/a	n/a	n/a	31	22	17	11	8	8	4	7
Pollution/environment	5	4	5	4	5	4	14	9	6	5	4	5
Public transport	6	4	13	8	7	12	9	14	9	9	6	4
Taxation	4	7	11	6	13	9	9	7	6	7	5	4
Drug abuse	10	8	6	6	3	7	5	7	6	5	5	6
(Others below 10% on every survey omitted)												

Source: MORI/ *The Times*
Base: c. 1,000 British 18+ in each survey

Europe

Europe remained the King Charles's head of Tory policy makers throughout the Parliament.

It was a touchstone policy for most of the MPs and most of the grassroots members. Opposition to joining the Euro, and frequently a more general antipathy to the EU, was almost the defining characteristic of Conservatism. It was the most significant issue on which the public was clearly in tune with Tory policy. Furthermore, it was easy to draw a clear contrast with Labour's position. Apparently it was the obvious key plank of the next election platform, and Hague duly adopted it as such.

But Europe lacks the characteristic of a good election fighting issue, saliency with the public. Just once, in the very month of the Euro-elections, Europe topped the public's monthly list of important issues facing Britain, for the first time ever in MORI's polls; but only 37% named it. At the 1997 election, when asked about the issues that would be important in considering which party to vote for, Europe was in only ninth place. Come the 2001 election, as we and many other commentators predicted at the time, it was again be replaced with such electoral stalwarts as health, education, and law & order. The vision of winning a general election, as they had won the 23% turnout European election, by appealing solely to a mainly latent sense of mistrust of the European Union, was a mirage.

Nor was it only MORI that found this. An ICM poll[61], after an intensive weekend devoted to acres of newsprint and hours of debate on radio and television on the subject of Europe and the Euro, found Britain's membership of the EU only 10th place in the list of important issues people said would be important to them in deciding how they would vote on 7 June, and Joining the Euro in eleventh place, following on from Asylum and immigration in ninth place and Taxation in seventh. Even the Tories' own pollsters were telling us that the party had picked the wrong issues on which to fight this election. So why on earth were they doing it?

Worse, the fact that the party was fundamentally split over the issue was always a bigger problem. Much was made of the Conservatives' "victory" in the European Parliament election. Yet the Tories lost more voters between 1992 and 1997 (c. 4.5 million) than voted Tory in the Euro Election (c. 3.8 million). Europe is not now, and has not been, an 'issue-issue' with the public; instead, it is an 'image-issue', for it splits the Tory Party.

So the Tories stayed split over Europe, and divided parties don't win elections. Tony Blair's failure to call a referendum on the Euro, whatever his reasoning, had at least the effect of ensuring that one of the weakest

---

[61] *Guardian*, 30 May 2001. ICM interviewed 1,000 British aged 18+ on 26-28 May 2001.

oppositions in modern British history stayed weak right through the Parliament. Certainly there was little indication that they had learned any of the lessons of 1997.

Yet even given Europe's limited utility as an issue, the Tories still managed to misplay it. One danger of the European issue was that many of the public, though Euro-sceptical by instinct, kept an open mind on the subject, and were sometimes unpredictable. One detail on which the Tories, and the Euro-sceptic press, misjudged the public mood was over the proposal for a European Rapid Reaction Force. It is plain that they felt that this idea could only further strengthen and intensify public feelings against the EU, yet when it came to the point, the majority of the public actually thought the proposal was a good idea.[62]

Not that this should have been a surprise: MORI as far back as 1987 have also found support for integrating armed forces[63], even when other European developments have been strongly opposed. This is, no doubt, partly because the Tories have failed to get the content of their argument across. For example, the MORI/*Mail on Sunday* poll[64] found 51% thought British forces should not fight under a non-British commander. (Since British troops do so already on NATO or UN operations of which the Tories are generally supportive, perhaps this is an argument they prefer not to pursue.) Our earlier polls found majorities supporting integrated European forces but opposing an integrated foreign policy. It seems clear that many of the Euro-sceptic public see a combined European army not as a threat to British sovereignty but a useful co-operation and perhaps a contribution to British interests by our European partners.

Undoubtedly the Tories were hampered in establishing Europe as an issue on the agenda by the apparent acceptance by much of the media of Labour's argument that Eurosceptic positions – ruling out joining the

---

[62] MORI poll for the *Mail on Sunday*. MORI interviewed 1,006 British aged 18+ by telephone on 24-25 November 2000. A Gallup/*Daily Telegraph* poll came to a similar conclusion.
[63] A MORI poll for the European Democratic Group (the Conservative bloc in the European Parliament) in August-September 1987 found 58% of Britons would support "a fully integrated armed services to defend Europe".
[64] MORI interviewed 1,006 British aged 18+ by telephone on 24-25 November 2000.

Euro for ever, especially ever contemplating leaving the EU – were "extremist". On several occasions during the Parliament we, and the other pollsters, produced polls finding a narrow plurality saying they would vote to leave the EU if there were a referendum. On each occasion it was met with virtual incredulity. Media memories can be short when the facts do not fit the preconceptions, and the next time it happened it was the same story over again. It was almost as if we had produced a poll showing that the British thought the world was flat.

Most of the public keep an open mind on the European issue; we're not sure every journalist does.

Figure 12

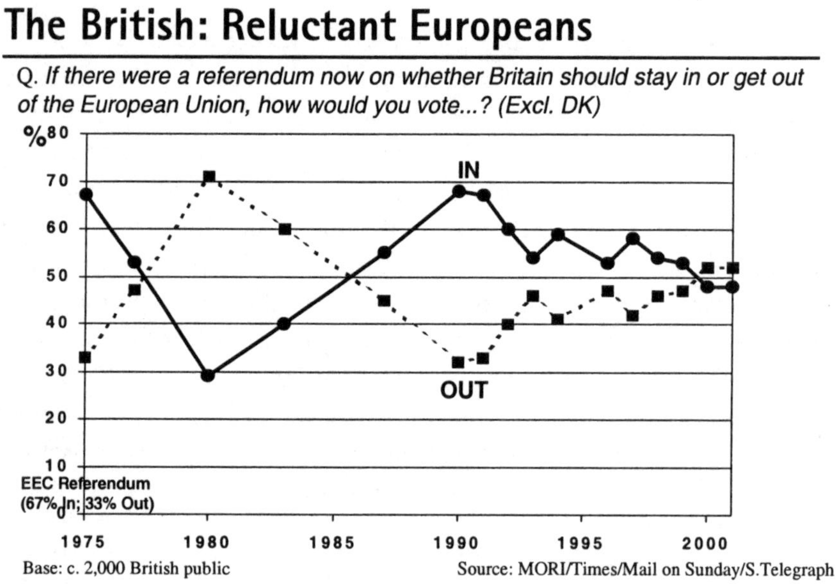
The British: Reluctant Europeans
Q. If there were a referendum now on whether Britain should stay in or get out of the European Union, how would you vote...? (Excl. DK)
%
80
70
60
50
40
30
20
10
IN
OUT
EEC Referendum
(67% In; 33% Out)
1975
1980
1985
1990
1995
2000
Base: c. 2,000 British public
Source: MORI/Times/Mail on Sunday/S.Telegraph

Though the majority are opposed to joining the Euro, they also reserve the right to change their minds. MORI has always found more than two in five, and on occasion three in five, keeping an open mind (see p 312). Similarly, ICM found[65] that while people remained cautious about joining the Euro in the short term, there was only limited support for a

[65] *Observer*, 13 May 2001. ICM interviewed 1,011 adults by telephone on 10-11 May 2001.

policy which stated that Britain should never join: 7% said Britain should join as soon as possible, 36% advocating joining "when the time is right", 24% wanted to rule out joining for the next few years, while only 28% took the firm position that Britain should never become part of the single currency. In a later ICM poll, although 61% said they would vote against joining when asked a simple question, a more detailed question found the majority preferring to postpone the decision: 57% said "we should wait and see how things develop and then take a decision"; 29% said "we should definitely stay out", and 12% said "we should definitely join". 2% did not know.[66]

In any case, many opponents judge it a lost cause. More than half the public, 53%, said they expected Britain to join the Euro during the next Parliament, while 35% thought she would not join, according to an NOP poll for the *Sunday Times*.[67] They don't like being taken for granted, though. Peter Mandelson spoke out at the Monday lunchtime meeting at the Labour Party conference in 2000 that he was "certain" that the British public would vote on joining the single European currency when they decided to hold it. I happened a guest speaker on a platform at the Labour Party conference the following Wednesday with Peter Mandelson, and took the opportunity to warn him that if he wanted a bloody nose from the British public all he had to say to them that he was "absolutely certain" that they would do what he told them to do when he told them to do it.

Be that as it may, Europe was early defined as one of the Tory battlegrounds for the election, and it was an unproductive choice. Europe never took off as an issue in the campaign, either for the Tories or even for the dedicated anti-Euro party, UKIP. UKIP never looked at any stage likely even to emulate the Referendum Party's modest success in 1997, let alone match the 7.0% of the vote they themselves had garnered in the European Elections in 1999. In the end only one constituency result (7.8% in Bexhill and Battle) was as good as their national result two years before, which of course had been in a proportional representation election which ensured such vote were not

---

[66] *Guardian*, 30 May 2001. ICM interviewed 1,000 adults by telephone between 26-28 May 2001.
[67] *Sunday Times*, 27 May 2001. NOP interviewed 1,001 adults by telephone on 24-25 May 2001.

wasted. The party saved six deposits. Nevertheless, the UKIP vote was greater than the margin by which a second-placed Conservative candidate lost in 13 seats; but if we were to assume that had there been no UKIP candidate, half the UKIP support would have voted Tory and the other half not voted at all, that would mean UKIP cost the Tories only three seats.

Table 32: Effect of UKIP votes

	Winner	% Majority over Con	% UKIP vote	Ratio
Cheadle	Lib Dem	0.1	1.4	18.2
Dorset South	Lab	0.3	2.0	6.0
Braintree	Lab	0.7	1.5	2.1
Weston-Super-Mare	Lib Dem	0.7	1.4	1.9
Monmouth	Lab	0.9	1.5	1.7
Dorset Mid and Poole North	Lib Dem	0.9	1.4	1.6
Lancaster and Wyre	Lab	0.9	1.4	1.5
Northampton South	Lab	1.7	2.4	1.4
Somerton and Frome	Lib Dem	1.3	1.7	1.4
Guildford	Lib Dem	1.1	1.5	1.4
Kettering	Lab	1.2	1.6	1.3
Norfolk North	Lib Dem	0.9	1.1	1.3
Hereford	Lib Dem	2.2	2.7	1.2

Asylum, Race and Patriotism

Another issue which the Tories toyed with before abandoning it as a major campaign theme was asylum and immigration.

Of course, there is considerable interlinking between "patriotism", "Euroscepticism", resistance to immigration and other less reputable attitudes to national and racial issues. A politician may hold right-wing views on one and not the other – those who know William Hague are unanimous that he is entirely opposed to racism – and yet a campaign on one aspect may inadvertently appeal to the baser instincts of some voters, whether or not they read into it a subtext that is not there. No Conservative politician can ignore the question of national identity, yet even to mention it can lead to the immediate accusation that he is "playing the race card".

A few months before the election, a think tank report[68] was published which apparently suggested that the concept of Britishness was racist. It was widely ridiculed, and repudiated by Jack Straw who was theoretically its sponsor. On the other hand, Trevor Phillips, Labour chairman of the Greater London Assembly, and a member of the commission which wrote the report (and black himself), said criticisms of the report were the "knee-jerk reactions of little Englanders".[69] The degree of controversy that was aroused suggests that we need to investigate what "British" is taken to mean before we try to draw any conclusions about campaigning based on "Britishness", or the threat of becoming "a foreign land".

There is certainly a "British" stereotype, though of course the way in which the British might like to think of themselves is by no means necessarily the way others think of them. In 1999, MORI interviewed members of the "successor generation", those expected to be the decision makers and opinion formers of future years, in 13 countries round the globe on behalf of the British Council. The images that to them "best sum up" the countries of the United Kingdom are mostly trivial or superficial ones, and overwhelmingly visual: kilts, mountains and whisky for Scotland, castles and rugby for Wales, the Royal Family, Big Ben and the Tower of London for England. But they also have strong views on the nature of British society and the British people: they agreed by a big majority that Britain is "truly multicultural" and disagreed that it is a classless society; by more narrow pluralities they also thought that Britain is not very welcoming to foreigners, and that the British are not racially tolerant.

But how do we characterise ourselves? The first thing to emerge is that "Britishness" is very much another name for "Englishness" – these days,

---

[68] The Commission on the Future of Multi-Ethnic Britain was set up the Runnymede Trust. In the vanguard of the press coverage was Philip Johnston, "Straw wants to rewrite our history", *Daily Telegraph*, 10 October 2000.
[69] Philip Johnston, "Straw beats a very British retreat over race report", *Daily Telegraph*, 12 October 2000.

at least (was it ever really different?) it is only the English who tend to think of themselves as British in any numbers; most Scots think of themselves primarily as Scottish, most of the Welsh as Welsh. The English, on the other hand, are more likely to describe themselves as British than as English. (The whole question is rather different in Northern Ireland, but as MORI and the other Great Britain based polling companies do not normally poll there, and as Messrs Blair and Hague do not campaign for votes there, we shall leave it well alone.)

These identifications were explored in a MORI poll for the *Economist* in September 1999. Scots were most likely to identify primarily with Scotland (72%) and their region (62%), less with their local community (39%), and only rarely with Britain (18%). Even more overwhelmingly, the Welsh identify first with Wales (80%), then region (50%) and community (32%); 27% of the Welsh identify with Britain. But among the English, there is an almost even split between the importance of region (49%), Britain (43%), local community (42%) and England (41%).

Perhaps even more revealingly, the same poll asked which flags respondents identified with. In England, 88% identify with the Union Jack and only 38% with St George's Cross (perhaps because it has been discredited by its frequent association with football and adoption by football hooligans); but in Wales the dragon outscores the Union Jack by 85% to 55%, and while 75% of Scots identify with the Saltire only 49% do with the Union Jack. This "Britishness", if not exactly an English invention, is now primarily an English survival.

There is certainly little feeling that we are European, except in a purely geographical sense. The European Commission's Eurobarometer survey in Autumn 1998[70] asked samples across the EU whether "In the near future, you see yourself as (nationality) only, (nationality) and European, European and (nationality) or European only". Across the EU, 43% admitted only their own nationality, and 43% to their nationality first but also to seeing themselves as European. Only 11% felt European first

---

[70] European Commission Eurobarometer *Report Number 50* (1999), p B39.

(7%) or solely (4%); 2% didn't know. In 7 of the 15 member states, more felt at least partly European than not European at all. But in Britain, by contrast, 62% said they felt British only, 27% British and European and just 9% European and British or only European.

Nationalism and Europeanism

Q In the near future do you see yourself as ..?

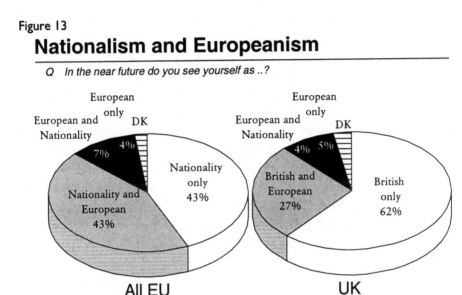

All EU   **UK**

Source: European Commission Eurobarometer 50
Base: 16,155 across the EU including 1,066 in GB, 327 in Northern Ireland, October-November 1998

But we are able to make a wider and more profound analysis of what Britons think with the help of the 1999 MORI/Socioconsult monitor, the British section of a wide-ranging multi-national survey which attempts to diagnose and link trends in public opinion, and point up their relevance for companies operating in the British market. Analysis of mostly unpublished data from the survey reveals an underlying tension.

MORI/Socioconsult detected an increasing polarisation up to 1999 between the broad bands of British opinion which on one hand hold to a distinct national identity and on the other embrace internationalism, the European Union and multiculturalism. One of the purposes of the Socioconsult monitor is to be able to identify and track 'currents' in opinion – underlying trends that tie together answers to similar or related questions, and which can give a coherent pattern to the numerous attitudinal and behavioural strands of Britain's national character. The current identified as "National Superiority", basically the conviction that Britain is different through its unique culture and heritage and in many ways better than other nationalities, is one that showed a distinct increase between the 1997 and 1999 surveys. These attitudes seem to have particularly high resonance among the population groups that MORI/Socioconsult classifies as "Traditional Working Classes" and "Traditional Poor", as well as "Corporatists" – in general, those whose values would identify them as being Labour's natural 'heartland' core vote. Of course, for much of the past century it has been the ability of the Conservative Party to divert many of this group away from Labour support with the more seductive appeal of patriotism and nationalism that has made them the "natural party of government" even in a country where the middle-class has until recently been much in a minority. If Tony Blair could successfully wrap the Labour Party in the Union Flag without at the same time compromising its socialism or its Europeanism, he could consolidate his electoral position; failing that Hague's perceived "patriotism" is potentially a strong card.

Similarly, the "patriotic" strand of opinion is closely allied to Euro-scepticism. Consider two of the characteristic questions defining the National Superiority current: 49% of the public agree that "It is important that the British remain very different from all other nationalities", and 71% that "What I love about Britain is our heritage". These are two attitudes that correlate strongly, and five in six who agreed with the first statement also agreed with the second. At the same time, 47% of adults agree that "I support Britain's involvement in the European Union. It's the way ahead in the nineties", a sentiment with which the government made it plain enough that it agreed; but, unfortunately for Mr Blair's ambition to appear patriotic, most of the public seem to feel pro-EU sentiment is diametrically opposed to a distinctive national identity – only 18% of British adults agree both that "It is important that the British remain very different from all other nationalities" and that "I support Britain's involvement in the European Union. It's the way ahead in the nineties".

This group of pro-EU patriots are not demographically distinctive – they are fairly evenly distributed through all groups and classes of the population, and indeed in their political support are spread between the various parties in the same proportions as everybody else.

But those voters who set store by their "Britishness" are not Tony Blair's natural constituency. Three in five of those who strongly agree Britain should remain different also say "I would like Britain to be the way it used to be". By aligning the Tories with Euro-scepticism and patriotism, Hague is only going with the grain of opinion among "conservatives with a small 'c'".

Unfortunately, this same bloc of opinion also tends to the right on immigration, and more generally (though for the most part with more genteel discretion) on race. The Socioconsult analysis suggests how strong the relationship between the two issues is: 75% of those who agree that "It is important that the British remain very different from all other nationalities" also think that "There are too many immigrants in Britain" (although, it should be noted, so do 57% of the whole adult population – and this rose as high as 66% in a separate MORI survey for *Reader's Digest* in July 2000). Hence the accusations of "playing the race card", even when that is far from a leader's mind. The issues may be distinct in the minds of the politicians, but they are closely aligned and feed on each other among the voting public. Although the Conservative Party is not, to use a current buzzword, "institutionally racist", it is an institution with a good many latently racist supporters.

The surprising thing is that, despite the depth of feeling on the issue, "playing the race card" (advertently or inadvertently) doesn't seem to work. In July 2000, 80% of the British public said they agreed with the statement that "Refugees comer to Britain because they think Britain is a 'soft touch'", and 63% that "too much is done to help immigrants at present".[71] Yet the Tories' failure to establish asylum as a winning issue by the time of the election was charted by an ICM survey for the

---

[71] MORI survey for *Reader's Digest*. MORI interviewed 2,118 British aged 15+ on 20-24 July 2000.

Guardian[72] conducted just before the election was called. More of the public, 20%, thought Labour's policy on the issue was best than favoured the Tories, 16%. However, the majority of voters either believed that no party has the best policies to deal with asylum (29%), or that they were unable to choose between party policies (also 29%). Three-quarters of voters were against the abolition of all immigration controls, with 18% in favour; however, more than half, 51%, said they would support a decision to allow unskilled economic migrants into Britain if done on a quota basis, such as the 'green card' system operated in the United States. Asked whether they supported such an approach if it could be proven that economic migrants would not be a burden on the state, 67% were in favour, rising to 70% support for migrants with skills in occupations currently suffering skills shortages in this country, such as GPs, nurses and teachers.

While Hague did not make a major issue of immigration during the campaign, his "foreign land" speech – aimed at the European Union, not immigrants – was widely taken as being a coded attempt to do so, and the matter was of course exacerbated by the furore over the CRE declaration and by John Townend's speech to his East Yorkshire constituency association. It was rumoured that a Tory election broadcast on asylum seekers was planned, and cancelled at the last minute when wiser thoughts prevailed, though other sources have denied this.

Being seen apparently to "play the race card" naturally damaged the Tories among ethnic minority voters. An Asian Marketing Group survey[73] found that only 7% of Asian business people said they had confidence in William Hague, and less than a quarter, 23%, thought that the Tories were committed to not playing the "race card", Asked about the speech made by William Hague in which he referred to Britain becoming a "foreign land" if Labour stayed in power, two-thirds thought the wording "clumsy" and 21% believed it was "racist". In the final outcome, though the Conservative share of the national vote rose, the share of the non-white vote dropped sharply.

---

[72] *Guardian*, 21 May 2001. ICM interviewed 1,022 adults aged over 18 by telephone on 4-7 May 2001.
[73] *Daily Telegraph*, 25 May 2001.

There is little sign from the constituency results that the asylum issue helped the Tories much. Kent is perhaps the county most disrupted by asylum seekers, and a MORI poll for the *Mail on Sunday* in April 2000 had found that whereas across England 27% thought the Tories and 22% Labour had the best policy on "immigration and asylum seekers", in Kent the Tory lead was 40% to 15%.[74] More than a quarter of the Kent residents, 27%, had said that race relations, immigration or asylum was one of "the most important local issues facing your part of the country", well ahead of any other issue in prominence. Yet at the election the swing to the Tories in Kent was only 1.2%, whereas the national (GB) swing was 1.8%.

Tax

Another consistent theme for the Tories was an old favourite, reducing taxes; but they showed little awareness that this policy does not have the pull with voters that it did in the eighties. During the Thatcher years, low taxes for their own sake looked like a vote winner and a natural Conservative policy. But those days are beginning to seem a very long time ago.

The Tories had made tax one of their key messages in the election run-up, and it was the issue with which they started their campaign – impressively, many commentators thought. They seem to have succeeded in getting their message that taxes had risen under this government home to the electorate. As early as December 1999, the public were convinced that taxes had risen under Labour: 28% thought that since it had been elected the government had kept taxes down while 57% thought it had not. By January 2001 the figures were a little better for Labour, but still expressed widespread scepticism: "thinking about all forms of taxation", 48% thought taxes had gone up since 1997 "for most people" and 41% that their own personal taxes had increased. Furthermore, few expected a re-elected Labour government to have a better record keeping its tax

---

[74] MORI interviewed 501 British adults aged 18+ across England, and a further 201 across Kent, by telephone on 27-29 April 2000.

promises: at the end of May[75], 74% said they thought that if Labour was re-elected it would increase taxes, and only 16% that it would not.

But that belief brought no increase in support for the Tories, nor was tax one of the issues of most concern to the public (see Table 31). They may have believed that Mr Blair had raised taxes, and would do so again, but it was not preying on their minds. It is true, of course, that all other things being equal most taxpayers would prefer to pay less tax; but most are also concerned about the standard of public services.

There is a myth in Labour circles, and perhaps in Tory ones, that Neil Kinnock lost the 1992 election because he promised to raise taxes, and Tony Blair won the 1997 one because he promised not to. There is a gaping flaw in this argument: Tony Blair may have made his famous "Five Year Pledge: No Increase in Income Tax Rates", but the key voters didn't believe him anyway. In MORI's 1997 final pre-election poll for *The Times*, 63% said they expected that a Labour government, if elected, would increase income tax, only 3% lower than the 66% who had expected a Kinnock government to do so in 1992.

So why did Kinnock lose in 1992 and Blair win in 1997? As far as the tax issue is concerned, the polling evidence from the British Election Survey strongly suggests that the sticking point for the key voters was responsible spending. It was not so much the threat of higher taxes in John Smith's Shadow Budget that 'middle England' rejected as the fear that the money would simply be wasted. Of course, 'Black Wednesday' (when sterling fell out of the European Exchange Rate Mechanism) shortly afterwards destroyed all Tory claims to fiscal credibility, and made it much easier for Labour in 1997 to be considered a serious alternative. Trusting Labour's tax pledges really didn't come into it: tax is no longer the bogy that once it was.

The Tory "You paid the taxes" campaign was playing on the wasted money argument, and probably hit home, but only in reminding the public of their dissatisfaction with the standards of public services, not in

---

[75] MORI survey for *The Times*, published on 31 May. MORI interviewed 1,013 British aged 18+ on 29 May 2001.

swaying them towards a party promising lower taxes and therefore, by implication at least, lower public spending. The Tories had to convince the public that current spending levels were not delivering adequate public services, and that therefore taxes should be cut. There was clear public sympathy for the first proposition, much less for the second. "You paid the taxes" talked about a problem, not a solution. The public might have been enthused by an opposition they believed would draw from this that the same promises had to be made but this time the promises had to be kept; but they were not interested in the argument – which had been a winning one in 1992 – that since Labour's taxes were not delivering good public services the proper alternative was to abandon the quest for better public services, and to cut taxes instead.

Even in the weeks after the petrol crisis, when there was widespread condemnation of one aspect of government tax policy and it was briefly socially acceptable and not politically incorrect to question the utility of taxes, the Tories failed to convince the public against the principle of higher spending to improve public services. Our poll for the *Mail on Sunday* in November 2000 found a slight lessening of the tax and spend mentality since the 1997 election, but not nearly sufficiently so to be of any electoral impact.

Table 33: Tax and Spend

Q. *People have different views about whether it is more important to reduce taxes or keep up government spending. How about you? Which of these statements comes closest to your own view?*

	25-28 April 1997 %	2-3 Nov 2000 %
Taxes being cut, even if it means some reduction in government services, such as health, education and welfare	7	12
Things should be left as they are	14	20
Government services such as health, education and welfare should be extended, even if it means some increases in taxes	76	61
Don't know	3	7

Source: MORI/*Economist/Mail on Sunday*
Base: c. 1,000 British adults aged 18+ on each survey

The solid and uncomfortable fact for the Tories is that the vast majority of British voters, these days, are entirely committed to the idea of public services, especially the NHS, distrust the Tories on the issue, and do not want tax cuts as an alternative. That is not to say that they are entirely hostile to any alteration in the arrangements. For example, according to an NOP poll, two in three, 66%, would be prepared to pay for some NHS care if it meant an overall better service.[76] But improving the service remains the aim.

Nevertheless, the Tories stuck to their guns. Most of them probably still don't believe that the voters will really stand for increased taxes, however laudable the spending that results; they feel they've heard that one before, and take with a pinch of salt polls that seem to suggest the converse. The people only say that to interviewers because they are embarrassed to admit being tightwads, they argue.

Such arguments can be partly countered by asking the poll questions in a different way. If respondents are answering disingenuously because they feel social pressures to conform, it may be better to ask them what they feel other people think – this is an approach which can sometimes uncover a 'silent majority' where one does exist. But there is no sign of this on the tax and spend issue. For example, in ICM's pre-budget poll for the *Guardian* in 2000[77], more than three-quarters said that "thinking about the people you know", they thought most people would prefer extra NHS funding to tax cuts, and two in three also thought that more money to the NHS was more likely to win the next election for Labour than a tax cut.

Or, it is sometimes argued, the voters don't understand what 1p in the £ income tax means, and think the sums involved are much more trivial than is the case; but in fact surveys spelling out the cost to each taxpayer or household find similar endorsements of higher taxation to fund the NHS.

---

[76] *Sunday Times*, 27 May 2001. NOP interviewed 1,001 adults by telephone on 24-25 May 2001.
[77] *Guardian*, 21 March 2000. ICM interviewed 1,207 British aged 18+ by telephone on 17-19 March 2000.

As another instance, in an interesting and under-reported experiment, in February 1999 Milton Keynes Council rather than taking an opinion poll organised a binding referendum of their residents, and were given a direct and convincing mandate to increase council tax so as to improve services. However, similar exercises organised by other local authorities drew votes in favour of cutting services rather than raising council taxes. This could be the age-old problem governments have of disentangling the question of higher taxes, hypothecation and effective service delivery.

But, in any case, even were this not so, the Tories had so failed to convince the public of their own tax and spending credentials that, regardless of Labour's poor showing, the Tories were hit by a "double whammy": more of the public believed that a Conservative government would raise income tax than believed it would not[78], and more expected public services under the Tories to deteriorate than to improve: NOP in the *Sunday Times* found that the electorate had more confidence in public services improving under Labour, and remained unconvinced that they would end up paying less in tax under a Conservative administration. Almost half (46%) expected to see public services improve under a second Blair term, with 32% expecting them to stay about the same, and 18% believing they would get worse. In contrast, barely one in five (21%) anticipated improvements under the Conservatives, with 35% expecting public services to stay about the same and 36% saying they would get worse.[79]

---

[78] By 45% to 40% in MORI's poll for the *Sunday Telegraph* on 10-12 May 2001.
[79] *Sunday Times*, 13 May 2001. NOP interviewed 1,003 adults by telephone on 10-11 May 2001.

Figure 14: Public Services and Tax under a Tory government

If the Tories were to win the election...

Q ...do you think that the overall level of taxation would be...?

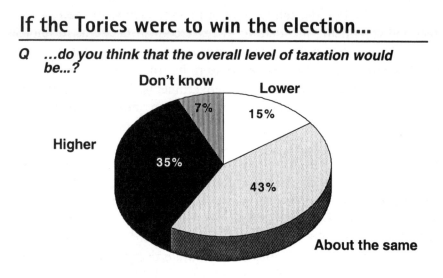

Base: 1,007 British 18+, 11-13 January 2001. Source: MORI/*Sunday Telegraph*

If the Tories were to win the election...

Q ...do you think that public services would..?

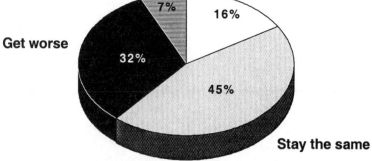

Base: 1,007 British 18+, 11-13 January 2001. Source: MORI/*Sunday Telegraph*

Setting the agenda

The opposition cannot hope to win an election on the issues without seizing the initiative and setting a news agenda that highlights their arguments. We have already seen (Table 14) which issues the public picked from our list of 17 as important to their vote. But more revealing in many ways is to ask them the same question without prompting them with a list. The answers to an unprompted issues poll depend on what is 'top-of-the-mind' when it is conducted, and that in turn is very dependent on the news coverage.

Table 34: Issues important in deciding vote

Q. *Looking ahead to the General Election, which, if any, issues do you think will be very important to you in helping you to decide which party to vote for?*

	10-12 May 2001	31 May-2 Jun 2001 All	"May change mind"
Unprompted answers:	%	%	%
Health care	40	50	47
Education	35	39	37
Pensions	16	15	13
Europe	7	14	15
Taxation	16	11	13
Law and order	10	10	12
Managing the economy	7	7	7
Public transport	5	7	7
Asylum/immigration	6	6	7
Protecting the natural environment	2	3	4
Unemployment	3	3	4
Animal welfare	1	2	1
Foot & mouth disease	2	2	1
Housing	2	2	2
Defence	1	1	*
Northern Ireland	*	*	0
Trade Unions	*	*	0
Other	14	11	12
None/Don't know	18	11	11

Source: MORI/*Sunday Telegraph*

Agenda setting is a vital part of party strategy in a modern election campaign, and if these are the issues on which the Tories believe they can win votes it is up to them to ensure they raise their salience in the public mind. (Sometimes that's easier said than done, even when the public is receptive – remember "The War of Jennifer's Ear" in the 1992 election, when the media's insistence on reporting the conduct of Labour's campaign rather than its substance effectively derailed their attempt to achieve any serious debate on the NHS.)

Table 34 shows how the Tories had not succeeded in getting their issues onto the agenda. However receptive the public might have been to the Tory messages if they heard them, the Tories' chosen issues were not the issues the public was thinking about. Even after what was widely seen as a strong start by Hague on tax, only 16% of the MORI sample named taxation as 'very important' to them in helping them to decide for whom to vote. Also sleeping to begin with was Europe, with only 7% mentioning Europe and the Euro at the start of the campaign. It rose, but only to 14%, still an inadequate platform for an election-winning campaign. In fact the "Labour issues" of health and education – in other words, improving the services rather than finding a way to spend less on them – were so far ahead in the public's priorities as to be out of sight.

Why the Tories were short of campaign issues

But perhaps the biggest difficulty for the Tories in finding election issues was that their record in government had already queered their pitch too comprehensively, blocking many avenues which it would otherwise have been natural to pursue. Tax was an example – much of the distrust of William Hague's tax promises must have been at least strengthened by memories of John Major's perceived broken promises on the same subject up to 1997. So also were the two issues which unforeseen events thrust to the forefront of the news agenda over the last six months before the election, the state of the railways and the Foot and Mouth outbreak.

The Hatfield rail crash and the consequent decimation of Britain's rail services followed hard on the petrol crisis. It might in other circumstances have been a clear opportunity for recriminations against the government, indeed an unprecedented opportunity to kick Blair while he was down. But it was never going to work out that way; the baggage of past Tory misdeeds was too encumbering. Attacks on government policy were blunted by the public's memory of earlier Tory policy in the same field. When NOP asked[80] about the issue of rail safety, far more of the public blamed the last Conservative government for the problems than blamed the present Labour government (though only 14% thought Labour was not to blame at all). Similarly, the public were critical of the management of rail services by Railtrack and the franchise holders: a Gallup poll for the *Daily Telegraph* at the start of November 2000 found that 54% of the public thought that Railtrack was "greatly to blame" for the rail crisis and 47% said the same about the rail operating companies. But 42% also blamed the previous Conservative, government; only 15% attributed the same degree of blame to Labour incumbents.[81] In short, rail disasters, and the disruption to services that followed, were blamed mainly on privatisation, not on the government, and 56% in an NOP poll for the C4 programme *Powerhouse* in November wanted the railways renationalised. The government had no intention of doing that, but it was the Tories who had devised the "poll tax on wheels" in the first place, and they could hardly make political capital by abandoning it now.

Much the same scenario was going on in miniature in the capital over the government's proposals for the London Underground. According to a MORI survey in November 2000 for the Greater London Authority[82], more than half of Londoners opposed the government's plan of a Private Public Partnership for the Tube. Furthermore, among these opponents more than twice as many said they opposed "strongly" as said they "tend to oppose", a considerably greater intensity of feeling than polls usually find on public policy issues. Nor is it hard to see reasons for the public's

---

[80] *Evening Standard*, 9 November 2000. NOP interviewed 501 electors on 8 November 2000.
[81] *Daily Telegraph*, 13 November 2000. Gallup interviewed 1,010 British aged 18+ on 1-7 November 2000.
[82] MORI Telephone Surveys interviewed 801 London residents aged 18+ on 9-12 November 2000.

attitudes. Almost half of Londoners in the MORI/GLA poll (47%) thought that if the PPP were to be introduced, value for money for passengers would get worse; perhaps more importantly still, 42% thought safety would deteriorate, and 38% that reliability would be worse. But it was Ken Livingstone, not the Tories, who was able to ride the crest of this wave of disapproval of the government.

Take a third policy. Four-fifths of Londoners, according to an ICM/*Evening Standard* poll[83], thought the Millennium Dome was a failure. Yet while seven in ten thought the present government should be blamed for the fiasco, six in ten also blamed the Tories (who, certainly, had the initial idea, but passed over the reins of power to Labour long before it was too late to stop and do something else with the money). (It wasn't even really Labour's policy, but Tony Blair's: indeed, it is said by those involved that of Blair's first Cabinet, only three members, including himself, were active supporters of the Dome.)

And whatever happened to Foot and Mouth as an election issue? The Tories never even attempted to raise it except with regard to delaying polling day, despite the anger against the government from farming communities in some of their strongest seats. Perhaps they had done their own private polling on the issue and decided not to risk it; probably they were wise not to do so. It is certainly not beyond the bounds of possibility that the public would have resented a partisan campaign on the handling of Foot and Mouth by the party that when in government had mishandled BSE. But if an opposition is forced by its own past record to remain mute on an issue such as this, what hope have they of dislodging the government?

But there may have been an even wider problem. In two clear cases at least, the Tories found themselves on the popular side of the debate with complete consistency and ought to have had every prospect of drawing whatever political benefit was available, yet the public would not associate support for the policy with support for the party.

---

[83] *Evening Standard*, 1 December 2000. ICM interviewed 1,002 London residents aged 18+ by telephone on 27-28 November 2000.

The first instance was the question of repealing Section 28 of the Local Government Act (the law that prevented local authorities from promoting homosexuality, especially in schools, strictly speaking called Section 2(a) in Scotland). The controversy became a cause célèbre, and was at its height when the first by-election to the Scottish Parliament took place, at Ayr in the Spring of 2000. The Conservatives had made much play of their support for retaining Section 28, which all the other Scottish parties were committed to repealing, and clearly hoped to benefit from the issue in the by-election. Polls confirmed that the Conservative stance was much the more popular, both across Scotland as a whole and, specifically, in the Ayr constituency.

The Conservatives comfortably gained Ayr from Labour, it is true. But it was clear that the Section 28 issue contributed little or nothing to the Tory victory. In fact, the Conservative share of the vote barely rose since 1999 (from 38% then to 39% in the by-election); the victory was secured because there was a 13% swing from Labour to the SNP, with Labour's share of the vote slumping from 38% to 22%. Yet the SNP was as supportive of repealing Section 28 as was Labour. Polling evidence confirmed the unimportance of the Section 28 issue – an ICM constituency poll[84] looked at all the Ayr voters who said they had supported Labour in 1999, and divided them by whether they wanted Section 28 repealed or retained – they found 44% of the repealers and 40% of the retainers sticking with Labour, not a statistically significant difference.

In other words the Tories, having found an issue on which most of the electorate felt very strongly, and having positioned themselves on much the more popular side of the debate with all their opponents on the unpopular side, still could not win votes by it. Whether it was because they failed to get across their message of who stood where, or because the voters didn't consider it an issue relevant to a Scottish Parliament by-election, or because they simply refused to vote Tory regardless, we cannot tell.

---

[84] *Scotsman*, 13 March 2000. ICM interviewed 1,001 adults in the Ayr constituency, by telephone on 9-10 March 2000.

But Section 28 might be considered a minor issue. Opposing entry to the Euro, by contrast, is the Conservatives' most fervently-held creed. A Gallup poll in the *Daily Telegraph*[85] showed that the policy was popular: in a referendum, 69% of the public would vote against joining the Single Currency and abolishing the pound. Yet 45% of the public thought Labour more closely represented their views on Europe, while only 40% thought the same of the Tories.

This failure to communicate policy arguments and positions to the electorate applied to other issues as well. An ICM poll for the *Guardian* a week before the election illustrated this dramatically in the field of education, a key issue for voters and potentially a major election battleground. When shown the Conservative, Labour and Liberal Democrat manifesto pledges on education, two-thirds of those intending to vote Conservative (68%) were unable correctly to identify the Tory policy – 32% correctly did so, but 31% misattributed Labour's policy to the Tories. Perhaps worse, only 37% of Tories were able to correctly identify their party's policy on the Euro, and 45% its policy on health.[86]

There seemed to be many voters who would not connect policy and party if it means being sympathetic to the Tories. While this continues to be the case, the Tories cannot hope to find an agenda for forging victory and are clearly condemned to further defeats.

---

[85] *Daily Telegraph*, 10 May 2001.
[86] *Guardian*, 6 June 2001. ICM interviewed 1,009 adults across Britain by telephone on 2-4 June 2001.

2. Not just apathy: why two in five didn't vote

Why was the turnout so low?

Why was the turnout so low, just 59% of the electorate?

We can discern a number of threads of public opinion, each of which led some electors not to vote in 2001.

- For some Britons, especially the young, elections simply don't matter. They may consider politics itself entirely unimportant, or party politics irrelevant to the real problems facing society, and may be disillusioned with politicians and the political system. This is the attitude typified by the old American bumper sticker, "Don't vote, it only encourages them". Consequently there is less attachment or identification with to political parties than was the case in the past, and as a corollary lower registration to vote. This is the explanation for low turnout that is most feared by politicians, and poses a real potential threat to democracy. It may be part of a world-wide trend. And yet there have always been those uninterested in politics, and the young have always been rebellious and not necessarily engaged with the system. How much greater was this cause of abstention in 2001 than at previous elections?
- Many seem to have felt that while they accept that elections in general are important, or can be important, this one was not, or that they could best achieve what they wanted from this election by not voting. They may have seen little difference between the parties, or wished to make a positive statement about current political trends by denying their vote to all candidates. This is where we classify those voters who felt all the parties were as bad as each other, that the issues between the parties are too trivial. We note that fewer of the public thought it important who won this election than was the case in the past. Furthermore, for many young citizens who have never had the chance to get into the habit of voting, what they feel is a

rejection of the whole political system may in reality only reflect rejection of the choices on offer in a specific election. Who did we think wouldn't vote in 2001? As I explained to the Institute of Directors Annual Conference and elsewhere[87] before the election, a mixture: **Old Labour,** feeling they had to vote Labour in 1997, but damned if they'd give Blair another landslide, and not, now, fearing that abstaining would risk something worse; **One-Nation Tories,** dismayed with the right-wing slant to the current Tory policies, hoping that a sizeable Labour victory would result in moving the Tories leftward, leading to the replacement of William Hague by a more moderate leadership; **New Labour idealists,** disappointed by the failure, as they saw it, of Labour's 1997 promises; and finally – and here I was certainly wrong in the event – **Tactical Liberal Democrats** from 1997, especially in the South and South-West, followers of Paddy Ashdown unimpressed by Charles Kennedy;.

- Perhaps the most significant group, who have so far received little attention, are those who might have voted in the 2001 election but for the campaign itself. We found many people whose attitudes to this election were probably little different from their attitudes to previous elections in which they did vote, who were *not* bored with the election as such but frustrated with the information they were receiving from the parties and the news media and the apparent over-control by the parties on **who,** said **what.** Both coverage and campaigning were more lacklustre than in any other recent election.

- Fourth, there were those who agreed not only that elections in general are important and that the outcome of this specific election was important, but that their own vote was not. If the result nationally was a foregone conclusion, there was less incentive to turn out; and those living in safe seats, increasingly ignored even by the parties, are perhaps beginning to get the message that in their case voting is no more than a gesture, and the walk to the polling station a waste of shoe leather.

- Finally, of course, as always, there were a few who would have voted but could not, or thought they could not. The introduction of postal voting on demand was meant to ameliorate this problem, but there is

---

[87] Notably in Robert Worcester, "Crying Wolf", *Red Pepper*, April 2001.

little evidence that it helped very much. Some didn't receive their polling cards, and thought they couldn't vote. Some didn't receive their postal ballot papers, and really couldn't vote – including a few who then presented themselves at the polling station only to discover that because they had been issued with a postal vote they were barred from voting in person. Some, naturally, were ill or prevented from voting by some unexpected and unavoidable commitment. But that is true in every election, and is unlikely to have been significantly worse than usual in 2001.

Our surveys found some evidence that all of these factors were keeping people away from the polling stations on election day, but certainly all were not equally causes of the *fall* in turnout. Our survey for the Electoral Commission found that the public's interest in politics has remained very stable over the past three decades, suggesting that people are no more 'turned-off' by politics per se than they were in the past and that people said they were no less interested in the 2001 election than in politics generally. But there is some evidence that the 2001 election did not connect with people and made them view it differently to previous ones. Certainly it seems it was more short-term factors than a long-term decline that were the immediate cause of the fall in turnout.

Perhaps one red herring should be discarded. The electoral register, it is true, is imperfect – though perhaps the newly introduced rolling register will begin to address those imperfections over time. It can be – and has been – argued on the one hand that since a significant proportion of entries on the register are "dead names" (those who have actually died since the register was compiled, or are no longer, or never were, in fact eligible to vote), and many others are double entries (since it is perfectly legal to appear on the register more than one, at different addresses, so long as you only vote once in a general election), the actual percentage of those that could vote who did vote was higher than 59%. But on the other hand it can also be argued that there are many adults in Britain who should be on the register, but are not; since in most cases one of the reasons they are not on the register is because they have insufficient interest in voting to claim the right to do so, these also must be counted as non-voters, and the turnout is much worse than it looks. Both arguments are true, but taken together they neutralise each other. The total registered electorate, that is the number of names on the list however valid, is within a few hundred thousand of the best estimates of the total adult population, whether registered or not; and, indeed, this has been the case for many years. The 59% figure is a reasonable estimate of the real turnout in the 2001 election; and, more to the point, is fair comparison and consistent with similarly-calculated figures for the official turnouts in other recent elections[88].

In purely statistical terms, that makes it the worst turnout since 1918; and, as a number of commentators have pointed out, the circumstances of the 1918 election were so unusual as to be an unreasonable comparison. Besides, that was before full adult suffrage. The turnout in 2001 was the lowest *ever* in a modern, democratic, British General Election.

---

[88] A side issue is that – until the introduction in 2001 of a "rolling" register, the register has been updated only once a year, compiled in October and used from February to February. The quality of the register naturally deteriorates with age, and in an Autumn election, for example, there would be considerably more dead names, which would complicate the calculations slightly. However, all the elections since 1979 have been between April and June, minimising the effect.

Why people vote

But by jumping straight into the question of why people didn't vote, we are perhaps putting the cart before the horse. Aren't we taking too much for granted? The first question we need to ask ourselves is why people do vote. It is a question so obvious that it has received little attention in the past, but the Electoral Commission were astute enough to have us include questions on precisely that topic in our surveys for them during and after the election.

Overwhelmingly the main reason that voters gave was that they felt an obligation to do so. Five in six of the public agreed with the statement "I feel it is my duty to vote", and among those who said in the first week of the campaign that they were certain to vote, the commonest unprompted reasons were along the lines of "It is my civic duty", "Everyone should vote" or, which may amount to the same thing, "I always vote".[89]

The importance of habit should not be under-estimated, and of course it is much stronger with older voters, who have turned out in many elections, than with the young who have yet to establish the habit. Of those who said they certain to vote, 42% of those aged 65+ gave "I always vote" as their reason, but only 29% of the 18-24 year olds.

Those hoping to achieve something specific with their vote are fewer, and the majority of these are essentially making gestures – "I want to have a say" or "send a message". Only 5% said they were voting to defeat the government, and 4% so that their own party would win. The

---

[89] In fact there are two ways of interpreting these answers. Our respondents may have been telling us that they vote through simple habit, without consideration of any other particular reason for doing so. But it may also be that they interpreted our question "Why do you say that you are certain you will vote" as being a question about their basis for predicting that they would vote rather than their motivation for voting. The latter interpretation seems supported by the post-election recall, when only 11% said "I always vote" in response to the question "Why did you vote", compared to the 36% who before the election gave it as the reason for having stated that they were certain to vote. Similarly, when those who had said they were not certain to vote were asked why they were not certain, the most frequent response (15%) was "I will probably vote", i.e. they had taken the question as being a prediction about the future, and had answered accordingly, rather than an expression of their feelings towards voting. This suggests that the post-election figures may be the better measure of motivation.

reasons given post-election for having voted followed a very similar hierarchy.

Table 35: Reasons for voting

Q. *People give many reasons for voting at elections. Why did you vote at the General Election on the 7th June?*

	%
It is my civic duty/everyone should vote	42
I wanted to have a say	14
It is my right to vote	13
I always vote	11
So that my preferred party won	8
If people don't vote then they have no right to complain/have an opinion	8
People fought to win the right to vote for me/others	5
To defeat/remove the government	3
To prevent a party from winning	2
So that my preferred candidate won	2
To prevent a candidate from winning	1
Liked/pleased with the government	1
I was urged/persuaded to vote by a family member/friend	1
To defeat/remove my MP	*
Liked/pleased with a particular candidate	*
Other	6

Base: All who say they voted (951)
Source: MORI/Electoral Commission

One in five said they were 'certain to vote' because "It is my right"; again, this was most common among young voters, and perhaps reflects the way in which political thought has tended more to concentrate on rights than duties in recent years. Whether the exercise of a right, for no better reason than that it exists, is as powerful a motivator to vote as the acceptance of a duty to do so, is an interesting question. On the one hand, one might feel that the exercise of a right is optional and that no harm is done by the failure to exercise it, so one might expect turnout to be lower among the "rights" group than the "duty" group. On the other hand, the duty is to the state or to civil society, and it may be that increasing disillusionment with the state and the political system will tend to encourage abrogation of the duty, whereas for the rebellious young the exercise of a right untrammelled by the political classes might come to seem more rather than less valuable if disillusionment sets in. But this is of course speculation; but what does seem at least possible (and it cannot be put more strongly than that on the basis of age comparisons from a single survey rather than a longitudinal study) is that the basic view of motivation for voting among those who think it important may be undergoing a significant evolution.

At any rate, voting is not purely driven by the politics of the day. It is clear that many of the public vote even though they do not feel strongly involved with political issues. More than half, 56%, of those who said they were 'not at all interested' in politics nevertheless claimed to be likely to vote, and a similar proportion, 58%, agreed that "It is my duty to vote". Nearly three in ten, 29%, of those who said they "always vote" in general elections nonetheless admitted they were "not particularly interested" or "not at all interested" in politics. More than half of those who said they were "not at all interested" in politics still claimed to have voted on June 7, and 68% still voted despite being "not at all interested" or "not particularly interested" in news about the election. Moreover, two-thirds of those who did not vote *disagreed* that "I didn't think it was important to vote".

'Elections aren't important'

Many commentators have assumed that the principal reason for the fall in turnout in 2001, in line with the very low turnouts in other British elections since the mid 1990s, is simply that an increasingly large section of the public feels elections are irrelevant or pointless, and this is part of a global trend. Our survey for the Electoral Commission suggests that this is not the case. Although a proportion of the public, indeed, rejects the value of elections, they are far too few to explain a 41% non-vote in a general election, let alone the even lower turnouts in local and European elections.

In fact most of the British public have a strong belief in voting. On balance, they think it is important and that it makes a difference. Nine in ten disagree that "I don't think voting is very important" with three-quarters disagreeing *strongly*; only 10% agree with the statement. Similarly, 78% disagree that "I don't think voting makes much of a difference" with more than half, 55%, disagreeing *strongly*; only just over one in six, 18%, agree with the statement. Furthermore, despite the general assumption that the young tend to dismiss elections as unimportant, and notwithstanding the very low turnout of 18-24 year olds (just 39% on MORI's figures), the vast majority of them also fall into line with their elders.[90]

But when we asked much the same questions after the election – to as many of the same sample of electors as we were able to re-interview – we found that the responses were rather different. Almost twice as many said that they "did not believe that voting would make much of a difference" as had said beforehand that "I don't believe voting makes much of a difference"; among the youngest group the switch was even more dramatic. Furthermore, while among the sample as a whole there was no more sympathy with voting being unimportant in the second survey than in the first, among the 18-24 year olds twice as many agreed afterwards as agreed before. This ought to be worrying if only because

---

[90] Even if there is some exaggeration here, the only reason we can see for it is that respondents felt a social pressure to conform by admitting the importance of voting. If that perception of social pressure is there, the point is made.

the vast majority of those aged 18-24 are first-time voters; every young citizen who goes into his or her first general election as an adult believing that voting is important yet comes out of it thinking it is not may be another nail in the coffin of democracy.

Table 36: The importance of voting

Q. I am going to read out a number of statements. Please tell me how much do you agree or disagree with each.

Pre-election		All			18-24 year olds		
		Agree	Dis-agree	Neither / don't know	Agree	Dis-agree	Neither / don't know
I feel it is my duty to vote	%	83	14	3	67	26	7
I don't believe voting makes much of a difference	%	18	78	4	17	76	7
I don't think voting is very important	%	10	89	1	13	84	3

Source: MORI/Electoral Commission
Base: 1,801 UK adults 18+, 9-15 May 2001

Q. I am going to read out a number of statements some people have made about the General Election campaign this year. Please tell me how much do you agree or disagree with each.

Post-election		All			18-24 year olds		
		Agree	Dis-agree	Neither / don't know	Agree	Dis-agree	Neither / don't know
I did not believe that voting would make much of a difference	%	34	64	2	46	52	2
I didn't think it was important to vote	%	9	89	2	26	70	4

Source: MORI/Electoral Commission
Base: 1,162 UK adults 18+, 9-18 June 2001

The way in which the older age groups draw a distinction in their changing attitudes to the two questions while the 18-24 year olds do not is an important lesson to note. To the older voters, the importance of voting is not necessarily dependent on whether it can make "much of a difference", so a dull and perhaps insignificant election will not shake their belief in the importance of voting as a whole. To the young, it may not be like that.

However, we must not go too far in drawing conclusions about the effect of the 2001 election on attitudes to the electoral process. The pre-election questions had addressed general attitudes to voting, the post-election recall attitudes to voting specifically in the 2001 election. Those who answered the two pairs questions differently *may* have suffered a permanent disillusionment, but the surveys offer us no evidence of that. What they do show is a failure of the 2001 election to connect with millions of voters who were quite prepared to take it seriously; we examine this in more detail in the next chapter.

Of course, there is a section of the public which rarely votes in general elections, and for whom abstention in 2001 was not a new experience. What are their motivations? Even among those who say they 'never' or 'rarely' vote in general elections, there is a sense that voting is important – 62% believe it is. However, this group differs from the rest of the public in that they are only slightly more likely to disagree than agree that "voting does not make a difference" (47% against 43%), and more likely to agree than disagree that "none of the parties stands for the policies I would like to see" (39% against 34%). Agreement with this latter statement might in many people's cases refer specifically to current political conditions, but presumably in the case of those who rarely vote they see it as a longer-term malaise. If they never feel attracted to the choices on offer, it would help explain why they rarely vote even if they think voting is – in theory – important.

But there always are, and always will be, some who feel politically disengaged. If we are looking for explanations of the increased abstention in 2001, we need to discover something that has changed dramatically since 1997. Do the parties as abstract entities, rather than in their concrete present forms, appeal less than they once did? We have no sign of a sudden disengagement from political means of thought since 1997. The 'Michigan' Question for determining the public's party identification found a lower number than in 1997 thinking of themselves as Conservatives, but no very substantial increase in the numbers saying they identified with no political party or didn't know. If there were a permanent alienation from the party system taking place, we would expect it to show itself here; it has not.

Table 37: The 'Michigan' Question

Q. *Generally speaking, do you think of yourself as Conservative, Labour, Liberal Democrat, or what?*

	1963* %	21-24 Mar 1997 %	22 May 2001 %	29 May 2001 %	5 Jun 2001 %
Conservative	36	29	24	24	25
Labour	44	36	41	42	41
Liberal (1963)/Liberal Democrat (1997-2001)	10	11	7	10	10
Scottish/Welsh Nationalist	n/a	2	1	2	2
Green	n/a	1	1	1	1
Other	n/a	1	2	2	1
Don't know	2	5	6	4	6
None of these	8	14	16	15	12
Refused	n/a	1	1	2	2

* "Q. Generally speaking, do you usually think of yourself as Conservative, Labour or Liberal?"

Source: British Election Study, reported in D. Butler & D. Stokes, *Political Change in Britain* (Macmillan, 1969), p 469 (data for 1963); MORI (1997-2001)

Nevertheless, as comparison with the first British Election Survey, which asked a very similar question almost forty years ago, shows, there has been some long-term decline. Around twice as many of the public now decline to identify themselves with any of the parties as was then the case. Although it cannot explain the precipitous drop in turnout between 1997 and 2001, this degree of dealignment may point towards a steadier long-term fall.

This goes hand-in-hand with evidence of decreasing involvement in party politics, and it may also be relevant that the political class is held in very low esteem. For many years, MORI has regularly asked a series of questions on 'Socio-Political Activism', measuring the degree to which Britons become involved with activities in the public sphere, either voluntary or party political. Comparison of the figures in 1972, 1999 and for the first quarter of 2001 shows a significant fall in those activities connected with the political parties, especially among the young; but other activities, which are political in a broader sense, have held up or indeed increased: substantially fewer young people say they have voted, or encouraged others to vote, and far fewer have been involved in a political campaign; but fund-raising, making speeches and – tellingly – contacting elected members have all increased. This fits in well with other evidence that the public are increasingly turning to single-issue pressure groups, NGOs or other channels for their political expression rather than the political parties.

Table 38: Socio-Political Activism

Q. Which of the things on this list, if any, have you done in the last two or three years?

	All 16+			Aged 16-24		
	1972	1999	2001	1972	1999	2001
	%	%	%	%	%	%
Voted in the last general election	74	73	64	43	30	19
Helped on fund-raising drives	22	29	26	24	24	21
Made a speech before an organised group	11	17	18	10	14	13
Urged someone outside my family to vote	18	17	13	18	12	6
Urged someone to						
get in touch with a local councillor or MP	14	16	15	9	7	4
Been an officer of an organisation or club	14	14	13	12	6	5
Presented my views to a local councillor or MP	11	15	15	4	5	5
Written a letter to an editor	6	8	7	6	5	4
Taken an active part in a political campaign	4	3	3	6	2	2
Stood for public office	*	1	1	*	*	*
None of these	17	17	22	34	44	55

Source: MORI
Base: 2,062 British 16+, 1972; 46,143 British 16+, January-December 1999; 14,010 British 16+, January-March 2001

The 1999 figures probably give the fairest comparison with 1972 on electoral matters, being about the same period of time after the previous general election. But even some of the changes between 1999 and 2001 have been quite dramatic, more so than we would expect even given that strictly speaking the previous election is not within "the last two or three years". The significant jump in the number – among all age groups – prepared to admit that they have not voted suggests a weakening of a social taboo. The 'activism question' has constantly over the years found a slight exaggeration in the numbers claiming to have voted when compared with the actual turnout, and only once before in thirty years had the number claiming to have voted fallen below 68%, even towards the end of a parliament. But it may also be important that immediately after the 2001 election, MORI and the other pollsters found a substantial 'overclaim', of more saying they had voted than could really have done so. It may be that, if the public were briefly complacent about non-voting, the turnout in 2001 has shocked them out of it.

If the public is turning its back on party politics and elections as a means of political expression, why should this be? One possible explanation is disillusionment with the system based on the low regard in which politicians and the political system are held.

It is understandable that people may be little interested in the parties' promises if they do not expect those promises to be kept. Before the 1997 election, two in five, 42%, expected a Blair government to keep its promises but almost as many, 40%, did not; and two-and-a-half years on (according to MORI's December 1999 poll for *The Times*), 49% thought that they hadn't done so. By the time of the 2001 election, just 31% thought Labour would keep its promises if elected for a second term[91]. This extends beyond failure to deliver after honest effort. When electors see firm promises being directly repudiated, as with David Blunkett's "read my lips" fiasco[92], which will have done no more for his administration's trustworthy image than it did for the first President Bush's, no doubt their trust is shaken.

The sad truth is that politicians, parties and the whole political process have allowed themselves to fall into disrepute. In March 2001, MORI found[93] that fewer than one in five of the public, 17%, said they generally trust politicians to tell the truth, and just 20% trust government ministers. Even journalists, who more often than not in past polls scored worse than politicians, were trusted by more, 18%. By contrast, in a period when a series of medical scandals reported in the

---

[91] MORI survey for *The Times*, published on 31 May. MORI interviewed 1,013 British aged 18+ on 29 May 2001.

[92] At the 1995 Labour conference, David Blunkett had explained his education policy "Watch my lips – no selection". Later, as Education Secretary, he repudiated his earlier pledge on the grounds that it was a "joke".

[93] MORI survey for the British Medical Association. MORI interviewed 1,918 British adults aged 15+ on 1-6 March 2001.

media culminated in a doctor being convicted of murdering countless numbers of his patients, 89% trusted doctors to tell the truth. Although both politicians generally and ministers scored a little better under Blair than during the Conservative government, these are dismal figures.

Table 39: Trust in people to tell the truth

Q. *Now I will read you a list of different types of people. For each would you tell me if you generally trust them to tell the truth, or not?*

	1983	1993	1997	1999	2000	2001
	%	%	%	%	%	%
Doctors	82	84	86	91	87	89
Teachers	79	84	83	89	85	86
Television news readers	63	72	74	74	73	75
Professors	n/a	70	70	79	76	78
Judges	77	68	72	77	77	78
Clergyman/Priests	85	80	71	80	78	78
Scientists	n/a	n/a	63	63	63	65
The Police	61	63	61	61	60	63
The ordinary man/ woman in the street	57	64	56	60	52	52
Pollsters	n/a	52	55	49	46	46
Civil Servants	25	37	36	47	47	43
Trade Union Officials	18	32	27	39	38	39
Business Leaders	25	32	29	28	28	27
Journalists	19	10	15	15	15	18
Politicians generally	18	14	15	23	20	17
Government Ministers	16	11	12	23	21	20

Source: MORI/BMA (1999-2001); MORI/*The Times* (1983-97)
Base: c. 2,000 British adults aged 15+/18+

Electors and their MPs

Yet it is not quite so simple. Even when the public is cynical about the political class in general, they may find it harder to condemn individual figures, especially those they feel they know. Asked just before the election[94] whether they thought Tony Blair and William Hague "honest"

---

[94] MORI survey for the *Sun*, published on 2 May. MORI Telephone Surveys interviewed 1,008 British aged 18+ on 30 April-1 May 2001.

or "dishonest" and "principled" or "unprincipled", 62% said Blair was honest and 65% principled, while Hague scored 59% and 58%.

Furthermore, there has been no sudden collapse of satisfaction with the way that MPs are doing their job. Far from it. When we asked the public[95] how satisfied or dissatisfied they were with "the way MPs are doing their job", we found that satisfaction has significantly *increased* since we last asked this question in October 1992. Then 32% were satisfied and 56% dissatisfied, a net score of −24; in 2001, 39% were satisfied and only 37% dissatisfied, a net +2 and a 13% swing in MPs' favour.

As in 1992, respondents were more positive when asked about their own MP than about MPs in general. In fact, satisfaction with the local MP stayed absolutely steady over a decade: 43% satisfied in 1991, 44% in 1992, 43% in 1995 and 42% in May 2001.

Nevertheless, it is clear that there is a link between satisfaction with MPs and turnout. While 42% of all electors said they were satisfied with the way their own MP was doing his or her job, 49% of those "certain to vote" were satisfied. Furthermore, 51% of those who had definitely decided how they would vote were satisfied, but only 31% of those who said they might change their minds. Interesting also, for those who like to blame the low standing of politicians on the smears and negativity of the tabloid newspapers, that satisfaction stood at 45% among broadsheet readers but 48% among readers of the popular press.

But then we also found that only 41% of the public could accurately recall the name of their Member of Parliament – even with an election campaign in full swing, which ought to help a bit! – and it dropped to 36% in London. In Conservative seats 42% know the name of their local MP, in Labour seats 38%, and in the Lib Dem seats, 55%. In March 1991, 52% could give a correct answer to the same question and in 1973, in the 'State of the Nation' survey for Granada TV, 53% could.

---

[95] MORI survey for *The Times*, published on 17 May. MORI interviewed 1,019 British aged 18+ on 15 May 2001.

This, again, suggests the public is less politically aware than a few years ago.

On the other hand, when asked the name of the Parliamentary Constituency that they live in, though only 43% could name it correctly, this is the same figure as in 1991; another 15% gave an answer but it was wrong. In Conservative seats 47% know the name of the constituency they live in, as do 44% of people living in Labour seats. It is much higher, interestingly, in London (57%). Possibly the lower knowledge of MPs' names reflects not a real loss of political engagement, but the simple fact that the 1997 landslide put a lot of new MPs in the Commons, and hence the average period that the MPs have served their constituents is significantly lower than when we asked the question in 1991. (But 38% of electors in seats gained by Labour in 1997, which by definition have new MPs, knew their MP's name, while only 36% did in the Labour "heartland" seats where many of the MPs have served for years.) The alternative is that MPs have been interacting less well with their constituents than ten years ago. But in that case we would have expected a significant fall in satisfaction with the local MP which, as we have seen, has not been the case. At any rate, something has been lost somewhere.

Lack of interest is not the 'problem'

It is not, simply, apathy. As we have already seen, non-party socio-political activity seems to be as high as ever. The same emerges when we ask the public directly how interested they are in politics. Media comment to the contrary, among the public as a whole, interest in politics has remained remarkably stable over the past three decades.

Only one in ten say they are 'not at all' interested in politics, fewer than the 14% who say they are 'very' interested. Indeed, the 2001 figures are not significantly different in any respect from those found for Granada TV in 1973, or in 1991 in our survey for the Joseph Rowntree Reform Trust. Four measures of public opinion over nearly three decades, and no significant difference in any study, in each case taken in the year before, or during, a general election.

Table 40: Interest in politics

Q. *How interested would you say you are in politics?*

| | 1973 | 1991 | 1997 | 2001 |
	%	%	%	%
Very interested	14	13	15	14
Fairly interested	46	47	44	45
Not very interested	27	26	29	29
Not at all interested	13	13	11	11
Don't know	1	*	*	1

Source: MORI/various

Figure 15

Interest in politics over time

Q How interested would you say you are in politics?

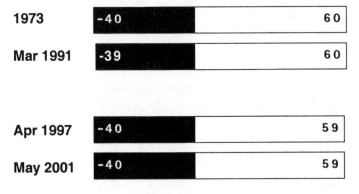

Base: c.1,000 British/UK adults 18+, 9-15 May 2001   Source: MORI/JRRT/Electoral Commission

There is some demographic variation. Women are significantly less likely than men to say they are 'very' or 'fairly' interested in politics: 52% to 66%. ABC_1s are more interested than C_2DEs. Younger age groups are less interested, especially 25-34 year olds (49% "very" or "fairly" interested compared with 53% among 18-24s, and 68% among those aged 55+). However, there are no significant differences in levels of interest by ethnicity; non-whites are just as interested as whites, and Asians are only slightly less interested than Black people.

Of course, lack of interest feeds abstention. Three-quarters of those who 'rarely' or 'never' vote in general elections say they are *not* interested . But again, it is plain there is nothing new here. We are simply explaining the non-voting of the hard core who do not normally vote even at the best of the times; it is not revealing why this should have been so much the worst of times.

The scale of the fall in turnout took almost everybody by surprise – including us. But it should not have done. The clear evidence of the poll trends throughout the first months of 2001 was that by comparison with the corresponding point in 1997 the fall in percentage points was in double figures. But we, and almost everybody else, believed optimistically that the figures would pick up eventually.

Table 41 shows the equivalent data at corresponding points in the 1992 and 1997 campaigns. (January 1997 is compared with January 2001 as, at that point, it seemed probable that the election would be held on 3 May; March 1997 is compared with both March and April 2001.)

But while the polls from January 2001 onwards were pointing to a turnout as low, or almost as low, as eventually occurred, this was not the case with a MORI poll for *The Times* in August 2000, which found that 59% said they were certain to vote at the next election; taken by comparison with the 55% who had been certain to vote in September 1996, this pointed towards a modest upturn in the turnout; adding in those "very likely to vote", there were 70% certain or very likely in August 2000, whereas there had been 71% in September 1996.

Although it is a lot to draw from a single poll, this would point towards the conclusion that there was nothing in the general attitude of the public towards elections at that point which would tend towards a 59% turnout; the malaise set in later.

Table 41: Turnout projections from MORI's polls

Q. From this card, can you tell me how likely you are to get along to vote in the general election?

1992 election					11-12 Mar 1992	16 Mar 1992	23 Mar 1992	30 Mar 1992	7-8 Apr 1992	9 Apr 1992
Certain to vote					69%	67%	72%	71%	82%	
Certain/very likely					80%	79%	82%	82%	90%	
Actual turnout										78%
1997 election	Jan 1997	Feb 1997	Mar 1997		1 Apr 1997	8 Apr 1997	15 Apr 1997	22 Apr 1997	29 Apr 1997	1 May 1997
Certain to vote	57%	61%	66%		63%	62%	64%	68%	71%	
Certain/very likely	72%	77%	78%		75%	75%	77%	80%	81%	
Actual turnout										71%
2001 election	Jan 2001	Feb 2001	Mar 2001	19-24 Apr 2001	8 May 2001	15 May 2001	22 May 2001	29 May 2001	5 Jun 2001	7 Jun 2001
Certain to vote	48%	50%	49%	50%	46%	53%	52%	54%	63%	
Certain/very likely	64%	67%	66%	66%	65%	70%	69%	71%	76%	
Actual turnout										59%
Difference from 1997 (certain to vote)	-9	-11	-17	-16	-17	-9	-12	-14	-8	
Difference from 1992 (certain to vote)					-23	-14	-20	-17	-19	

Source: MORI/ *The Times*

On the other hand, as the table shows, the rot had certainly set in by the start of 2001, when MORI began to ask the likelihood of voting question regularly as part of the election run-up: the figures were below even those of 1997 by ten points or more. What happened to make a change between August and January? Clearly, there must be the strongest suspicion that the precipitate fall in confidence in the government in September, apparently caused by the petrol crisis and perhaps also the

125

Dome deficit, shook the resolve of many to record their votes. If so, it is clearly primarily a short-term phenomenon, related to the circumstances of this particular election, and not part of a longer-term trend against public participation.

In general, we must reach a negative verdict on our first hypothesis. Certainly there has been increasing disillusionment with the system over some years, and equally certainly the reason for some non-voters' abstention was political disengagement. But this explains little more than the constant term in the equation – there is little evidence that it made more than a minor contribution to the sharp fall in turnout in 2001.

Party Values

Finally, we must be quite clear that turnout has not fallen because the public can't, won't or don't think in political terms. Much cant is talked about regarding 'Old' and 'New' Labour, 'One-Nation' Tories and 'Thatcherites'. But to our knowledge, no one up until now has asked the public how they see *themselves*. Like right/left characterisations, these are the stuff of the chattering classes, but who 'out there' thinks in these terms? As it turns out, many do, and the measure of them throws an interesting light on how people position themselves on the dimensions which describe to political scientists how the three major parties divide among themselves, and the profile of each camp.

Certainly taking the Tories first, while a third of the voters, only one in five of the electorate, we see the contenders for the leadership of the Conservative Party leading wings which are not only divided by the candidates' stance over the Euro, but on many other issues as well. While the election for the Tory leadership is still going on as we write, to discover that in the country (not necessarily among party members of course), the 'One-Nation' Tories outnumber the 'Thatcherites' among party supporters by four to three. Yet the position on the issue that is seen most to divide their party is remarkably similar

Among Labour supporters, over four in ten of the electorate, 'New' Labour are nearly three times as prevalent as those who identify with 'Old' Labour. And among the merged Liberals and Social Democratic Party, the 'Liberals' outnumber the 'Social Democrats' by two to one.

Table 42: Political identification by vote

Q. *Which one of these definitions, if any, comes closest to your political views?*

		Voting intention		
	All	Con	Lab	LD
	%	%	%	%
New Labour	29	2	62	10
Old Labour	12	4	21	16
One-Nation Tory	11	42	0	4
Thatcherite Tory	9	29	*	1
Liberal	12	6	4	41
Social Democratic	7	2	8	19

Source: MORI/ *The Economist*
Base: 1,010 British 18+, 4-5 June 2001

Figure 16

The Political Pie

Q *Which one of these definitions, if any, comes closest to your political views?*

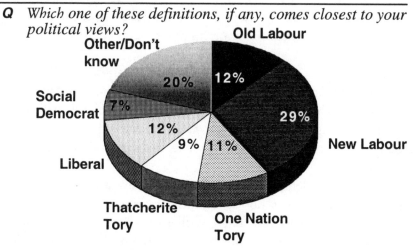

Base: 1,010 British 18+, 4-5 June 2001. Source: MORI/*Economist*

One is immediately struck when looking at how these political typologies are segmented not at their differences, but their similarities, especially when considering the Conservatives' split over Europe. When you put to the Thatcherite Tories whether then support or oppose joining the European Single Currency, 89% say they oppose it and just 6% say that we should, for a net opposition score of –83%, as indicated in the table below; when we put the same question to the One-Nation Tories, by a remarkably similar score, 82% against, just 9% for, for a net opposition of –73%, it does make one wonder what the fuss is all about.

Other issues are by far more contentious among Conservative supporters, as shown in the table. Those that most divide the Tories is the proposal to require companies to give fathers paid time off work when their children are born, with One-Nation Tories on balance in favour of this by +10% while the Thatcherites oppose it by a net –23%; another nearly equally contentious among Tories is PR, with a net +26% of One-Nationers favouring a change in the voting system that would give parties seats in Parliament in proportion to their share of votes while the Thatcherites who are also on balance in favour of it now, but by only a net +10% margin.

Where the Conservative wings of the party are fairly united is in renationalising the railways, selection at secondary schools and in their opposition to raising income tax on highest earners to 50%.

Also interesting is that the Thatcherites, despite their generally libertarian tinge, are less strongly opposed to banning fox hunting than the One-Nation Tories. The One-Nation strain of Toryism has always been especially associated with the more traditional, land-owning and aristocratic wing of the party, and it seems this may still be true.

Among Labour's identifiers, the dividing issues are allowing private companies to run state schools, while both wings are against this, the differences between them are huge, with a net –65% of those who think of themselves as old Labour while a –23% is the position of new Labour. Another big difference is found when considering the new-born baby bonus, which finds New Labour in on balance in favour of this idea by a net +21%, while Old Labour opposes it, by a net –13%, a difference of 34 percentage points. This may be accounted for partly by the differences in the age profiles of the two groups.

Table 43: Political identity and issues for the second term

Q. I am now going to read out a list of policies that a new Labour Government might carry out. Please tell me whether you support or oppose each. (Net Support)

% net (support minus oppose)	British Public (100%)	Old Labour (12%)	New Labour (29%)	One-Nation Tories (11%)	Thatch-erite Tories (9%)	Lib-erals (12%)	Social Demo-crats (7%)
Bring the railways back into public ownership	+53%	+87%	+61%	+21%	+18%	+62%	+44%
Have more NHS patients treated in private hospitals	+43%	+29%	+58%	+52%	+41%	+26%	+25%
Adopt a new voting system that would give parties seats in Parliament in proportion to their share of votes	+43%	+55%	+46%	+26%	+10%	+61%	+56%
Ban fox hunting	+26%	+42%	+54%	-31%	-13%	+32%	+42%
Increase income tax to 50% for highest earners	+23%	+57%	+33%	-23%	-24%	+25%	+60%
Let secondary schools select pupils who are good at certain subjects	+3%	+2%	+2%	+24%	+19%	-6%	-11%
Put up to £800 of taxpayer's money into an account for every newborn child. They would be able to spend this money as they like when they are 18.	-15%	-13%	+21%	-53%	-48%	-38%	-1%
Require companies to give fathers paid time off work when their children are born	+38%	+54%	+64%	+10%	-23%	+41%	+44%
Join the European Single Currency	-31%	-14%	*	-72%	-85%	-19%	*
Allow private companies to run state schools	-39%	-65%	-23%	-27%	-23%	-54%	-60%

Source: MORI/*Economist*
Base: 1,010 British adults 18+ 4-5 June 2001

Obviously, where an issue is straddled with one group for it and the other opposed it has greater possibility to cause internal conflict within the party, although that isn't the case with the Tories over Europe!

Labour's two groupings are united in their luke-warm support for secondary state school selection (+2% for both groups), and in their substantial support for PR (+26% among Old Labour but only, surprisingly +10% among the New).

The Liberals and the Social Democrats are most united in their massive support for paternal paid leave (net +41% for Liberals and +44% among the Social Democrats, and for PR (+61% for the Liberal wing, and +56% among Social Democrats). They are also united in their support for treating NHS patients in private hospitals (+26% and +25% respectively).

Where they are split is on baby bonds, with −38% opposition among the Liberals and only a −1% among Social Democrats. On joining the Euro, the Social Democrats are split down the middle, with about as many in favour as opposed, while the Liberals are fairly heavily opposed to Britain's joining (−19%).

It is when we look at the demographics, geographics, and readership that the difference that split the wings of each of the three parties becomes particularly interesting, after looking at how they divide on the issues of the day.

Those who identify with either wing of the Labour Party, Old or New, are dominated by the women, while the Thatcherite Tories are even more dominated by the men, as is the Social Democratic wing of the Liberal Democrats.

The party wing identifiers are in terms of gender support are most in balance in the One-Nation Tories and the Liberal wing of the LibDems.

That New Labour is of greater attraction to the young, under 35 and proportionally even more to the under 25s, will be of no surprise as will

130

not the tilt of 'Old' Labour to the older generation, but not so much, interestingly, the OAPs, but the 35-54 age cohort. The One-Nation Tories have the higher proportion of the elderly, but the Thatcherite Tories are weakest with the young, with only 21% support among the under 35s, compared to 35% of the electorate who are 18-35.

The Liberal identifiers are the best proportionally among the parties in attracting the grey vote. This may help to explain their picking up the extra point or two at the recent election. On the other hand, their 23% support profile among the younger electors is only two points higher than the Thatcherite Tories. Just under half the support of the Social Democrat identifiers, 46%, are in the 35-54 age group, most of whom will remember their near-miss of second place 18 years ago in the 1983 general election.

That Britain's political parties still remain indebted to their historic class supporters gains some support from this analysis, with Labour still the party of the working class, but much more true of Old Labour identifiers than those who feel more comfortable with the New Labour label. As indicated in the table, nearly two-thirds, 63%, of Old Labour identifiers are objectively determined 'working class' by the nature of their occupation, while among those who chose to label themselves as 'New' Labour are very close to the balance by class found in the electorate as a whole. Both wings of the Liberal Democrats are tilted to the middle classes, and the Social Democrats heavily skewed to ABs, more than half again likely to be found among the professional and managerial occupation group.

The analysis throws an interesting light on Blair's capture of the middle-class vote. For while Old Labour and New Labour have similar numbers of ABs (19% and 17% respectively), there is a very significant difference among the other classes. Old Labour is 18% C_1, 63% C_2DE; New Labour is 31% C_1, 52% C_2DE. Blair's new creed has brought in the vital C_1 voters – lower middle-class, in many cases upwardly mobile and not long ago blue-collar rather than white collar.

Full-time workers tend to have a greater proportion of those who identify with either the Thatcherite Tory group or the Social Democrats.

New Labour is wonderfully evenly dispersed regionally, almost a match for the electorate as a whole, while both wings of the Tories concentrated in the South, as are the Liberals, while the Social Democrats and Old Labour people are in greater proportions in the North and Scotland.

Table 44: Political identity by demographics

Q. *Which of these definitions, if any, comes closest to your political views?*

	British Public* (100%)	Old Labour (12%)	New Labour (29%)	One-Nation Tories (11%)	Thatch-erite Tories (9%)	Liberals (12%)	Social Demo-crats (7%)
Incidence	100%	12%	29%	11%	9%	12%	7%
Men	49%	43%	46%	51%	61%	51%	63%
Women	51%	57%	54%	49%	38%	49%	37%
18-24	12%	9%	16%	8%	7%	15%	3%
25-34	21%	19%	25%	18%	14%	18%	20%
35-54	34%	40%	32%	35%	42%	35%	46%
55+	33%	33%	27%	39%	37%	42%	31%
AB	23%	19%	17%	32%	22%	25%	37%
C1	27%	18%	31%	28%	30%	34%	23%
C2	22%	25%	22%	19%	25%	19%	21%
DE	28%	38%	30%	21%	23%	22%	19%
ABC1	50%	37%	48%	60%	52%	59%	60%
C2DE	50%	63%	52%	40%	48%	41%	40%
Full-time workers	46%	42%	44%	43%	53%	45%	53%
Not full- time worker	54%	58%	56%	57%	47%	55%	47%
North incl.Scotland	34%	41%	34%	35%	30%	30%	43%
Midlands incl. Wales	25%	28%	27%	24%	23%	20%	19%
South incl. London	40%	30%	39%	40%	45%	50%	38%
Greater London	12%	11%	15%	8%	11%	14%	14%
South excl. London	28%	19%	24%	32%	34%	36%	24%

Source: MORI/ *The Economist*
Base: 1,010 British 18+, 4-5 June 2001
*British Public Demographic Profile Source: Election Aggregate, 8 May-6 June 2001,
18,567 interviews weighted to election result

Readership by Political Values

It is in the readership tables below that some of the most interesting and surprising findings came, for instance that the highest incidence of *Times'* readers (26%) identify with New Labour, and that with 35% of Times' readers identify with Labour against 33% with the Conservative identities. Also, that 36% of *Guardian* readers identify either with the Liberal designation or think of themselves as Social Democrats.

Table 45: Political identity by readership

Q. Which one of these definitions, if any, comes closest to your political views?

	All	Regular readership						
		Mid-Market		Broadsheets			RedTops	
		Expr'ss	Mail	Times	T'graph	Guardn	Sun	Mirror
	100%	5%	15%	5%	8%	4%	16%	11%
Old Labour	12%	7%	10%	9%	7%	27%	15%	22%
New Labour	29%	37%	22%	26%	10%	25%	31%	43%
One-Nation Tories	11%	12%	17%	18%	31%	8%	8%	4%
Thatcherite Tories	9%	15%	16%	15%	15%	0%	13%	3%
Liberals	12%	9%	13%	14%	14%	17%	10%	10%
Social Democrats	7%	1%	5%	8%	7%	19%	0%	7%

	All	Regular readership						
		Mid-Market		Broadsheets			RedTops	
		SExpr	MoS	STimes	STel	Obs	NoW	SMirror
	100%	4%	13%	8%	5%	3%	16%	8%
Old Labour	12%	10%	9%	5%	8%	27%	16%	27%
New Labour	29%	29%	24%	23%	13%	18%	33%	47%
One-Nation Tories	11%	12%	16%	21%	16%	6%	6%	3%
Thatcherite Tories	9%	14%	20%	11%	16%	0%	11%	4%
Liberals	12%	8%	8%	14%	23%	18%	13%	8%
Social Democrats	7%	0%	5%	11%	8%	20%	1%	4%

Source: MORI/ *The Economist*
Base: 1,010 British 18+, 4-5 June 2001
Readership Source: Election Aggregate, 8 May – 6 June,
18,567 interviews weighted to election result 7 June 2001

The recasting of the political stance of the *Daily Express* has brought with it a recasting of its traditional profile: in this typology over a third of their readers, 37%, say that 'New Labour' comes closest to their political views, and another 7% say 'Old Labour, totalling 44% of its readers, compared with just 27% in total who identify with either wing of the Tory Party.

Whereas some 41% of the electorate say that one designation or the other comes closest to their political view, 65% of *Mirror* readers, 52% of *Guardian* readers, 46% of *Sun* readers do; while 20% say they identify with Tory Party identifiers overall, 46% of *Telegraph* readers and 39% of *Mail* readers do (the surprise here was that 32% of *Mail* readers either identify with New (22%) or Old (10%) Labour. Only just over a quarter of Daily *Express* readers, 27% as noted above, say they are closest to one or the two Tory designations; and no surprises that among these papers (the sample size for the *Independent*, as well as the *Daily Star* and the *Financial Times,* being too small to report) the *Guardian* captures the highest incidence of Liberals and Social Democrats.

Of course a third of the public don't read any daily national newspapers regularly.

Among readers of the Sunday national newspapers, the *Sunday Mirror* and the *Observer* have the most Labour readers with nearly half of the *Sunday Mirror*'s readers saying that they are New Labour (47%) compared to Old (27%) while the balance tilts to Old Labour over New by a ratio of 27% to 18%.

We suspect that it will come as a surprise to the editors of the *Sunday Times* to find that analysed this way, their modal reader is closest to New Labour (23%), followed by One-Nation Tories (21%). Overall there are third of *Mail on Sunday* readers who identify with Labour's two wings, just short of the 36% who identify with the Tories' identifications. That 45% of *Observer* readers identify with Labour will come as no surprise, but that this group is so closely followed by the combination of Liberals (18%) and Social Democrats (20%) surely will.

Again, the *Independent on Sunday* readership as well as *People* and *Sunday Business* have sample sizes too small to analyse with confidence.

'This election wasn't important'

But if the public have not necessarily rejected electoral politics as a whole, perhaps they are unhappy with the choice they are currently offered, or alternatively sufficiently content with both the alternatives, or feel it is not important at all. Of course this, as much as the start of a long-term trend, would explain the low turnouts in all forms of British elections in recent years[96].

While, on balance, people said they disagreed that "I did not believe that voting would make much of a difference" (by 64% to 34%), that "none of the parties stood for policies I would like to see" (61% to 32%) and that "there was little difference between what the main parties were offering" (58% to 38%), it can be seen that in each case significant minorities were of the contrary opinion. Furthermore, non-voters were more likely to agree than disagree with the first two of these statements, though even among the abstainers opinion was evenly divided on whether the parties were offering a real choice.

What is more, it is plain that some of the negativity was specific to the current election. More than a quarter, 27%, of those who at the start of the campaign had said they thought voting makes a difference later agreed that they "did not believe that voting would make much of a difference" this time. In other words, a significant proportion of those who were positive about the efficacy of voting in general were nevertheless negative about it at this election: that is to say the 2001 general election was viewed differently to the 'norm'.

Fewer of the public than at any of the preceding three elections said it was personally important to them who won, though the fall since 1997 was only slight. In 1987 just one in eight said it was not important to them who won; this time it was one in three. Little wonder turnout was low.

---

[96] Of course in theory European and local elections are entirely separate from Westminster politics, and ought not to be affected by its unpopularity. But we know in practice that this is not the case, and a high proportion of voters in both are swayed primarily by their views of the national, parliamentary parties.

Table 46: Importance of who wins

Q. *How important is it to you personally who wins the General Election?*

	Jun 1987 %	Apr 1992 %	Apr 1997 %	Jun 2001 %
Very important	55	55	36	32
Fairly important	30	31	33	34
Not very important	9	10	18	25
Not at all important	3	3	10	8
No opinion	2	1	3	2
Important	85	86	69	66
Not important	12	13	28	33
Net important	73	73	41	33

Source: MORI
Base: c. 1,000 at each election

Lower interest in the result leads naturally to lower commitment in other ways. In 1997 some four million people, one elector in ten, enlisted in "Tony's Army", saying that they supported the Labour Party so much that they would encourage others to vote Labour without being asked; a further 21% would encourage others to vote Labour if asked for their opinion. Only a quarter as many were canvassing others on behalf of John Major's Conservative Party.

This innovative analysis, which was employed for the first time in the 1997 campaign, was developed from the MORI Excellence Model, used by a number of major corporations to test their corporate image in a system 'beyond customer satisfaction'. It showed how powerful a factor word of mouth advertising was in the last election.

We asked the public the same questions again in 2001, in our first election poll for *The Times*. There was considerably less enthusiasm this time – not only for Labour, but for the other parties as well, although the parties' relative levels of support were similar. Four in ten of Tony's foot soldiers deserted the field of battle in the 2001 election, though he still had an army of advocates, some 2.6 million people, trying through word of mouth to convince others that a second Blair term was to be desired.

That was three times as many as the roughly 900,000 who were slogging away for William Hague to become Prime Minister.

Table 47: MORI Excellence Model – "Word of mouth"

Q. *Thinking of the ... Party, please pick one statement from each section on this card according to which best reflects your behaviour and opinions with respect to the .... Party.*

	Con		Lab		Lib Dem	
	1997 %	2001 %	1997 %	2001 %	1997 %	2001 %
I support the Party so much I encourage others to vote for it, without being asked	3	2	10	6	2	1
If someone asked my opinion I would encourage them to vote for the Party	11	10	21	17	9	7
If someone asked my opinion I would be neutral about voting for the Party	42	57	45	57	60	68
If someone asked my opinion I would discourage them from voting for the Party	22	16	11	11	11	11
I am so strongly opposed to the Party that I discourage others from voting for it without being asked	12	10	3	4	4	5
Positive Response	14	12	31	23	11	8
Negative Response	34	26	14	15	15	16
Net	-20	-14	+17	+8	-4	-8
Don't know /No opinion	10	5	9	4	14	8

Source: MORI/ *The Times*

As a measure of the overall fall in enthusiasm, if we total the first two options for each party, we find that only 43% of the public would encourage somebody else to vote for one of the three main parties, even if asked; in 1997 the corresponding figure was 56%.

And while somewhat under two million people said they were so strongly opposed to the Labour Party that they would discourage others from voting for it without being asked, some four and a half million so despised the Tories they were going out of their way to rubbish them. Even so, negative advocacy against the Conservatives had fallen. There was a significant drop in the number who would discourage somebody else from voting Tory, whereas both Labour and the Liberal Democrats fare fractionally worse than they did in 1997. Nevertheless, the anti-

Conservatives still outnumbered the pro-Conservatives – by five-to-one on "without being asked", and by more than two-to-one if we include those who would only give opinions if asked for them; by contrast, both Labour and the Liberal Democrats come out on the right side of the ledger on either criterion.

Further evidence of Tory weakness, or perhaps just of low morale, comes from cross-analysing this data by voting intention. Of the already small band who were intending to vote Conservative, only 39% would encourage somebody else to do the same (and only 7% would give such advice without being asked); but 50% of Labour voters would advise others to vote Labour, including 15% who would need no prompting to do so. The Lib Dems, though, were as shy as the Tories – only 39% of the their supporters would advocate voting for the party, and just 3% would do so if not asked for advice.

Can we tell what is behind the fall in enthusiasm for the parties? One explanation that looks suspiciously convincing is public attitudes to the prime ministerial contenders. We have already seen how William Hague's leader image was always poor (Table 24), and how Tony Blair's declined sharply during 2000 (Table 11). When we combine the two, we discover that for the first time in four elections both the Prime Minister and the Leader of the Opposition were viewed predominantly negatively by the British public in the immediate run-up to polling day, as Table 48 shows.

By contrast, before the 1987 election, both Mrs Thatcher and Mr Kinnock had positive net scores, as did Mr Major and Mr Kinnock in 1992; in 1997 Mr Major's score was negative but Mr Blair's positive.

It is certainly not fanciful to link the image of the leaders with electoral turnout, although it must be borne in mind that the leaders' images are in part themselves a product of more general feelings about the political system, so it could be argued that poor leader image and low turnout might be both symptoms of the same malaise rather than that one is a cause of the other. At any rate, the turnout in 1987, when both leaders had a positive rating, was good; in 1992, when their combined score was better still, it was very good indeed. But in 1997, with only one of the two achieving a positive score turnout touched what was then a post-war low and in 2001, with both leaders scoring negatively, the turnout fell far below that to its lowest level ever in real terms.

Table 48: Leaders' average scores on positive and negative attributes

	Conservative leader			Labour leader			Combined
	Positive	Negative	Net	Positive	Negative	Net	
		Thatcher			Kinnock		
May 1987	40.8	36.2	+4.6	31.2	20.6	+10.6	+15.2
		Major			Kinnock		
March 1992	40.6	22.2	+18.4	30.8	22.0	+8.8	+27.1
		Major			Blair		
March 1997	18.2	23.0	-4.8	23.6	14.0	+9.6	+4.8
		Hague			Blair		
April 2001	11.0	24.0	-13.0	20.1	20.4	-0.3	-13.3

Source: MORI/ *The Times*

We can carry out a similar analysis for party image, but here the public have always been more prepared to pick negative descriptions and attributes, and party net scores on the 9 positive and 5 negative descriptions in the MORI party image test have often been lower than those for the leaders. Conversely, the final party image test of the 2001 election found Labour with a slight positive rating (a sharp contrast to the –14.8 the party scored in October 2000), and although the very low Conservative rating meant that the combined net rating of the parties was at its worst level for the past four elections, this was only just the case. In fact in 1987 – when the turnout was perfectly respectable – both parties had a negative net score.

Table 49: Parties' average scores on positive and negative attributes

	Conservative party			Labour party			Combined
	Positive	Negative	Net	Positive	Negative	Net	
May 1987	26.2	31.8	-5.6	21.1	29.0	-7.9	-13.5
March 1992	27.1	27.2	-0.1	29.3	25.8	+3.5	+3.4
April 1997	11.1	30.8	-19.7	25.7	14.0	+11.7	-8.0
May 2001	10.9	27.4	-16.5	21.6	19.8	+1.8	-14.8

Source: MORI/ *The Times*

That the standing of the leaders should have an effect on turnout while the general standing of the parties seems not to do would fit the general finding already discussed of the "Political Triangle", that leader image is more significant than party image in a modern election. But it must be admitted that the correlation between turnout and the overall standing of the leaders, though compelling, may be no more than coincidence.

Table 50: Public attitudes to manifestos

Q. *How likely or unlikely are you to read or look at any of the party political manifestos in this election campaign?*

	2-3 Apr 1997 %	17-22 May 2001 %
Very likely	21	16
Fairly likely	32	23
Not very likely	22	23
Not at all likely	25	35
Don't know	*	3
Very/fairly likely	53	39
Not very/not at all likely	47	58
Net likely	6	-19

Source: MORI

Q. *Which of these statements best describes your attitude to the party election manifestos?*

	2-3 Apr 1997 %	17-22 May 2001 %
They are important for everybody to read	36	30
I wouldn't read them but I would hope to hear about them in the media	46	37
I think they are a waste of time and I wouldn't pay any attention to them	14	26
None of these	2	3
Don't know	2	4

Source: MORI

If fewer Britons think the contest is important or have any regard for the leaders, of course it will be harder to make them take an interest in the campaign. As a case in point, we can take their attitudes to the party manifestos. The public confessed itself considerably less interested in the parties' election manifestos at this election than in 1997[97]: then, more than half said that they were at least "fairly likely" to read or look at some of the manifestos; in 2001, fewer than two in five thought it likely they would do so. Similarly, fewer than in 1997 said they thought it was important that everybody should read the manifestos, and fewer were interested in hearing about the manifestos from the media; more than a quarter now think that they are "a waste of time".

So had the parties so failed to interest the public by the start of the campaign that it was doomed to be a boring election with the public unreceptive to information or campaigning materials? The press clearly thought so. But maybe it wasn't as simple as that.

---

[97] The survey was conducted as part of the MORI Financial Services Omnibus. A representative quota sample of 1,960 adults aged 18+ were interviewed face-to-face, in home, on 17-22 May 2001.

The lacklustre campaign

In the 2001 election, fewer of those who voted said that they had made up their mind during the campaign than was the case in other recent elections: in 1992, only 63% said they had made up their mind before the campaign began; in 2001 it was 74%.

There are two ways to interpret this figure. It could be argued that because most of the public had already made up its mind, the result was a foregone conclusion and there was little to play for, the campaign was less necessary than usual and perhaps boring as a consequence. But for that to hold water, we would expect to find more of the public than usual decrying the campaign, saying that there was too much coverage of the election and that they were uninterested in it. In fact, the opposite was true, and this points to the alternative explanation for the high proportion of voters that had made up their minds before the campaign. If the campaign was poor, so that many of those who normally decide how to vote during the campaign came to no decision and failed to vote, that would cause both an increase in the proportion who had already made up their minds (since those who had not didn't vote), and a decrease in turnout – turnout was low because the campaign failed the floating voters.

Interest in the campaign

We were told, of course, *ad nauseam* that "This is the most boring election in this century/decade/since the war/lately/whatever". How many elections is it that I've been hearing that? Nine is it? Every election news editors send some tyro journo out to stir up apathy, and prove once again that this is the most boring election since the year dot.

Since only about one in six of us are at the best of times 'very' interested in politics, and about one in eight always wish it had never been invented, it's easy to take tape recorder in hand and go out on the high street and highjack some feckless youth or old dear to moan about how bored he or she is with the election...already. Perhaps one thing that has changed is that the journalists are reaching this stage ever earlier in the campaign, and can then take it as an excuse to stop reporting the election issues and progress altogether. Not all the papers admitted their boredom as openly as *The Mirror* (whose front page on the Tuesday of election week pictured the three party leaders apparently asleep or yawning with the headline "P.S. Exciting, Isn't It?"), but the mood was all-pervasive. (In *The Times*, for example, Tom Baldwin[98] had decided that "Tony Blair has announced the longest, and possibly dullest, election campaign in British political history" by 2 April.)

Figure 17:

Was the Election interesting?

Q   How strongly do you agree or disagree that . . . it was an interesting election campaign?

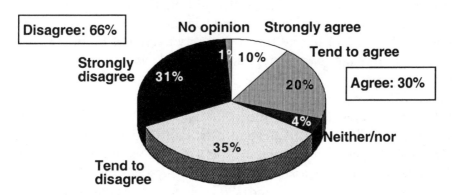

Base: Phase 2 - 1,162 UK adults 18+, 9-18 June 2001

In fact, the public were far from bored. But the lacklustre way in which the election was fought, and in which the campaign was reported, failed to give many of them the stimulus they needed to turn out and vote. Despite the record low turnout and the clear impression that the 2001 election was the most boring ever, with few people taking an interest, interest in news about the election was actually at a higher level in 2001 than in some earlier elections. It is certainly true that there were a lot of

---

[98] Tom Baldwin, "Longest election fight has already cost millions", *The Times*, 2 April 2001.

Britons who were taking no interest in the election at all. But it didn't follow that the diminished number who were intending to vote were less interested in the election than in the past.

When we re-interviewed our Electoral Commission panel after the election, more than two-thirds recalled that "thinking back to the campaign", they had been very or fairly interested in news about the election. As this was as many – indeed, fractionally more – than had originally said they were interested in politics it does not appear that the 2001 election faced the public as an atypically boring prospect. It suggests, indeed, that declining turnout is not a function of declining interest in politics or elections but rather a failure of the campaign to connect with the electorate.

This is reflected in the finding that although the majority said that they had been interested in news about the election, the majority disagreed by more than two-to-one that "It was an interesting election campaign". Even of those who had said they were *"very* interested" in politics, 61% said that, looking back, they did not find the election campaign interesting.

Of course impressions after the event can be fallible, and we cannot compare the Electoral Commission data with similar polls from earlier elections. However, in our poll for *The Times* in the fourth week of the campaign (29 May) we asked a bank of four questions that we also posed at similar stages of the 1992 and 1997 campaigns, measuring how many of the public said they were "very interested" or "fairly interested" in news about the election, what the polls were saying, the party election broadcasts and politicians' speeches. Surprisingly, in view of the general impression of apathy, more of the public said that they were interested in each of these four than was the case in 1997. In fact, more of the public were interested in politicians' speeches than in 1992, one of the highest turnout elections of modern times!

Why should this be the case? One noticeable feature of this election was how early in the entire proceedings the media came to the unanimous conclusion that they were bored, and so must be their readers or viewers.

Could it be that that part of the public which takes an interest in politics and will vote – still a majority, apathy notwithstanding – far from feeling sated by the coverage simply found it whetting their appetites? And as for politicians' speeches, they rarely had the chance to hear them – only soundbites, and then mostly from the leaders.

Table 51: Interest in election coverage 1992-2001

Q. *How interested would you say you were in each of the following?*

	Apr 1992 %	Apr 1997 %	May 2001 %
News about the election			
Interested	60	52	58
Not interested	38	48	41
Net	22	4	17
Politicians' speeches			
Interested	43	40	46
Not interested	56	60	54
Net	-13	-20	-8
What the opinion polls say about the election			
Interested	40	33	35
Not interested	58	66	64
Net	-18	-33	-29
Party election broadcasts			
Interested	36	32	35
Not interested	63	67	64
Net	-27	-34	-29

Source: MORI/various
Base: c. 1,000 British aged 18+ in each survey

The public's thirst for information

The election campaign period carries out a very important function for the majority of citizens in Britain. For most of the time, between elections, few pay deep attention to political issues. They may have impressions, good or bad, of the parties and the politicians, and a good idea which way they are likely to vote when the time comes. But many still feel they do not know enough, and want to be better informed before they cast their votes.

MORI research consistently finds a correlation between familiarity and favourability – generally, the more people feel they are informed about an institution or company, the more they tend to be satisfied with it. The Electoral Commission research suggests that information is a key driver in framing attitudes to voting and this is a particular issue among key, 'hard-to-reach' groups such as young and non-white citizens.

MORI's first survey for the Electoral Commission survey confirmed that a substantial proportion of the population feel short of information. More than half, 53%, agreed that "I don't know enough about the candidates who stand at general elections", and 34% that "I don't know enough about what the parties stand for at General Elections". Two-thirds of young people (18-24 year olds), 66%, agree that they don't know enough about candidates and the majority are also more likely to agree than disagree that they don't know enough about the parties.

Table 52: Why undecided

Q (To all "undecided" about voting intention) *Why do you say you are undecided?*

Unprompted answers:	%
Don't know enough about the election/politics	28
Waiting to see manifestos	15
Don't know what the parties stand for	11
Not interested in the election/politics	9
Don't know the candidates	6
No difference/they are all the same	6
Waiting to see candidates in my area	5
Waiting to see what happens during the campaign	5
Don't trust them/any of them	4
Refused	3
Other	8
Don't know	5

Source: MORI/*Sunday Telegraph*
Base: 128 British 18+ who said they were undecided about their voting intention, 10-12 May 2001

Lack of information is a key reason for people saying they are undecided about who to vote for. A MORI/*Sunday Telegraph* survey in the first week of the campaign found that information-related reasons – "Don't know enough", "Am waiting to see manifestos", "Don't know what the parties stand for", "Don't know the candidates" – were more often given than those relating to scepticism, mistrust or simple lack of interest in explanation of why the respondent was unsure how he or she would vote. We strongly suspect that the vast majority of this group did not vote in 2001; in other elections, a significant proportion of them might have done so.

If information is lacking, from what sources do the public expect to get it? And which sources do they trust?

Table 53: Trusted sources of political information

Q. *From which, if any, of the sources I am going to read out, do you obtain information and news about politics and current issues?*
Q. *And from which one of the sources do you obtain most information and news about politics and current issues?*
Q. *And which one of the sources do you trust most to give accurate and impartial information and news about politics and current issues?*

	Any %	Most %	Trust %
TV including satellite TV	88	48	49
Daily newspapers	74	28	12
Sunday newspapers	54	5	3
Radio	48	10	12
Leaflets through the door	42	2	2
Friends	30	1	1
Family	26	2	3
Work colleagues	21	1	1
The internet	13	1	1
Magazines	*	*	*
Local papers	*	0	0
Nowhere/none	*	0	9
Other	1	1	1
Don't know	*	1	6

Source: MORI/Electoral Commission
Base: 1,801 UK adults aged 18+, 9-15 May 2001

Television is the most used source of information and news about politics and current issues, used by seven in eight of the adult population as at least one of their sources of information, and by almost half as their single most important source. Daily and Sunday newspapers are also important, and the daily paper is the principal information source for one in four. Just under half the public also use the radio as a source.

These patterns are consistent among all groups but younger people are more likely than others to get information through family and the internet: 38% and 22% respectively, twelve and nine points higher than the public as a whole.

When we consider which sources are most trusted, the domination of broadcasting is even more marked, with three in five naming either TV or radio as their most trusted source of information.

In fact, more generally the broadcasters are Britain's most trusted media. The vast majority of the public believe the political reporting of the BBC and ITV to be neutral and fair. Perhaps as a result, by comparison with radio and television, the newspapers score very poorly on trust – much worse than in most of the rest of the EU, as demonstrated in the European Commission's Eurobarometer survey in 1999.

Table 54: Trust in the media

Q. *For each of the following institutions, please tell me whether you tend to trust it or tend not to trust it.*

	All EU	UK
% "tend to trust"	%	%
The press	49	24
Radio	66	66
Television	67	71

Source: Eurobarometer 51.0, March-April 1999

This order of preference puts a great deal of significance, of course, on the Party Election Broadcasts, the one opportunity that the parties have directly to address the electorate through the information medium of choice of the majority of its members. PEBs are often much maligned, but having asked those of the public who watched them on TV what they thought of them, we can give them a mixed report card. Among those who say they saw at least one broadcast, the PEBs were on balance seen as 'interesting' (51% to 33%) and 'informative' (48% to 34%) but they are *not* seen as being particularly 'useful' (38% to 45%). They are also thought to have had minimal influence on what people decided to do on election day: 77% say broadcasts had 'not very much' influence or 'none at all', similar to 1997 (74%) and significantly higher than equivalent figures for the effect of "election coverage on television" (50%) and in the newspapers (61%).

Media coverage of the election campaign

Asked if there was too much or too little coverage of the election in the media, more said there was too much than too little both on television and in the newspapers. (Far fewer had an opinion of the radio coverage.) This is of course always true. Given that there is always part of the population with no interest whatever in the election, it is inevitable. (Remember that in past elections we have found as many as 24% prepared to support a ban on all coverage of the election on TV and radio, and 16% who would ban all newspaper coverage!) But the numbers feeling coverage to be too high were significantly lower in 2001 than in recent previous elections; and this was much truer of the press coverage than of television.

In the Electoral Commission survey, we asked about the content of election information received. In this case, it is important to remember that we are dealing with a panel survey: respondents were those who were prepared to be interviewed once at the start of the campaign then re-interviewed afterwards. One result of this (a "panel effect") is that our sample were significantly more interested in politics than the public as a whole; we would therefore expect to find many fewer hostile to the propagation of election information than in a fresh sample like the *Sunday Telegraph* poll. Yet as many as one in five panel members felt they received too much information about the party leaders and one in eight too much about the parties' campaigns nationally. Nevertheless, the majority felt they got 'about the right amount of information' on both these subjects. They were less satisfied with information on the policies of the parties – 44% too little, 48% about right – and the candidates in their constituency – 55% too little, 39% about right.

Table 55: Degree of media coverage – public attitudes

Q. How do you feel about the amount of coverage newspapers have been giving to the election campaign? Have they given much too much coverage, a little too much coverage, about the right amount of coverage, a little too little coverage or much too little coverage?

Q. And how do you feel about the amount of coverage given to the election campaign on television?
Q. And how do you feel about the amount of coverage given to the election campaign on radio?

	1983 %	1987 %	1992 %	1997 %	2001 %
Newspapers					
Much too much	18	30	34	20	17
A little too much	18	22	22	21	20
About the right amount	46	35	32	41	48
A little too little	3	2	1	2	3
Much too little	1	1	*	*	1
No opinion	13	9	10	16	12
Too much	36	52	56	41	37
Too little	4	3	1	2	4
Television					
Much too much	24	49	45	29	18
A little too much	26	22	23	24	20
About the right amount	40	24	27	37	51
A little too little	2	2	2	1	3
Much too little	1	*	*	1	1
No opinion	7	3	3	8	7
Too much	50	71	68	63	38
Too little	3	2	2	2	4
Radio					
Much too much	4	12	13	8	2
A little too much	4	6	8	4	3
About the right amount	25	30	32	33	31
A little too little	3	3	4	3	4
Much too little	2	2	2	1	1
No opinion	61	46	41	51	58
Too much	8	18	21	12	5
Too little	5	5	6	4	5

Source: MORI

All in all, this suggests that if the public did not necessarily want more information in total, they *did* want different *types* of information, that is to say more candidate-focused and more policy-focused information, less on the daily campaigning circus in front of the cameras and notebooks.

Instead, media coverage focussed too much on the leaders. The Electoral Commission report records[99] that the Communications Research Centre at the University of Loughborough found Blair featured in 35.4% of all election news items, with Hague in 26.4%. Kennedy was third. Nobody else hit double figures. The leaders were not in any case what the viewers wanted to see. An NOP poll in the *Sunday Times* asked the public which party leader they would rather sit down and watch on TV: Tony Blair was well ahead of William Hague by 38% to 17%, but "neither of these" scored a winning 42%.[100]

Table 56: Satisfaction with level of election information

Q. *Did you receive too much, too little or about the right amount of information about the following aspects of the General Election?*

		Too much	Too little	About right	Don't know	Net
The candidates in your constituency	%	5	55	39	2	-50
The policies of the parties	%	6	44	48	2	-38
The parties' campaigns nationally	%	12	31	53	4	-19
The party leaders*	%	22	25	52	1	-3
What the party leaders were doing†	%	22	23	52	3	-1
*: Asked to part of sample only (base: 376)		†: Asked to part of sample only (base: 786)				

Source: MORI/Electoral Commission
Base: 1,162 UK adults aged 18+, 9-18 June 2001. (Re-interview of panel)

It would be natural to blame the parties for this over-concentration on their leaders. But, when challenged, the party strategists blame the media: if a party leader took part in an event, they could be guaranteed coverage, while a more junior minister or shadow minister would simply be ignored and the opportunity lost.

Too much of the media coverage, too, covered electoral process and procedure rather than issues or politicians' conduct, as the Electoral Commission noted in its report. The Loughborough research found that consistently around 40% of media coverage was about the process of the

---

[99] Electoral Commission, *Election 2001, The Official Results* (Politico's Publishing, 2001), p 19.
[100] *Sunday Times*, 13 May 2001. NOP interviewed 1,003 adults by telephone on 10-11 May 2001.

election and the campaign rather than substantive issues, though this was also true in 1997.[101]

Another aspect of the media coverage of the election that we, at least, noticed, was the reduced commissioning of opinion polls – so that, for example, there were just 30 published national voting intention polls over the four week campaign, compared to 47 in 1997 (though that was a six week campaign), and 50 in 1992 (when the campaign was the same length as in 2001). A few months before, it was expected that the *Mail on Sunday* would be polling every week as would the *News of the World*, *Observer*, *Sunday Telegraph* and possibly the *Sunday Mirror*. As the flat-lining continued month after month from the beginning of November, each cut down their commitment to measure the mood of the electorate each week during the campaign. Instead, some of them did a weekly 'focus group', as made famous by Philip Gould, which make pretty boring reading to even an election junkie like me.

Surely one important factor in public attitudes to the press coverage, and perhaps in the turnout itself, was the degree of sheer negativity of the reporting. The work that Echo Research has been doing, and making available to Brian MacArthur of *The Times* and others, has proved instructive.

The negative nature of journalism in Britain is measured by the net scores for the two major parties, -13 for Labour and a massive –25 for the Tories. Only the Liberal Democrats came out on balance favourably mentioned according to the Echo analysis, with a net score of +10.

---

[101] Electoral Commission, *Election 2001, The Official Results* (Politico's Publishing, 2001), p 11.

Table 57: Summary of Newspaper Bias

	Total	Fav-ourable	Unfav-ourable	Neutral	Net fav-ourable	Rating
Labour	3693 (48%)	957 (26%)	1445 (39%)	1291 (35%)	-488 (-13%)	48.7
Conservative	2897 (37%)	506 (17%)	1222 (42%)	1169 (40%)	-716 (-25%)	47.3
LibDem	1182 (15%)	325 (27%)	205 (17%)	652 (55%)	+120 (+10%)	50.9

Source: Echo Research (Summary of Coverage 8 May – 7 June 2001)

According to Echo, some 18% of all the articles pertaining to the election were published in the *Guardian*, 17% in the *Daily Telegraph*, 16% in the *Independent* and 15% in *The Times*. The *Financial Times* coverage was only 10% of the total. Among the mid-market papers, the *Daily Mail* published just 7% of the total number, while the *Express* only 4%. Of the red tops, the *Mirror* accounted for 7%, the *Sun* for 5% and the *Daily Star* for just 2%.

Table 58: Scale of election coverage in national daily newspapers

	Reader-ship (% of adult public)	Con		Lab		Lib Dem		Total	Share of coverage %
The Sun	16%	142	40%	187	53%	26	7%	355	5%
Daily Mail	15%	165	35%	258	55%	49	10%	472	7%
The Mirror	11%	187	42%	206	46%	53	12%	446	7%
Daily Telegraph	8%	433	38%	538	47%	168	15%	1,139	17%
The Times	5%	382	38%	468	46%	160	16%	1,010	15%
Daily Express	5%	114	38%	148	50%	36	12%	298	4%
Guardian	4%	445	37%	556	46%	209	17%	1,210	18%
Independent	2%	416	37%	476	42%	232	21%	1,124	16%
Daily Star	2%	49	36%	67	49%	20	15%	136	2%
Financial Times	1%	250	38%	316	48%	99	15%	665	10%
TOTAL		2,583	38%	3,220	47%	1,052	15%	6,855	

Source: MORI (readership figures); Echo Research (Summary of Coverage 8 May – 7 June 2001)

It is interesting also that the overall coverage in terms of number of articles without regard to 'bias' equates closely to the outcome of the election, if 'others' are taken into account, and that there was not great variation in the proportion of space given to the different parties by the various newspapers. The *Daily Mail* (35%) had least about the Tories and the *Mirror* (42%) the most, but the difference is hardly huge. However, it is certainly worthy of note that the *Independent* gave substantially more coverage to the Liberal Democrats than any other newspaper.

Of course, quality and prominence as well as quantity of coverage is relevant, and perhaps not all the figures in the table can be taken entirely at face value. The *Daily Star*'s front-page election coverage, for instance, apart from two stories about John Prescott punching an egg-throwing demonstrator, consisted entirely of four stories: "Geri [Halliwell] Goes into Labour" (14 May), "Britney [Spears] backs Labour" (16 May), "Jordan [a topless model] stands as an MP" (23 May), and "Jordan: I've Got 'Em by the Ballots" (24 May), with accompanying pictures in scanty dress. (That is, scantily dressed pictures of Britney Spears and Jordan. The scantily-dressed pictures of John Prescott were a *Mirror* exclusive.) [102]

In fact, the Prescott story was – perhaps predictably – much the most widely covered story, judging from MORI's own analysis of the front page coverage[103]. Only on four weekdays during the four-week campaign did the average front page coverage exceed 35% – 9 May (coverage of the election announcement), 7 June (election day itself) and 17 and 18 May, the first day with coverage of the punch itself and the second with follow-ups of that story. It should be noted that 17 May was also the day after Labour's manifesto launch: only *The Times* and the *Guardian* found room for front-page headlines on the manifesto (though the *Mirror* did

---

[102] The *Mirror* on 18 May had a front-page picture of John Prescott in the boxing ring in 1958, in singlet and shorts, together with a presumably faked photo of the modern Prescott ("Britain's raging bulk") in boxing pose with bare torso.

[103] It also seems to have been the most read. On the day after the punch, newspaper sales rose by 150,000 — though that might also have owed something to Liverpool's UEFA Cup final victory, reported in the same day's papers. (Brian MacArthur, "Talked up and dumbed down", *The Times*, 8 June 2001.)

headline its Prescott picture "ManiFISTo" and mention the manifesto launch in the caption). Every single national paper had a second Prescott story on the front page the following day and only the *Daily Mail* and *Daily Record* didn't lead on it.

Table 59: Stance of articles in national daily newspapers

Number and percentage of favourable, unfavourable and neutral stories about each party in each daily newspaper

	Conservative			Labour			Liberal Democrat		
	Fav	Unfav	Neut	Fav	Unfav	Neut	Fav	Unfav	Neut
The Sun	38	66	38	75	59	53	7	8	11
	27%	46%	27%	40%	32%	28%	27%	31%	42%
Daily Mail	51	21	93	16	204	38	4	9	36
	31%	13%	56%	6%	79%	15%	8%	18%	73%
The Mirror	11	143	33	118	33	55	9	19	25
	6%	76%	18%	57%	16%	27%	17%	36%	47%
Daily Telegraph	84	92	257	69	193	276	28	17	123
	19%	21%	59%	13%	36%	51%	17%	10%	73%
The Times	27	99	256	56	126	286	21	14	125
	7%	26%	67%	12%	27%	61%	13%	9%	78%
Daily Express	37	64	13	77	56	15	24	4	8
	32%	56%	11%	52%	38%	10%	67%	11%	22%
Guardian	43	231	171	127	231	198	71	36	102
	10%	52%	38%	23%	42%	36%	34%	17%	49%
Independent	62	214	140	117	191	168	62	52	118
	15%	51%	34%	25%	40%	35%	27%	22%	51%
Daily Star	7	18	24	27	15	25	1	5	14
	14%	37%	49%	40%	22%	37%	5%	25%	70%
Financial Times	99	103	48	157	95	64	55	12	32
	40%	41%	19%	50%	30%	20%	56%	12%	32%
TOTAL	451	1,051	1,073	839	1,203	1,178	282	176	594
	18%	41%	42%	26%	37%	37%	27%	17%	56%

Source: Echo Research (Summary of Coverage 8 May – 7 June 2001)

As Table 59 shows however, even the most even-handed newspapers seem to feel they have to put a spin on the majority of their articles; only *The Times* and the *Daily Telegraph* ran more neutral articles than those leaning one way or the other. For instance, the *Financial Times* was even-handed on its coverage of the Tory Party during the election, but of the 250 stories they carried about the Conservatives, Echo coders rated the roughly 40% favourable, 40% unfavourable and only 20% neutral. The *FT*'s coverage of Labour was on balance favourable, with 50%

positive, 30% negative. The *Indy*, which was launched with the slogan 'It's independent, are you?', covered the Tories' campaign with a third neutral but half unfavourable.

It must seem to the political parties that no matter what they do, they can't get a favourable story out of some of the newspapers! Even the *Daily Telegraph*, regarded as the "house journal" of the Conservative Party, had more negative than positive to say about the Conservatives; on the other hand, the *Observer* was more negative about Labour than the *Daily Telegraph*! Certainly the 'Poison Index' we've invented is an indication how even the most partisan papers sometimes have difficulty saying a nice thing about anybody, even the side they are supporting. Using the data provided by Echo, we constructed an Index of positive minus negative reporting, leaving aside the neutral material which might be thought as an ideal way in which newspapers should report an election.

Most negative of the daily papers, by some way, was the *Daily Mail*, with a poison index of –65, ahead of the *Mirror* (-49) and, perhaps surprisingly for a broadsheet, the *Independent* (-49). The only two papers which proved to be on balance positive in their coverage were the *FT*, and, intriguingly, the *Express*.

But the vitriol is really strong on Sunday, with the *Sunday Mirror* the most negative by far, but somewhat skewed by their three out of three negative articles about the Liberal Democrats during the election. On balance, the Sundays were more negative about both the Conservative Party and the Labour Party, but were equally favourable to the Lib Dems. Not only did not a single Sunday paper have more positive than negative coverage, but the least poisonous of them, the *Independent on Sunday* (–38) and *Sunday Express* (–39), had net negative scores by a long way.

It is often commented on, and not only by the politicians, that the newspapers follow the maxim that 'good news is not news', and won't cover what they want to let the public know about, and in our work for the Electoral Commission, this complaint seems to be felt by the public as well. Perhaps the editors of the newspapers might consider their coverage of general elections in light of the findings of these figures. Certainly the feeling of the public in this election is that there were far fewer complaining about too much coverage of the election in 2001 than in earlier contests.

Table 60: The Poison Index and Con-Lab bias Index

	Overall stance* towards:			Poison index	Con-Lab Bias index
	Con	Lab	LD		
Daily Mail	+18	-73	-10	-65	+91
Daily Telegraph	-2	-23	+7	-18	+21
The Times	-19	-15	+4	-30	-4
The Independent	-37	-16	+4	-49	-21
Financial Times	-2	+20	+43	+61	-22
The Guardian	-42	-19	+17	-44	-23
The Sun	-20	+9	-4	-15	-29
Daily Express	-24	+14	+56	+46	-38
Daily Star	-22	+18	-20	-24	-40
The Mirror	-71	+41	-19	-49	-112
Total for national dailies	-23	-11	+10	-24	-12
Mail on Sunday	-6	-69	-25	-100	+63
Sunday Telegraph	-24	-41	+19	-46	+17
Sunday Times	-30	-46	+17	-59	+16
Sunday Express	-20	-11	-8	-39	-9
The Observer	-70	-27	+35	-62	-43
News of the World	-47	-3	-44	-94	-44
Independent on Sunday	-52	-7	+21	-38	-45
Sunday Mirror	-85	+5	-100	-180	-90
Sunday Business	-85	+5	0	-80	-90
Sunday People	-82	+30	-50	-102	-112
Total for national Sundays	-45	-25	+11	-59	-20

"Overall stance" calculated as percentage positive minus percentage negative articles.
"Poison index": Total positive or negative score on overall stance for all three parties
"Con-Lab bias Index": net favourable to Conservative minus net favourable to Labour
Source: Calculated from Echo Research Summary of Coverage (8 May – 7 June 2001)

Table 60 also shows the Con-Lab bias index, combining the net positive or negative percentage scores for the two parties to show to what extent each paper's overall reporting leant to one side or other of the fence. The most partisan papers, predictably, were on the Conservative side the

Daily Mail among the dailies, and the *Mail on Sunday* among the Sundays, and the *Mirror* and *Sunday People* for Labour.

Does a newspaper's bias affect the opinions of its readers? Ever since Burke characterised the Press as a Fourth Estate more important than the Three Estates in Parliament, the power of the Press, and especially its political power, has been debated. From the Zinoviev Letter of 1924 to the *Sun* Wot Won It in 1992, newspapers have been accused of having swung the results of elections – and they have not always repudiated the allegations. But does the Press today really have the power to swing the public mood?

Perhaps not in 2001. The papers didn't really seem to have their hearts in it. There was hardly a headline or front page that was really memorable. Of course, no newspaper could conceivably have swung the result of this election.

How closely does the voting behaviour of readers coincide with the editorial lines or bias pushed by their newspapers? In general terms, it is true that the party political inclinations of readers tend to match those of their newspapers – the Tory papers have the highest Tory support, and the consistently Labour papers the highest support for Labour. The *Sun* occupies a median position. Is it possible to tell whether such coincidence, when it occurs, is because the papers have influence over their readers or simply that members of the public tend to prefer to read the newspapers with which they find themselves most in agreement?

The table of voting by readership presents the titles in the same order as the bias table, for ease of cross-reference.

It is clear that there is close correlation between the papers' partisan bias and their readers' votes. Only the two *Express* titles, the *FT* and *The Times* saw more of their readers vote for the major party they were 'biased' against than for the one that they favoured. The *Independent* wrote positively about the Liberal Democrats, negatively about both the major parties, and further gave a bigger proportion of its coverage to the Liberal Democrats than any other paper; its readers voted in greater numbers for the Lib Dems than for the other two parties, and the increase in the Lib Dem share among *Independent* readers was greater than the increase in the share of any party among the readers of any other paper.

Table 61: Voting by national newspaper readership
(Percentages in brackets after titles are the percentage of the adult British population who were regular readers of the title during the 2001 election campaign)

Newspaper (Readership)	Vote share 2001					Change since 1997				
	Con %	Lab %	LD %	Oth %	Lead %	Con %	Lab %	LD %	Swing	Turn-out %
Daily Mail (15%)	55	24	17	4	+31	+6	-5	+3	+5.5	65
Daily Telegraph (8%)	65	16	14	5	+49	+8	-4	-3	+6.0	71
The Times (5%)	40	28	26	6	+12	-2	0	+1	-1.0	66
Independent (2%)	12	38	44	6	-26	-4	-9	+14	+2.5	69
Financial Times (1%)	48	30	21	1	+18	0	+1	+2	-0.5	64
Guardian (4%)	6	52	34	8	-46	-2	-15	+12	+6.5	68
Sun (16%)	29	52	11	8	-23	-1	0	-1	-0.5	50
Daily Express (5%)	43	33	19	5	+10	-6	+4	+3	-5.0	63
Daily Star (2%)	21	56	17	6	-35	+4	-10	+5	+7.0	48
The Mirror (11%)	11	71	13	5	-60	-3	-1	+2	-1.0	62
Daily Record (3%)	8	59	10	23	-51	-4	+2	0	-3.0	57
No daily paper (33%)	27	45	22	6	-18	-2	+2	+1	-2.0	56
Evening Standard (5%)	29	42	21	8	-13	-7	-3	+9	-2.0	51
Mail on Sunday (13%)	53	25	17	5	+28	+4	-3	+2	+3.5	65
Sunday Telegraph (5%)	63	17	13	7	+46	+7	-2	-4	+4.5	71
Sunday Times (8%)	40	29	24	7	+11	-3	-1	+3	-1.0	67
Sunday Express (4%)	47	29	20	4	+18	-6	+2	+6	-4.0	67
Observer (3%)	4	53	34	9	-49	-7	-10	+12	+1.5	71
News of the World (16%)	27	55	12	6	-28	-1	0	+1	-0.5	52
Indep't on Sunday (1%)	10	47	37	6	-37	-4	-1	+5	-1.5	70
Sunday Mirror (8%)	16	72	9	3	-56	-2	+5	-3	-3.5	62
Sunday People (5%)	19	65	13	3	-46	-2	+3	+2	-2.5	60
Sunday Mail (4%)	14	53	13	20	-39	0	0	+2	0.0	59
Sunday Post (3%)	22	43	18	17	-21	-1	-2	+5	+0.5	64
No Sunday paper (42%)	30	42	22	6	-12	0	0	+1	0.0	55

Source: MORI election aggregate 2001
Base: 18,657 adults aged 18+, interviewed 8 May-6 Jun 2001

Statistical analysis confirms how closely the two tables are related. The r^2 correlation co-efficient between the Con-Lab bias index of the newspaper's reporting and the Conservative lead over Labour among its readers is 0.65: 65% of all variance in the voting behaviour can be explained by the bias index. From the derived regression equation, we find that the Labour lead can be expected to rise by 1.15 points for each increased point in net bias. Put another way, for every extra 1% of coverage that leans to Labour rather than being neutral, an apparent swing to Labour among the readers of almost 0.6% can be detected.

However, we must be wary of assuming a causal relationship here – a newspaper's readership is not a captive audience, and such a correlation can arise just as well from voters choosing to buy a newspaper they agree with as from the paper having the power to sway the opinions of its readers.

Also striking are the differences in abstentions across the various titles, with the *Sun* and *Daily Star* standing out from the rest of the press, including more non-voters even than those who read no paper regularly. Interestingly, these were by no means the papers most negative in their coverage, but they were two of the three which carried fewest stories about the election at all. It is worth noting that turnout by *Express* readers, the other title with low coverage, was much more respectable. This presumably shows the papers reflecting the preferences of their readers (or, in the case of the *Express*, of their target market).

If a paper is really able to influence its readership, however, it is perhaps more useful to consider changes over time rather than a snapshot of readers' opinions. Perhaps the most obvious case study is the *Express*, once a Conservative paper, then owned by Lord Hollick's United Newspapers and pursuing a Labour line under Rosie Boycott's editorship, now sold again to Richard Desmond and paying little attention to party politics at the 2001 election. Yet its readers have not co-operated. In 1997, the *Express* was still a Conservative paper and its readers voted almost identically to those of its mid-market rival, the *Daily Mail*. But this stayed true well into the Boycott editorship, its readership remaining stubbornly Tory supporting. In the second quarter of 2000, 45% of those *Express* readers who gave a voting intention were still Tory, 15 points higher than the public as a whole, and 34% of *Express* readers were Labour, 16 points lower than the average. But at the 2001 election, when its coverage was lower than that of any other daily except its stablemate the *Star*, the Tory share was only ten points higher than the national 33%, and Labour's nine points lower. Compared to the national trend, its readers swung disproportionately to Labour over precisely the period when it was covering least newsprint in parading its Labour preferences – or, more likely, many of its Tory readers simply switched to reading another paper altogether.

Table 62: Readers' perceptions of newspaper bias, 1992-2001

Questions asked only to the regular readers of each title:
Q. *Do you think the ... mainly supports or opposes the Conservative Party, or neither particularly supports or opposes it?*
Q. *Do you think the ... mainly supports or opposes the Labour Party, or neither particularly supports or opposes it?*

	1992			1997			2001		
	Con	Lab	Bias	Con	Lab	Bias	Con	Lab	Bias
Daily Telegraph	+67	-46	+56.5	+73	-51	+62.0	+72	-53	+62.5
Daily Mail	+80	-63	+71.5	+65	-48	+56.5	+62	-49	+55.5
The Times	+31	-26	+28.5	+41	-19	+30.0	+29	-5	+17.0
Daily Express	+66	-54	+60.0	+63	-51	+57.0	+18	-1	+9.5
Independent	+4	-4	+4.0	-13	+15	-14.0	-16	+8	-12.0
Daily Star	+20	-12	+16.0	+10	+9	+0.5	-18	+26	-22.0
The Sun	+59	-52	+55.5	-53	+61	-57.0	-22	+34	-28.0
Daily Record	-70	+75	-72.5	-52	+75	-63.5	-48	+51	-49.5
Guardian	-41	+27	-34.0	-57	+63	-60.0	-57	+55	-56.0
The Mirror	-52	+59	-55.5	-70	+75	-72.5	-56	+61	-58.5
Sunday Telegraph	+80	-61	+70.5	+61	-45	+53.0	+83	-47	+65.0
Mail on Sunday	+65	-44	+54.5	+68	-56	+62.0	+58	-47	+52.5
Sunday Express	+59	-45	+52.0	+62	-52	+57.0	+25	-2	+13.5
Sunday Times	+61	-40	+50.5	+41	-26	+33.5	+22	-4	+13.0
Independent on Sunday	+1	-4	+2.5	-30	+55	-42.5	-33	0	-16.5
News of the World	+40	-30	+35.0	-23	+28	-25.5	-14	+22	-18.0
Sunday People	-29	+36	-32.5	-24	+35	-29.5	-33	+35	-34.0
Observer	-21	+16	-18.5	-52	+55	-53.5	-54	+48	-51.0
Sunday Mirror	-65	+70	-67.5	-59	+65	-62.0	-43	+49	-46.0

Con: Net Conservative score (% saying supports Conservative minus % saying opposes)
Lab: Net Labour score (% saying supports Labour minus % saying opposes)
Bias: Average derived from Con and Lab. Positive score overall perceived bias to Conservative, negative to Labour
Source: MORI

One obvious factor limits the newspapers' influence. At recent elections, the vast majority of regular readers have been able to correctly characterise the party politics of their paper, giving them the potential to see through editorial spin and to discount it. (Even a few years ago, this was not always true). And, as we have seen, trust in the press is low in any case.

The Echo Research figures allow us for the first time to test readers' perceptions against an objective measure. At first glance, it is surprising how poorly the readers performed at identifying their papers' current biases. There were nine dailies and nine Sunday titles where we asked readers to say whether it was generally favourable or unfavourable to each of the two main parties, giving us 36 chances to match the verdict of the plurality of readers against the dispassionate assessment of Echo's experts. The readers failed 13 of those 36 tests.

But when we consider the details, it is more understandable. Can we blame the readers of the *Daily Telegraph, Sunday Telegraph* or *Mail on Sunday* for saying that their paper is generally more favourable than unfavourable to the Conservative Party? Yet they were not in this election, at least when judged by numbers of stories. The sheer negativity of the coverage defeated them.

Perhaps more relevantly, only three titles were so misjudged by their readers that they assessed the overall direction wrongly – the *Daily Express, Sunday Express* and *The Times*, all believed by more of their readers to favour the Tories overall than to favour Labour, when their net tendency in fact was the opposite. (This was so only very narrowly in the case of *The Times,* but it did also endorse Labour before polling day.) All three had switched party support. More significantly, all three readerships voted Tory in 2001, but on the other hand all three swung to Labour while the country as a whole swung to the Tories.

But, as we've seen, although what election coverage there was in the *Express* tended to Labour, its volume was minimal. For that matter, it may well be that readers have failed to note the slant of the coverage not because they are unable to tell the difference but simply because they have ignored it. It is possible to question how much attention readers pay to coverage of politics or public affairs in their newspapers. A 1996 MORI study for Linda Christmas of the City University Graduate School of Journalism[104] asked a representative sample of the British public what they thought they were "very interested" in reading in the national daily newspapers. Overall, the category (from a list of 59) selected by most respondents was "TV and radio listings" (42%). However, there were very distinct gender differences – the single most popular category among men was football reporting (50% of men but only 12% of women), while women were more likely to be interested in medical/health news, food & recipes and the letters page. But reporting of parliamentary news, analysis of current affairs and (sadly) opinion polls scored poorly with both men and women.

Echo also provided a count of articles by issues, and by personalities. The party leaders led the coverage of course, with Blair's score reaching 1,697, half again Hague's 1,230, and four times Kennedy's 457. In fact, the Chancellor, Gordon Brown, with 727 articles during the election, had a great deal more coverage than the LibDem leader. Portillo, with 387 articles, and Prescott, 378, had the next greatest coverage.

Of the broadsheet political journalists scored by Echo Research on their articles about the Conservatives and Labour (they didn't publish any scoring on the individual journos writing about the LibDems), the most prolific in terms of numbers of articles published during the election was the *Daily Telegraph*'s Political Editor George Jones, who was also the most pro-Tory, indeed the sole pro-Tory, with a bias index of +38, while the *Guardian*'s Michael White tilted most to Labour, with 50% of his articles on the Tories negative to only 14% positive, but 29% to 17% positive about Labour for a net index of -48. The *Guardian*'s team was easily the most partisan, the *Independent*'s duo just the most balanced. The most balanced individual journalist was the *Indy*'s Paul Waugh, scoring a perfect zero on the bias index.

---

[104] MORI interviewed 2,026 British aged 15+ on 19-22 January 1996.

Table 63: Stance and negativity of articles, by journalist

	Articles		Stance of articles covering:						Con-
			Conservative			Labour			Lab
								Poison	Bias
	Total	%	Fav	Unfav	Neut	Fav	Unfav	Neut	index	index
Robert Shrimsley	96	4%	33	20	3	23	9	8	+28	-12
Brian Groom	73	3%	12	7	3	31	14	6	+30	-11
Cathy Newman	88	4%	14	18	6	19	17	14	-2	-15
Rosemary Bennett	60	3%	7	10	5	20	10	8	+12	-40
Financial Times total	317	13%	66	55	17	93	50	36	+17	-16
Michael White	78	3%	5	18	13	12	7	23	-10	-48
Patrick Wintour	65	3%	3	10	12	8	15	17	-22	-11
Kevin Maguire	62	3%	3	11	12	10	10	16	-13	-31
Nicholas Watt	66	3%	6	20	9	6	12	13	-30	-21
Guardian total	271	11%	17	59	46	36	44	69	-18	-29
Andrew Grice	121	5%	10	26	21	19	22	23	-16	-23
Paul Waugh	75	3%	14	16	9	11	13	12	-5	+0
Independent total	196	8%	24	42	30	30	35	35	-12	-14
George Jones	131	5%	18	13	33	12	32	23	-11	+38
Andy McSmith	70	3%	4	9	18	6	12	21	-16	-1
Benedict Brogan	67	3%	4	9	16	9	14	15	-15	-4
Daily Telegraph total	268	11%	26	31	67	27	58	59	-13	+17
Philip Webster	87	4%	3	8	29	9	8	30	-5	-15
Tom Baldwin	69	3%	1	11	20	3	6	28	-19	-23
Roland Watson	69	3%	3	10	20	5	11	20	-19	-5
Peter Riddell	67	3%	1	10	23	7	9	17	-16	-20
The Times total	292	12%	8	39	92	24	34	95	-14	-16
Broadsheets total	1344	100%	141	226	252	210	221	294	-7	-12
Trevor Kavanagh	51	12%	10	7	6	13	6	9	+20	-12
George Pascoe-Watson	53	12%	8	13	2	14	9	7	0	-38
Sun total	104	24%	18	20	8	27	15	16	+10	-25
James Hardy	54	13%	2	18	5	24	1	4	+13	-143
Oonagh Blackman	44	10%	0	20	3	0	16	5	-82	-11
Paul Routledge	43	10%	0	16	5	8	6	8	-33	-85
Mirror total	141	33%	2	54	13	32	23	17	-30	-88
Patrick O'Flynn	62	14%	10	19	2	27	3	1	+24	-106
Kirsty Walker	32	7%	8	4	3	11	4	2	+34	-15
Alison Little	30	7%	6	6	3	8	5	2	+10	-20
Daily Express total	94	22%	18	23	5	38	7	3	+28	-75
David Hughes	51	12%	9	3	11	2	22	4	-27	+98
Paul Eastham	40	9%	3	3	12	2	18	2	-40	+73
Daily Mail total	91	21%	12	6	23	4	40	6	-33	+87
Tabloids total	430	100%	50	103	49	101	85	42	-9	-33

Totals refer only to those journalists listed in this table

Source: Calculated from Echo Research Summary of Coverage (8 May – 7 June 2001)

Surprisingly, Nicholas Watt of the *Guardian* turned out to be the most poisonous, with an index of -30; Brian Groom and Robert Shrimsley on the *FT* were the most positive, with a +30 and a +28 vying to come out on top as Mr Nice Guy.

Turning to the tabloids, our advice to the political parties at the next election is to stay away from the poison pen of Oonagh Blackman on the *Mirror*, who doesn't have a good word to say about anybody or anything! She wrote no fewer than 44 articles during the election that the folks at Echo coded: 20 out of the 23 that were about Labour were graded as negative, and 16 out of the 21 about the Tories were negative also; the remainder were neutral with not one story scored positive for either party. Paul Routledge did what he could to put the boot into the Tories as well, with 16 out of his 21 stories thumbs down, but 6 out of his 22 stories about Labour were also unfavourable (no doubt those mentioning Mandelson). The third member of the *Mirror* team, James Hardy, easily the most partisan of all the journalists coded with a score of −143, had at least one unfavourable story about Labour, and two favourable to the Tories. Wonder how they slipped past the editor?

The *Sun* on the other hand was not nearly so partisan in this election. Their powerful political editor, Trevor Kavanagh, wrote a total of 51 articles in all (not counting the leaders he also wrote) which was 12% of all the tabloid articles in the table, and most were on balance favourable, both to Labour and to the Tories. His colleague George Pascoe-Watson did about the same number, but was more partisan for Labour.

On the *Express*, Patrick O'Flynn led the battle for Labour, and all three of their journalists had a Labour bias, though they were also overall more positive than negative. The *Mail*'s political editor David Hughes and his colleague Paul Eastham's were the only tabloid writers tending to the Tories.

The party campaigns

But the press were not the only culprits in failing potential voters' thirst for information and contact. Very little attention has been paid to how effectively the parties put their case across on the ground in the traditional way, canvassing and leafleting.

Table 64: Campaign penetration 1979-2001

Q. *During the past few weeks have you...?*

% saying "yes"	1979 %	1983 %	1987 %	1992 %	1997 %	2001 %
...had any political leaflets put through your letterbox?	50	78	80	86	89	69
...seen any party election broadcasts on TV?	78	83	68	71	73	58
...seen any political advertisements on billboards?	35	45	43	55	70	50
...watched the leaders debate on TV?					36	43
...seen any political advertisements in newspapers?						37
...heard any party election broadcasts on the radio?	12	27	18	18	15	16
...been called on by a representative of any political party?	25	29	32	30	24	14
...received a letter signed by a party leader individually addressed to you?			8	13	20	12
...been telephoned by a representative of any political party?					7	5
...helped a political party in its campaign?			5	6	4	3
...visited a political party's website?						2
...used the internet to access information on candidates or parties?						2
...attended a political meeting addressed by a candidate?		2	2	1	2	1
...received a video through your letterbox from a political party?					27	1
...received an e-mail from a political party?						1

Source: MORI

In each of the past six elections, we have asked the public towards the end of the campaign about the various ways in which they might have been in contact with the campaign – have they seen the party broadcasts or the advertisements, been canvassed in person or had a leaflet through the door, been to a meeting where a candidate spoke or actively helped in a campaign. We found, as you might expect if the public was simply bored or unreceptive, that there had been a sharp drop in the number that watched the party election broadcasts, from 73% last time (and an

83% peak in 1983, which was the last election that was considered such a "foregone conclusion") to 58% this time. (There was no corresponding drop in the figures for election broadcasts on the radio, but this may simply reflect radio's growing audience share.)

But there are other figures that can't be blamed on public boredom. The most startling falls in the figures are those in direct contact between the parties and the voters. It is true that the poll was conducted a week before polling day, and the final figures for contact may have been higher (our Electoral Commission surveys suggested that they probably were, a little)[105]; but the surveys from previous elections with which we are comparing were also a week or more before polling day, so the comparison is exact. In 1992, 86% had had a political leaflet through their door by this stage of the election, in 1997, it was 89%; in 2001, just 69% said that they had done so.

Even more dramatic is the fall off in canvassing: in the elections of 1983, 1987 and 1992 the parties between them managed to call in person on around three in ten of the electors; in 1997 it had fallen to only a quarter; but in 2001 the figure was only 14%, less than half what it had been eight years before. Furthermore, there was little overlap, so the canvassers were presumably concentrating more on their core vote within each constituency rather than the doubtfuls: just 7% of electors had been called on by Labour, 6% by the Tories and 2% by the Lib Dems. Of course, this is how canvassing often works out – aimed at "getting the vote out", it is far the most efficient use of a party's resources to concentrate on its known supporters. But in the wider sense of getting the vote out, not simply with party objectives in mind but maintaining the overall turnout, this is of course the worst of all worlds.

---

[105] In any case, with perhaps more than a million-and-a-half votes being cast by post, maybe we should wonder when the parties should aim to end their campaigns. If postal ballot papers are to reach the Returning Officer by Thursday evening, it would be unwise to wait until Thursday morning to post them – especially if, as was the case in 2001, there was the looming threat of a postal strike. Many voters, no doubt, returned them much earlier – indeed, by return of post once they arrived. If there really was a blitz of leaflets in the final few days, then for many it may already have been too late.

Then there is canvassing by telephone. In the preliminary skirmishes before the election, when the question of whether it was possible to fight an election campaign properly with a Foot and Mouth epidemic raging, we were told by those who did not want the election delayed that modern elections no longer relied on personally meeting the voters, since telephone canvassing was now far more important. We ventured to disagree at the time, noting that in 1997 only 7% of the public had been contacted by telephone by a party representative. And in 2001? Just 5%. So much for the modernisation revolution! In fact there was no difference in the level of canvassing in person between urban (13%) and rural (14%) areas, though it was slightly higher in our semi-rural sampling points (17%); in all three categories, 5% said they had been contacted by telephone.

What impression does such a campaign give to the electors? A poor one, we suggest. One of the authors lives in a safe Labour seat but a marginal county council ward. Throughout the election campaign he received through the door, to serve the five adults living in the house who are registered to vote, two leaflets – one from the Labour Party, one from the Greens, and both concerned only with the county council. Quite apart from the six other parties with parliamentary candidates in the constituency who did not succeed – even with the availability of free delivery in an unaddressed envelope to every household by the Royal Mail – to have a single piece of election literature delivered between them, what is he supposed to make of the party workers from Labour and the Greens who took the trouble to walk up to the door, push a county council leaflet through the letterbox, and yet didn't bother to drop off an election address for their parliamentary candidate at the same time? No wonder some of the public don't feel there is much point voting, if the parties can't be bothered to ask for their votes! [106]

How much of this fall-off in campaigning was the result of "targeting", concentrating effort and resources on key seats, and perhaps on the key

---

[106] In the parties' defence, we should perhaps add that the question has been raised of whether the Royal Mail may have simply failed to deliver all the campaigning material, or that some of it was delayed by postal strikes. The Electoral Commission refers to such complaints in its report (Electoral Commission, *Election 2001, The Official Results* (Politico's Publishing, 2001), pp 54-5), and adds that it is pursuing the various issues that emerged from the general election with the Royal Mail.

voters within those seats? It is true that more voters were contacted in the marginal seats than in the safe ones. Whereas only 69% of the whole electorate had had a leaflet through the door, 76% of those in Labour-held marginals[107] had done so. In Labour's safest "heartland" seats[108], just 50% were leafleted. Similarly, 14% overall were canvassed in person and 5% by telephone, but it was 21% in person and 14% by telephone in the Labour marginals, just 5% and 1% respectively in the safest Labour seats. But even so, this level of targeting does not explain the fall in the campaigning figures since 1997; after all, a much higher proportion of the entire electorate, 89%, was leafleted in 1997 than the proportion even in the key marginals in 2001.

Labour's targeting on constituencies was the more effective, increasing the advantage which they already had in the overall figures. In the Labour marginals (which, remember, were the Tory targets), 10% said they had been telephoned by Labour while only 4% had been by the Tories, 12% had been canvassed in person by Labour but only 8% by the Tories. On leaflets, even though the Tories had done slightly better than Labour across the country (43% to 40%), Labour led in its marginals (52% to 49%). Of course this may partly reflect that the Labour marginals were the only group of key seats for Labour, while the Tories also had to worry about the Conservative-Lib Dem marginals, too small a group for us to analyse separately in the survey.

Nor does it seem tenable that there was concentration on the key floating voters, as we have repeatedly defined them throughout the life of this and earlier parliaments and repeated in the introduction to this book. As already noted, if the campaign was being concentrated on the key swing voters, we would expect there to be much overlap in campaigning – the swing voters are, after all, the same for the two parties who think they can win a marginal seat, and we should expect them to be targeted by both of these parties. Yet not only was this not the case, but it was comparatively less so than in 1997. Perhaps this should not be a surprise. Canvassing, at least, has always been aimed primarily at getting the vote out and therefore concentrated on the core vote; but

---

[107] Defined for this analysis as those constituencies where the 1997 majority was 10% or less.
[108] With a majority of 35% or more.

there can be few excuses in this day and age for not at least getting a leaflet sent to everybody. Meanwhile, if the personal touch is confined to the solid voters and ignores the less committed – who are precisely those who may not vote at all – then an overall fall in turnout would be the predictable result.

Of course, there is always the faint possibility that what has fallen away is not the level of campaigning but the electors' reporting of it. The surveys in 1992 and 1997 were part of panel studies, and we know that panels, especially the later waves, will tend to comprise those more interested in politics and hence over-represent measurements of voluntary activities, for example. We would not be surprised if a panel found a higher proportion who had watched the PEBs. Yet after the election our Electoral Commission survey, which *was* a panel, found 55% saying they had seen the broadcasts on TV, which was actually lower than the 58% who said so in the stand-alone Omnibus survey. So that pig won't fly.

In any case, should the panel effect interfere with the measurement of a factual event (the delivery of leaflets) that were not within the respondent's control? Only if, for some reason, the sort of people who drop out of or decline to join panels – the apathetic and uninterested, perhaps – mistakenly don't think they have been leafleted when in fact they have. This is by no means as ridiculous as it might sound. Is it possible that electors are increasingly treating election communications as junk mail that they are not even bothering to open, so that questioned later they don't realise that they have been leafleted? If so, it would be a serious hurdle for the parties in future elections which might hamper the achievement of a more respectable turnout. It may be worth researching this point.

Election advertising

It was interesting to note, also, that the impact of poster advertising on billboards was considerably less than 1997, only 50% of the public having seen them as opposed to 70% four years ago. The fall was not simply in the overall figures, but was similar for both the main parties when we asked which party or parties' posters had been seen – 31% thought they had seen a Tory poster (53% in 1997), and 35% a Labour poster (55%). It takes a second look at the data to realise what this implies for voters having seen more than one party's posters. In 1997, three-quarters of those who had seen any poster had seen a Labour one, and three-quarters of them had also seen a Conservative one; in 2001, not only had fewer seen posters at all, but only seven in ten of those had seen a Labour poster and barely three in five a Conservative one.

How effective is election advertising? A survey from The Chartered Institute of Marketing (CIM) published during the campaign found that for every elector who admitted being influenced by a negative campaigning advert to vote for the party publishing the advertisement, five more said they were irritated into voting against that party. It is questionable how realistic such figures are, especially in the case of a sustained campaign of negative advertising. Some may not realise how far they are unconsciously influenced; others may not wish to admit it.

In the CIM survey, only 8% admitted that advertising helps them decide which party to vote for. In the MORI survey of campaign penetration towards the end of the election[109], only 2% of the public said that posters on billboards had influenced the way they intended to vote (down from 4% at a similar stage of the 1997 campaign), and after the election in MORI's survey for the Electoral Commission, 2% said that political advertisements on billboards had "a great deal" of influence on their decision "about what you would do on the day of the election", while 8% said they had "a fair amount" of influence. Yet 61% of that panel said they had seen political advertisements on billboards during the election campaign.[110]

In all probability, much of the huge sums spent by the parties on their advertising campaigns reap little reward in votes. But perhaps the parties

---

[109] Unpublished MORI Omnibus survey, fieldwork 24-30 May 2001.
[110] MORI panel survey for the Electoral Commission, second wave. MORI Telephone Surveys interviewed 1,162 UK adults aged 18+on 9-18 June 2001. Respondents had previously been interviewed on 9-15 May 2001.

suffer from the same problem as the great soap magnate, Lord Leverhulme, who once admitted that half the money he spent on advertising was wasted – but, unfortunately, he didn't know which half. (It is instructive that fewer of the public said they had noticed political posters than at the previous two elections even though, because the unexpected postponement of the election came after the parties had booked their advertising space for a May election, the posters were in place far longer at this election than would otherwise have been the case.) The new spending restrictions on the national party campaigns are probably beneficial to all concerned, except the ad agencies and owners of poster sites. In 1997, the Tories probably spent more in real terms than any party in British electoral history, yet could not prevent their worst defeat since before Queen Victoria was crowned.

Then there was Sir James Goldsmith, whose inventive campaigning innovation provides a footnote to political marketing history. The use of videos delivered purportedly to every household in the country in the 1997 General Election by the Referendum Party was only 'received', in the sense of being aware and recalling they'd received it, by one person in four (27%). We didn't measure who had watched it, and we had resigned Sir James' account long before the campaign had begun. If there were poll findings measuring the impact of the video blitz from Harris, to whom he turned after we rejected his demands to write his own questions (our unbiased questions not appealing to him), we've never seen them. In the event, they can't have done him much good, as his party failed to gain a single seat, and lost most of their deposits. Its only effect was to cost the Tories votes, as of the order of half a million usual Tory voters deserted their traditional voting patterns to support Sir James' party.

The election and the Internet

We were told this would be the e-election. It was not. It was a TV election, like each of the ten that preceded it.

There will be no e-election without universal unmetered access to the web. While most regular internet users are young, uninterested in politics and paying by the minute for their web access, surely political campaigning on the net will not take off. Political advertising does poorly enough on television, as party broadcasts inserted between the regular programmes, without asking the target audience to pay to see it!

Having said that, now more than a third of the public, and over half of those under 35, have access to and use the internet either at their place of work or at home, according to the monthly e-MORI Technology Tracker (which can be found on the www.mori.com web site). The data in the graphs below are taken from the survey done during the 2001 British general election campaign. Note that only a quarter of 55-64s use the internet and, despite the much commented upon 'e-mails to the grandchildren' of the OAPs, only 8% of the over 65s say they use the net.

Access is one thing; use is another. Only some 7% of the public said they used the internet to access information on the election in our post-election recall survey of the panel we conducted for the Electoral Commission, and as stated earlier, this would likely be an overstatement of the use by the public generally, because of the panel effect on Phase 2 respondents. In any case, only one percent of people interviewed on the MORI Omnibus survey the final week of May, a week to ten days before polling day, said that the internet had any effect at all on the way they intended to vote. That included 1% of Labour supporters and 1% of Tories, but 2% of those who at that time said it was their intention to vote for the Liberal Democrats.

One percent also said they had received an e-mail from a political party during the campaign.

Men were more likely to use the internet than women, as shown on the graph below, by a substantial margin. Again, its use for obtaining information was much greater among the young than the old, and three times more likely to be used by middle-class people than those in the working class.

Figure 18

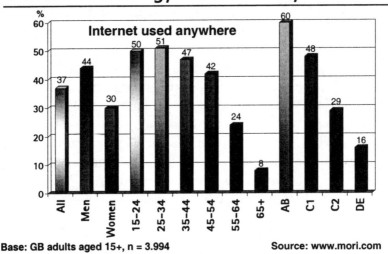

e-MORI Technology Tracker – May 2001

Base: GB adults aged 15+, n = 3.994   Source: www.mori.com

In the post-election panel recall we also asked '...how much influence, if any, did each of the following had on your decision about what you would do on the day of the General Election?', and found that only one percent said it had 'a great deal', but another 3% said 'a fair amount' and 5% 'not very much'. Seven in eight, 87%, said 'none at all'. This compares with 13% who said a 'great deal' of influence came from the election coverage on TV, 8% from newspapers, 6% from PEBs and from the views of their family and friends, 5% from election coverage on the radio, and 2% each from opinion polls, political advertisements on billboards and from personal calls from representatives of the parties.

Two percent of the electorate said they had visited a political party's web site, 2% the Tories', 1% Labour's, and 1% the Lib Dems'. But the most encouraging figure for the internet advocates came from the Phase 1 initial wave of the survey for the Election Commission, carried out from 9-15 May when we asked 'From which of these sources do you obtain information and news about politics and current issues?' In that survey we found 13% said they had used the internet (some time in the past, not necessarily about the election or during the first two or three weeks of the campaign) to obtain information and news about politics and current issues (as broadly as that), but we also found that only a single one percent said they received 'most' of their information and news from the internet, and one percent also felt the internet the most trustworthy source of such information and news. (See Table 53).

Figure 19

Use of the Internet?

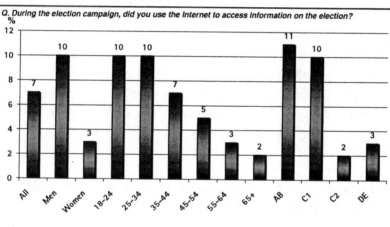

Q. During the election campaign, did you use the internet to access information on the election?

Base: Phase 2 - 1,162 UK adults 18+, 9-18 June 2001   Source: MORI/Electoral Commission

Post election, we were commissioned by the Hansard Society to discover in more detail how the public used the internet during the election campaign, to provide hard data for inclusion in the Hansard Society report by Dr Stephen Coleman, Director of the Hansard Society E-Democracy Programme, and Nicola Hall who is Researcher on the E-Democracy Programme[111].

---

[111] Questions were placed on MORI's General Public Omnibus Survey and were asked to a representative sample of 1,999 adults aged 18+, face-to-face, in home, on 21-26 June 2001.

In it, they report[112]:

"How many of them had access to the internet?
- 33% reported having home internet access.
- 33% said that they had access to e-mail.
- 69% had mobile phones.
- 32% used text messaging (SMS).
- Only 13% said that they used digital television for interactive services - such as shopping, games or e-mail.
- Men were 11% more likely to have internet access at home than women.
- Members of socio-economic group ABC_1 were more than twice as likely to have home internet access than C_2DEs.
- 46% of Liberal Democrat voters, 37% of Conservative voters and only 29% of Labour voters had home internet access.

"US polls about e-politics have tended to find that online citizens are significantly more likely to vote than those without internet access. This was not the case in the UK election of 2001, where 23% of respondents without internet access did not vote as against 25% who were online. This is explained by the high number of young non-voters with internet access being outweighed by the high number of older voters who are least likely to be online.

"The only party that had significantly more votes from online than offline voters were the Liberal Democrats.

"We then asked those respondents who did have access to the internet or e-mail what they used it for during the election campaign:
- 82% of them did not use the internet or e-mail for any election-related activities. But almost one in five did.
- Over one in 10 (11%) said that they visited a media web site, such as BBC Online, to read about the election.
- 7% used web sites or e-mail to find out information about the election, parties or candidates.

---

[112] The report, *2001: Cyber Space Odyssey: The internet in the UK election*, is on the Hansard Society web site, www.hansard-society.org.uk/cyberodyssey.htm

- 5% sent or received e-mails about the election.
- 4% sent or received e-mails or visited web sites with humour or games about the election.

"Men were more likely to do most of these activities than women (for example, twice as many men as women visited media sites to find out about the election), but more women than men sent or received e-mails about the election.

"5% of Labour and Lib Dem voters went to the humour and games sites, but only 3% of Conservative voters. But, interestingly, visitors to the irreverent humour sites were not mainly disaffected non-voters – only 1% of non-voters went there compared to 6% of those who voted.

"What kind of information were those who were online looking for?
- Over one in 10 (11%) were searching for the parties' policies.
- Almost one in 10 (9%) sought information about the parties' national campaigns or the candidates in their constituencies.
- 3% of respondents sought information online about how to vote tactically – with women being more likely than men to do this.

"We would have predicted that Liberal Democrat and Labour voters would have been considerably more interested in using the internet to find out more about tactical voting, but found that exactly the same number of respondents from each main party did this – perhaps Conservatives were visiting such sites to size up the threat. Interestingly, one in five (21%) of 18-24 year-old respondents used the internet to find out what the parties' policies were, compared with only 8% of 25-44 year-olds and 12% of 55-64 year-olds. Young people are more used to the internet as a source of information and are turning to it in significantly high numbers to make sense of the policies on offer to them.

"We then asked how important overall the internet and e-mail were in providing our respondents with information that helped to decide how they voted.
- 6% said that it was very or fairly important;
- 66% said that it was not at all important.

"The internet and e-mail influenced the voting choices of twice as many Liberal Democrats (9%) as Conservatives (5%) and had much more influence upon 18-24 year-olds (17% of whom reported that the internet was a very or fairly important influence on their voting) than upon older voters, under 5% of whom reported any e-influence upon their voting.

"These findings point to a trend: younger voters are much more interested in the internet as a route to politics than are older voters; these are the voters of the future, so e-politics is here to stay and in future elections this generation of voters and those following them will be targeted much more successfully by e-campaigners. The lesson for the euro referendum, if it happens, is that there will be many younger voters, whose votes may well be decisive, looking to the internet to explain the issues to them in their own terms."

At least that is the view of Dr Coleman; we shall see.

'My vote doesn't count'

What about those citizens who accepted that there was a real choice o offer but felt they had been disfranchised from it?

A foregone conclusion?

The certainty of a Labour victory must have had some effect in depressing the turnout, but it proved a surprisingly elusive effect to measure. Only 5% of those who had said that they were certain to vote and afterwards admitted they had not done so cited "foregone conclusion" as their reason for changing their minds. Of those who were already uncertain whether to vote, just 1% said it was because "my vote will not make any difference to the outcome", though perhaps some of the 8% who said "There is no point voting" felt the same.

In one of our polls for the *Sunday Telegraph*[113], we asked the public what effect, if any, they thought Labour's large poll lead might have on their voting behaviour. As expected, the tendency was again to favour the underdogs rather than the leader.

Table 65: Effect of Labour's poll lead on voting intention

Q. As you may know, the Labour Party has had a large lead in the opinion polls throughout the Election campaign. Does this make you more likely to vote Conservative, less likely to vote Conservative or does it make no difference to you? Does this make you more likely to vote Labour, less likely to vote Labour or does it make no difference to you? Does this make you more likely to vote for the Liberal Democrats, less likely to vote for the Liberal Democrats or does it make no difference to you?

		More likely	Less likely	No difference	Don't know	Net
Conservative	%	9	6	85	0	+3
Labour	%	8	12	79	I	-4
Liberal Democrat	%	I I	6	82	I	+5

Source: MORI/*Sunday Telegraph*
Base: 1,021 British aged 18+, 31 May-2 June 2001

---

[113] MORI survey for the *Sunday Telegraph*, published on 3 June. MORI interviewed 1,021 British aged 18+ by telephone on 31 May-2 June 2001.

Not surprising – there was plenty of other evidence that the public while broadly happy for Tony Blair to return to Downing Street were less happy with the idea of his being returned with a second landslide.

Nevertheless, there is little evidence here of an overall tendency to depress the turnout – if anything rather the opposite, as the poll suggests a potential boost to opposition parties so as to limit the scale of Labour's landslide.

The electoral system

At a conference on the election and the Internet a few weeks after the election, the columnist Polly Toynbee pontificated at length on the first-past-the-post electoral system as a cause of electoral apathy and low turnout; without electoral reform and the introduction of proportional representation, she argued, other attempts to re-invigorate electoral participation are almost doomed to fail.

Sorry, Polly, but that is not what the non-voters are telling us. The electoral system didn't register as a reason for not voting either in our pre-election or post-election surveys. Nor would we really expect it to do so. The vast majority of the public are more interested in outcomes than process, in who wins the election rather than how it is conducted, and they are never likely to get very worked up about proportional representation or any other fundamentally technical part of the process. The minority who really care, either way, about the electoral system are mostly well-educated, well-informed, politically active and enthusiastic. A high proportion of them probably read Polly in the *Guardian*. And almost certainly, though perhaps under protest, most of them vote.

Nevertheless, it appears electoral reform would not be unpopular: in our survey two days before the election for *The Economist*, nearly two thirds, 63%, of the public agreed that "This country should adopt a new voting system that would give parties seats in Parliament in proportion to their share of the vote"; only one in five, 20%, disagreed. The figures were similar in previous surveys in 1995 and 1997. However, electoral reform is a good example of a subject where survey outcomes can be much influenced by how the question is asked. Other questions emphasising popular aspects of the "first-past-the-post" system can just as easily achieve a majority in favour of its retention. On our scale running from opinions through attitudes to values, proportional representation is for the vast majority a subject on which they only have an opinion, not deeply thought through and easily swayed by argument or extra information. For similar reasons, there are only very few who decline to vote because of the voting system.

Labour's stay-at-homes in the safe seats

It is true, though, that one consequence of the first-past-the-post system is that many electors live in safe constituencies where their votes are unlikely ever to influence the outcome. That is a dangerous argument, though – who would have thought Labour could lose in Rhondda at the Welsh assembly elections? If turnouts fell too far the supposedly safe seats might not be safe at all, especially "safe Labour" seats in a year of Tory resurgence or vice-versa.

But it's true that turnout in 'safe' seats is, and has been for many years, lower than in the marginals. Moreover it fell further in the safest seats in 2001 than elsewhere. Part, at least, of this effect must surely be attributable to the increasing targeting of campaigning resources on the key seats by the parties. But it is probably also true that in the safest seats Labour's vote was soft, partly because these tend to be Old Labour strongholds and partly because the seats were safe, making a protest abstention or apathetic abstention (the distinction may not be a wide one for Old Labour voters feeling let down by Blair) sufficiently risk-free to consider.

How soft was the Labour vote? It seems clear that the party's support was soft in the sense that, in the end, it was less likely to turn out and vote, even though we were not able to consistently demonstrate this with questions on likelihood of voting. In terms of vote share, that was also the case in 1997. But, as we noted before polling day, there was no guarantee that a low turnout, even a low turnout of Labour supporters, would harm Labour in terms of seats. In 1997, turnout fell most in Labour's safe seats, almost certainly among voters who if they had voted would have voted Labour. (And, we believe, most of those were disillusioned 1992 Tory voters, though some other analysts are equally convinced that the switchers turned out while it was Labour's "core" voters who stayed at home.) So although turnout reduced Labour's share of the vote in 1997, it didn't cost them many seats. The same happened again in 2001, though the differential between safe and marginal seats was lower – turnout fell most in the safe Labour seats and least in Conservative-Lib Dem marginals.

Before the election the received wisdom, which seemed to be accepted almost universally, was that a low turnout would harm Labour. The Tory vote was less soft than Labour's it was argued – partly because the Tories had been reduced to their core supporters while all the floating vote was in the Labour column; conversely, other commentators suggested that it is Labour's "core" voters who were less likely to turn out, because the party's heartlands were disillusioned with a government that had made too many compromises of principles in its search for the political centre ground. Whatever the reason, it was certainly the case that the Conservatives made substantial gains at both council and European Parliament level in elections which plumbed new depths of poor turnout in British elections.

Surveys in the run-up to the election offered some support to the thesis that Labour had most to lose from a low turnout: our survey for *The Times* in January, for example, found 63% of Tories and 62% of Lib Dems but only 52% of Labour supporters saying they were certain to vote; the difference in voting intention between all those who named a party and those who said they were certain to vote was the equivalent of a 3.5% swing to the Tories.

During the election this differential faded, but it seems clear that in the final event it was indeed Labour's supporters who were most likely to stay at home. It is plain that the low turnout cost Labour votes relative to the other parties. The fall was greatest in their safest seats, and turnout much lower among their strongest groups of the population. Only 47% of ethnic minority electors voted; only 52% of council or housing association tenants; 44% of the unemployed; 53% of DEs; 36% of 18-24 year old women.

Table 66: Average change in percentage turnout by type of seat

	All	Margin 0%-10%	Margin 10%-20%	Margin 20%+
All	-12.5	-11.0	-12.1	-13.2
Con-Lab seat	-11.7	-11.5	-12.2	-11.1
Con-LD seat	-10.7	-9.9	-10.9	-11.2
Lab-Con seat	-13.1	-11.2	-13.1	-13.6
Lab-LD seat	-12.8	-12.3	-12.0	-13.0
LD-Con seat	-10.9	-10.4	-10.8	-12.6
LD-Lab seat	-11.1	-11.5	-10.3	-11.6

Source: MORI analysis of election results published by the Electoral Commission

An ICM poll for the BBC *Today* programme, some two months after the election, asked non-voters which party they thought they would have voted for if they had gone to the polls: 53% said they would have voted Labour, only 19% Conservative. Even allowing for some bandwagon effect in favour of the winners, this is a huge differential. The Tory MP Bob Spink's response to the survey was "This is nothing but *Today* programme bias towards the Conservative Party"![114] While the Tories continue to take this blinkered attitude to public opinion and disregard for objective evidence of what the potential voters think of them, not only will they not win elections, but they will not deserve to do so.

Nevertheless, the implications are not quite as hopeless for the Tories as the Today programme suggests, and there is more than an element of truth in Iain Duncan Smith's comment that "Whilst the election defeat was a bitter blow to the Conservatives, the low turnout is also a signal of the despair people feel about the political process under Mr Blair." Even if the non-voters split almost three-to-one for Labour, among the key group – those who didn't vote but under other circumstances might have done so – the margin was probably much less dramatic. Even the most optimistic would never expect turnouts above 80%, and it has probably

---

[114] Quoted at http://www.bbc.co.uk/radio4/today/reports/politics/non_voters.shtml

always been the case that the residual 20% is composed largely of groups who would naturally back Labour.

During the election, we found that among the 11% who said that they were "very likely" (but not "certain") to vote, Labour supporters outnumbered Tories by a little less than two-to-one, 49% to 26% of those who expressed a voting intention. This is the group that we believe did not vote, but would have been the next group to vote had the turnout been higher. Therefore a higher turnout would probably have been worse for the Tories in terms of share of the vote, but not so dramatically as the ICM post-election survey suggests.

But the question that was asked much more rarely was, even if Labour's vote were to be disproportionately reduced by a low turnout, would this cost the party many seats? Naturally, with the first-past-the-post electoral system, that all depends in which constituencies the Labour voters fail to turn out. The poll indications were always that the fall in turnout would be worst in Labour's safe seats, and this indeed came to pass. In this case, even supposing that Labour's vote share was cut by a differential turnout, the party would lose many fewer seats than a simple projection of the vote shares would suggest.

From an analysis of the interaction between differential effect by party support and differential effect by constituency type in the first four MORI polls of the year, Roger Mortimore was able to predict the likely pattern whereby the swing was least in the marginals. "In the seats the Tories already hold," he wrote on MORI's website on 4 May, "a low turnout will tighten their grip. (Many of these seats, of course, are rural seats that have suffered from Foot and Mouth Disease in recent weeks). In Labour's heartland seats, the Tories will gain ground in votes, but not, of course, nearly enough to make any unlikely gains. But in the marginals all parties will suffer equally from low turnout – those who are most certain to vote are no different in their allegiances to those who are not. There are no sweeping gains to be had." [115]

---

[115] Roger Mortimore, "Low Turnout – Who Loses?", commentary column for www.mori.com., 4 May 2001.

Table 67: Certainty to vote by marginality, January-April 2001

		Con	Lab	LDem	Others	Con lead
Conservative-held seats						
All	%	40	40	18	2	0
Certain to vote	%	46	33	20	1	+13
Difference		+6	-7	+2	-1	+13
Labour marginals (majority < 10%)						
All	%	31	53	12	4	-22
Certain to vote	%	31	52	15	2	-21
Difference		0	-1	+3	-2	+1
Labour semi-safe (majority 10-35%)						
All	%	27	58	8	7	-31
Certain to vote	%	26	60	8	6	-34
Difference		-1	+2	0	-1	-3
Labour super-safe (majority 35%+)						
All	%	16	66	12	6	-50
Certain to vote	%	19	63	12	6	-44
Difference		+3	-3	0	0	+6

Source: MORI

Which, broadly speaking, is what happened.

Table 68: Average change in Conservative share by type of seat

	All	Margin 0%-10%	Margin 10%-20%	Margin 20%+
All	+1.0	+1.6	+0.6	+0.8
Con-Lab seat	+2.9	+4.0	+2.0	+1.7
Con-LD seat	+2.0	+3.2	+1.5	+1.8
Lab-Con seat	+0.5	+0.5	-0.2	+0.7
Lab-LD seat	-0.7	-1.7	-3.3	-0.2
LD-Con seat	-0.4	-1.3	-0.4	+2.3
LD-Lab seat	+0.9	-0.9	+1.0	+6.4

Source: MORI analysis of election results published by the Electoral Commission

What this means, incidentally, is that the supposedly "misleading" large Labour lead of the pre-election polls were not really misleading at all. Not only did they reflect real voters' feelings in vote share, but they pointed to a realistic distribution of seats.

Table 69: MORI final <u>pre</u>-campaign poll and result, 1997 and 2001

	1997		2001	
	MORI/*Time* s 21-24 Feb 1997	Election result I May 1997	MORI/*Sun* 30 Apr-1 May 2001	Election Result 7 June 2001
	%	%	%	%
Conservative	31	31	32	33
Labour	52	44	50	42
Liberal Democrat	11	17	13	19
Other	6	7	5	6
Labour lead over Conservative	+21	+13	+18	+9

The fall of the lead in votes did not help the Tories in seats. This was just as it had been in 1997. Suppose the result in 1997 had been exactly as the figures in that last MORI poll before the campaign. If there had been perfect national uniform swing, Labour would have won 438 seats instead of the 419 they did win – a modest improvement in their majority. But on the same basis, the Tories would have won 180 seats even though the Labour lead at 21 points was much more than Labour actually achieved; in fact they only won 165. The Tories did *worse* than the pre-election polls would have suggested, even though the Labour lead fell, because the fall in the lead didn't significantly cut Labour strength in the Con-Lab marginals, it merely added Lib Dem votes in the Con-Lib Dem marginals where a Labour vote would have been wasted anyway.

In 2001, much the same story. Uniform swing and an 18-point lead would have given the Tories 158 seats, Labour 443 and the Liberal Democrats only 30. Again, concentrating on the lead was misleading, because although the lead was halved by election day it was the Liberal Democrats and not the Tories who benefited; the Conservatives won just eight seats more than the 158 that projection would have given them, less than one seat for each one-point fall in the lead.

Moral: Watch the Tory share, not the gap.

'I wanted to vote but I couldn't'

We now turn to the practical mechanics of recording a vote. In our post-election panel recall survey for the Electoral Commission, the unprompted explanations of those who said they hadn't voted focused less on the parties or lack of interest than on practical considerations. A fifth of non-voters (21%) said that they didn't vote because "I couldn't get to the polling station because it was too inconvenient"; women and those *not* in full/part-time employment were most likely to give this reason, but surprisingly there was little difference between urban and rural non-voters. A further one in six non voters (16%) said they did not vote because they "were away on election day." Taken together, these represent more than a third of the abstainers.

But we should not necessarily take these answers entirely at face value. There are degrees of inconvenience, after all – how many of those who couldn't make it to the polling station or were away or otherwise "too busy" would have managed to vote if the result had been more important to them? This may represent just as much a perceived lack of importance of this election, or of elections in general, as a failure of the system to facilitate voting.

On the other hand, more than one in ten (11%) said they did not vote because they "Did not receive a polling card/postal vote". Again, this may be in many cases only an excuse for apathy, and of course you do not need to have received a polling card to vote, but it nevertheless represents a failure of the system to give electors all due encouragement.

Voting by post

Changes to the law since 1997 made it much easier to claim a postal vote than hitherto; all electors were now entitled to vote by post if they preferred, and had simply to contact their local council before the deadline (also later than in the past) to ensure they received their ballot papers. After the election, despite an expansive advertising campaign, we found 23% of the public said that they had been unaware of this. But perhaps that is par for the course. More relevantly, 44% of those who admitted they had not voted said they were unaware of the new postal voting rules.

Naturally, we tracked the take-up of postal votes through our polls. At the peak of the findings[116], 5% of the population said that they had already applied for a postal vote, and another 3% that they intended to do so. (A further 1% were intending to apply for a proxy vote, to which legal restrictions still apply.) If the 8% total were correct, that would involve almost three-and-a-half million postal votes being issued. By the time of the final poll, when it was too late for good intentions, half that number, 4%, said that they had actually voted by post; we await the official returns, but given the overall turnout that would suggest that around one-and-a-three-quarter million postal votes, making up 6% of the total turnout, were cast. Rallings and Thrasher's estimate for the Electoral Commission[117], based on 85% of statistical returns, was a little lower, 1.7 million papers issued and 1.4 million postal votes counted.

This is a dramatic increase: in 1997, the total number of postal ballot papers issued was only 937,205, of which 738,614 were duly returned in time to be included in the count. Despite successive loosenings of the rules, including allowing holidaymakers a postal vote, there had been no dramatic increase in the number of postal votes cast up to 1997: indeed, in the close election of October 1974, when all the restrictions still applied, more than 850,000 were included in the final count. But it is clear that from now on it will be a very different story. It is also worth noting that the turnout problem did not apply to those who took out postal votes, around 82% of those issued actually being returned.

Of course, there was some exaggeration of the impact. On the Today Programme at one point in the election, a spokesman for Consignia/the Post Office said that they thought as many as 20% of the electorate would vote postally. And pigs will fly.

---

[116] MORI survey for *The Times*, published on 24 May. MORI interviewed 1,066 British aged 18+ on 22 May 2001.

[117] Electoral Commission, *Election 2001, The Official Results* (Politico's Publishing, 2001), p 33.

Taking the postal ballots and proxies together, the highest use of postal/proxy voting is among the elderly and unskilled working class (DE) category (which are of course highly correlated, as persons living only on state support fall into the DE category). But though the latter is also correlated with voting Labour, the overall benefit from postal voting – as has been the case more often than not in the past – seems to have been with the Tories. The MORI final election aggregate suggests that while those voting in person gave Labour a ten-point lead (Labour 42%, Conservative 32%, Liberal Democrats 19%), postal voters were evenly split (Conservative 39%, Labour 39%, Liberal Democrats 19%) and proxy voters gave the Tories a big lead (Conservative 48%, Labour 35%, Liberal Democrats 13%) – always assuming their proxies voted as those on whose behalf they voted would have wished!

I recall that back in my first election, 1970, the late Iain Macleod at the Tory press conference on Jun 16 stated that the Conservatives would get 30 seats simply through their superior organisation of the postal vote. At that election there were 32 seats where the number of postal voted included in the count exceeded the Conservative majority. According to Butler and Pinto-Duschinsky[118], it was decisive in just six seats, but could have been the margin of victory of as many as 17. It won't have made that much difference this time, but it may have saved the Tories a seat or two.

Of course, one of the main reasons for widening the availability of postal votes was the hope that it might counter falling turnout. Just over half, 51%, of non-voters say that voting by post would have made them more likely to vote, but this surely exaggerates the potential impact.

In fact, there seems little evidence that postal voting helped the turnout much. In a survey for the Institute for Citizenship before the election was called[119], we specifically tested whether reminding respondents of the new regulations would increase their propensity to vote. When told that "The Government has changed the law so that registered voters can

---

[118] David Butler & Michael Pinto-Duschinsky, *The British General Election of 1970* (Macmillan, 1971), p 332.
[119] MORI interviewed 892 British aged 18+ on 19-24 April 2001.

obtain a postal vote if they want one by ringing their local Council and asking for a postal vote" some 2% more people said they were "certain to vote" than without that knowledge, raising the "certain to votes" from 52% to 54%, with the "very likely" respondents dropping from 17% to 15%. Other categories shifted a point or two, but the likely overall effect on turnout had to be judged minimal. It seems that, while many citizens took advantage of the convenience of being able to vote by post, it was almost entirely those who would have voted in any case.

Similarly, after the election when we asked those who had voted how they had done so, take-up of postal voting was considerably higher among those who had told us that they always vote than among those who claim to vote less frequently. (While 7% of those who "always vote" took the chance to vote by post, only 4% of those who say they voted and vote "usually" or "sometimes", and 3% of those who said they vote "rarely" or "never" but voted in 2001, did the same. Of course part, at least, of this differential can be explained demographically, since those who say they "always" vote are likely to be older and therefore more likely to need a postal or proxy vote.)

Other means of voting

Despite the support by non-voters that we found (in our survey for the Electoral Commission) for various changes to the voting regulations or procedures to make it easier to cast a vote, it must be doubtful whether this does more than scratch the surface. The superficiality of many of the explanations of why non-voters did not vote suggests the same conclusion – in the vast majority of cases it wasn't because they couldn't, but because they didn't want to, or felt it wasn't important enough to take the trouble. Indeed, in such cases there is an argument – as with the argument against compulsory voting – that compelling or persuading citizens to vote when they care so little about the outcome might actually be harmful rather than beneficial to the health of democracy, by trivialising the process and the outcome.

A number of modifications to the established methods have been suggested, and experiments have been tried in other elections, with mixed success. In the English local authority elections of 2000 a number of councils, for the first time, used powers recently granted to them to experiment with different means of making it easier to vote. The intention is in the long run that any initiatives that are a clear success at local level will be extended to future parliamentary elections as well. In some, the polls opened a week early to cater for those who couldn't make it on the designated day; in others there were travelling polling stations or polling stations in supermarkets. One council wired up its polling stations so that it could try electronic voting.

The outcome of the experiments in 2000 were mostly inconclusive[120], but all-postal voting (i.e. without the option of voting at a polling station) seemed to boost turnout. The same has been true in the USA. In Oregon, nobody went to the polls on 7 November to vote in the presidential election, as voting was entirely postal. The closing of the ballot places and going over entirely to postal voting lifted the turnout significantly.

A MORI survey for the Local Government Association in 1998 investigated non-voting in local elections and the appeal of various alternatives for facilitating voting, and it suggested that potential benefits might be real but small.

The key group would seem to be the 18% who say they "usually vote" in local elections. (The obvious implication from the turnout figures is that in fact this group usually do not vote in local elections but probably do vote in most general elections.) What would encourage this group to turn out? The MORI/LGA poll offered twelve possible options, and asked for each whether it would make respondents more or less likely to vote. By far the most popular option among the "usually votes" was voting from home using the telephone, which 54% thought would make it more likely that they would vote; voting from home via digital TV or

---

[120] For details see *Elections – the 21st century model* (LGA research, report 14). A summary of the experiments and their outcomes is also included in House of Commons Library Research Paper 00/53.

the internet was popular with 31%. With access to telephones virtually universal, this option has a much more obvious appeal, and if the obvious problems of security and initial set-up costs can be overcome looks a much more obvious means of permanent long-term reform than tinkering with the details of voting time or polling station location which may only meet the short-term needs of particular social problems that may easily change in the future.

During the general election we were able to take this investigation a good deal further in our surveys for the Electoral Commission. The first wave of the research found support for reforming the mechanics of voting. Similarly, for each of several specific suggestions for reform, significant proportions of non-voters say that had it been in place on 7 June, they would have been 'more likely' to have voted and as mentioned earlier, many of the reasons given for non-voting do relate to inconvenience and difficulties 'getting along'. Most popular among the suggestions was, again, voting using the telephone/mobile phone with 66% of non-voters saying that this would have made them more likely to vote on 7 June.

There is support for reforming the mechanics of voting among those who did vote, too, but it will be important to reassure people that these are reliable and in particular that they are fraud-proof. When our whole sample was asked pre-election which would be most likely to encourage them to vote at the forthcoming election, voting using a telephone is chosen by 36%, followed by voting at supermarket, 27% and 24 hour voting and voting by internet, both 21%.

There were some notable differences by sub-group: 43% of 18-24 year olds said that internet voting would encourage them, whereas older people were more likely to say 'don't know'.

Respondents were also asked whether they supported or opposed polling stations being replaced wholly with voting by other methods such as voting by post, by telephone and by the internet. More than half, 53%, supported this but a third, 34% were against. Support was relatively low among older age groups who are the most likely to vote but is higher among younger people and those who say they rarely or never vote general elections.

When asked why they supported the idea, the main reasons given relate to "Convenience/ease of voting" mentioned by 52% and "will encourage people to vote" by 17%. Among those who rarely/never vote and support the idea, convenience is mentioned by 63%.

The main opposition to the idea is based on the idea that "people should go/prefer going", mentioned spontaneously by 46%. The other main concern focuses on "identifying fraud/hard to identify voter" which is given as a reason for opposition by 31%. It is interesting that this concern should be so common. It is not, superficially an obvious answer to the question, although awareness of the possibility of fraud may have been heightened by media investigations reported during the campaign. It suggests that not only do electors care about the integrity of the voting system, but that they have given some thought to the merits of existing mechanisms even before we called it to their minds in our survey.

Slightly more oppose than support making voting in elections compulsory, 49% to 47%, which represents a 4.5% swing against since the question was last asked a decade ago in 1991, when 49% supported the idea and 42% opposed it. Among those who usually/sometimes vote in general elections opposition is higher at 60% and this rises to 72% among those who say they never or rarely vote.

Non-registration

Of course, those not on the register couldn't vote in any case. But here the question arises of why they were not registered.

Among non-voters, one in six (15%) claimed they were not registered to vote, a figure rising to 29% of 18-24 year old non-voters and 27% of blacks (although in the case of the latter this is based on a small base size). However, it is instructive that only 6% of non-voters spontaneously gave non-registration as a reason for non-voting. In Phase

1 the reasons given for *anticipated* non-vote focused on "There is no point/all parties are the same" (8%), "no interest in politics" (8%) and "being away on election day" (7%). Probably a high proportion of those who are not registered failed to register because they do not want to vote – a different problem entirely.

In our final poll, 3% of our representative sample of adults told us they were not on the register and 1% said they didn't know, but that is almost certainly an underestimate, A further 2% told us they were registered to vote, but not in the constituency where we were interviewing them. Of those who said they were not on the register at all, 65% were aged 18-34, and 70% had already told us that they would not vote. The rate of non-registration was twice as high among ethnic minority respondents (6%) as among whites, but again the sample size is too small (only 112 non-whites in total) for these figures to be more than indicative. Improbably, the rate was also higher among readers of broadsheet newspapers (4%) than of tabloids (2%), which may simply indicate greater awareness of the registration process among the former, or greater reluctance to admit non-registration among the latter.

Nevertheless, inadvertent failure to register remains a significant problem. In MORI's surveys for the Electoral Commission, 8% of those who had said before the election that they were certain to vote but said afterwards that they had not done so gave as their reason that they had discovered that they were not registered to vote. We can only hope that a rolling register will reduce this problem, but it seems unlikely that it will.

3.   The Result

Middle ground, Middle England

Labour was once a predominantly working-class party with a working-class agenda. The driving force behind the Labour Representation Committee's foundation was the trade union movement, with the intention of getting working men into Parliament, and thereby better to represent working class voters.

But then, Britain was once a predominantly working-class country. There has been a remarkable shift in the social class mobility of the nation since I came here over 30 years ago. When I came over from America in time to work for Harold Wilson in the 1970 General Election, over seven in ten electors were classified as 'working class' (the 'blue collar' C_2DEs) by the occupation of the head of the household (male), and fewer than three in ten were in the 'white collar' middle class (ABC_1).

For the first decade of the existence of MORI, during which we were the private pollsters for the Labour Party, we were conscious (even if they were not) of the conflict between our client's identification as a class-based political movement and the need to attract middle-class votes to win elections. In those days, the middle-class 'only' represented a third of the electorate, so that the Labour votes of middle-class electors, about one in five of them, accounted for a support for Labour of only about 6% of the total voting public. No big deal.

However, with the deindustrialisation of Britain which took place after Mrs Thatcher's 1979 election victory, the middle class became an increasingly important sector of the population in an electoral system that still closely correlated voting with class. As shown in the table, in the first decade, the class profile didn't move; but starting in 1979, Britain moved from being largely a working-class nation to becoming a nation evenly balanced between working-class households and middle-class households. The growth in the middle class has been greatest among the

C_1s, not professionals or managers, but routine office and clerical workers.

The electoral significance of this was profound, and its importance not lost on the party strategists. Gone were the days when their Director of Publicity could say "We don't want and don't need middle-class support to win British elections", as he had in 1974. By the 1980s and even more in the 1990s it became increasingly obvious that if the Labour Party didn't capture a significant proportion of middle-class votes, they would never win another election.

And so after the catastrophic loss of the 1983 election, a group intellectually led by Patricia Hewitt, working out of the leader's office, set about preparing arguments which Labour leader Neil Kinnock could use to bring the party of the working class into the real world of politics. He started it; John Smith continued it; Tony Blair finished the job. It took two decades, but the dropping of Clause Four of the Labour Party constitution, abandoning their commitment to "common ownership of the means of production, distribution and exchange". was more than symbolic. It represented the difference between more than 'Old' and 'New' Labour, it represented the difference between achieving government, and languishing in opposition.

Table 70: Voting by social class

	Vote share 2001					Change since 1997				
	Con %	Lab %	LD %	Oth %	Lead %	Con %	Lab %	LD %	Swing	Turn-out %
Total	33	42	19	6	-9	+2	-2	+2	+2.0	59
AB	39	30	25	6	+9	-2	-1	+3	-0.5	68
C_1	36	38	20	6	-2	-1	+1	+2	-1.0	60
C_2	29	49	15	7	-20	+2	-1	-1	+1.5	56
DE	24	55	13	8	-31	+3	-4	0	+3.5	53

Source: MORI election aggregate 2001
Base: 18,657 adults aged 18+, interviewed 8 May-6 Jun 2001

A century on from the party's foundation, Keir Hardie and his fellow pioneers might find many characteristics of his party's voting support unfamiliar. Labour support that, far from its origins as a sectional pressure group, is now spread throughout British society. Not much over half, 55%, of Labour's voters come from working class households; not much more than a fifth (22%) are trade union members. Furthermore, what would perhaps be more startling to the party's founders, two-thirds (68%) of their supporters own their own homes.

The 2001 election showed a significant narrowing of class differentials in voting. The middle class ABC_1s – who, of course, were less likely to vote Labour in 1997 than their working class counterparts – swung to Labour, though only by 0.5%. C_2s swung 1.5% to the Tories, DEs 3.5% the same way. Mr Blair seems to be winning over those who were initially least supportive of New Labour, while losing a little ground among his "core supporters". In 1997, C_1s were evenly split between Conservative and Labour; in 2001, Labour led among C_1s for the first time.

Between 1974 and 1992 the Tories took more than half the middle-class vote election after election, while only around one in five voted Labour (ranging from 16% in 1983 to 24% in 1979); indeed, in three of those five elections more middle-class voters supported the Liberals or the Alliance than Labour. In 1997, the gap narrowed, with more than a third voting Labour; in 2001 they did so again.

Table 71: Middle-class (ABC_1) voting 1974-2001

	Oct 1974 %	1979 %	1983 %	1987 %	1992 %	1997 %	2001 %
Conservative	56	59	55	54	54	39	38
Labour	19	24	16	18	22	34	34
Liberal Democrat	21	15	28	26	21	20	22
Other	4	2	1	2	3	7	6
Conservative lead (ABC_1)	+37	+35	+39	+36	+32	+5	+4
Conservative lead (All voters)	-3	+7	+16	+11	+8	-13	-9
Percentage of electorate ABC_1	35	35	38	40	45	49	50
Percentage of electorate ABC_1 and voting Labour	7	8	6	7	10	17	17

Source: MORI

Why the decline in class voting? Part of the reason for this is certainly political as 'New Labour' has moved to the middle ground, and the Tories have responded by leaping rightwards. In an NOP poll for the *Daily Express*, when asked about the political slant of William Hague's party, 27% of respondents thought the Tories too right wing, 7% thought it too left wing, whilst 28% thought the party had the right mix. But among AB voters the proportion who think the Conservatives are too right wing rose to 41%.[121] The Tories are no longer the natural and only choice for the middle choices, but merely one of two acceptable alternatives and the one which, at the moment, is the least ideologically appealing to many.

---

[121] *Daily Express*, 10 May 2001. NOP interviewed a representative sample of 1,000 voters between 4-7 May 2001.

The gender gap

Historically, from the very earliest British elections when women were allowed to vote, Labour has been at a disadvantage – the party has always appealed less successfully to women than to men. This 'gender gap' has been a persistent theme in Labour's electoral history, though at some periods the discrepancy has been smaller than at others, and indeed fleetingly disappeared altogether at the 1987 election. For the past few years now the gap has been slight, and at the 1997 general election Labour's share of the vote was only one percentage point lower (and the Tory share one point higher) among women than among men. In 2001 the gap closed further: Labour's share was the same, 42%, among women as among men, though the Tories did one point better among women (33% as against 32%) and the Lib Dems correspondingly one point worse.

Table 72: The Gender Gap 1974-97

	'Gender Gap' *
1974	+12
1979	+9
1983	+8
1987	0
1992	+6
1997	+2
2001	+1
*Con % lead over Lab among women minus Con lead over Lab among men	

Source: MORI election aggregates

This will presumably be of comfort to those campaigners in the Labour Party who have argued that the re-opening of the gender gap was a threat, that the party had to pay more specific attention to women's concerns, and that women's votes were "bleeding away" from Labour during the last Parliament.

But of course it is not that simple. Not all groups of women are more Tory or less Labour supporting than otherwise similar groups of men.

Age is – and has been for as long as we have had MORI data to analyse it – a very significant complicating factor.

Table 73: Voting by sex, age and class

	Vote share 2001					Change since 1997				Turn-
	Con %	Lab %	LD %	Oth %	Lead %	Con %	Lab %	LD %	Swing	out %
Men	32	42	18	8	-10	+1	-3	+1	+2.0	61
Women	33	42	19	6	-9	+1	-2	+1	+1.5	58
Men 18-24	29	38	26	7	-9	-1	-7	+10	+3.0	43
Men 25-34	24	52	19	5	-28	-4	+5	+2	-4.5	47
Men 35-54	29	43	19	9	-14	+1	-4	+2	+2.5	64
Men 55+	39	39	16	6	0	+4	-1	-1	+2.5	73
Men AB	38	31	25	6	+7	-2	-1	+3	-0.5	68
Men C$_1$	36	39	14	11	-3	0	+2	-5	-1.0	62
Men C$_2$	28	49	14	9	-21	+2	-2	0	+2.0	56
Men DE	23	55	14	8	-32	+4	-5	+2	+4.5	56
Women 18-24	24	45	23	8	-21	0	-8	+8	+4.0	36
Women 25-34	25	49	19	7	-24	-3	-1	+4	-1.0	46
Women 35-54	31	43	20	6	-12	-1	+1	0	-1.0	60
Women 55+	40	38	18	4	+2	+3	-2	+1	+2.5	67
Women AB	41	28	26	5	+13	-2	-2	+4	0.0	68
Women C$_1$	37	37	20	6	0	-1	0	+2	-0.5	59
Women C$_2$	30	48	17	5	-18	+1	+1	-1	0.0	56
Women DE	25	56	13	6	-31	+4	-3	-1	+3.5	50

Source: MORI election aggregate 2001
Base: 18,657 adults aged 18+, interviewed 8 May-6 Jun 2001

Younger women (18-24 year olds) are in fact much more likely than men of the same age to support Labour; this has been the case at each election since 1987, though the reverse was true in 1983. In the three older age bands, women are more Tory, but much less dramatically so than was once the case. The difference is so sharp that, but for the derisory turnout of 18-24 year olds of both sexes in 2001, the young pro-Labour gap would have cancelled out the older pro-Tory difference, and the overall gender gap would have vanished altogether. Furthermore, although the overall gender gap narrowed in 2001, Table 74 shows this was almost entirely a change among the 35-54 year olds, while the behaviour of other age groups remained steady.

Table 74: Gender Gap by Age, 1983-2001

	1983	1987	1992	1997	2001
All	+8	0	+6	+2	+1
18-24	+5	-17	-18	-14	-12
25-34	+14	-4	0	+3	+4
35-54	+9	+11	+10	+9	+2
55+	+5	0	+12	+2	+2

Source: MORI aggregate surveys

Furthermore, more detailed analysis of the data than we have attempted at previous elections shows that there is an interaction between age and class. Among both 18-24 year olds and those aged 55 and over, the gender gap operates in the same direction for ABC_1 and C_2DE women, but much more dramatically in the latter case. Perhaps this partly reflects that the life experiences and perhaps also economic interests of women are much more different from those of their men in working class than in middle class homes, though this is only speculation.

Table 75: Gender Gap by Age and Social Class, 2001

	Con	Lab	LD	Other	Con lead	Gender gap
	%	%	%	%	±%	
All	33	42	19	6	-9	
ABC_1 M 18-24	30	35	29	6	-5	-5
ABC_1 W 18-24	27	37	28	8	-10	
ABC_1 M 25-34	24	49	24	3	-25	+9
ABC_1 W 25-34	27	43	23	7	-16	
ABC_1 M 35-54	32	38	23	7	-6	+5
ABC_1 W 35-54	35	36	24	5	-1	
ABC_1 M 55+	49	27	19	5	+22	+4
ABC_1 W 55+	50	24	21	5	+26	
C_2DE M 18-24	28	42	21	9	-14	-29
C_2DE W 18-24	17	60	13	10	-43	
C_2DE M 25-34	24	57	12	7	-33	-1
C_2DE W 25-34	23	57	15	5	-34	
C_2DE M 35-54	25	50	14	11	-25	-5
C_2DE W 35-54	24	54	15	7	-30	
C_2DE M 55+	26	54	13	7	-28	+10
C_2DE W 55+	31	49	15	5	-18	

Source: MORI election aggregate 2001
Base: 18,657 adults aged 18+, interviewed 8 May-6 Jun 2001

Among the middle age groups, ABC_1 women are more Tory than ABC_1 men, but for C_2DEs the difference is reversed.

It is only fortuitous that with all these various dynamics applying, the total result is to cancel out and leave virtually no gender gap overall. If we look at what has changed since 1997, again it is the middle age groups that are most intriguing. Among both 18-24 year olds, and the 55-and-overs, the swing among men and women was similar, with changes in vote shares for both the main parties differing by no more than a single percentage point. But for 25-34 year olds, although there was a similar loss of support for the Tories among men and women, while the men switched mostly to Labour the women preferred the Liberal Democrats. For 35-54 year olds, there was little change between 1997 and 2001 among women, but the men swung from Labour to both the other main parties.

The general pattern gives little justification for the soul-searching over the gender gap which has been a feature of New Labour thinking over the last couple of years. It is easy to see where this concern comes from. Up to the mid 1980s, especially under Margaret Thatcher, the gender gap was very wide – women were much more likely to vote Conservative than were men, and much less likely to vote Labour. In the last four elections that gap has been narrower, though except in 1987 still perceptible. Between 1992 and 1997, the gap closed from six points to two points; put another way, women swung to Tony Blair 2% more than did men. Not unnaturally, those concerned with women's issues in the Labour Party considered this a triumph and looked to consolidate and build on it at this election.

Some of the arguments that have been produced to encourage greater concentration on women's concerns have been weak or mistaken. For example, it is suggested that women may be more easily swung by the election campaign, on the basis that more female voters say they are "undecided" when faced with the voting intention question. Not a very useful finding, since we know that the vast majority of the undecided respondents, male and female, don't vote.

A more useful analysis might be based on the "definitely decided" question included in almost all MORI's polls through the election. At the end of March[122], 29% of the men but 36% of the women said that they had not definitely decided how to vote and that there was "a chance" that they might change their mind. But, in any case, is this really evidence that women are more likely to change their minds, or simply that they are more prepared to admit when their minds are not made up? It may be significant that in most polls, not just purely political polls, we tend to find more don't knows among the women than among the men.

If women are really more easily swung, shouldn't they be politically more volatile? Many commentators assume that they are. But the polls don't bear that out: looking at MORI's monthly polls between March 2000 and March 2001 and comparing the month-on-month changes in voting intention of men and women, it is men who prove marginally more changeable. (The average change in Labour's lead among men was 6.7 points, among women 5.3 points; both men and women changed most between August and September – the period covered by the petrol crisis – but the change among men was 26 points, double that of the 13 point move among women.) In a *Guardian* article just before the election[123], Yvonne Roberts quoted Deborah Mattinson: "During last year's fuel crisis and pensions row the female vote just bled away". Well, yes, but according to our polls just half as fast as the male vote did.

(In passing, our nomination for the most entirely meaningless statement masquerading as psephological analysis of the 2001 election comes from Roberts, reporting research by Harriet Harman and Mattinson in the same article: "Two million more votes were cast by women than men [in 1997], almost all to Labour". What is this supposed to mean? How does one identify which two million women were the "extra" voters?)

But far more significant to the argument is the evidence of how differently the various age groups reacted. Of course it is true that women are likely to have a different political agenda to men. But there is

---

[122] MORI poll for the *Sunday Telegraph*. MORI interviewed 1,034 British aged 18+ by telephone on 30-31 March 2001.
[123] Yvonne Roberts, "Over to you boys", *Guardian*, 12 May 2001.

no single agenda of "women's issues" which appeals to all of them – differences in their age and circumstances can make their electoral needs and desires just a different from each other's as from those of their male counterparts. There is no magic formula to win the female vote.

The "grey" vote

Older voters are the group least supportive of New Labour, and winning them over is perhaps Tony Blair's biggest remaining political challenge. For much of the time, far more attention is paid to attracting the support of young voters, especially first-time voters, than is paid to attracting the votes of those who have retired. There is a superficial attraction to this: after all, young voters are generally less strongly attached to their party allegiances – if, indeed, they have any at all – and ought to be easier to swing. If their loyalties can be captured at a young age, perhaps they will subsequently offer their party a lifetime of voting service.

And yet such calculations ignore the reality of what I have characterised as "grey power". There are twice as many adults of pensionable age as there are 18-24 year olds, and the older group are twice as likely to vote, meaning that at any given election the grey vote is four times as big as the youth vote, quite an imbalance. This four-to-one ratio of power[124] should indicate to the parties the importance of giving due consideration to the particular needs and concerns of the older age group. Indeed, when we add in all those aged 55-64, who share many of the same attitudes, values and interests as those aged 65+, we are talking about a third of the electorate.

The higher propensity of older electors to turn out and vote becomes of increasing significance as turnouts fall. Furthermore, of course, their election agenda is in many respects distinctive, forcing those who hope for their votes to give them separate consideration. At the time of the 1997 General Election we calculated that the youth vote had only a quarter of the political power of the over 55s; but with 70% of the 65-and-overs voting and only 39% of those aged 18-24, old age pensioners alone had almost four times the voting power of the youngsters in 2001.

Received wisdom over the past thirty years is that the older voter is pretty fixed in his or her ways and stable, tending to support the Conservative Party. But of course this is a considerable simplification;

[124]Analysed in Robert M Worcester "Grey Power: the Changing Face" (1999). Available in pdf format on MORI's website at http://www.mori.com/pubinfo/pdf/greypowa.pdf

Labour needs, and gets, votes from senior citizens as well. Labour won only 38% of the vote among the 55+ age group, 39% among the 65-and-overs. To put that in perspective, despite being in a landslide victory it is lower share of this age group's vote than Harold Wilson won in October 1974 when he barely avoided a hung Parliament.

In almost every other demographic aspect, New Labour has narrowed the differentials between the parties, encroaching onto the Tories' traditional territory while giving up a little of its own core groups. Labour is doing in relative terms better with the middle classes, women and rural and suburban voters than ever before. But older voters have been less attracted, and the size of the "grey gap" – the difference in voting behaviour between the 55+ voters and the overall trend – has doubled since Tony Blair became leader.

Table 76: "Grey Power": voting by electors aged 55+

	Oct 1974 %	1979 %	1983 %	1987 %	1992 %	1997 %	2001 %
Conservative	42	47	47	46	46	36	39
Labour	40	38	27	31	34	40	38
Liberal Democrat	14	13	24	21	17	17	17
Other	4	2	2	2	3	7	6
Conservative lead (55+)	+2	+9	+20	+15	+12	-4	+1
Conservative lead (All ages)	-3	+7	+16	+11	+8	-13	-9
"Grey gap"	5	2	4	4	4	9	10

Source: MORI

Between October 1974 and 1979 the 55-and-overs swung a little less to Margaret Thatcher's Tories than did the rest of the country; but at each election since then the Tories have done as well or a little better among the "grey voters". In 1997 the third of the adult population aged 55 and over swung 8% to Labour – a substantial shift but less than the overall swing of 10.5%. Nevertheless, the scale of Labour's landslide was such that even this reduced swing left Labour the largest party among those aged 55 and over, probably for the first time since 1966.

In 2001, they swung back to the Tories by 2.5% – a little more than the 2.0% swing among all voters and returning the Tories to a minimal lead among the age group. Consequently the relative Conservative performance among the oldest third of the population is now stronger than at any time in the last quarter century. Put another way, their voting is the most out of step that it has ever been in that period.

While many of the concerns of older voters are the same as those of the rest of the electorate, they have some distinctive interests. When we asked[125] at the start of the campaign which issues would be very important to the public in helping decide how to vote, the issues most frequently named by those under 55 were health care (39%), education (38%) and taxation (17%); for the 55+ group the order was health care (42%), pensions (33%), education (27%) and taxation (14%). By the end of the campaign[126], the ranking was unchanged. Further down the list, law and order scores more highly with the older group (12% against 8%), but is nevertheless not one of the top of the mind concerns for any age group.

Labour did its best during the election campaign, and indeed seems to have got a good reception for the manifesto pledges aimed at older voters. An NOP poll[127] of pensioners found, perhaps unsurprisingly, that 92% supported the new winter fuel payments, and 86% the provision of free television licences to the over 75s. In MORI's poll for the *Economist*[128], Labour was chosen as having the best policy on pensions by almost three times as many of those who named the issue as important to their vote as chose the Tories.

This was something of a turnaround. Labour support among older voters took a severe knock in 2000, when the government announced a 75p a

---

[125] MORI survey for the *Sunday Telegraph*, published on 13 May. MORI interviewed 1,021 British aged 18+ by telephone on 10-12 May 2001.
[126] MORI survey for the *Sunday Telegraph*, published on 3 June. MORI interviewed 1,021 British aged 18+ by telephone on 31 May-2 June 2001.
[127] Nigel Nelson, "Grey Britain backs Blair!", Sunday People, 20 May 2001. NOP interviewed 500 pensioners on 17 May 2001.
[128] MORI survey for the *Economist*, published on 18 May. MORI interviewed 1,846 British aged 18+ on 10-14 May 2001.

week annual pension rise. They were fortunate that the effect faded. Nevertheless, the pensions issue had an effect at the time, and the dangers of further alienating the grey vote by future policy misjudgments is real.

The petrol crisis created a similar jolt. In August 2000, among the over-55s Labour had a four point lead with the Conservatives at 38%, Labour 42%, the Liberal Democrats 17% and others 3%[129]. Just under a month later[130], there had been a 7% swing "home" with the figures then recorded as 41% for the Conservatives, 31% for Labour, 20% for the Liberal Democrats and 8% for others. Dissatisfaction with the government among older people went up from 60% in August to 72% in mid September; dissatisfaction with Tony Blair doing his job as Prime Minister went up 13 points from 53% to 66% among the over 55s.

Among this most stable third of the electorate, Labour's vote is fragile; nevertheless at the moment the Conservatives are not the prime beneficiaries. While the Tory voting intention went up by three points, so did the Liberal Democrats', and the others jumped five. Many of the 55-and-overs that the Tories have lost since 1992 seem, so far, unwilling to return even when disappointed by Blair.

But the fact remains that they have not flocked to New Labour in the same numbers as their younger counterparts. Cutting the "grey gap" should be New Labour's next task.

---

[129] MORI poll for *The Times*. MORI interviewed 1,916 British aged 18+ on 17-21 August 2000.
[130] MORI poll for the *News of the World*. MORI interviewed 1,006 British aged 18+ on 14-15 September 2000.

Rural constituencies and rural voters

One of the biggest political red herrings of the Parliament was the question of whether the Tories posed a particular threat to Labour's rural seats. Although the debate eventually crystallised around the possible electoral effects of the Foot and Mouth outbreak, it started long before that. Earlier, it had become tied to the rural impact of petrol prices, with the suggestion that the September fuel boycott crisis would hit Labour especially hard in their rural seats, but the question had been raised even before that.

We call the debate a red herring simply because Labour had virtually no rural seats, in the sense of constituencies with a high rurally-based vote, to lose. Most of the confusion comes from the bandying-about of vague terms without any clear idea of how they are defined, and the lack of an accepted definition of a "rural" seat or, indeed, rural voter. As Peter Riddell explained in *The Times*[131], "Defining what is rural Britain lies in the eye of the beholder. There is no objective measure. A tiny number of people live and work on farms, but many more regard themselves as living in rural areas."

There are at least two definitions of a rural constituency which are reasonably established and have a lengthy pedigree; but neither are very useful as discriminating categorisations to pick out the constituencies where rural interests really have significant influence. One, the nearest thing to an official definition, is the designation of constituencies by the Boundary Commissions as "borough" ("burgh" in Scotland) or "county" constituencies. This is a historic distinction left over from the days when it affected the franchise, and these days has no real effect except that candidates' legal spending limits are a little higher in county constituencies. But a county constituency is defined as any one with more than a token rural element; on this basis around half the constituencies in the country are rural.

---

[131] Peter Riddell, "Tiny minority are living the truly rural life", *The Times*, 29 March 2001.

An alternative which has been much used and is a little nearer to the mark is to classify constituencies by their population density. If population density were uniform, this would be a perfect solution – but of course it is not, and some constituencies mix substantial areas of remote land and little population with adjoining towns or cities that in fact contain virtually all of the constituency's population. In effect, since the populations of constituencies are at least approximately equal, this equates to categorising constituencies by geographical size, regardless of the distribution of the population within them. On this basis, Sheffield Hillsborough, for example, would normally be classified as a semi-rural seat. Although the population density classification is useful for other purposes, it is too crude for useful analysis of political behaviour.

In the absence of an agreed definition, other classifications naturally arose. William Rees-Mogg depended upon perhaps the most extravagant, saying that "The Conservatives are likely to win rural marginals. About 60 per cent of Labour marginals have some rural content" [132]; having carried out the exercise of identifying the most rural 60% of Labour's marginals, we came to the conclusion that he must be including seats such as Hornchurch, Watford, Dudley North and Harrow East – in all of which the impact of any rural swing was never likely to be severe!

Peter Bradley, chair of The Rural Group of Labour MPs, classified 180 of Labour's 419 seats as rural or semi-rural constituencies[133]; in other words, 43% of all of Labour's seats. As a basis for forming a group of MPs with common constituency interests, such a wide definition may be reasonable enough. Naturally, any MP with even token rural interests in his or her constituency will be concerned about rural affairs – that is part of their responsibility to the electors they represent, to bear in mind the needs of the minorities as well as the majority.

But, as a basis for considering voter behaviour, it is a different matter. For, in almost every case, a tiny minority is what the rural element in Labour's constituencies actually comprises. In any electorally meaningful

---

[132] William Rees-Mogg, "Forget this silly talk of a Tory meltdown", *The Times*, 7 May 2001.
[133] House of Commons *Hansard*, 26 January 2001, col 1215.

terms, this is a huge over-estimate of the number of Labour constituencies where the rural vote is influential.

Using the MOSAIC geo-demographic marketing classification, which can be used to categorise every census enumeration district (ED) in the country as rural or not rural, only 7.5% of the adult population live in rural areas. On this strict definition, fewer than a dozen constituencies across the whole country have a majority of the electorate living in rural areas; indeed, there are just 86 constituencies in Great Britain where more than a quarter, 25%, of the electorate are rural. All the rest may have wide swathes of verdant countryside dotted with farmhouses and farm animals, but few people live there. Even in most constituencies that include rural areas and rural voters, the majority of voters live in the towns and experience rural issues only second hand.

Of the 86 constituencies where a quarter of the vote is rural, only ten were held by Labour, and a further 20 by the Liberal Democrats (and almost all of these non-Conservative rural seats are in Scotland or Wales); the remaining 56 were Conservative already, or held by the Nationalists. So it was always a nonsense to suggest that the fall of rural seats could have any significant effect on the election outcome; there were just not enough.

This is not to say that non-rural voters may not take the concerns of their rural neighbours seriously, and their vote might be swung on a high-profile issue such as Foot and Mouth even though living in towns. Further, of course, in a finely-balanced constituency contest even a small rural element might theoretically hold the balance of power – but the same could be said of any other sectional interest, most of which were far more predominant in marginal seats.

During the petrol crisis, when Labour's support briefly plummeted and was overtaken by the Tories, many commentators felt that this was an issue that would hit home especially hard in rural areas. Consequently, we analysed our end of September and end of October polls[134],

---

[134] This analysis was originally conducted for the BBC TV programme *On The Record*

comparing them with an aggregate of all our polls during August, to see what the effect in the rural areas had been, and whether it was lasting. Somewhat to our surprise, we found that far from the Tories benefiting in the rural constituencies during the fuel crisis, their share of the vote *fell* here, though less sharply than Labour's; it was the Liberal Democrats who (briefly) gained support, their share in the 86 constituencies with 25% or more rural voters doubling from 14% to 28%. But we also found that most of the effect had worn off again by the end of October.

Analysis of the general election results shows that the Conservatives in the end performed marginally better in the more rural constituencies, the difference in swing between the most urban and most rural seats being 1%. The pattern of vote gains, though, are a little misleading as they fell in with the story of the rest of the election, that the Conservative advance was concentrated where it could do the party no good.

Table 77: Change in vote share 1997-2001 by rurality

	All		Entirely urban 219 seats		Token rural only (0-5%) 198 seats		Minor rural (5%-25%) 138 seats		Major rural (25%+) 86 seats	
	1997	2001	1997	2001	1997	2001	1997	2001	1997	2001
	%	%	%	%	%	%	%	%	%	%
Conservative	31.4	32.7	25.4	25.1	30.0	30.7	37.6	39.6	38.1	41.1
Labour	44.4	42.0	55.2	52.3	48.0	45.7	35.9	34.8	26.1	24.6
Liberal Democrat	17.2	18.8	13.3	16.1	15.5	16.9	19.2	20.2	26.4	26.4
Other	7.0	6.5	6.1	6.5	6.5	6.7	7.3	5.5	9.4	7.9
Conservative lead	-13.0	-9.3	-29.8	-27.1	-18.0	-15.0	+1.7	+4.9	+12.0	+16.6
Swing		+1.8		+1.3		+1.5		+1.6		+2.3

Source: MORI analysis of election results published by the Electoral Commission

The eventual fall of seats in the election indicates how insignificant the rural seats were in determining the overall result. There was no cull of rural Labour MPs. In the most rural category Labour lost only one seat to the Tories, Norfolk North West; they also gained one from and lost another to Plaid Cymru. The Tories also took Galloway & Upper Nithsdale from the SNP, but lost Norfolk North and Ludlow to the Liberal Democrats, so had no net gain to show for their three point increase in share.

It was in the "minor rural" category that most seats changed hands, but again the results made a nonsense of Labour fears, with the loss of Newark to the Tories compensated by the gain of Dorset South. The Tories gained three other seats in this category (Tatton, where the Independent Martin Bell had not stood for re-election, and two from the Liberal Democrats), but at the same time lost four others to the Liberal Democrats.

Of course, this analysis is constituency based. It is a different question to ask whether rural *voters* (rather than all voters, urban or rural, living in rural constituencies) behaved distinctively. It may be that the genuinely rural voters have one agenda, have reacted sharply against Labour and are likely to vote more strongly against them than in 1997, but that these are swamped by the urban voters who predominate even in most "rural" constituencies. However, that is the point – they are swamped when it comes to election time as well. Rural issues can only count if they can be given wider resonance to attract the support of the urban electorate as well – as happened with the petrol price protest and the Foot and Mouth outbreak.

But in any case, are rural voters really that different in their priorities from urban voters in the first place? To take the obvious example of fox-hunting, polls have persistently shown that a majority even of rural voters would favour a ban (though the majority is somewhat less than in urban areas, and those rural areas where hunting actually takes place may be an exception.)

In our poll for Carlton TV on 13-14 October 2000, we asked our respondents for a (subjective) assessment of where they lived: 9% described themselves as living "in the middle of the countryside", and we can analyse their political views separately. They turned out to be no more Tory than the rest of the country – the Conservatives got 37% in these countryside areas, 38% elsewhere. Labour did worse than average here (31% as against 40% nationally), but the beneficiaries were the Lib Dems, Nationalists, Greens and anti-EU parties. 64% in the rural areas thought the Prime Minister was "out of touch with what ordinary people think", compared to 57% of those living in the middle of a town or city.

Meanwhile 55% of town and city dwellers thought William Hague was out of touch, and 49% thought so in the countryside. A small differential in Mr Hague's favour, it is true, but tiny when one considers it as a comparison of the two parties' supposed natural heartlands.

Foot & Mouth

Thus far, we have considered rural as opposed to agricultural constituencies. When Foot and Mouth became an issue, the considerations were different. This was an issue affecting livestock farmers and their areas. The distinction is a significant one, because many of Labour's "rural" areas have few farming interests – the villages on the former Durham coalfield, some in Tony Blair's own constituency, are certainly rural, but not by any stretch of the imagination agricultural. The genuinely agricultural vote is smaller even than the rural vote.

Again, most of the commentators greatly overestimated this. The former Tory MP Michael Brown, wondering in the *Independent* whether the Tories might eventually derive some electoral benefit from the crisis, talked casually of "100 or so seats with an agricultural character that are held by Labour" [135]. Since he once sat for one himself, only to be defeated in the 1997 landslide, he might be supposed to know what he is talking about. But, in fact, there are not that many other seats of the same type – certainly not a hundred unless you stretch your definition of "farming" well beyond breaking point.

Taking the figures from the 1991 Census, which among many other details classifies the population by the sector of industry in which they work, we might take as a, very generous, definition of a constituency with a significant farming presence one where the census found at least a thousand "engaged in agriculture, forestry or fishing industries". Just one thousand. Even if we assume that for every farmer on this definition there is a spouse and 2.4 children, all economically dependent on farming but not listed as working in agriculture, that adds up to a fairly

---

[135] Michael Brown, "Mr Hague may emerge the real winner from this oddest of crises", *Independent*, 2 March 2001

small vote in the constituency. Of course, in such areas local service industries will also be dependent on the prosperity of the farmers for their business, and even those locals with no direct personal involvement may still have the best interests of the farming community at heart and vote accordingly, but we can surely say that a constituency with fewer farmers than this cannot really be thought of as being agriculturally dominated. And we are not even considering what kind of farming (or forestry, or fishing) the farmers here are actually involved in, because of course arable farming areas were not affected by Foot and Mouth.

So, on this very broad definition, how many farming constituencies are there? Exactly 150. And how many of those had Labour MPs prior to the election? Only 28. Not enough seats to make any significant impact even if there were a huge Foot and Mouth inspired swing to the Tories.

Delaying the election

Although in retrospect it is no surprise than an ultra-cautious Prime Minister like Tony Blair should have chosen to delay the election for a month rather than risk fighting it at the height of the Foot and Mouth Disease outbreak, there was little in the polls at the time that suggested that the political effect on an immediate election was likely to be very damaging. Although MORI's poll for *The Times*, conducted on 22-27 March and published just before the weekend when Mr Blair made his decision, showed that the public was profoundly unimpressed with the government's handling of the Foot and Mouth crisis, and that opinion on the issue had deteriorated over the previous week.[136] But this dissatisfaction had not fed through into any adverse change in voting intentions, and although the outbreak topped the poll as the most important issue facing the country in both March and April, it barely registered as an issue voters said would be very important to them in deciding how to vote.

---

[136] 69% were dissatisfied with the way the Government was handling the Foot and Mouth outbreak on 22-27 March, compared with 52% dissatisfied on 15-17 March when we polled for the *Mail on Sunday*; by 19-24 April there were still 64% dissatisfied.

But even apart from the exaggeration of the electoral significance of the rural areas, was Tony Blair right to postpone the election (and the county council elections) for a month on account of the Foot and Mouth outbreak?

The consensus of public opinion from mid-March was, for sure, solidly in favour of delaying the election, as half a dozen polls indicated. The risks of calling the election while Foot and Mouth still raged through the countryside – and, more importantly, across the front pages – were real, but slight. While only 6% of the public said that Foot and Mouth would have been very important in deciding their vote had the election been held on 3 May[137], things might have been different had a 3 May election come at the end of a month-long campaign in which the government's opponents had sought to blame the government's handling of the crisis for its severity. Indeed, at the end of March, 49% of the public said it was one of the most important issues facing the country, the first issue to push NHS/hospitals out of top spot in almost two years, and 13% that if the government were to hold the election on 3 May that it would make them less likely to vote Labour as a result.

But the epidemic disappeared from the front pages if not from the farms, the Tories made no effort to exploit it as a national election issue (perhaps fearing that with their own record on BSE it was unwise to bring it up), and by the start of June only 2% were naming it as an important vote-determining issue.[138] (It was higher in the countryside of course, 6% of those who described themselves as living "in the middle of the countryside" – but, as we have seen, very few of those lived in the key Labour marginals.)

Before the final decision on the date was made, government spokesmen were reassuring the country that Foot and Mouth would not severely disrupt as general election, or indeed the county council elections, because these days telephone canvassing has almost entirely supplanted

---

[137] MORI survey for the *Sun*, published on 2 May. MORI Telephone Surveys interviewed 1,008 British aged 18+ on 30 April-1 May 2001.
[138] MORI survey for the *Sunday Telegraph*, published on 3 June. MORI interviewed 1,021 British aged 18+ by telephone on 31 May-2 June 2001.

face-to-face campaigning. Those demanding a delay argued that not only was this not true, but the presence of foot and mouth was certain to cause a catastrophic collapse in turnout in the affected areas. We note without further comment that in the event:

(i) just 5% of the adult population said at the start of the last week of the campaign that they had been telephoned by a representative of a political party in the previous few weeks, and

(ii) Hexham, the constituency where the Foot and Mouth outbreak is thought to have started, had the second highest turnout in England, 70.9%. This does not appear to have been a mass protest by the rural population against the government's handling of the epidemic, since the Labour candidate marginally *increased* his share of the vote. (The availability of postal voting on demand, of course, must have helped the purely logistic problem of allowing those in infected areas, especially busy farmers, to register their votes. But the point is that there is no sign that disruption to campaigning inhibited turnout here more than elsewhere.)

Incidentally, high marks for prescience, or for knowing the Prime Minister well, to Charlie Whelan who, in March 2000, wrote commenting on the bookies having quoted a May 2001 election as odds on that "the decision is Blair's alone; and, given his dithering over what to do about the London mayor, I would not put my mortgage on a May date." [139]

---

[139] Charlie Whelan's Racing Card, *New Statesman*, 20 March 2000

Religion and voting

A clear distinction between British elections and those in many other countries is how small a role religion plays either in the candidates' campaigning or, apparently, in voting behaviour. It was reported at one point during the 1997 Parliament that William Hague had had meetings with a leader of the American religious right, to explore what use might be made of such factors in the Conservative cause.

As is well known, religion can be a potent force in American politics; but the positions are not really comparable. A poll in 2000 by the Opinion Research Business found that 62% of Britons say that they believe in God (a decline from 76% in a poll in 1980); only 32% believe in the Devil and 28% believe in Hell.

Compare this with the USA[140]. A 1998 Louis Harris poll is the nearest to ORB's poll in question wording, and found that 94% of Americans say they believe in God; and a 1999 Opinion Dynamics/Fox News survey found that of registered voters, 50% say they believe the Biblical account of creation, compared to 15% who prefer the theory of evolution and 26% who say both are true. Hardly surprising that in American society the voice of the preacher can sometimes swing votes; yet even there, most polls find half or fewer of voters think elected officials or presidential candidates should be guided by religious principle in their decisions or discuss their religious beliefs in public.

Over here, we have no constitutional guarantees to separate the Church from the State – quite the contrary – but the declining belief in God reflects an increasing secularisation of society and attitudes in other ways, which make it improbable that any overtly religious appeal will succeed. Only 62% even claim to believe in God, and active participation is much lower; last year, just 14% of the public said[141] they would be

---

[140] The figures cited were reported in the May-June 2000 issue of *The Public Perspective*, the Roper Center's indispensable review of public opinion and polling in America.
[141] MORI survey for the *Mail on Sunday*, published on 23 April 2000. MORI interviewed 503 British aged 18+ by telephone on 14 April 2000.

going to Church on Easter Sunday, even though it is the single most important festival in the Christian year; indeed, only 55% could correctly say what Easter commemorates.

That is not to say that issues of morality cannot cause controversy, or to deny that many voters derive their values from their religious beliefs; but the one does not necessarily drive the other. The argument over the repeal of Section 28 is a good example of this. The polls showed that public opinion in both England and Scotland was opposed to repeal, and the campaign against it was led by, among others, the head of the Catholic Church in Scotland, Cardinal Winning. Yet the public has rejected his leadership: although 60% of Scots said in the MORI Scotland/*Sunday Herald* poll[142] that they were opposed to repeal, 60% also, told that Cardinal Winning had described homosexual relationships as 'a perversion' said that they disagreed with him.

There are certainly some religious differences in voting behaviour, though no denomination votes *en bloc* for any party. The Church of England is no longer, as it was once described, the Conservative Party at prayer.

During each of the last three elections, MORI has included a question on religious affiliation in one or more of the election polls, enabling this to be cross-tabulated with voting intention. The only religious groups big enough in our samples to consider separately were Church of England (just over half the sample), Roman Catholics (around one in eight), and those who said they had no religion (one in six). The Tories certainly do very much better among Anglicans and worse among Catholics and atheists than average. Much of this simply reflects the demographic characteristics of religious belief. Christians, especially Anglicans and above all active Anglicans, are on average older and more middle-class than the population as a whole. Furthermore, for these same reasons, they are considerably more likely to vote, and are more Conservative.

---

[142] MORI Scotland interviewed 500 Scottish residents aged 18+ by telephone on 20-21 January 2000.

The scale of religious belief in Britain is gradually declining not because believers are losing their faith but because fewer of the youngest generations than in the past are setting out in life as believers in the first place. The change is generational, and short of a significant social upheaval looks set to continue in the future.

Table 78: Voting by religion

	All			Church of England (c. 50%)			Roman Catholic (c. 12%)			No religion (c. 17%)		
	1992	1997	2001	1992	1997	2001	1992	1997	2001	1992	1997	2001
	%	%	%	%	%	%	%	%	%	%	%	%
Conservative	38	29	27	43	38	33	40	28	19	25	20	22
Labour	41	50	52	38	39	50	48	53	60	48	50	52
Liberal Democrat	17	14	16	17	19	14	9	13	16	23	21	21
Nationalist	3	3	3	*	*	*	2	3	1	4	3	3
Others	1	4	3	1	4	2	1	2	5	1	7	3

Source: MORI
Base: c. 2,000 British 18+ in 1992 and 2001, c. 4,000 British 18+ in 1997

The consequence of this is that, like most other Tory policy initiatives in the run-up to the 2001 election, any religious-based message would have spoken more to the Conservative core vote than to floating voters.

Even so, it is worth noting that the Conservative share of the vote has dropped since 1992 much more sharply than average among Catholics, and very much less than average among those declaring no religion. The discrepancy is much more than can be accounted for by any demographic factors, and the reasons are not obvious, unless Tony Blair's open Christianity and Catholic wife are the cause. (Unlikely.) It is a trend worth keeping an eye on in the future.

How the Lib Dems won the campaign

The Liberal Democrats went into the election with a new leader, and defending a swathe of seats taken from the Tories in 1997.

Plenty of the poll pickers noticed that in the election run-up the Lib Dem share in the polls was lower than the 17% they had won in the 1997 election; far fewer compared the figures with the polls at the same stage in 1997. (William Rees-Mogg in *The Times* was one exception, correctly noting "Elections give them exposure. Early polls naturally underestimate the Lib Dem outcome".) [143]

The position of the Lib Dems was not as weak as it looked at the start of the campaign when you realise that the party nearly always picks up support significantly in the last few weeks before an election.

Table 79: Change in party support during the campaign

		Con %	Lab %	LD %	Other %	Con lead %
20-22 Apr 2001	ICM/*Guardian*	33	47	14	6	-14
30 Apr-1 May 2001	MORI/*Sun*	32	50	13	5	-18
1-6 May 2001	NOP/*Daily Express*	31	51	13	5	-20
2-8 May 2001	Gallup/*Daily Telegraph*	32	49	13	6	-17
Average pre-campaign		32	49	13	6	-17
Result		33	42	19	6	-9
Campaign change		+1	-7	+6	0	

Source: MORI/ICM/NOP/Gallup

The 2001 election ran true to form. In terms of the change in vote shares, the Liberal Democrats won the campaign, as they usually do. The final pre-campaign poll from each of the four main polling companies averaged shares of Conservative 32%, Labour 49% and Lib Dems 13%, with remarkably close agreement on the figures. Comparing this with the final result, the Lib Dems gained six percentage points, almost increasing

---

[143] William Rees-Mogg, "Forget this silly talk of a Tory meltdown", *The Times*, 7 May 2001.

their strength by half; the Tories picked up just one point during the campaign, and Labour lost seven.

Nevertheless, during the election, the public felt that the Labour Party had won the campaign hands down. Asked in two polls[144] around a week before polling day "In your view, which of the political parties has run the most effective campaign so far?", just over a third (35% and 37%) named Labour, three times the number who chose the Conservatives (12% and 11%). Even among Tory supporters when analysed separately in the later of these two polls, only 31% said that their preferred party has run the best campaign. The Liberal Democrats scored 13% and 19% respectively in the two polls.

But the Liberal Democrat increase, coming both from tactical voting and from voters who forget to consider the third party as an alternative until the eve of the election but when they do so like what they see, is reflected when we ask the campaign question a little differently. Two days before the election, we asked "Which political party, if any, has impressed you most during the election campaign?"[145]; on this criterion, the Lib Dems were clear winners, picked by 30%, compared to 20% for Labour and only 11% for the Tories; the Lib Dems were the choice not only of 62% of their own supporters, but of 21% of those intending to vote Tory and 30% of those who intended voting Labour. Indeed, barely a third of Tories, 34%, said that they had been most impressed by their own party, while 31% said they had not been impressed by any of the parties.

At the start of the campaign, far more of the Liberal Democrats than supporters of the other parties said that they might change their minds. But during the campaign the Liberal Democrat vote especially, but also the Conservative vote, hardened more than did the Labour vote. In our first campaign poll, conducted for *The Times* on 8 May, more than half of those saying they would support the Liberal Democrats thought that

---

[144] MORI surveys for *The Times*, published on 31 May (MORI interviewed 1,013 British aged 18+ on 29 May 2001) and for the *Sunday Telegraph*, published on 3 June (MORI interviewed 1,021 British aged 18+ by telephone on 31 May-2 June 2001).

[145] MORI survey for the *Economist*, published on 8 June. MORI Telephone Surveys interviewed 1,010 British aged 18+ on 4-5 June 2001.

they might change their mind; and slightly more Conservative supporters than Labour supporters said so.

By the turn of the month the position was reversed. Not only were there considerably more Lib Dem supporters than at the start of May, but two-thirds of them say they have definitely made up their minds. The Tories had cut their proportion of waverers by a third, while for Labour there had been no statistically significant difference in swing.

Table 80: Definitely decided or may change mind

	30-31 Mar	8 May	10-12 May	15 May	22 May	29 May	31 May-2 Jun	4-5 Jun	5 Jun
Conservatives	%	%	%	%	%	%	%	%	%
Definitely decided	65	66	65	67	68	72	78	76	81
May change mind	32	32	29	31	30	27	22	23	17
Don't know	2	3	6	2	2	1	0	1	2
Labour									
Definitely decided	70	69	65	72	69	69	73	79	80
May change mind	27	28	31	25	28	29	26	20	18
Don't know	2	4	4	3	3	2	1	1	2
Liberal Democrats									
Definitely decided	41	42	50	42	51	63	64	71	66
May change mind	55	54	47	56	48	36	35	28	31
Don't know	4	4	3	2	1	1	1	1	3

Source: MORI/ *Times/Sunday Telegraph*

The Labour vote slipped in the final week (from a 50% share in the 31 May-2 June *Sunday Telegraph* poll to 43% in the *Economist* (4-5 June) and 45% in *The Times* (5 June) polls just before polling day, but what remained hardened to the same level as that of the Tories, with four in five of each party's supporters saying they had now definitely decided; yet even this late only around two-thirds of Liberal Democrats were sure that they would stick with the party, confirming the finding of the post election poll[146] that 10% of Liberal Democrat voters decided which party to vote for in the final 24 hours, compared to 7% of Tories and only 4%

---

[146] MORI interviewed 1,349 British adults aged 18+ who said that they had voted on 14-19 June 2001.

of Labour; a further 13% of Lib Dems made their mind up within the last week.

Figure 20

The campaign does matter!

Q   When did you decide which party to vote for? Was it . . . ?

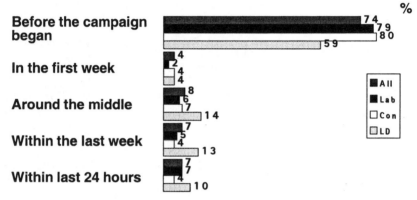

Base: 1,877 British adults aged 18+, 14-19 June 2001

As Figure 20 shows, voters questioned in our post-election survey confirmed the general pattern of decision making and especially the degree to which the Liberal Democrats gain from late decisions: 7% of all those who voted said they made up their mind in the last 24 hours, but 10% of Lib Dem voters decided this late, and a further 13% within the final week.

Tactical voting

It is clear that much of the Liberal Democrat increase in support during campaigns must be tactical. Before the campaign started, the Lib Dem share had fallen away from the 1997 result to a far greater extent in the party's strong regions, especially the South West, than elsewhere. Almost all the increase in support during the campaign was, similarly, concentrated here.

224

The Romsey by-election's most important indication was that there was still enough anti-Tory feeling to fuel tactical voting. It has been widely held that anti-Tory tactical voting peaked in 1997, and that the party could expect to capture seats back – especially from the Liberal Democrats but also from Labour – purely on the basis of some non-Tory voters returning to their 'natural home'. Romsey gave the lie to this, and suggested that as subsequently transpired at the general election there would be no easy pickings for the Tories in the Lib Dems' 1997 gains. Furthermore, being a south of England seat, the by-election demolished the myth that the Lib Dems' replacement of a leader from the South-West with a Scot would necessarily endanger their popularity in that key part of England.

Reported tactical voting in 2001 was at around the same level achieved as in previous elections. In 1997 we found that when asked "Which of these comes closest to your reasons for voting for [party indicated], 'It is the party which most represents your views', or 'The party you support has little chance of winning in this constituency so you vote for the [indicated] party to try and keep another party out'?", a week before the election 9% said it was more to keep another party out. This time[147] the figure was 10%. It had also been 10% in 1987 and 11% in 1992, so there has been no statistically significant change over four elections, despite their different political circumstances.

The most interesting aspect of this analysis is in the comparison by party support: among Labour and Conservative voters alike, 7% said they were voting to keep another party out, while among Liberal Democrats, one in four (25%) of intending Lib Dem voters said they were doing so to try to keep another party from winning in their constituency. This may well be a slight underestimate, for the Liberal Democrats stood on only 17% of the vote in the *Sunday Telegraph* poll, while they ended with 19%.

Interestingly, contrary to popular assumptions, tactical voting was not exclusively between Labour and the Liberal Democrats. Though 29% of

---

[147]MORI survey for the *Sunday Telegraph*, published on 3 June. MORI interviewed 1,021 British aged 18+ by telephone on 31 May-2 June 2001.

those switching tactically said they had switched from Labour and 29% from the Liberal Democrats, 20% had switched from Conservative. We understand the experience of the tactical voting websites was not dissimilar.

After the election, in our survey for the Electoral Commission, 15% of those who said they had voted told us they voted tactically. (However, this was a panel survey, which carries the risk that those respondents sufficiently interested to agree to be re-contacted might have been more sophisticated than the average elector.)

The potential for further tactical voting should it be needed is probably there. According to an ICM poll for the Observer, two-thirds of all Labour supporters would be prepared to switch to the Lib Dems if the party was better-placed to defeat the Tories. [148]

The Lib Dem appeal

It should be noted, though, that Lib Dem success is not purely built on good campaigning over a two-week period every four years. We found convincing confirmation of the often asserted success of Lib Dem MPs in building up a constituency vote: 72% of those living in LibDem held seats were satisfied with their local MP, compared to 40% in Labour seats and 38% in Conservative. Satisfaction was 39% in the seats Labour gained at the last election, 49% in their rock solid heartland seats, flying in the face of the stereotype of growing disillusionment in the safest seats; but, of course, many of those heartland MPs have served the same constituents for many years, giving them the chance to build up a core of personal support, while the MPs in the Labour gains are, by definition, new faces.

Nor did the leader prove to be the weakness that we had thought he might. Towards the end of the election campaign, Charles Kennedy's ratings as most capable Prime Minister (see Table 17) picked up

---

[148] Source: Observer, 3 June 2001. ICM interviewed 1,005 electors by telephone on 30 May-1 June 2001.

noticeably. His final 14% rating was only one point below the 15% that Paddy Ashdown had achieved in his final election, 1997, against Tony Blair and John Major – though, of course, John Major was seen as a less risible alternative than William Hague. Both ratings, of course, were a long way short of the 25% David Steel managed in 1983 (when only 15% picked Michael Foot as the most capable, and a further 6% chose the other Alliance leader, Roy Jenkins.)

The Lib Dems eventually took 18.8% of the vote and their 52 seats were their highest total since the days of Lloyd George. Perhaps of all the parties in the 2001 election, they have most reason to feel satisfied with a job well done.

The first devolved election

At the first general election after governmental power was devolved to a Scottish Parliament – and to a lesser extent to the Welsh Assembly and Greater London Authority – it is fascinating to try to read how, if at all, devolution affected voting patterns, turnout, and the issues which Scottish, Welsh and London voters considered in making their choice.

Some commentators suggested that turnout was likely to be lower in Scotland and Wales than in England following devolution. Perhaps that would have been true had turnout in England been respectable. However, in the event 58% voted in Scotland and 61% in Wales, compared to 59% in England.

Table 81: Issues important to vote in Scotland, Wales and London

Q . *At this General Election, which, if any, of these issues do you think will be very important to you in helping you decide which party to vote for?*

	England %	Scotland %	Wales %	London %
Health care	73	73	67	69
Education	63	63	60	68
Law and order	50	49	50	46
Pensions	39	45	42	29
Taxation	38	38	29	33
Unemployment	30	35	30	32
Managing the economy	30	30	22	30
Public transport	31	27	25	43
Asylum seekers	30	25	18	30
Protecting the natural environment	25	22	21	25
Europe	26	21	15	28
Housing	20	21	17	32
Animal welfare	12	13	7	8
Defence	11	12	8	7
Constitution/devolution	6	8	7	7
Trade Unions	6	8	3	9
Northern Ireland	7	6	4	8
Other	3	2	3	3

Source: MORI/ *The Times*
Base: 2,088 British 18+ (166 in Scotland, 104 in Wales, 244 in London), 5 June 2001

Devolution seems to have had little impact in modifying the terms of the election debate, except that the constitution itself is longer an issue. There was remarkably little difference between Scotland and England in the issues that electors said would determine how they would vote. Even though the issues that most concerned English voters, the NHS and education, now come under the control of Holyrood and should not, in theory, be affected by who is sent to Westminster, these were also the issues that were very important to Scots in deciding how to vote. The same was true in Wales.

It has been very clear since 1999 that many voters make a clear distinction in their party preferences between the two Parliaments. The monthly System Three polls for the *Herald* regularly ask the same sample of Scots how they would vote for Westminster and how for Holyrood; invariably, Labour performs better and the SNP worse for Westminster; the difference is usually at least five points, and has touched double figures. Scots are divided on the relative importance of Westminster and Holyrood (32% told ICM[149] that Holyrood is "more relevant in dealing with issues that affect you", 21% that Westminster is more important and 42% that they are of equal importance), but they don't necessarily accept that devolution has removed Westminster's influence over devolved policy areas such as education and the NHS. (38% think Westminster has most influence over the quality of the NHS and schools in Scotland, only 27% Holyrood.)

And who is to say they are wrong? Government spending in Scotland is tied to the Barnett formula, which governs the allocation of central government money round the UK and gives Scotland more than its per capita share. An NOP poll during the election[150] found more than half the British public think Scottish spending should be brought down to English levels. If Scots want to prevent that, should they vote Labour or SNP?

---

[149] *The Scotsman*, 15 May 2001. ICM interviewed 1,000 residents in Scotland aged 18+, by telephone on 12-13 May 2001.
[150] *Herald*, 14 May 2001.

If the Nationalists could poll their Holyrood strength for Westminster, they would be breathing down Labour's neck in the race for most votes in Scotland – but in seats they would still struggle to reach double figures and Labour could still hold two-thirds of the seats in Scotland even if level on votes with the SNP.

There were few election surveys published in Wales, and the Welsh sub-samples in the national polls are usually too small to be of much use. The *Western Mail/Wales on Sunday* survey though[151], carried out by Market Research Wales, gives some indications on the devolution issue.

Asked what they would like to see happen to the Welsh National Assembly, more (35%) would like to see it be given primary law-making and tax-levying powers as in Scotland than those who would like to see it scrapped (27%). One in five (19%) believe it should remain with the powers it now has; 7% believe it should be given primary law-making powers, and 5% believe it should give way to an independent Welsh Parliament.

If the political tensions unleashed by devolution were likely to damage Labour, perhaps it was potentially most likely to happen in London. The government was openly at loggerheads with the Mayor, Ken Livingstone, over the issue of transport for London. London voters had already once supported Ken at the polls, to the humiliation of Frank Dobson who as Labour candidate finished third, and on the same occasion they had given the Tories most constituency seats in the Assembly – though that was on a very low turnout.

The powers of the Greater London Authority are, of course, more restricted than those of the Scottish Parliament. But, as it turned out, this in no way diminished the scope for ambiguity over the boundaries of power and hence the appearance that the government was encroaching on the matters that had been devolved to the Mayor and Assembly. By far the most significant remit of the GLA, in the public's opinion, is transport. When Londoners were asked, in a MORI poll for London

---

[151] *Western Mail*, 28 May 2001. Market Research Wales interviewed 500 adult residents of Wales by telephone on 14-21 May 2001.

News Network on the eve of the Mayoral election, "What do you think are the two or three most important issues facing London for [the Mayor] to deal with?", public transport was named, without prompting, by 70%. Reducing crime was the second priority (39%), the traffic congestion (19%). It should have been plain that London's voters would not take kindly to government interference with Ken's attempts to solve the capital's transport problems.

By the time of the election, Londoners still sided with Livingstone over the issue of dealing with London Underground, according to an ICM/*Evening Standard* survey[152]. 57% stated that they supported, and only 22% said they opposed, the Mayor's decision to go to court to attempt to block the government's plan of running the tube under the proposed PPP (public-private partnership). Similarly, when asked to rate how the three main players handled events surrounding the future of the London Underground, 51% thought Ken Livingstone had handled them well, compared to the 20% and 26% who did so for John Prescott and Gordon Brown respectively.

But even this survey showed that public transport was unlikely to affect voter's party choice. Repeating a question posed by MORI in the run up to the 1997 election, ICM found only 8% thought the issue "very important in helping you decide which party to vote for", compared to 11% recorded by MORI in 1997. Additionally, more respondents lay blame on the Tories rather than Labour for the current state of public transport in their area. As Table 81 shows, public transport was much more of an election issue in London than elsewhere, but in the end Labour survived it.

---

[152] *Evening Standard,* 15 May 2001. ICM interviewed 507 voters in London by telephone, on 11-13 May 2001.

4. Pundits and Pollsters

Predicting the result

There are still many commentators who prefer to think that the political world would be a better place without opinion polls, that they could make better assessment of the way the political wind was blowing without us, or perhaps even that everybody would stop trying to predict the future altogether. Hardly.

We are indebted to David Butler's research published in the *Financial Times* on 4 June to put both the politicians' nous and the punters in perspective before the invention of the modern opinion poll. In 1906, he reported, just before the Conservatives lost 240 seats in the Liberal landslide, Liberal politicians, yes Liberal politicians, were predicting a Conservative victory. Was that an example of spin, early 'lowballing'?

And in 1924, 100 to 1 was quoted against the Conservatives winning 400 seats (they got 428). Wonder if anybody took the bet?

In 1931, spread betting even then suggested 350 seats for the National government (they got 550). On election eve in 1935, Clement Attlee could declare: 'We are on the eve of a great victory' (Labour only won 151 seats).

And despite the *News Chronicle*'s two Gallup polls of the 1945 election showing clear Labour leads, the Labour victory with a majority of 140 was a surprise to both sides, so reported Butler in the *FT*.

I reported the reaction of Churchill to the Gallup findings in an article in *BBC History Magazine*[153] just as the election began:

"Public Opinion Polling in Britain began just before the War. British Gallup, originally known as BIPO (British Institute of Public Opinion),

---

[153] Robert Worcester, 'Going to the Polls', *BBC History Magazine*, May 2001, p 41-42.

was founded in 1937, just two years after its American stepfather. In October 1938 it began the series of political questions that continue today, testing the public's satisfaction with the Prime Minister (57% were then satisfied with Neville Chamberlain, 43% dissatisfied, setting aside the 'don't knows'), and the first national voting intention questions came in February 1939 (64% said they would vote for the Government 'if there were a general election tomorrow'). [154]

"Gallup's first associate in Britain was the late Dr Henry Durant, who was one of three post-docs listed by the LSE as available for hire. He reminisced forty years on:

> 'Not [George] Gallup himself, but an associate of his, Henry Field, came from the USA in 1936 looking for someone to start up part-time Gallup work from home... For a lordly £150 a year I did postal surveys, till the *News Chronicle* became interested. They said, "We want you to forecast the by-election to show that the system works." West Fulham: Edith Summerskill was the Labour candidate. It was a Conservative seat and she upset the Conservative, as I had forecast, and by a miracle I got it on the nose within 1%; beginner's luck.' [155]

"During the war, Dr Durant and his colleagues largely focused on government work, but they also continued to publish poll findings regularly in the sparse pages of the *News Chronicle* during those paper-rationed times, and when the election was called in May 1945 they were ready to predict it. As Durant remembered:

> 'Gallup showed us that Attlee was going to win with the Labour Party. Nobody believed us, including all the *News Chronicle* people.' [156]

"Nor did Conservative Central Office believe it: according to the memoirs of Lord Moran, Winston Churchill's physician, Churchill

---

[154] George Gallup, *The Gallup International Opinion Polls: Great Britain 1937-1975*, (Random House, 1976), pp 9, 14.

[155] Brian Chappell, 'Founding Fathers: Henry Durant', *Market Research Society Newsletter*, numbers 157-8 (April-May 1979).

[156] *Ibid.*

recalled that the Central Office view was that the Tories would be returned with a substantial majority. According to Churchill:

> 'I had not burdened myself unduly with the subject (of the election) while occupied with the grave business of the [Potsdam] conference. On the whole I accepted the view of the party managers and went to bed in the belief that the British people would wish me to continue my work.

> 'My hope was that it would be possible to reconstitute the National Coalition Government in the proportions of the new House of Commons. Thus slumber. However, just before dawn I woke suddenly with a sharp stab of almost physical pain. A hitherto subconscious conviction that we were beaten broke forth and dominate by mind... I was discontented at the prospect, and turned over and went to sleep again.' [157]

"We have the recollection of Lord Moran[158], Churchill's doctor, who reports that in a conversation with the then former Prime Minister in the year after the great man's defeat, tried to argue that Churchill's defeat was only the swing of the pendulum, but finding his mind elsewhere, told him of the Gallup polls carried out at intervals throughout the war by the *News Chronicle* and when he did, got Churchill's attention: 'Tell me about them,' Churchill commanded. Moran says he told Churchill that 'two questions were put to the readers (sic). To the first, "Who do you think should be responsible for the conduct of the war" there was only one answer: 'Winston Churchill.' The second brought out their hostility to the Tories. Churchill interrupted at this point, according to Moran. 'I don't understand.'

"Moran reported that he then said that all the time the percentage of voters who wanted a Tory government after the war was steadily falling. Churchill had been listening intently. And then, as he mused, the light went out of his face. "

Nowadays, politicians, pundits, punters (and bookies) alike are better informed, one reason for which is the polls. Of course, polls are not

---

[157] Winston Churchill, *The Second World War, Volume VI, Triumph and Tragedy*, (Cassell & Co. Ltd., 1954).
[158] Lord Moran, *Winston Churchill: The Struggle for Survival* (Constable, 1966).

predictions. They measure the present. (If you want to know the future, buy a crystal ball.) But they are the best available guide to the present and as such an important prediction tool.

The Reuters' 'Kalends' panel of 66 leading political scientists and commentators' predicted an average 143-seat majority for Labour[159]. I was initially asked to participate in their surveys, but when I suggested a fee might be appropriate if they were going to ring weekly for over the election period, I never heard from them again, and in fact had great difficulty finding them on the web. This is a shame, for the data from its 1997 predecessor, the Reuters' 'Panel of Experts' gave us great fun and some useful data, reported in *Explaining Labour's Landslide* on pp. 214-218.

What else did they predict? "The general election will go ahead on May 3 despite the foot-and-mouth crisis and the government will win with a 97-seat majority." Three in four of the 'talking heads' Reuters canvassed up to 21 March thought 3 May was still on, up from 51% a few weeks earlier. Indeed, 83% of their 'expert respondents' said if the general election was to be delayed as a result of the foot-and-mouth crisis, it would have little or no effect on the outcome.

In 1997 the Reuters 20 'experts' anticipated a Labour majority of 92; but as we reported in *Explaining Labour's Landslide*, those whose reasoning took account of what the polls were showing tended to perform a lot better than those who had other prediction methods. John Curtice's forecast (one of the better ones on the panel) was 131, 48 seats adrift, and he's critical in so many papers of the pollsters' 'failure' to get it spot on! The only Curtice forecast we saw this time was for a Labour majority of 105, in an *Observer* feature in the first weekend of the campaign – an interesting mix of pollsters, journalists, academics and bookies. It's arguable who won, but Nick Cohen definitely lost, on Labour and the Tories at any rate, though he had the best turnout prediction and shared the honours on the Lib Dems.

---

[159] Source: www.kalends.com

Table 82: Pundits' predictions in the *Observer*, 13 May 2001

	Labour majority	Con seats	Lib Dem seats	Turnout
Nick Cohen (*Observer/Spectator*)	100	230	50	63%
John Curtice (Strathclyde University)	105	212	35	67%
John Stevens (Pro-Euro Conservative Party)	110-115	210	38	66-67%
Andy Clifton (Ladbrokes)	119	208	33	67%
Bob Worcester (MORI)	120	215	32	66%
Ben Pimlott (Goldsmiths College)	120	200	50	70%
Graham Sharpe (William Hill)	125	190	44	65%
Mark Seddon (*Tribune*, ex-Labour NEC)	130	190	35	66%
Peter Wilby (*New Statesman*)	150-200	Fewer than 200	40-50	Below 70%
Peter Kellner (*Observer/Evening Standard*)	150	177	48	68%
Richard Burkholder (Gallup)	175	183	31	66%
Election result	167	166	52	59%

Source: *Observer*, 13 May 2001

Peter Wilby, editor of the *New Statesman*, was nearest to getting all his predictions right, but then he left himself plenty of leeway!

At the outset of the election, the punters were anticipating another Labour landslide, following the opinion polls as punters do. The spread betting shops, led by IG Index, kept careful track of the election, offering spread betting facilities on line, on phone, by post and fax, and no doubt on the back of a packet of fags.

By 28 May, the IG Index has risen to Labour at 404, Conservatives at 177 and Liberal Democrats 48. Just a couple of days later, but after the publication of an ICM poll which gave Labour its biggest lead[160] since 1999 jumped Labour to 415, Conservatives at 151, down 26 seats, and the LibDems at 50, virtually the same as in the 1997 election. By polling day, the Index mid-point gave Labour 403, back to the end of May figure, Conservatives 173 and boosted the LibDems to 55. But by polling day there wasn't a lot of money to be made either way, and only the stalwart supporters of the parties, betting with their hearts rather than

---

[160] *Guardian*, 30 May 2001. The poll showed a Labour lead of 19% from fieldwork on 26-28 May,

their heads, were betting against the polls and the punters who followed them so closely.

As indicated above, my own forecast for the four years leading up to the election, made on countless radio and television programmes and many platforms from the Institute of Directors' Annual Conference in the Albert Hall to articles in, of all places, *Red Pepper*, was 100-120 before the election began, then in the second week upped my guesstimate to 140-150 majority and then on 1 June to 180 –200, and on 6 June said at the KPMG Non-Executive Directors' business breakfast with around 80 in the audience that '166' would be the number I'd put my money on, splitting the difference between 165 and 167. And on vote share? In an article for the May 2001 issue of *The House Magazine*, written before the election was called, I said: "My bet's on Labour at about 44% again, the Tories on 34%, the Liberal Democrats on 16%, and 6% other."[161]

---

[161] Robert M Worcester, "The Impact of Modern Polling Techniques on Campaigning in the 2001 General Election', *The House Magazine,* 7 May 2001.

The polls in the 2001 election

The pollsters

The four established polling organisations were joined in 2001 by two new entrants to the field: as well as Gallup, ICM and NOP, using conventional telephone polling methods with a form of random digit dialling, and MORI, conducting some polls in that way as well but also using face-to-face interviewing for our "flagship" series of polls in *The Times*, the American company Rasmussen Research had joined the fray and the academic-led British Election Study (with fieldwork by Gallup), were publishing their results as the election went along for the first time.

The new entrant to British media polling was Rasmussen Research, polling by computer 'speaking clock' for the *Independent*. We were dubious about the system they were using, which in the 2000 American Presidential election left them 15th out of the 16 polls polling in the final week of the campaign in terms of their accuracy in reporting the outcome.

As the *Independent* explained the system[162]:

> 'It is designed to overcome some of the problems of polling - that people can be reluctant to tell a stranger their political views, or inclined to give what they think is the "correct" answer rather than their real feelings. So, Rasmussen uses a computer, not interviewers, to read out the questions. Respondents then type in a number on their phone to signify their answer. This greater anonymity encourages respondents to say what they really think. Similar technology is already used in Britain to sell cinema tickets. But this is the first time it has been used to find out what voters think about the hot political issues of the day.'

Their automated system conducts an interview with whoever answers the phone, so long as they are aged 18+. After corrective weighting (typically, they interview too many women and older people), they

---

[162] "A new kind of polling", on-line edition of the *Independent* (www.independent.co.uk), 15 May 2001.

conduct a 'sanity check' to make sure their data is comparable with other results. Interviewing a no doubt bemused British electorate over the telephone, they consistently found the narrowest margin throughout the campaign, with the Tories on 32% or 33% in each poll and Labour on 44% to 46%. The BBC, adhering to its rigid policy of covering only "approved" polls, did not report Rasmussen's results, even in their otherwise comprehensive polls section on the BBC News Online website.

There was also the British Election Survey[163], funded by the Economic and Social Research Council (ESRC), based at the University of Essex, and directed by Professors David Sanders, Paul Whiteley, Harold Clarke and Marianne Stewart. Throughout the election the BES (with fieldwork by Gallup but designed by the academic team at Essex) asked c. 150 people each day a number of questions relating to the election, including how people intended to vote, their certainty of voting, interest in the election, issues of importance, liking and disliking of political leaders, etc. It was little reported in the media, but the rolling results were posted on the University of Essex web site. Once we discovered them, we included the findings in our poll digests and reported some of the findings in our commentaries on the polls. I reported the BES findings on the *Powerhouse* (Channel 4) programme, and also mentioned it on my regular BBC 5 Live *Drive Time* slot. As far as we can tell, this was the only coverage the BES findings got on the BBC except for one interview with Professor Paul Whiteley on *Newsnight*.

The rolling design of the BES poll is one used by Marplan for GMTV in the 1992 General Election, and proved highly 'bouncy', using a three-day rolling poll design. In the US elections last year, the Gallup poll and one or two others used a similar rolling design (the Americans call this a "tracking poll", but we use that term differently in Britain); these, too, had a tendency to hop about a lot and to give an impression of an electorate far more volatile than was suggested by viewing all the poll evidence. The BES proved more stable (over seven days until the final poll, which was over three days but still based on c. 1,000 respondents),

---

[163] The details of the findings can be found at www.essex.ac.uk/bes.

Table 83: The campaign polls, 2001

Fieldwork	Agency	Client	Public-ation Date	Sample	Con %	Lab %	LD %	Oth %	Lab lead ±%	Swing since 1997 ±%
8 May	MORI	*Times*	10 May	1,046	30	54	13	3	24	-5.5
10-11 May	NOP	*S. Times**	13 May	1,003	32	49	13	6	17	-2
10-11 May	ICM	*Observer**	13 May	1,011	32	48	15	5	16	-1.5
8-14 May	British Election Study†		14 May	1,100	32	53	11	4	22	-4.5
10-12 May	MORI	*S. Telegraph**	13 May	1,021	31	51	13	5	20	-3.5
11-13 May	ICM	*Eve. Standard**	14 May	1,437	32	48	14	6	16	-1.5
12-13 May	Ras.	*Independent***	15 May	1,030	32	46	13	9	14	-0.5
13-14 May	ICM	*Guardian**	16 May	1,004	31	46	16	7	15	-1
10-14 May	MORI	*Economist*	18 May	1,846	26	54	14	6	28	-7.5
14-15 May	Gallup	*D.Telegraph**	17 May	1,004	32	48	13	7	16	-1.5
15 May	MORI	*Times*	17 May	1,019	28	54	12	6	26	-6.5
17-18 May	NOP	*S. Times**	20 May	1,107	30	49	14	7	19	-3
14-21 May	British Election Study†		21 May	1,156	25	55	14	6	30	-8.5
19-21 May	ICM	*Guardian**	23 May	1,000	32	45	17	7	13	0
19-22 May	Ras.	*Independent***	25 May	3,162	32	44	16	8	12	0.5
21-23 May	Gallup	*D. Telegraph**	24 May	1,439	32	48	15	5	16	-1.5
22 May	MORI	*Times*	24 May	1,066	30	55	11	4	25	-6
24-25 May	NOP	*S. Times**	27 May	1,001	30	49	14	7	19	-3
22-29 May	British Election Study†		29 May	1,000	28	54	13	5	26	-6.5
26-27 May	Ras.	*Independent***	29 May	1,227	32	44	17	7	12	0.5
26-28 May	ICM	*Guardian**	30 May	1,000	28	47	17	8	19	-3
29 May	MORI	*Times*	31 May	1,013	30	48	16	6	18	-2.5
28-29 May	Gallup	*D. Telegraph**	31 May	1,462	31	47	16	6	16	-1.5
30 May-1 Jun	ICM	*Channel 4**	1 Jun	1,007	31	43	19	7	12	0.5
31 May-1 Jun	NOP	*S. Times**	3 Jun	1,105	30	47	16	7	17	-2
31 May-1 Jun	ICM	*Observer**	3 Jun	1,005	34	46	15	5	12	0.5
31 May-2 Jun	MORI	*S. Telegraph**	3 Jun	1,070	27	50	17	6	23	-5
30 May-3 Jun	British Election Study†		3 Jun	1,000	26	53	14	7	27	-7
2-3 Jun	ICM	*Eve. Standard**	4 Jun	1,332	30	47	18	5	17	-2
2-3 Jun	Ras.	*Independent***	5 Jun	1,266	33	44	16	7	11	1
2-4 Jun	ICM	*Guardian**	6 Jun	1,009	32	43	19	6	11	1
4-5 Jun	MORI	*Economist**	7 Jun	1,010	31	43	20	6	12	0.5
4-6 Jun	British Election Study†		6 Jun	1,000	25	55	14	6	30	-8.5
5-6 Jun	MORI	*Times*	7 Jun	1,967	30	45	18	7	15	-1
6 Jun	Gallup	*D.Telegraph**	7 Jun	2,399	30	47	18	5	17	-2

* telephone poll
** telephone automated response poll
† rolling telephone poll (fieldwork conducted by Gallup)

but could still be forecast in the same way as we did in 1992, by knowing in advance when an extreme result was about to drop out.

We are also sceptical of any poll findings being reported to a decimal point, suggesting spurious accuracy, as no poll of a national population can be said to deliver results with that degree of accuracy.

Internet polling

This election also saw, for the first time, polling using the internet. First up were the "BBC News Online 1000". These were conducted by ICM, initially based entirely based on "a random sample of ... adults [interviewed] via the Internet", later mutating to interviewing "via the internet and by telephone", although the BBC's website didn't specify what proportions the mix between telephone and internet interviews. This is new and unproven methodology; it is a great pity that the many secondary reports of its findings across the media made no mention that the surveys were not conducted by ICM's usual methodology, simply reporting them as "an ICM poll for the BBC".

The internet has not been used before for political polls in Britain, though Harris Interactive achieved impressive results during last year's US elections; one is inclined to be a little wary until the methodology has also established a track record here. In the one case when it was possible to get an approximate comparison of results – polling during March on whether the election should go ahead on 3 May – as Table 84 shows, the BBC Online findings were a long way out of line with other polls on the same subject, and although it is possible that the course of events did indeed bring about such an abrupt change of opinion between 8-10 March and 13-14 March, it must give rise to pause for thought; the sharp difference between the ICM/BBC poll and the remainder is obvious – amounting to an apparent 23% "swing" over considerably less than a week between that poll and the next.

But the BBC On-Line poll did not, in line with the BBC anti-poll guidelines, attempt to measure voting intentions.

Table 84: Polls on delaying the election, March 2001

	ICM/ BBC OnLine 8-10 Mar %	NOP/ C4 13-14 Mar %	ICM/ News of World 14-16 Mar* %	NOP/ Sun. Times 15-16 Mar %	MORI/ Mail on Sun. 15-17 Mar %	ICM/ Guar- dian 16-18 Mar %
Hold election on 3 May	63	36	37	43	34	40
Delay election	28	47	53	53	61	52
No opinion/don't know	9	18	10	4	5	8

*ICM/News of the World poll conducted only in marginal seats

Where the internet is used merely as a means of contacting and questioning a sample reliably drawn as representative on some other basis, there is no reason to doubt its reliability – though given the current penetration of usage it is probably a more efficient tool for polls of, say, business leaders than of the general public. (Probably this was why ICM mixed telephone interviews with their internet interviews in the BBC Online panel, to maintain representative coverage of that part of the population not yet connected to the internet.)

But where the net itself is the basis for sampling as well as the interviewing tool, it might be wise to be more cautious. There are no reliable directories of e-mail addresses from which you could generate a representative sample, as you can do with telephone numbers.[164] The vast majority of "polls" on the web are in fact what we call voodoo polls, with self-selecting samples.

This seems to have been the case with the yougov internet poll, which nevertheless claimed a more accurate forecast than any of the conventional polls. For the record, here is what yougov published on the eve of poll, based on their 'BES online survey and subsequent surveys': Labour 43%; Conservative 33%; Liberal Democrat 17%; Other 7%; Labour lead 10%. A brave and impressive effort.

---

[164] In fact this is not how most modern telephone sampling works – because of the large number of ex-directory numbers, directory sampling is practical but prone to bias. Consequently most modern telephone polls use some form of random digit dialling – not yet an option when sending e-mails.

The similar Harris Interactive poll in the USA last year, with quarter of a million "respondents", was also very accurate. These were not of course crude voodoo polls. Not only were careful steps taken to prevent multiple voting, but demographic details were collected which allowed weighting to correct for the obviously unrepresentative aspects of the net-connected population (younger, more male and more affluent than the average). As yet we have no solid theories why this method seems to work.

Non-national polls

There were also, as always, regional polls in Scotland, Wales and London, though fewer than in the past.

Table 85: Non-national polls

Scotland					Con	Lab	LD	SNP	Oth
Fieldwork	Agency	Client		Sample	%	%	%	%	%
4-10 May	Scottish Opinion	*Daily Record*		?	12	58	9	20	1
12-13 May	ICM	*Scotsman*		1,000	16	44	12	25	3
18-21 May	System Three	*Herald*		3,019	12	50	9	25	4
24-28 May	System Three	*Herald*		1,048	13	47	11	26	3
4-5 Jun	ICM	*Scotsman*		1,013	14	43	14	24	5
Result (Scotland)		7 Jun			15.6	43.9	16.4	20.1	4.0

Wales					Con	Lab	LD	PC	Oth
Fieldwork	Agency	Client		Sample	%	%	%	%	%
14-21 May	Market Research Wales	*Western Mail*		c. 500	18	58	10	14	*
30 May-3 Jun	NOP	HTV		1,000	18	53	12	14	3
Result (Wales)		7 Jun			21	49	14	14	2

London					Con	Lab	LD	Oth	
Fieldwork	Agency	Client		Sample	%	%	%	%	
11-13 May	ICM	*Evening Standard*		507	32	52	13	3	
2-3 June	ICM	*Evening Standard*		502	26	53	14	7	
Result (London)		7 Jun			30	47	17	6	

Unusually, there were very few constituency polls – only two that we know of by a major polling company. (Discussed below, p 295).

244

What a pity nobody commissioned a serious poll[165] in Hartlepool to give guidance to those many folks who would like to see the end of Peter Mandelson. When the NOP poll in the *Mail* in 1983 gave Simon Hughes a one-point lead over the Labour Leader of the Southwark Council John O'Grady, he went on to defeat Peter Tatchell, the gay, draft-avoiding Australian whom the left-wing Labour selectors in Bermondsey decided that working-class, Catholic, dock-yard constituency should have as their Member of Parliament. NOP/*Daily Mail*, where were in 2001 when we needed you? Never did I think I might wish to a) give up my American citizenship, b) move to Hartlepool, and c) vote for Arthur Scargill!

Were you up for Mandelson? Extraordinary performance it was. Shades of the late Sir James Goldsmith's performance at Putney on election night 1997.

---

[165] We don't count the *Independent on Sunday*'s do-it-yourself poll, reported on 18 February, which interviewed 1,000 Hartlepool electors by telephone using a named list of researchers "with help from the NCTJ pre-entry journalism course at Darlington College".

Accuracy of the polls

Like it or not – and we don't, much – the polls tend to be judged almost solely by their final forecasts. Despite the inevitable carping of the Curtices and Glovers (see Appendix II), in terms of the overall error it was the best performance since 1987, with an average error in share for the four final polls less than 1.6% – well inside the standard 3% "margin of error". (These figures exclude the special case of the British Election Study's rolling poll, and NOP, who did not publish from fieldwork in the final week, and therefore can't be said to have produced a final forecast. Their poll for the *Sunday Times* the previous Sunday, with fieldwork done 31 May-1 June, showed a large lead for Labour, typical of all the polls taken before William Hague sounded the warning of a huge Labour landslide.) The poll of polls came closer still[166], with an average error of only 1.3%, and within 3% of the final share for every party.

Table 86: The Final Polls, 2001

	Con	Lab	LDem	Other	Lab Lead	Lead error	Average share error
NOP/*Sunday Times* (31 May-1 Jun)	30	47	16	7	17	7.7	2.75
ICM/*Evening Standard* (2-3 Jun)	30	47	18	5	17	7.7	2.5
MORI/*Economist* (4-5 Jun)	31	43	20	6	12	2.7	1.1
British Election Study (4-6 Jun)	25	55	14	6	30	20.7	6.5
Rasmussen/*Independent* (2-3 Jun)	33	44	16	7	11	1.7	1.4
ICM/*Guardian* (2-4 Jun)	32	43	19	6	11	1.7	0.6
MORI/*The Times* (5-6 Jun)	30	45	18	7	15	5.7	1.75
Gallup/*Daily Telegraph* (6 Jun)	30	47	18	5	17	7.7	2.5
Average errors	*1.6*	*2.8*	*1.2*	*0.75*		*4.2*	*1.56*
Poll of polls (final four only)	31.3	44.8	17.8	6.3	13.5	4.2	
Error in poll of polls	*-1.4*	*+2.8*	*-1.0*	*-0.2*			
Result	32.7	42	18.8	6.5	9.3		

---

[166] The error in the "poll of polls" is of course often lower than the average error in the individual polls, since errors by different polls in opposite directions can cancel each other out.

Congratulations are due to ICM for coming closest, with an average error of 0.6% for their poll in the *Guardian* published on Wednesday, although their poll for the London *Evening Standard* published on Tuesday was one of the furthest out, with an average error of 2.5%.[167]

MORI's two final polls were also well within the margin of error, with the poll for the *Economist* within 1.1% and the poll for *The Times* 1.75%.

Rasmussen Research's "speaking clock" computer telephone poll turned in a creditable 33%/44%/16% share for the *Indy*, with an average error of 1.4%, and was the only one of the final polls to overstate the Tory share rather than understating it.

Table 87: Accuracy of the polls, 1945-2001

Year	Average error in lead %	Average error in party share %	Number of polls
1945	3.5	1.5	1
1950	3.6	1.2	2
1951	5.3	2.2	3
1955	0.3	0.9	2
1959	1.1	0.7	4
1964	1.2	1.7	4
1966	3.9	1.4	4
1970	6.6	2.2	5
1974 Feb	2.4	1.6	6
1974 Oct	4.5	1.4	4
1979	1.7	1.0	4
1983	4.5	1.4	6
1987	3.7	1.4	6
1992	8.7	2.7	5
1997	4.4	2.1	5
2001	4.2	1.6	4
Average	*3.7*	*1.6*	*65*

---

[167] The measurement of a poll's accuracy by the average of its errors in measuring each of the party shares is the "Rose method", first utilised several decades ago by Professor Richard Rose of Strathclyde University.

The worry for the pollsters is that now well-established British phenomenon of the underdog effect was at work in 2001. In every recent election save one, 1987, the party ahead in the polls in the last week has ended up with fewer votes than forecast. Why? Critics say it is Labour bias (but in that case it was Conservative bias in 1983), and that sampling is primarily to blame. We are convinced it is primarily a form of "late swing", though this is frequently dismissed by critics, unfairly in our view. By "late swing" we mean all forms of last minute changes of mind, including voters staying at home or differential turnout.

Table 88: Error in the "Poll of Polls", 1945-2001

	Conservatives	Labour	Liberal Democrats
	%	%	%
1945	+2	-2	+1
1950	+1	-3	+1
1951	+2	-4	+1
1955	+1	+1	-1
1959	0	+1	0
1964	+1	+1	-1
1966	-1	+3	-1
1970	-2	+4	-1
1974 Feb	0	-2	+2
1974 Oct	-2	+2	0
1979	0	+1	0
1983	+2	-2	0
1987	-1	+2	-1
1992	-5	+4	+1
1997	0	+3	-1
2001	-1	+3	-1
Average	*-0.19*	*0.75*	*-0.06*

All we can say is at the moment there is a clear tendency to over-estimate Labour, which seems to be related to late swing or differential turnout – but it is not clear whether the bias is to Labour as such or to Labour as the party ahead in the polls. Perhaps there is both. Any analysis is complicated by the fact that the biggest over-estimate was in 1992, when there were clearly other distorting factors as well. All other things being equal we would expect the underdog effect to be least in 1992, when the race was perceived to be a close one.

We think we are interviewing the right people, but not always getting the right answers. We don't think that the samples are the problem. Why? Let's look at the evidence, and how it is related to the methodologies of the polls.

Methodology

Polling is a simple business, all you have to do is ask the right sample the right questions and add up the figures correctly. For fifty years and more, the questions asked were more or less the same by all polling organisations, the sampling was more of less the same type of quota samples or taking names at random off the electoral roll, and the figures were added up in the same way. It isn't like that any more.

Polling is a marriage of the art of asking questions and the science of sampling. At MORI, since its entry into the public polling arena in 1975 for the *Sunday Times*, we have made our methodology transparent, and open to inspection for anyone who wishes to see how we obtain the findings which our clients publish in their newspapers, radio and television. Before discussing the details of how the various current methodologies differ and why, let us explain in detail how MORI's methodology works.

Basic nuts and bolts of polling

To begin with the pure mechanics, how do we ask respondents their voting intention? The British pollsters for some years have followed the Gallup method of determining voting intention, asking a two part question. This is the traditional way, which MORI has used for more than 30 years. These are usually the first questions asked on the questionnaire, and the procedure is the same whether the interview is being conducted face-to-face or by telephone.

The first question is:

Q. *How would you vote if there were a General Election tomorrow?*

or, once the election has been called

Q. *How do you intend to vote in the election on June 7th?*

Our interviewers record responses to this question as one of the following:

Conservative
Labour
Liberal Democrats
Scottish National Party/Plaid Cymru
Green Party
Democratic/UKIP/Referendum Party
Other
Would not vote
Undecided
Refused

Note that in our traditional methodology we don't prompt our respondents by suggesting the parties that they might pick, or by reading them a list. Although we have a single category for "other", in our regular face-to-face polls we record in every case which particular party this response represents – there are no parties missed out or excluded from our polls, and if any supposedly minor party made a sudden breakthrough in support, our polls would detect it. But in practice the "other" category rarely accounts for even 1% of responses, and consequently we don't always feel the need to distinguish between the very minor parties in our telephone polls.

Leaving aside those who say at that point they would not vote, we ask those who say that they are undecided or refuse to say for which party they would vote for,

Q. *Which party are you most inclined to support?*

As a frame of reference, figures of 30% undecided, 10% would not vote and 3% refused would not be unusual at the first question, and when asked the second, the undecideds drop to 10% and the refusals to 2%.

This follow-up question, often called the "squeeze" question, tends to find that many of those whose initial reaction is not to plump for any party have, nevertheless, a clear inclination or party preference. The voting figures that are reported are, therefore, the "combined voting" figures calculated by taking together the answers from Q1 and Q2. (Past experience at elections has shown that the combined figures are a better guide to the electorate's voting behaviour than the figures from Q1 alone – at most general elections most of the "incliners" still vote. The separate breakdown of figures for Q1 and Q2 is not always reported, but is always available if required by contacting MORI.)

For the combined voting figures we simply add together for each party those who named it in response to either question. Those who said they "would not vote" at either question are similarly added together, while the residual "undecided" and "refused" respondents are those who still gave this response having been asked both Q1 and Q2.

For the final two *Times* polls of the 2001 campaign, MORI used a different questioning method, exactly as we had done in the final poll of 1997. Instead of asking the questions without prompting respondents with any possible answers, our interviewers showed them a list of all the candidates standing in their constituency, in the order in which they would appear on the ballot paper. (We couldn't do this before the penultimate week, of course, as we had to wait until nominations had closed before we knew who the candidates would be.) The details of the methodology and the change in showing the names on the ballot was helpfully explained in Peter Riddell's column in *The Times* the day the poll was published.[168]

The next stage is weighting the data. Weighting is a statistical procedure, carried out by computer, which simply compensates for any known

---

[168] Peter Riddell, "Labour loses from change to polling method", *The Times*, 31 May 2001.

unrepresentativeness in the sample. For example, women make up 52% of the British adult population; if we were to find that in one poll they made up 55% of the sample, the computer would downweight their answers slightly to ensure that in the final figures the opinions of women contributed the correct 52% of the numbers and men the other 48%. In practice the effect of weighting is almost always very small, and represents fine-tuning of the data rather than anything more drastic.

The final stage is to "repercentage" the data to exclude the "don't knows", so that the final "headline figures" that we report are percentages of those who have a party preference, rather than of the whole population. This is for comparability with election results (which, of course, measure only those who have voted for a party or candidate, not those who have abstained) and with other voting intention polls. This practice has been standard in Britain for many years; in the USA, by contrast, there is no generally accepted convention and each company reports its figures in different ways – some exclude don't knows and some do not. The result is confusion and a situation in which no two poll results are comparable with each other.

Table 89: Calculation of Voting Intention Figures

	Q1 (unwtd)	Q2 (unwtd)	Q1+Q2 (unwtd)	Q1+Q2 (wtd)	Whole sample	Reper-cent-aged (head-line)
	n	*n*	*n*	*n*	%	%
Total	2,082	446	2,082	2,062		
Conservative	422	74	422+74=496	500	24%	31%
Labour	713	99	713+99=812	795	39%	50%
Liberal Democrat	185	35	185+35=220	218	11%	14%
SNP/PC	62	9	62+9=71	57	3%	4%
Green	9	4	9+4=13	15	1%	1%
Ref/UKIP/Dem	7	2	7+2=9	7	*	*
Other	4	0	4+0=4	3	*	*
Would not vote	234	10	234+10=244	257	12%	
Undecided	410	179	179	177	9%	
Refused	36	34	34	33	2%	

n.b. The 446 who were asked Q2 were the 410+36 who were either undecided or refused at Q1.

Source: MORI/ *Times* January 2001

Because we exclude "don't knows" from the final results, we are often accused of ignoring the don't knows. Not true. The omission of don't knows reflects the experience of more than sixty years of polling that the vast majority of this group will not eventually vote, and those that do generally split between the parties in similar proportions to those that give a voting preference. Our aim is clarity: we believe that presenting the data in this way makes its meaning and implications most easily comprehensible. Nevertheless, the percentages of don't knows are always published. In the reports of our polls for *The Times*, these figures are invariably given in the small print technical note at the end of the article; some other papers don't always report these figures (although we try to enforce it as far as we can, at least with our clients), but the full figures will always be available on request, and are published on our website.

Table 89 illustrates the entire process of calculating the figures, taken from the January 2001 poll.

A separate problem is to determine at what point in the questionnaire the voting intention questions should be asked. Before the foundation of the Social Democratic Party, the voting intentions questions were asked as the fourth or fifth question(s) in the questionnaire by Gallup, Marplan (the predecessor to ICM[169]), NOP, Harris (originally ORC) and MORI, following after leader satisfaction and issues questions. However, when the SDP was established, empirical tests showed that asking about satisfaction with the party leaders, including David Steel for the Liberals and David Owen for the SDP, boosted the SDP's share of vote by around 3% when asked afterwards.

ASL, polling on the telephone in the 1983 general election, continued to ask the voting intention question(s) in the traditional fifth place, but the others started asking voting up front (somewhat to the consternation of interviewers) in both face-to-face interviews and on the telephone. In the election that year, the final polls by Gallup, Harris, MORI and Marplan said they expected the SDP-Liberal Alliance to get 26% of the vote; ASL 29%. On the day, the Alliance got 26%.

---

[169] Marplan is still in existence as a market research company, but does not do political polling

Since then all the established companies have normally asked voting intention at or near the head of the interview (though likelihood of voting sometimes comes first). An exception this time was the British Election Survey. The BES asked voting intention in questions 6 and 7, after asking first interest in the election, the single most important issue in this election, which party they thought best able to handle this issue, likelihood of voting (using an 11 point scale from 0 to 10), if the respondent had decided, and then they ask: "Which party will you vote for?" of those who say they are decided, and then "Which party do you think you are most likely to vote for?"

The most obvious methodological variation between the polling companies these days is the difference between face-to-face and telephone interviewing. The distinction is not just the physical one of how questions are asked and answered, but it dictates the possible sampling methods. Up to 1992, all the major companies interviewed face-to-face, often in street.[170] After the 1992 election, when all the polls were further adrift than they should have been, a Market Research Society Enquiry investigated various aspects of the polls. A great deal of methodological testing was undertaken, including an examination of telephone against face-to-face, one-day polls against multiple day polls, weekend interviewing against weekday interviewing, in-street against in-home interviewing, etc., and no statistical difference was found between any of these methodologies. However, there was general agreement that one of the problems had been in the sampling. Since then, MORI has completely redesigned its face-to-face samples; meanwhile all the polling organisations other than MORI have moved to telephone polling, with its entirely distinct sampling methods, usually described as 'quasi-random'.

Only MORI continues to interview in home, face-to-face, now using CAPI (Computer Aided Personal Interviewing), in its polls for *The Times*

---

[170] None of the companies now conducts election polls in street, even though this is the wide-spread assumption fostered by the predilection of TV companies for filming in-street interviews. The popular misconception was picked up by the *Daily Express* (6 June 2001), which claimed "Monday lunchtime, Oxford Street... there, in the middle of the throng, stands Clipboard Girl, a nervous representative of one of our major polling companies. 'Excuse me,' she says timidly, 'have you got five minutes you could spare?'".

– though it also undertakes telephone polls for its other media clients. These are three-stage samples, the first selection of a representative set of constituencies, the second a random selection of a ward within each of these constituencies, though with a limiting condition to require that the ward selected should be sufficiently representative of the constituency, and finally a selection by our interviewers of respondents within the designated sampling point to fit a quota tailored to that sampling point's population.

Before we can look at this in more detail, we need to discuss the basics of sampling. Perhaps the question we are asked most often is "How can a sample of only 1,000 or 2,000 possibly reflect the opinions of 42 million Britons within a 3% margin of error?".

There is time-honoured answer to this question that goes back to George Gallup, the American who first developed opinion polling in the 1930s: if you have a large bowl of soup, you don't have to drink the whole bowl to decide if it has too much salt in it – just stir it well, and one spoonful will suffice.

Of course, finding a representative sample is not really as easy as stirring soup. The theory of representative samples is derived from the mathematical science called statistics, which dictates how to judge the probability of different events. The study of probability was originally developed to understand the gambling odds involved in various permutations of dice throws or playing cards, and we can use a simple example to illustrate the theory behind sampling. Suppose you have four playing cards in front of you, a heart, a club, a diamond and a spade. If you were to shuffle them together and pick two of them at random, it is not too hard to work out how likely it is that you will pick one red and one black card. There are six different possible pairs that you could pick, each equally likely: two of those six are pairs of the same colour, the diamond and the heart or the spade and the club, the other four are mixed. So there are four chances in six, or 66.6%, that you will pick one red and one black card.

Now suppose you have the whole pack of 52 cards. You can work out in exactly the same way how likely you would be to pick one red and one black card, although it will take you a lot longer to count all the possible pairs; but instead of counting, a simple mathematical calculation will tell you how many pairs there must be. (The first card can be any of 52, and the second any of the remaining 51, so there are 52 x 51 possibilities. This is double the total number of possible pairs, because you can pick each possible pair two ways depending on which of the two cards comes out first.) From here it is a simple step to working out the formula that will tell you how likely it is that any six cards you pick will be split equally between red and black, or any fourteen cards. Or, indeed, how likely you are to get any other combination of red and black.

Now suppose you don't know for certain that the 52 cards in front of you are necessarily a full pack: there may be more than 26 red cards, or there may be fewer. But if you pick, say, ten of them at random and find that five are red, you can work out how likely that would be if 26 of the whole pack were red, and how likely if 30 were red, and how likely if 35 were red, and so on. In short, it gives you a best guess for the number of red cards in the whole pack, and a margin of error (or "confidence interval"). Then, when you know how likely it is that any given number of randomly drawn cards will have the same split of reds and blacks as the whole pack – what we call being representative – you can work out how many cards you need to pick before you reach a given level of certainty.

Sample survey reliability works the same way – but on a much larger scale. Instead of 52 cards, we have 42 million adults to pick from. Using exactly the same mathematical principles (although the formulas have got a great deal more complicated now), we can find that 19 out of 20 of all the samples which could possibly be drawn will yield an outcome within 3% of the true percentage among the population. The most likely outcome is the true percentage of whatever it is we are measuring; next most likely are outcomes very close to this true percentage. One in 20 of the possible samples are outside this 3% range. This is what is meant by the "3% margin of error" that is often – especially in the USA though sometimes here as well – tagged onto the end of news reports of poll stories.

The important rule in sampling is how the respondents are selected. In theory, the most reliable sample selects poll respondents randomly – which does not mean haphazardly! A random sample, also called a probability sample, is one that ensures that everybody in the population being surveyed has an equal chance of being selected for interview. In reality, a pure random sample is not always practical – apart from any other considerations, it takes a lot of time because once you have selected your target respondents you have to make repeated attempts to contact them; even after weeks, the chances are that the response rate will be a long way short of 100%, and those that have not been contacted or who have refused to take part may well be systematically different from those who have been interviewed ... besides which, of course, an opinion poll which takes weeks to conduct may be out of date by the time it has been completed, of very little use when issues or political opinions which might change daily are in view! For this reason, most face-to-face polls in Britain use quota sampling which pre-determines the demographic make-up of the sample to ensure it matches the profile of the whole adult population, as indeed do many of the quasi-random telephone polls. Both usually incorporate elements of random sampling as well, such as selecting telephone numbers by random digit dialling or, in the case of face-to-face interviews, randomly selecting the areas where the interviews are conducted. The quotas ensure, in theory, that we don't over-represent any groups that are easier to find, and that for every potential respondent who won't take part we replace them with somebody of similar views who will. Historically in Britain, the record of quota samples in predicting elections has been better than that of random samples.

ICM and Gallup interview on the telephone, which gives a potential random sample, excluding of course the small number who are not on the telephone, though raising extra difficulties in giving everybody a theoretically equal chance of being polled, since one single telephone number may reach a household containing several adults, while other people can be called on several numbers.

For any given sampling design, in theory the larger the sample the more accurate the survey can be expected to be; but the benefits of increasing the sample size beyond a certain point are small. In the case of pure random samples, the mathematics dictates that doubling the sample size only makes the margin of error half as good again, so there is a point beyond which the extra expense of larger samples is wasted. One frequent reason for larger samples, which does justify the expense, is to allow small subgroups of the population (first-time voters, for example, or readers of a particular newspaper) to be examined and compared.

The Tories would very much like to believe that there is something fundamentally wrong with the polls, so that they have an excuse to disregard them. But shooting the messenger is rarely the wisest solution.

In line with Central Office thinking, the *Daily Telegraph* has several times attacked the credibility of the polls in general, and on occasion when we published a poll result particularly worrying to the party, MORI in particular. Fair enough, perhaps, if the criticisms were accurate; but they were not.

The *Telegraph* stated "face-to-face interviews ... tended to be biased because Tory voters spend more time at work."[171] This is nonsense. Any competent pollster can allow for such factors in the quotas or weighting used in the poll design, so that the sample accurately represents all work patterns. (If it were a problem, polling by telephone would be little better, since different groups of voters are at home and available to be telephoned for different fractions of time). Incidentally, at the time this attack was published, the pollsters – whether using telephone or face-to-face interviewing – were in complete agreement on the current standing of the Tories! [172] Another *Telegraph* editorial[173] later in the year again suggested that face-to-face polls tend to find lower Conservative support

---

[171] "Tory vote", *Daily Telegraph*, 14 February 2000.
[172] MORI's last two published face-to-face polls (in *The Times*) had put the Conservative share at 28% and 30%, and our last telephone poll (in the *Daily Mail*) on 29%; ICM's last two telephone polls (in the *Guardian*) put them at 29% and 30%, and Gallup's (in the *Telegraph* itself) at 30% and 28%. In other words, 29% plus or minus 1% in seven polls, two in person and five over the telephone.
[173] "The Tories can win", *Daily Telegraph*, 5 December 2000.

than telephone polls. Not so. We wrote to the paper correcting these errors, but it failed to publish our letter.

We might hope that the telephone versus face-to-face, quota versus random myth will be finally laid to rest by the final polls in 2001 with the predicted Conservative shares being NOP (telephone/quasi-random) 30%, Gallup (telephone/quasi-random) 30%, ICM (telephone/quasi-random) 32% and – agreeing with two of the three telephone pollsters – MORI (face-to-face/quota) 30%. (Indeed, ICM's second-last poll also had the Tories on 30%).

But no doubt some will dismiss this as a fluke, so let us take a more robust body of evidence. Throughout the year 2000 three regular monthly poll series measured voting intention in Great Britain: MORI for *The Times*, with samples of c. 2,000, conducted face-to-face, in home, with a quota sample; Gallup for the *Daily Telegraph*; ICM for the *Guardian*. Both Gallup and ICM interviewed telephone samples of c. 1,000. The table shows the average results over the year of each of the three main monthly poll series[174].

Table 90: Poll averages (monthly series), 2000

	Sampling	Con %	Lab %	LDem %	Other %
MORI/ *Times* (face-to-face)	Quota	31.3	47.7	14.9	6.1
Gallup/ *Telegraph* (telephone)	Quasi-random	31.9	47.3	14.3	6.3
ICM/ *Guardian* (telephone)	Quasi-random	33.3	42.3	17.7	7.2

It is plain that there is no systematic difference between face-to-face and telephone poll results; in fact, there is virtually nothing to choose between MORI and Gallup. In many months, indeed, all three polls were in close agreement; and, as they are conducted at different times of the month, where there were differences it may well simply have reflected real changes in public opinion between the fieldwork periods. Furthermore, of course, all polls are subject to sampling variation ('margin of error'), so some differences between any group of polls are

---

[174] There are twelve polls in each series (the extra poll Gallup published in the *Telegraph* in September has been excluded to ensure that the time spread is as even as possible).

259

only to be expected. While most of the effect of sampling variation is likely to cancel out over the course of year, the effect of differences in timing might remain.

One thing that is true, however, and is perhaps partly to blame for the misconceptions peddled by the *Telegraph*, is that MORI's telephone polls during the year 2000 tended to find a Labour share on average that was lower than the average of our face-to-face Times series. But the reason for this is not *how* the polls were conducted but *when* they were conducted.

Table 91: MORI Face to Face and Telephone Polls, 2000 – average findings

	Sampling	Con %	Lab %	L Dem %	Other %
MORI/ *Times* (face-to-face)	Quota	31.3	47.7	14.9	6.1
MORI telephone polls	Quasi-random	34.4	44.4	15.6	5.7

How can this be? At first glance it might seem it would be a highly unlikely coincidence that two sets of polls over the same year, differing only in the fieldwork dates, could both be accurately measuring public opinion and yet be this far apart. But this ignores the entirely different circumstances in which the polls are commissioned. Our *Times* polls are a fixed monthly series taking measurements at broadly regular intervals. The fieldwork dates are determined months in advance, and the poll goes ahead come rain come shine.

Our telephone polls, by contrast, are *ad hoc* affairs, usually commissioned at a couple of days' notice for one or another of our Sunday newspaper clients. Naturally enough, such polls tend to be commissioned when our clients think that they will give rise to a good story; and, equally naturally, given the course of politics over the last few years, a government in trouble is usually a more interesting news story than a government sailing serenely along. Consequently, our telephone polls have been disproportionately likely to be taken at periods of particular government unpopularity. (It is for this reason, among others, that we consider the trends from our regular monthly *Times* as the 'gold standard' among the polls; it is not that there is anything wrong with our other polls as snapshots of the public mood at the moment they are taken – which is what our clients want them for – but taken collectively they could present a selective and possibly distorted view of the course of events. The camera proverbially doesn't lie, but a photograph album shows those moments when the camera was on hand to take the snapshots.)

Table 92: MORI Face to Face and Telephone Polls, 2000 – comparison

	Con %	Lab %	LDem %	Other %	Lead %
25-27 Jan MORI/*Daily Mail**	29	49	15	7	-20
20-25 Jan MORI/*Times*	30	50	15	5	-20
	-1	-1	0	+2	0
17-19 May MORI/*Daily Mail**	33	46	14	7	-13
18-23 May MORI/*Times*	32	48	15	5	-16
	+1	-2	-1	+2	+3
22-23 Jun MORI/*News of the World**	34	47	14	5	-13
22-27 Jun MORI/*Times*	33	47	13	7	-14
	+1	0	+1	-2	+1
20-22 Jul MORI/*Mail on Sunday**	32	51	11	6	-19
20-24 Jul MORI/*Times*	33	49	12	6	-16
	-1	+2	-1	0	-3
17-18 Aug MORI/*News of the World**	32	51	12	5	-19
17-21 Aug MORI/*Times*	29	51	15	5	-22
	+3	0	-3	0	+3
21-22 Sep MORI/*Mail on Sunday**	39	35	21	5	4
21-26 Sep MORI/*Times*	35	37	21	7	-2
	+4	-2	0	-2	+6
24-25 Nov MORI/*Mail on Sunday**	34	47	13	6	-13
23-28 Nov MORI/*Times*	33	48	13	6	-15
	+1	-1	0	0	+2
13-15 Dec MORI/*News of the World**	32	47	16	5	-15
7-12 Dec MORI/*Times*	34	46	14	6	-12
	-2	+1	+2	-1	-3
Average telephone	33	47	15	5	-14
Average Times (face-to-face)	32	47	15	6	-15
Average difference	+1	0	0	-1	+1
Telephone average (exc. September)	32	48	14	6	-16
Times average (exc. September)	32	48	14	6	-16
Difference	0	0	0	0	0
*=telephone poll					

Source: MORI

The polls in September illustrate this perfectly. At the end of August when our *Times* poll was taken, the government was riding high on William Hague's 14-pint interview and other matters. Then came the controversy over Dome funding, followed by the fuel crisis, and we in common with the other polling companies found a brief Tory lead as the government's popularity plummeted. By the time of our next poll for *The Times* the government recovery had begun – again, the other pollsters' data agrees – so in that period our telephone polls on average found a much rosier picture for the Tories. But it certainly wasn't because telephone polls are methodologically more friendly to the Tories!

In fact, on the few occasions in the year when it was possible directly to test the two methods against each other – when we were commissioned to conduct a telephone poll over the same weekend when our face-to-face interviewers were in the field on our poll for *The Times*, or immediately after they finished – the results were very similar, as Table 92 shows.

Almost all the differences are within the normal limits of sampling error, and are not systematic – sometimes the telephone poll finds a bigger Labour lead, sometimes the *Times* poll does. The only big difference is in September, which was at a period when other polls were also finding sharp changes over short periods, and even the difference between a Thursday-Friday poll and a Thursday-Tuesday poll, with the bulk of interviews on the Saturday and Sunday, could perfectly plausibly account for the change. Excluding September, the figures are identical over the year to the nearest whole number, as the last line of the table shows.

Nevertheless, it is true that there were significant differences between the main poll series of the different companies during the last parliament. But as Table 90 shows, the odd man out is not MORI but ICM, and the biggest difference is not in the standing of the Tories but of Labour. ICM's Labour share has tended to be several points lower, with the Liberal Democrats usually correspondingly higher – hence the Labour lead over the Tories is lower in ICM's polls, even though the measurement of Conservative share is not too far out of line.

John Curtice, writing in the *Independent*'s "Rough Guide to the Election" concluded: "Throughout the last parliament ICM has consistently recorded a lower Labour lead than either MORI or Gallup. One of them, at least, is wrong." Not necessarily. Maybe they are measuring different things?

It is in the Labour rather than Conservative share that there is the most persistent discrepancy between ICM on the one hand and MORI and Gallup on the other. We have long argued that this was probably an effect of question wording (and were often glibly dismissed for our pains). Up to the 2001 election MORI, and Gallup, continued to use the traditional wording of the voting intention question as it has been used for most of the sixty-plus years that there have been opinion polls in Britain: *"Q. How would you vote if there was a General Election tomorrow?"*. ICM by contrast, have used a different question for several years, which names the parties: *"Q. The Conservatives, Labour, the Liberal Democrats and other parties would fight an immediate general election in your constituency. Please tell me which party you think you would actually vote for in the polling station."* Unlike the other pollsters, ICM are reminding respondents of the possibility of voting LibDem, and it has long been recognised that using such a preamble is liable to push up the LibDem share in any poll in mid-Parliament – the result is that there is a switch to LibDem from Labour as compared with other companies' polls.

Why? Pollsters have acknowledged for many years that between elections many potential supporters of the centre party (Liberal Democrats now, Alliance or Liberal as they once were) seem to forget its existence. Invariably questions about voting at the previous election after a couple of years have passed tend to find a much lower reported Liberal vote than was really the case. (And nobody has ever seriously suggested that there is a spiral of silence against the Liberals.) The same effect depresses Liberal Democrat voting intention – as can often be seen when a by-election raises their profile and causes a sudden upward blip in their national ratings.

However, during the 2001 election, both Gallup and MORI altered their question wordings. For the final few polls, all three companies prompted the respondents with the possible choices – with the names of the main parties, in the case of ICM and Gallup, or with the names of all the candidates and their parties standing in that constituency, in MORI's case. MORI made a change in the question methodology with the closing of nominations, as in the final poll in 1997; until the close of nominations, MORI used an open-ended question of "How do you intend to vote in the General Election on June 7?". The week-on-week comparison of the two MORI/*Times* polls before and after the change in question method would suggest that this cut Labour's share by 7 points and increased that of the Lib Dems by 5, though this probably exaggerates the effect as the shift in the figures may also incorporate sampling variation and a real swing in attitudes over the week independent of the polling method.

Immediately after MORI switched questioning methods, ICM, Gallup and MORI had near identical results. (Indeed, uncharacteristically, it was ICM that had the lowest Tory share).

Table 93: ICM, Gallup and MORI results, end of May 2001

	Fieldwork	Con %	Lab %	LD %	Other %
ICM/*Guardian*	26-28 May	28	47	17	8
Gallup/*Daily Telegraph*	28-29 May	31	47	16	6
MORI/*The Times*	29 May	30	48	16	6

Not, as they say, a cigarette paper between them.

So who is right, ICM or MORI? Depends what you are trying to measure. Following the Market Research Society's Review after the 1992 British General Election when the pollsters were castigated for their error in "forecasting" (sic) the result, some polling organisations started attempting not to measure public opinion at the time the interviews were conducted, but to forecast how people would vote in a hypothetical election some weeks or months or even years ahead before the general election is called, or once the Prime Minister does set the date, to forecast weeks and then days ahead what the outcome is likely to be.

We have always taken a different view. Between elections, the question on voting intention is effectively a hypothetical one. We try to measure the mood of the nation as a whole regarding the parties. We want to avoid adding any elements that might cause our respondents to be unrepresentative or different from the rest of the public; therefore we don't artificially remind them of the possibility of supporting other parties if such ideas are not in their minds already, because our respondents represent the wider public who do not have such thoughts either. We do not "prompt" as we believe we are taking the pulse of the nation at that point in time, not trying to judge in some abstract way what might happen if there had been an election on the following day, when the respondent knows full well that there will not be.

The function of the final polls in an election, though, is rather different. Once the election is called, there are some changes we have always made. We change our question wording from the "How would you vote if there were a general election tomorrow?", which is asked month in and month out until the Prime Minister calls an election, to "How do you intend to vote at the general election on [June 7]?"; already we have shifted from measuring a hypothetical election to a real one.

Our last poll has to be designed to provide as much information as possible to predict the result of the election; here we are interested in finding out what the voters will actually do in the polling booth, and need to confront them with the real choice that they will face so as to judge their reactions. Therefore a different measuring tool is needed, and the results may be different. This poll – and this poll alone – is a forecast, for the final polls taken on the eve of elections are designed to do just that, unlike (in our view) polls in between elections. Consequently, we don't simply report the raw figures, we take other measurements to help understand their implications as predictors of the future. In the past we have asked certainty of voting, care who wins, definitely decided, even will you vote if it rains, and of course we record those who say they will not vote, are undecided and those who refuse to say. We then look at the impact of each of these on the voting intentions recorded 'raw', and judge if there is an argument to apply all or any combination of these to our final projection. We also ring back some people who we have interviewed before to see if they have shifted and, if so, in which direction.

It is then, explaining openly what we have done, that we turn from being reporters of the views of the public, to forecasters of voting behaviour. Then, on the eve of poll, recognising that in those last 24 hours, even in the polling booth, some people will change their minds. But this final forecast is still tied to the polling data.

We work within the limits of sampling, and the vagaries of turnout, weather, last minute events, and other factors which limit the ability of anyone, whether they be weather forecasters or economists, to foretell the future. We try hard, and can never, except by luck, be spot on. Why some interviewers on the media expect us to be just says we haven't done enough to educate them in the limits of our trade.

And, as well as this extra interpretation that we apply to the figures, we change the way we do the poll as well. For one thing, we usually have a bigger sample size and extra sampling points, to reduce the statistical margin of error. But, more fundamentally, we shift to a replication of the ballot, with the names of the candidates in each constituency shown to the respondent. In 1997, we did this only in the final poll; in 2001, we decided to switch a week earlier, as soon as it was possible to do so. Between the moment where the election is first called and the final poll, it is something of a grey area in terms of exactly what we are measuring; we are no longer asking about an entirely hypothetical election, but nor are we predicting the future. We took the view that the most appropriate point to switch methods was once the final lists of candidates were available, at which point the various local factors can be properly brought into the equation. In particular, electors can begin to make their calculations about tactical voting and to realise which other parties apart from the big two are standing in their constituency. The difference from the previous week, as we said, was to cut Labour's share by 7 points.

Incidentally, it would be easy to misunderstand the implications of the difference in the figures by thinking in terms of the Labour lead over the Conservatives. Simply because the Labour lead is lower on the prompted poll figures, this does not imply better news for the Conservatives. In fact the Conservative share of the vote has not been affected; but there is a shift from Labour to the Liberal Democrats and smaller parties. If anything, this implies a worse position for the Tories as the Liberal Democrat increase is greatest in the seats where the Conservatives and Liberal Democrats stand first and second, where Labour votes would be wasted in any case.

To make things absolutely clear: MORI does not weight its samples for past voting. We did not change our sampling methods, and continued to interview face to face, in home. MORI switched to showing respondents a list of the candidates standing in their constituency. This was not copying ICM or anybody else: the method is not used by ICM or, so far as we know, any other pollster in Britain today (and is extremely difficult using current telephone sampling techniques), though Robert Waller has reminded us that he did it years ago when doing the Harris polls using of course the face-to-face methodology. Finally, MORI's switch in technique is not an adjustment for "shy Tories" – it had no effect on the Conservative share.

But it does reflect out discomfort at the way our polls are reported, especially the secondary reporting. Reluctantly we have come to the conclusion that although we believe the traditional way is purer, more informative, and abandoning it will effectively throw away 30 years of trend data, the perpetual misreporting and misunderstanding of the figures by the media in its secondary reporting means that the public is probably being misled. For all the excellence of Peter Riddell's reporting of our work in *The Times*, and several of his counterparts on other papers working with us and other companies, it is almost inevitable that most of those who hear about our polls read only the headlines, glance at the graphics or rely entirely on secondary reports. Our figures do not mean what the public have been led to think they mean, and we have eventually decided we must change the way we produce the figures so that they do mean what most people think they mean, however damaging that is to their underlying value. As we say, we do it with extreme reluctance.

The second major methodological difference is the question of whether the polls need to compensate for the alleged existence of "shy Tories". ICM "adjusts" its data by weighting on the basis of respondents' reported vote at the last election, to correct for a supposed "spiral of silence". Before the last election this adjustment was often of the order of several percentage points added to the Tory and subtracted from the Labour share. We have always believed that, even if the shy Tory phenomenon was real, the ICM adjustment was an overcompensation. After the 1997 election, ICM stopped publishing its unadjusted data, so we could only guess how much difference the adjustment was making; but since their figures for Conservative share were only a little higher than MORI's unadjusted data (and Gallup's), it seemed likely that the effect is now much smaller than it used to be. The 'spiral of silence', if it ever existed here, has unwound.

In February 2000, the *Telegraph* perpetuated another canard: "opinion surveys have tended to underestimate the actual level of Conservative support" [175] – they haven't, and this misunderstanding is at the heart of a proper diagnosis of what little was wrong with the polls in 2001. Apart from the exception of the 1992 general election (after which all the polling companies extensively reviewed and reformed their methodologies), the polls have measured Conservative strength remarkably well. More recently, the polls have measured Tory support perfectly well in both the European elections and by-elections. MORI's last poll before the European election found just over 8% of adults "certain to vote" and supporting the Conservatives, the measure we would have used had we produced a prediction (which we didn't, as the poll was more than a fortnight before the election) – that would project to a Conservative vote of 3.54 million, and the actual Tory vote was 3.6 million. Our poll in the Eddisbury by-election (again, more than a week before the contest and therefore not published as a prediction) measured

---

[175] "Tory vote", *Daily Telegraph*, 14 February 2000.

the Conservative share of the vote within 1% and the margin of victory within 2%. So where were those 'shy Tories'?

The *Telegraph* went on to say "most of them [the pollsters] were wrong again in 1997" – not so. Four of the five final polls in 1997 were within the accepted 3% margin of error for the Conservative share – two overestimates (Gallup and ICM), one underestimate (MORI), and one spot-on to the nearest whole number (Harris).

It is true that polls taken some time before an election currently seem to find more Labour supporters than eventually vote Labour. But there is no mystery about this: we know that as polling day approaches, some of those Labour supporters will switch to the Liberal Democrats or minor parties, and others will decide it is not worth their while voting at all.

William Hague had to say throughout this campaign that he didn't read the polls, didn't believe the polls, that what the polls were saying wasn't what they were finding on the ground, and that he was talking to "real people". We wonder who he thought we were talking to? And much more systematically and objectively than he was.

Now we know he was studying the polls carefully, as befits the serious and thorough person he is, and he took very seriously his ratings as long ago as 1999, when he set his own target for survival. He fought the good fight, and I don't begrudge him the cry that there is a "hidden majority" out there (which I first heard from the campaign manager of Barry Goldwater in the 1964 American Presidential Election when he was convincingly trounced by President Lyndon Johnson). But the "hidden majority" didn't exist then, and it doesn't now.

One reason sometimes given for believing that the polls are distorted by "shy Tories", and that the polls' samples under-represent Conservatives, is the response to the past vote question. MORI's political polls, and most others, frequently include a question asking respondents how they voted at the last general election.

Some critics are so naïve as to simply take the percentages saying they voted for each party and compare the poll to the result of the election. However, although the responses are useful to us in a number of ways, we do not expect them to be an entirely accurate reflection of how the respondents did, in fact, vote. Consequently the responses of a representative sample will *not* normally match the actual result of the last election, and the fact that a sample's recalled vote differs from the election result is not evidence that the sample is unrepresentative.

The phenomenon of inaccurate recall of past vote has been known in Britain for many years. It was noted in the Sixties that recall of Liberal vote tended to be lower than reality in polls between elections, and there has also been a general tendency for more respondents to claim to have voted than actually did so. MORI was aware of this back in the mid-1970s, and Peter Kellner, who was then our 'link' at the *Sunday Times*, wrote it up for that newspaper. Himmelweit, Biberian and Stockdale produced a seminal paper on the subject in the *British Journal of Political Science* in 1978. [176]

This phenomenon is not confined to Britain: in the USA, for example, where John F Kennedy won the Presidency by a tiny margin, the margin on recalled vote steadily increased during his term, and, after he was killed, some two-thirds recalled that they had voted for him!

That the failure of the recalled vote on surveys to match the actual result is caused by inaccuracy of recall, rather than by unrepresentativeness of the samples, is relatively easy to demonstrate. One obvious point is that the polls have a generally good record of final election prediction, which would not be the case if past voters for a particular party were systematically under-represented. In the case of the Liberals/Alliance/Lib Dems, whose share of the vote has been most consistently undercounted by the vote recall question, the average finding of the final election day polls has not been out by more than one percentage point in 'predicting' the share in any of the last seven elections. The unreliability of recall has also been demonstrated experimentally on a number of occasions using a

---

[176] H. Himmelweit, M. Biberian and J. Stockdale, 'Memory for Past Vote: Implications of a Study of Bias in recall', *British Journal of Political Science 8,* pp 365-375 (1978).

panel survey, where the same respondents are questioned about their past vote on more than one occasion, and can be shown to have given inconsistent answers.

The pattern of answers to the vote recall question from 1997 to 2001 was generally consistent, and in particular the proportion of people who say that they voted Conservative in 1997 (supposedly the group we weren't interviewing enough of!) is usually quite accurate; however people who did not actually vote in 1997 seem liable to say that they voted Labour even if they did not, and the number remembering having voted Liberal Democrat, though initially accurate, eventually became consistently lower than the number who actually did.

Table 94 shows MORI's findings from the vote recall question since 1997, which should be compared with the election result (expressed as percentages of the adult population rather than of those who voted) shown in the top line.

Some polling companies, including ICM, and now NOP, use recalled vote to help to establish a weighting factor for their polls. They do not, of course, simply weight to the actual result of the election, being fully aware of the phenomenon of inaccurate reported vote. But this raises the question, what targets do you set? How distorted should you expect the answers from a representative sample to be?

Weighting by past vote can be open to the criticism that the targets are entirely arbitrary. We could make the polls say anything we wanted by changing the past vote targets. Not, of course, that the companies who weight by past vote really do this. Though ICM is somewhat secretive about the details of its methodology, an article by John Curtice[177] implied that they used the British Election Panel Study as a source for target weights. (There is an obvious risk in this, since panel respondents tend to be more interested in politics than average, and their accuracy in vote recall may be higher than among the whole population, which would lead to exaggerated weighting factors.)

---

[177] John Curtice, "You can't believe what you tell the pollsters", *Sunday Telegraph*, 27 May 2001.

Table 94: Recall of past vote in MORI's polls 1997-2001

Q. *Which party did you vote for at the last General Election, in May 1997? If you are not sure, or did not vote, please say so.*

	Con	Lab	Lib Dem	Nat	Green	Referen- dumParty	Other	Did not vote	Too young	Can't rem- ember	Refused
	%	%	%	%	%	%	%	%	%	%	%
GE 1997 (Result)	22	32	12	2	*	2	1	29	-	-	-
1997											
June 20-23	22	42	14	2	*	1	1	15	*	*	2
July 25-28	21	46	13	2	*	2	*	14	*	*	2
Aug 21-25	23	44	13	1	*	1	*	14	1	1	2
Sep 26-29	23	45	10	1	*	1	*	16	1	*	2
Oct 24-27	22	46	10	1	*	1	*	15	1	1	2
Nov 21-24	22	45	13	2	*	1	*	14	1	*	2
Dec 12-15	21	45	10	2	*	1	1	16	1	1	2
1998											
Mar 20-23	22	46	10	2	*	1	1	14	1	1	2
July 17-21	23	43	12	2	*	1	*	15	1	1	2
Oct 23-26	20	45	12	2	*	*	*	16	2	1	1
1999											
Mar 19-22	19	47	12	2	*	1	1	14	2	1	2
July 23-26	21	41	10	2	*	*	*	19	4	1	2
Oct 22-25	20	47	7	2	*	*	*	18	2	2	2
Nov 19-22	19	45	9	2	*	*	*	18	3	2	2
Dec 10-14	21	43	10	2	0	1	0	17	4	1	1
2000											
Jan 20-25	21	42	11	2	*	1	1	15	3	2	2
Feb 17-22	20	47	8	1	*	*	*	16	3	2	2
Mar 23-28	20	44	10	2	*	*	1	17	4	1	1
Apr 13-18	19	41	10	2	*	*	*	22	3	1	1
May 18-23	18	40	9	3	1	*	1	21	4	2	1
Jun 22-27	20	41	8	3	*	*	*	21	3	2	1
Jul 20-24	21	45	8	2	*	1	1	16	3	2	1
Aug 17-21	20	44	10	1	*	*	1	16	3	2	2
Sept 21-26	20	44	10	2	1	1	*	15	4	2	2
Oct 19-23	22	38	10	2	*	*	*	18	4	2	2
Nov 23-28	21	43	10	2	*	*	*	18	3	2	1
Dec 7-12	22	42	9	2	*	*	1	17	4	1	1
2001											
Jan 18-22	19	45	9	2	*	1	*	15	5	2	2
Feb 15-20	18	42	11	2	1	*	1	19	4	1	2
Mar 22-27	21	44	9	2	*	*	*	15	5	1	1

Source: MORI

Normally we are not told how much difference this makes to ICM's results. However, for the ICM/*Guardian* poll of 13-14 May 2001, the full computer tabulations were published on the *Guardian*'s website, including the unweighted figures for the first time. The unweighted voting intentions of the entire sample of 1,004 were Conservative 29%, Labour 51%, Liberal Democrat 14%. But after applying weighting, which includes the ICM "adjustment" of setting a target weight for reported vote at the last election, the figures were shifted to Con 30% (up one point), Lab 47% (down 4) and LD 16% (up 2), a reduction in the lead of five points. (In the published headline figures, the lead was reduced by a further two points by taking the opinions only of those saying they were most likely to vote, giving final figures of Con 31%, Lab 46%, LD 16%.) Of course, the whole of this five-point reduction in the lead might not be attributable to the "adjustment", since it will also include any compensation required for demographic imbalance in the sample; but, at any rate, it gives some indication. (We should perhaps add that we will always make available for inspection the unweighted as well as weighted figures from any published MORI poll. We consider this a necessary part of the transparency of method which is the only way in the long-term to maintain confidence in the research industry. We include them on every set of tables.)

It also indicates another curious fact, of which we were previously unaware, that ICM's adjustment is apparently boosting the Lib Dems. And we understood it was all about shy Tories!

Weighting by reported past vote may be all very well if there is an imbalance in the samples. Although it may not be easy to decide what weights to use, weighting is the correct remedy for sampling bias – unless, of course, you can revamp the sampling to remove the bias. We believe this (removing the bias) is what we achieved in most respects after the 1992 election , and that although there may still be a bias – probably is, given the consistent over-measurement of the Labour share – it is not a sampling bias.

What is the alternative? A response bias or an interpretation bias. Despite having a representative sample, in one way or another the answers they are giving us are not helping us predict how they will vote sufficiently accurately. And a possible explanation for that response bias is not hard to find. What if people are consistently telling us they will vote, or have voted, Labour, when in fact they will not vote, or have not voted, at all?

We know, of course, that not everybody who expresses a voting intention will necessarily turn out and, furthermore, that in any particular election one party's supporters may be more likely to turn out than another's. Given a turnout of just 59%, with abstention that was clearly differential by party support, identifying which of the respondents would in fact vote was one pre-requisite to achieving an accurate prediction of the vote shares.

Turnout prediction has never been so vital a part of final poll projections in Britain in the past; but it is a familiar problem in the USA. For example, Humphrey Taylor, chairman of the Harris Poll, made this cogent analysis of the outcome analysed by various permutations in the US Presidential elections in November 2000.

> "The final nationwide telephone poll on the presidential election carried out by Harris finds that the two main candidates are so close that it is impossible to predict a winner. We don't know who will win.
>
> "The difficulty of predicting a winner is compounded by the fact that slightly different definitions of who will and who will not vote (i.e. the definition of likely voters) produces three different results:
>
> (1) Among those who say they are absolutely certain to vote, Gore has a 3-point lead;
>
> (2) Among those who are absolutely or quite certain to vote and say that the election result will make a great deal or quite a lot of difference, Bush has a 2-point lead;
>
> (3) Using a third possible definition, people who are absolutely certain to vote, and voted in 1996 or were too young to vote then, shows the two candidates tied.
>
> "It seems likely, therefore, that the results will depend on turnout. If the turnout falls below 50% as it did 4 years ago, that will be good for Bush. If, however, the Democrats are successful in turning out a higher proportion of some of their most loyal voters, such as African-Americans, then the

turnout might rise to 53 to 54% of all adults which would be good for Al Gore. The difference between a high and a low turnout could make the difference between a Gore and a Bush victory."

In Britain in 2001 we knew who was going to win, but in getting the numbers exactly right we faced the same problem – we needed to be able to spot which of the respondents in our final poll would vote.

Although the four established polling companies all attempted to do this, the details of their approaches differed. Three – MORI, ICM and NOP – relied on a direct question which asked respondents to assess their own likelihood of turning out, but the question wording and responses categories differed, as did the use that was made of the data derived.

Gallup's method, based on methods developed in their polling in the USA and helpfully described in some detail in an article on their website[178] (though not, unfortunately, expounded to readers of the *Daily Telegraph*), was more complex and perhaps more contentious. After screening for registered voters, they then used a battery of questions to discover 'the views, opinions and self-perceptions of the voters themselves as a mechanism for isolating likely voters', using a bundle of answers including "whether or not the individual voted in the last election" (notoriously inaccurate in the British polling history!), "how closely the person is following the election, how often they vote in elections, and so forth". From this they assign every respondent a numerical likelihood of voting, and then reduce the total sample down to a percentage that they think best estimates the percentage of the voting age population that will vote on Election Day. Thus they say if the turnout will be 70% in their estimation, they throw out the 30% of the sample least likely to vote, and that's what their voting intention figures is based upon.

Rasmussen also attempt to filter out likely voters, using screening questions on voting history, intention to vote, and 'other matters'.

---

[178] Frank Newport and Colleen Sullivan, "How Does Gallup Define 'Likely Voters'?", article at www.gallup.com.

Table 95: Likelihood of voting questions, 2001

Agency	Question	Response categories
NOP version (a)	Many people do not manage to vote at general elections, how certain is it that you will vote on June 7? Are you certain not to vote, very unlikely to vote, fairly unlikely to vote, fairly likely to vote, very likely to vote or certain to vote?	Certain not to vote Very unlikely to vote Fairly unlikely to vote Fairly likely to vote Very likely to vote Certain to vote
NOP version (b)	Many people do not vote in general elections, and some people expect turnout to be the lowest ever. How likely is it that you personally will vote on June 7?	Certain not to vote Very unlikely to vote Fairly unlikely to vote Fairly likely to vote Very likely to vote Certain to vote
Gallup*	How likely is it that you will go out and vote in the General Election?	Definitely will vote Probably will vote May vote Probably won't vote Definitely won't vote
ICM	How likely would you be to vote in an immediate general election?	On a scale of 1 to 10
MORI	(From this card), can you tell me how likely you are to get along to vote in the General Election?	Certain not to vote Not very likely to vote Quite likely to vote Very likely to vote Certain to vote

*Gallup question used in conjunction with information from other questions

There is surely an argument that this process is somewhat arbitrary. MORI, ICM and NOP all derive our estimates of expected turnout from our survey responses. Gallup guesses what the turnout will be, then applies it to manipulate the survey responses. Is this letting the tail wag the dog?

NOP, having not polled in the final week, published no final turnout projection. MORI (63%) and ICM (63%) both slightly overestimated – though ICM would have been much closer, 58%, if they had taken only those respondents giving themselves likelihood 10 of voting on a scale of 1 to 10, instead of taking points 9 and 10. It looks as if ICM's ten-point scale was a better discriminator than our verbal descriptive five-point scale, at least in this election.

MORI also differed from the other companies in reporting the results of the full sample, rather than those we expected to vote, as our headline figures, except in the final prediction poll; but the intentions of those certain to vote were also reported on most occasions in Peter Riddell's copy. ICM stuck to their filter throughout; Gallup, a little confusingly, switched from reporting all responses to those who they expected to vote part of the way through the campaign as they had done in earlier American elections.

Because we all over-estimated the final turnout, we would expect the party shares to be distorted if one party's supporters were more likely than another's to be identified as probable voters while not in fact voting. (The trouble with percentages is that if you get the base figure wrong, all the other figures are thrown out.)

We can understand this better if we do something that we never normally do, and consider the party support figures before re-percentaging.

Table 96: MORI, Gallup and ICM final polls 2001, not re-percentaged

Final polls without re-percentaging
(taking published turnout projections as prediction of non-voting)

	MORI	Gallup	ICM	Result
	Quota	Quasi-random	Quasi-random	
	%	%	%	%
Conservative	19	20	20	19
Labour	28	31	27	25
Liberal Democrat	11	12	12	11
Others	4	3	4	4
Non-voters*	37	34	37	41

*i.e. all assumed unlikely to vote and excluded from calculation of published "forecast"

Source: Estimates calculated from published poll forecasts

These percentages are estimates. MORI's final prediction poll had 63% certain to vote, the criterion that we use to distinguish those who are expected to vote from those who are not. ICM, using points 9 and 10 on their 10-point likelihood scale, also produced final figures based on a 63% turnout (though up to this stage they had used points 7 to 10 on the scale, and surprisingly Alan Travis did not draw attention to the change in his write-up of the poll for the *Guardian*). The Gallup projection seems to have been based on an expected 66% turnout[179].

Viewed in this light, it seems pretty clear that the method of sampling is not the problem. All three final polls have measured the Tories and Lib Dems right, either exactly or over-estimating by a single percentage point. But all three have also over-estimated Labour while under-estimating abstentions.

Of course it is *possible* that all three polls – based, remember, on different sampling methods with different corrections for the problems that are already understood – have in fact shared both a sampling bias in favour of Labour and at the same time a sampling variation that has fluked the Tory and Lib Dem shares right. Or perhaps we are oversampling Labour, undersampling the apathetic, yet the bias doesn't affect the other parties at all. But is hardly the simplest or most plausible explanation. (Note that in the same way MORI found exactly the right Tory vote in the European elections, while overestimating Labour support badly.) Far more likely is that our samples are representative, and that a significant proportion, about 4% of the total sample, are telling us they will vote Labour and then staying at home on the day.

Is this genuine last-minute decisions, or people who know they are unlikely to vote yet won't admit it? We think, but can't prove, it is predominantly the former.

William Hague's decision to play the "Queensland tactic" in the final week, effectively admitting defeat and asking the electorate to narrow the margin, seems to have been reasonably in tune with the public's mood. Although none of the polls found a significant shift towards the Tories before the final few hours of the election, there does seem at the very least to have been a differential abstention working against Labour

---

[179] Anthony King, "Four Weeks on Stump Fail to Sway Voters", analysis published on www.gallup.com.

that was stronger than most of the campaign polls suggested would occur. Our final phone recall found a definite softening of the Labour vote, and consequently our final figures forecast a narrower margin than the raw figures from the original face-to-face poll. Even so, the forecast over-estimated Labour. To be honest we expected this would be the case; but of course we don't allow ourselves to fiddle the figures even if we don't fully believe them. We have to publish what the poll tells us. The underdog effect bit us again.

Is there a solution to the underdog effect? Of course, we could weight by reported past vote, setting our weighting targets so as to reduce the Labour share by a couple of points while boosting the Tories, and it might get us nearer the result. But that would be fiddling the figures, because the only legitimate function of weighting is to compensate for an unrepresentative sample, and we don't believe that there is a consistent sampling error or bias. If you weight for an imbalance that isn't there, you distort the measurement of everything else in the poll. What we need to find is a better questioning method that successfully discriminates between abstainers and voters. We are working on it, of course, but we only get one chance every four or five years to try it out. What we do need is for the media – and their readers and viewers – to stop expecting the impossible, and accept that while polls are useful, they cannot predict what the public will do in the future if the public itself doesn't know. But we've been saying this for thirty years, and not enough people have heard.

Exit polls

In 1997, ITN's then political editor Michael Brunson used every warning device known to warn people watching the Election Night Programme on ITN to say not to pay too much attention to the MORI Exit Poll they'd spent so much money on, and we'd worked so hard to get right, as 'Exit polls have been wrong before...'. Interviewing me on *Powerhouse* during this election, he was generous in his apology for his scepticism four years earlier, but I suspect far fewer people were watching this excellent but unappreciated mid-day programme than were watching the 1997 ITN election-night broadcast.

In 2001, for once there was *nothing* at which the critics could carp in the performance of the exit polls. MORI's poll for ITN predicted Labour's final haul of seats within four, and NOP's for the BBC within five, neatly bracketing the actual result.

Table 97: Exit polls, 2001

Agency	Client	Sample	Con seats	Lab seats	LD seats	Other seats	Lab majority seats
MORI	ITV	13,667	154	417	58	30	175
NOP	BBC	17,368	177	408	44	30	157
Result			166	413	52	28	167

Both were purely prediction polls, to make the best estimate of the seats won by each party, without collecting demographic or attitudinal information which would have enabled deeper analysis of the result. In the poll designs, of course, MORI and NOP were simply meeting the requirements of their clients, who are more interested in having a reliable forecast to broadcast at the head of their election night coverage than analysis poll details. The trauma for the American networks of inaccurate forecasting in their coverage of the 2000 US Presidential elections no doubt reinforced this. Nevertheless, it is a pity that neither network felt the expense of a separate analysis exit poll justified – though the BBC, curiously, commissioned ICM to carry out an on-the-day national poll of similar content, yet having done so decided to suppress the results. Why? What on earth can the BBC gain by knowing more about the election than it is prepared to tell its viewers and listeners? Especially since we, the licence-fee payers, paid for it. We think we should be told!

For those interested in the details, MORI's exit poll was conducted in 100 polling stations, one in each of 100 constituencies chosen to be representative of the marginal seats – 70 of which were marginal between Conservative and Labour and 30 between Conservative and Liberal Democrat. Where we could, we polled in a polling station where we had polled at a previous general election, and could obtain a direct comparison of results. Where this was not possible (if the polling districts had been altered or abolished, so that comparison would not be valid, or where we had not polled in the constituency at the last election at all), we attempted to select the most typical ward in the constituency (using both local government electoral and census demographic data), and then the most representative polling district within that ward (relying purely on census data[180], and occasionally having to reject the first choice if the polling station proved physically unsuitable for the task – for example by having several doors through which voters could leave).

At each polling station throughout the day our team of interviewers selected emerging voters, using a fixed interval[181], and handed a ballot paper which we asked them to fill in and vote again, replicating the secret ballot and the choice of candidates that they had had in the real election. Just over 15% of those we approached declined to take part, and these we replaced by our interviewers approaching the next voter

---

[180] Observers of our exit polls from other countries are often unaware that British electoral law prohibits us from knowing the result of previous general elections at polling district or even ward level. Results may only be published for constituencies. This means that far more sophisticated psephological analysis (and a bit of educated guesswork) goes into designing British exit polls than is the case in, say, the USA where the result at the previous election in the precincts polled is a known fact.

[181] For example, we might interview every 7th elector to emerge. The interval was calculated for each polling station from the polling district electorate and our estimate of turnout, with the intention of interviewing c. 150 at each polling station during the day. As we slightly over-estimated turnout, our final total sample was a little smaller than the 15,000 we had chosen as our theoretical target.

(outside the fixed interval) of the same sex, broad age-band and apparent social class.

There will, inevitably, be comparisons drawn between the exit polls in Britain and those in the US elections of November 2000, which were widely blamed – almost entirely unjustly, as far as we can tell – for the fiasco of the TV networks calling the presidency first for Gore, then for Bush, before eventually admitting it was too close for them to call.

In fact the mis-projections in November depended little on the exit polls. To understand what happened, it is first necessary to understand how the American exit poll works. All five networks together with Associated Press rely on a single, jointly-sponsored, agency called Voter News Service (VNS), both to provide exit poll data and to collate and report the officially declared results, as well as to make psephologically-based projections from all of these. (There is a second national exit poll for analytical purposes, sponsored by the *Los Angeles Times*, but its findings are not available to the networks on the night for making projections.)

In recent elections, however, instead of relying totally on VNS for projected results, the networks have taken to employing their own desks of experts who examine the raw VNS data so that they can jump the gun and beat the competition by being the first to declare the result. So there are a number of teams of analysts, working from exactly the same data, but under considerable pressure to be the first to use it to reach the right result – which of course carries the risk that they may also reach the wrong result, although having several independent interpretations of the same data ought also to be a safeguard against misinterpretation. The record over the years, since Voter Research and Surveys (predecessor of VNS) was formed in 1990, has been very good: despite the plethora of elections reported, only one previous wrong call, when VNS was wrong in the New Hampshire Senate race in 1996.

Part of the confusion over the significance of the exit polls derives from the fact that "VNS data" is not just exit poll data, but also real election results; and that projections from VNS data are not necessarily made by VNS – who are, however, convenient scapegoats when the networks get it wrong.

At 7.50 p.m. Washington time, NBC used the VNS data to call Florida for Gore; CBS and CNN followed suit before VNS made the same pronouncement officially. It is not clear to what extent, if at all, inaccuracy in the exit poll data itself was a contributory factor. No exit poll data was involved when the networks called Florida for Bush at 2.15 a.m.; this was based on the declared results, both as published by the counties and as collated by VNS, and on the VNS estimate of the number of ballots still to be counted. In the belief that there were too few uncounted ballots in comparison to Bush's current lead for there to be a realistic chance of his losing, the networks declared a result. (VNS itself, in fact, never called Florida for Bush.) As it turned out, the number of ballots still to be counted had been underestimated, and once again the networks had to retract their calls.

One congressman has already announced that he plans to hold congressional hearings on the networks' misprojections, and various sources have demanded stringent new regulations on the exit polls and on the networks' reporting of election results. There was even, to our astonishment, a proposal to adopt a single-source exit poll here in Britain.

Perhaps the main reason why the errors of the American networks caused such controversy is that, because the USA is split into several time zones, the early projections of the vote are being broadcast well before all the polling stations have closed, perhaps potentially convincing some citizens that the election is already decided and that there is no point in their voting. But to pick on the exit polls for this reason seems misplaced, since the projections will in any case be made from the publicly declared official results from those precincts and counties which have already finished voting[182], and unless staggered voting times are

---

[182] This does not necessarily even involve waiting until the close of poll, since Dixville Notch and similar tiny communities considered traditional bellwethers normally count the votes and declare a result as soon as all the registered voters have voted, hours before the close (or even opening) of the poll elsewhere. It would probably take a constitutional amendment to stop them.

introduced the east coast results will always be ready before polling stations in the west have shut their doors.

But while there remain no restrictions in the USA there are now – somewhat unnecessarily, we believe – restrictions on the publication of exit poll data in Britain. Introduced in the Representation of the People Act 2000, it is now an offence to publish the results of any exit poll or other poll of how people have voted while the polling stations are still open. So much for Freedom of Information under this illiberal Labour Government which the British public re-elected with a landslide! There has never been a problem to my knowledge in the self-regulation agreed by the clients, BBC and ITN, and their polling organisations, that there would be no mention on air, and that the data would be closely held. Despite a good record, parliament has now decided that a ban is in order.

Just the Tuesday before polling day I learned that adding insult to injury, the Radio Broadcasting Authority has decreed, without so much as a word of consultation with the individual polling organisations or their association, the Association of Professional Opinion Polling Organisations, that no word about the election could touch the lips of any newsreader or commentator on radio from midnight Wednesday night until the polls closed at 10 p.m. on Thursday. ITN and the BBC TV have not been mandated by the ITC, but nevertheless, as usual, followed a policy not to discuss the election, including the results of the MORI and Gallup findings in the morning papers, after the polls opened at 7 a.m.

The broadcasting authorities have thus taken it upon themselves to substantially ignore the principles of freedom of information and free speech and impose these regulations without reference to either Parliament or the people

The polling industry has regulated itself perfectly well on this basis for more than 60 years; but, in the end, the new regulation on the exit polls only wounds our *amour-propre*, since it stops us doing something we don't want to do in the first place. And perhaps it will have beneficial effects if it prevents the spurious rumours of poll leaks that have too frequently in past elections swept the City in a blatant manipulation of share prices; a phenomenon that we were pleased (and surprised) to note did not occur, so far as we know, in the 2001 election. Because, we suspect, the expectation of a Labour landslide and the lack of financial fear of a Labour victory was thought by the fly boys to have left no margin for their manipulation of the stock market.

Private polls

Private polling for the parties is now a part of elections which is taken for granted, even though it is excoriated by those who consider that taking the voters' preferences into account is a betrayal of political principle and an abdication of the responsibilities of leadership.

At any rate, the principle is hardly new. The turning point came in 1832. "The indirect influences of the Reform Act has not been inconsiderable, and has led to vast consequences. It set men a-thinking; it enlarged the horizon of political experience; it led the public mind to ponder somewhat on the circumstances of our national history...and insensibly it created and prepared a popular intelligence to which one can appeal." To understand the demos, Disraeli's Lady Marney depended upon the nous of the political agents, Tadpoles and Tapers, in *Sybil*. Politicians today use polls and focus groups to sound the public mood more systematically than Tadpoles and Tapers could do then, but now, as then, there are those who ignore them, or misread them, or hope against hope they may be wrong, as they sometimes are. But not often.

Most of the private polls are never published. But as well as using the private polls for their own planning, of course, the parties sometimes find it useful to release the results. Several of the private polls during the 2001 election found their way into to the press.

On page two of the *Sunday Telegraph*[183], Joe Murphy reported an almost unnoted poll conducted privately for the Labour Party by NOP, leaked 17 days before the date of the election but almost unreported in the media, which had the Labour Party on 47%, Conservatives on 25% (sic) and the Lib Dems on 13%. The numerate reader will notice that these figures add up to 85%. Add 5% for "others", and you get to 90%, the remainder likely to be the "don't knows". Reallocate these, and you get a set of figures comparable to the published polling figures at the same period: 52%, 28%, 14%.

---

[183] Joe Murphy, "Tories in rift over Hague strategy as polls fail to shift", *Sunday Telegraph*, 20 May 2001.

At that morning's Tory press conference Francis Maude referred to Bob Worcester by name as doing Labour's private polling as if explaining away why MORI's figures were so gloomy for his party. This was questioned by Adam Boulton of Sky Television and some of the other journalists present, who reported it to me. Later that same evening Francis and I met in the Sky television studio when he courteously apologised to me for his misunderstanding. I was then pleased two days later when at the Tory press conference that morning's spokesman Michael Portillo gave me what journalists present described as a 'fulsome apology'. In fact, I have not done the Labour Party private polling since 1989, and since then have served as a polling advisor to the Conservative Party when Ken Baker was Party Chairman; subsequently I have done polls for the Referendum Party, the UK Independence Party and the Liberal Democrats among others.

Interesting also is that Michael Portillo at another Tory press conference said they were cutting back on their private polling, and hadn't commissioned their private pollsters (ICM) to do any polling for them in the three months leading up to the call of the election. After the election, one of the Central Office insiders not involved in the polling directly speculated that they'd cut back their polling so as to enable them to concentrate on getting their message out (sic)!

Later, the *Guardian* reported[184] that the Labour Party's private surveys showed the party on 46%, the Tories on 26%, and the Liberal Democrats up 3% since the campaign launch on 16%. (However, the figures suggest that "don't knows" have not been excluded from the voting intentions, and that they are hence not directly comparable with the other published polls).

The *Sunday Times* reported[185] that the Conservative Party was taking its canvass returns more seriously than the findings of published polls, because they had in this case – so they said – spoken to between 20% and 30% of voters in these seats. It is extraordinary the credence the

---

[184] *Guardian*, 29 May 2001
[185] Michael Prescott & Eben Black, "Tories fear worst ever defeat as Blair gives pledge on tax", *Sunday Times*, 6 May 2001.

parties apparently give to their canvass returns as a predictor – let alone as a favourable story to be leaked.

If the Tories had spoken to between 20% and 30% of voters, it is a fair bet that most of them were from the most Tory 20%-30% of the electorate – getting the vote out is one of the main aims of canvassing. But the 20% or 30% is doubtful anyway. Even three weeks later, across the country only 6% of the public said they had been called on by a Conservative representative.

But in any case on this occasion even their canvass returns couldn't cheer the Tories. Leaked details of the Conservative Central Office canvassing exercise found similar levels of Tory support within 15 target seats in or just outside of London to their 1997 national result of 31 per cent – much what the polls were showing.

The Lib Dems made more imaginative use of their tiny polling budget – to our chagrin. In February, the national Liberal Democrats had commissioned a MORI poll to find out what their vote might be if voters thought that the LibDems could win in their constituency, and discovered that more than a third of the public said they would vote Lib Dem under such circumstances. Fair enough, and we posted the findings on our web site, made the full question wording available, and so did they. The Lib Dems also published a projection of the poll result to constituencies on a regional basis, and turned it into a striking poster of the map of Britain turned largely yellow. A powerful use of the data, and acceptable so long as it wasn't presented in such a way as to obscure the obvious limitations of the poll. But in some local constituencies overzealous LibDem activists put out releases, and leaflets, which made it appear that a MORI poll had been conducted in their constituency, which showed that the local candidate could win. Naughty. We did our best to stamp out such sharp practice, but no doubt many electors were misled. In at least one case the leaflet claimed that "MORI predicted" that the sitting Tory MP would finish third. (He won.) We protested, and received an apology. But this incident has forced us to consider whether we must impose even more stringent contractual restriction on political party clients in the future.

Reporting the polls

Polling is, as far as we can achieve it, a scientific and objective means of measurement of people's views. Interpretation of the data, with the best will in the world, is another thing entirely. Reporting involves interpretation and it involves selection. Then come headlines, which usually also involve simplification. Then comes the secondary reporting of polls, often a ghastly game of Chinese whispers, in which other papers, and broadcasters, will probably repeat the figures out of context, misinterpret them, cherry-pick particular findings to bolster a different slant to the story, perhaps create further errors. This can leave us a long way from where we started. Many is the time when, as a result, a story begins "A MORI poll says .." when the MORI poll says nothing of the sort. (If, indeed, it is a MORI poll at all, for attributing the entire story to the wrong research agency is by no means unknown.)

We are not, we must emphasise, suggesting that all reporting of the polls is below standard. Peter Riddell's reports of our polls for *The Times*, we would say, are models of their kind, and a number of his counterparts on other papers, whether reporting polls that we have conducted or those of our competitors, are equally first-rate. But such standards involve hard work all round. We work closely with our clients in the press to ensure that the initial reports are as accurate as possible; indeed, we make it one of our contractual conditions that we see and approve all copy to ensure that it faithfully reports the poll and does not mislead about the findings, even inadvertently or by implication. Peter Riddell floats over to our offices faithfully for each and every poll, and joins a group of MORI analysts who gather together to go over the findings; following the conference, Peter's copy is e-mailed over to us and is gone through in word-by-word detail, and any qualifications or afterthoughts then dealt with by telephone. We work directly (and very happily) with the *Times*' graphics department, and check their artistic interpretations of our crude graphic suggestions to ensure the integrity of the data. This happy and symbiotic relationship has now existed for over 20 years, without acrimony, posturing or even serious disagreement over all that time. But not every poll report in the press or on television or radio reaches these standards.

289

Voting intention polls often suffer worst from the potential problems and pitfalls. Close readers of my essays during the campaign (published daily on epolitix.com) and of much else I have written over the years will recall that time and time again I have urged watching the share, not the gap, and especially the Conservative share, as that will best indicate the state of the election at the time the poll in question was taken. It seems that few listened.

How rare it was in this election to find any headline or opening paragraph mentioning share. Almost always it was the lead ("Labour by 30") – or, worse, it was a projection of the poll into seats ("Blair's 227 majority"), which multiplies the margin of error alarmingly.

Two polls, both by NOP, were the first out of the gate in the general election. We can draw some lessons from how they were reported.

The first, for Channel 4's *Powerhouse* Programme, had the Tories trailing by 15 points, while the other, published that same morning in the *Daily Express*, had the Tories 20 points behind. Both were done over the same period of time, with the one projecting to 253 seat majority (the *Express* said 250 on their 'splash') while the other to only (only?) 207, a 46 seat discrepancy. Both couldn't be right.

Or could they? Look at the results of the two polls: The first, 49%, 34%, 11%; the second, 51%, 31%, 13%. Within, well within, sampling tolerance of each other. So the lesson from this? Read the shares, not the gap, which doubles the sampling tolerance. And read either of those in preference to the seat projections.

Seat projections and the ICM/*Guardian* 'Variometer'

Opinion polls measure the electorate's intentions in votes, not in seats. We can – with a perfect poll and our fair share of luck – measure voting intention percentages directly, and would hope to be accurate within our margins of error. But projecting the number of seats that a given share of the votes would give, although it produces a better headline, involves much greater uncertainties, and we rarely have the information we need to produce such figures with anything approaching precision.

This is a consequence of Britain's first past the post electoral system. Under even the more complicated variants of proportional representation, a knowledge of the national vote shares dictates to within very tight margins the shares of seats that will ensue. But first past the post doesn't work like that – the relationship between total seats and total votes is arbitrary and unpredictable, varying from election to election. In many other democracies with first past the post systems, the attempt to predict seats from votes is rarely even made. In India, for example, where regional variation predominates, psephologists would never expect the national vote shares to indicate the seats won, and no American pundit would be likely to forecast the composition of the Senate or House from national rather than state polls.

However, in Britain this is not the case. Political change tends to be reflected across the nation, though with substantial local and regional variations. Ever since David Butler developed the concept of uniform swing in the forties, it has been taken for granted that it is possible for a given share of the votes to make a reasonably accurate prediction of the number of seats that each party would win. Once upon a time, swings really were relatively uniform, and this was broadly true. These days the variations are greater than they used to be, and seat projection cannot be done to any reasonable degree of accuracy without much more information than is provided by the overall national vote shares. But this doesn't stop journalists, and pundits, from doing it.

Projecting from an opinion poll finding widens these uncertainties because the poll itself can only be expected to be accurate within a given margin of error. As a small shift in votes can cause a large shift in seats, the margins of error sound much larger when translated into seats, and even very similar polls can produce substantially different seat projections. Consider the figures from our one of our polls for *The Times*. In votes, this had the Conservatives on 30%, Labour on 54%. Incorporating the margin of error, this means Conservative 30±3%, Labour 54±3%. But translating this into seats assuming uniform swing, it placed the overall majority anywhere between 231 and 363. (In fact the difference is between Labour winning 68% and 78% of the seats, so in percentage terms it is only a margin of error of ±5%, but it sounds like a lot more than that.)

One venture which we took all opportunities to question – in which we believe turned out to be fully justified by the election outcome – was the ICM/*Guardian* 'Variometer', apparently designed in collaboration with John Curtice who tried to defend it in a BBC radio debate with me to argue that the projections we were using would overestimate Labour's support.

The 'Variometer' was a votes-to-seats projection model displayed on the ICM and *Guardian* websites (from both of which it quickly disappeared the moment the polls closed, from ICM's website on the Friday and the *Guardian*'s on the Saturday following the election) and used ICM poll evidence to project differences in swing between different classifications of constituency to make up the overall vote shares.[186]

As any cautious pollster might have predicted, this in the event involved slicing the cake altogether too fine, leading to too great a margin of error in the individual cells of the design, with the consequence that it predicted massive deviation from uniform swing. ICM's model was "predicting" that if the vote shares were the same as in 1997, Labour's majority would be cut by 60; in the event there was a 2% swing to the Tories yet the Labour majority fell by only 12 seats. We preferred to stick to the simple – some would say simplistic – uniform change model as a basis for projection, though adding caveats where necessary.

The perils of the elaborate model were amply illustrated when applied to ICM's own final poll, which had a very creditable prediction of the final vote shares, Con 32%, Lab 43%, Lib Dem 19%. According to the variometer, this would have given Labour a majority of just 98 instead of

---

[186] The variometer on the ICM website, incidentally, was programmed so that it could only project from a Conservative share of 30% or higher – which must have been a little embarrassing when ICM's 26-28 May poll for the *Guardian* put the Tories on 28%, so it couldn't be run through their own model!

the 167 on the night. Much is made post-election of the MORI findings influencing people to think that Labour was further ahead than they turned out to be. We have seen no *mea culpa* from Curtice, ICM or the *Guardian* that their Variometer was misleading their readers and others who took it seriously in underestimating the likely size of the Labour victory.

Alan Travis, reporting the final poll for the *Guardian*, wisely ignored the variometer altogether, though not explaining how he made his own estimate from the same figures of a majority "somewhere between 170 and 190".[187] The MORI swingo model, using simple uniform change in party vote shares, would from the same figures have projected an overall majority of exactly 167. Yet Travis had quoted projections from their 'Variometer' in his write ups of the ICM findings on at least two earlier occasions, e.g. on 23 May when he reported a 13% lead which 'would see Tony Blair's second term majority cut by around 34 seats to 145' and on 20 May when ICM had blipped up to a 19 point Labour lead, which Travis reported 'would translate on the "variometer", which takes account of regional variations in swing, into a landslide majority of 267'.

The lesson seems to be that polls can be sometimes be very uncertain instruments for diagnosing fractional and regional effects which they have not been specifically designed to measure. This is probably especially true when a poll is as much "adjusted" as is the case with ICM's polls, or is otherwise heavily weighted, rather than relying on the unvarnished data. The careful calibration of the total adjustment to correct the overall headline figures may be masking substantial sectional differences in the factors being adjusted. If the error which is being corrected for in fact only affects a part of the sample, then after adjustment the headline figure may be corrected and yet all the sub-sectional data distorted. A correction for "shy Tories" (if such creatures still exist, of which we remain unconvinced as we have argued above) may be right nationally, yet give no indication that they are very shy in say, London, yet positively vocal and unembarrassed in the South-West; if such were the case then correcting the whole sample to compensate for

---

[187] Alan Travis, "Tories stage late recovery", *Guardian*, 6 June 2001.

the problem in London would overestimate Tory strength in the South West.

Of course, we use the uniform swing projection in full knowledge that strictly uniform swing is unlikely. We don't consider that our polls are "predictions", even of the vote shares, and we certainly prefer that our clients don't lead with a seat projection rather than a vote share measure. But uniform swing, though a probably inaccurate simplification, has the merit of being a straightforward and defensible basis for analysis. Vote shares on their own are somewhat abstract; it helps to explain them to express the figures in the terms that if everybody in the country behaved in the same way, the outcome in seats would be this.

Then you can go into the likely exceptions. There may be regional variations. Rural and urban seats may behave differently. The target marginal seats, where the parties concentrate their campaigning efforts, may swing differently from the neglected safe seats. There may be differential turnout. There may be tactical voting in some constituencies – or, rather, there may be more or may be less than at the last election.

But most of these factors are difficult to measure if you prefer to attempt a more sophisticated projection model. No single opinion poll can give you very much useful information about how far voting will deviate from uniform swing, although it may give some indication of differential turnout; even an aggregation of a number of polls gives only broad indications, and while it may detect systematic regional variations, it can't deal with tactical voting, let alone the peculiarities of individual constituencies. (This makes it especially hard to accurately project the number of LD seats).

Constituency polls – how not to do it

We are wary of seat projections from national or regional polls, and even more when such polls are used to "predict" the result in individual seats. An egregious example in 2001 was the *Herald*'s System Three poll across the Scottish regions, which was preposterously reported as showing Charles Kennedy in danger of losing his seat on the grounds of a fall in the Lib Dem vote across the Highlands[188].

But it is no better to report the data collected in individual constituencies, unless there is enough of it. Twice during the election the *Daily Record* carried polling results from six marginal seats in Scotland, broken down to give the findings in each constituency; both polls were conducted by Scottish Opinion. All very well, except that the first poll interviewed only 744 respondents in total (an average of 124 per constituency), and the later one interviewed 911 (average about 152).

Such tiny sample sizes mean that the margin of error is far too large for the findings in the individual constituencies to be of any practical use. Nor was the presentation of the figures ideal: percentages were calculated including don't knows (normal polling practice in Britain is to exclude don't knows, allowing direct comparison with actual election results) and figures given to one decimal place. (Use of decimals implies an entirely spurious level of accuracy: it is plainly ludicrous to report figures to the nearest tenth of a percentage point when the margin of error is eight points!)

By way of contrast, two other polls in the same constituencies using more realistic sample sizes, by ICM for *Scotland on Sunday*, are also shown.

---

[188] Robert Dinwoodie & Murray Ritchie, "Poll warning for Tories and LibDems from Herald's 3000", *Herald*, 23 May 2001. They described the threat to Kennedy "seems fanciful ... but that is a threat on paper", but the secondary reporting was less cautious.

Table 98: Scottish constituency polls, 2001

	Sample size	Con %	Lab %	LDem %	SNP %	Other %	Source
AYR							
Scottish Opinion Ltd (4-7.5)‡	c. 124	25	47	6	24	0	*D.Record*
Scottish Opinion Ltd (10-14.5)‡	c. 152	27	50	5	17	2	*D.Record*
Result		37	44	5	12	2	
EASTWOOD							
Scottish Opinion Ltd (4-7.5)‡	c. 124	25	52	9	12	2	*D.Record*
Scottish Opinion Ltd (10-14.5)‡	c. 152	19	65	12	14	0	*D.Record*
ICM (Week to 2.6)†	500	29	46	11	10	4	*Scot on Sun*
Result		29	48	13	9	2	
EDINBURGH PENTLANDS							
Scottish Opinion Ltd (4-7.5)‡	c. 124	16	56	2	12	0	*D.Record*
Scottish Opinion Ltd (10-14.5)‡	c. 152	33	50	8	14	4	*D.Record*
ICM (Week to 2.6)†	500	30	42	11	12	6	*Scot on Sun*
Result		36	41	11	11	2	
PERTH							
Scottish Opinion Ltd (4-7.5)‡	c. 124	25	25	2	45	1	*D.Record*
Scottish Opinion Ltd (10-14.5)‡	c. 152	24	19	9	36	1	*D.Record*
Result		30	25	13	30	2	
STIRLING							
Scottish Opinion Ltd (4-7.5)‡	c. 124	26	31	1	41	1	*D.Record*
Scottish Opinion Ltd (10-14.5)‡	c. 152	21	53	6	18	2	*D.Record*
Result		25	42	12	16	5	
TAYSIDE NORTH							
Scottish Opinion Ltd (4-7.5)‡	c. 124	16	19	0	50	1	*D.Record*
Scottish Opinion Ltd (10-14.5)‡	c. 152	22	35	2	38	1	*D.Record*
Result		32	15	11	40	2	

‡The Scottish Opinion/*Daily Record* figures are (approximately) re-percentaged to exclude the don't knows, for comparison with the final result in each constituency.

The low value that should be put findings such as those in the *Daily Record* is evident when we come to look at the differences in results between the two polls (we hesitate to refer to it as "change"). In Eastwood, Labour's share had apparently risen by twelve points in a week. In Edinburgh Pentlands, the first poll put the Tories (whose candidate was the former Foreign Secretary, Sir Malcolm Rifkind) on 16%, half his share at the last election; but that doubled in six days. In Stirling, meanwhile, there has apparently been a 22.5% swing from SNP to Labour. In Perth (not Perth and Kinross as the *Record* called it – Kinross has been in the neighbouring Ochil constituency since 1997), the Lib Dems seemed to have had an impressive week, more than quadrupling their support, but they also quadrupled support in Edinburgh Pentlands, and increased it six-fold in Stirling! Or not.

As the *Record* noted of Stirling, with massive understatement, "last week's SNP lead must have been a freak result, because they are now third". Well, no, not really a "freak result"; exactly the sort of result that will inevitably occur far too frequently when polls are based on inadequate sample sizes.

Headline News?

Headlines can encompass other pitfalls, especially when the "news" they convey is not new because the poll reported is out-of-date or not the latest available. Almost all the papers regularly fall into this trap when reporting the twice-yearly results of British opinion found in the European Commission's Eurobarometer polls – which, because the Commission takes several months to release the results, have frequently been superseded by more recent polls by MORI or ICM, both of whom produce regular polls on attitudes to the EU and the Euro.

To take a different example, on 9 June 2000 the latest monthly Gallup poll had Labour *up* two points since the previous month, the Conservatives down one, yet the front page headline in the *Daily Telegraph* was "LABOUR'S LEAD OVER TORIES IS HALVED". What does that convey, knowing that Gallup polls for the *Telegraph* monthly and is published within a couple of days of the end of fieldwork? Surely that the government has suffered a catastrophic loss of support in the last month, and that this was the position as measured a couple of days before.

The first false impression created is over the timescale. One tends to assume, and anyone seeing the headline without reading the poll probably would do so, that an unqualified statement about the change

297

revealed by a poll indicates the change since the last poll in the series; to headline the poll in this way when the change referred to is the change since this time last year is misleading, to say the least!

Worse, the poll figures cited were not only old news and not the most up-to-date figures available, but the more up-to-date figures directly contradicted the thrust of the story. Every month, Gallup produces two sets of figures: its "Political Index", data aggregated over the previous calendar month, and a "snapshot poll", over a single week. The snapshot poll is the newest data, and this is what is normally considered to be the new Gallup poll. In this instance, the Gallup Index consisted of just over 4,000 interviews on 3-31 May 2000, the snapshot of just over 1,000 interviews on 31 May- 6 June 2000. The Gallup Index figures are therefore for a period which has already been extensively polled for publication – twice by MORI, twice by ICM and once by Gallup. These polls all, like the Gallup Index, found the government's position deteriorating. But the new Gallup snapshot, the first published poll of June, found the opposite: Labour up two points since last month, the Conservatives down one. The *Telegraph* headlined the old poll, not the new one, with the first mention of the snapshot buried eight paragraphs into Political Editor George Jones's front page article.

Reporting focus groups

Since their use by the Labour Party in recent years has familiarised the political classes with focus groups, they have become very much flavour of the month. In the past they have been rarely commissioned by the press in its political reporting, if only because – properly used – they simply don't provide very interesting copy.

Too many journalists do not seem to know the difference between a focus group and a poll, or simply apply "focus group" as a generalised term of abuse with which to denigrate any survey which they wish to slang off.

Focus groups are tricky. They are subject to manipulation in a way that polls are not. The sample selection is not 'random' by any sense of the use of that word. A moderator can powerfully influence the way people talk, and can be selective in the recruitment of the panel, the questions that are asked, the way they are asked (eyebrows are powerful communicators), and what is reported. People have even been known to commission focus groups to get the answer they wanted, rather than what people really are thinking.

The late Percy Clarke, former director of communications at the Labour Party, several decades ago dismissed focus groups as a waste of time, saying he might as well go to the local Labour club and listen to the chaps at the bar. He underestimated their usefulness, as I believe Peter Mandelson overestimates them. I used to use them, when doing Labour's private polls, for two purposes: testing concepts, e.g., the design of the 'red rose' or of party literature, and for 'semantics', listening for the way people are talking about the issues and images of the day. They can be useful for the parties in this way, but their value for the press is less useful.

In 2001, some of the newspapers did commission focus groups, and the contrasts in the way in which they were used illustrate their right, and wrong, uses. Consider first the reasonably well conducted and analysed focus group done by Live Strategy Ltd for the *Telegraph*. Reasonably reported. It didn't turn a half dozen or so people (seven in this exercise, in Boreham Wood, Hertsmere, Cecil Parkinson's old seat, a Conservative marginal in 2001) into any kind of referendum on the standing of the parties. Instead it did what focus groups should do, gathering the views of a group of people in an informal but informative way, about the election. But we wonder whether the *Telegraph* really got much from it that its reporters couldn't have got themselves.

By contrast, consider the disgraceful way in which the *Financial Times* reported their focus groups (May 10). In one of the worst political analyses ever, Rosemary Bennett reported "40% (sic) of the sample (sic), interviewed last week by Banks Hoggins O'Shea FCB, the advertising agency, said they had already made up their minds how to vote in the

June 7 election, with two-thirds (sic) backing Labour." Later they said the panel was drawn from 76 floating voters...

So, we now know that, maybe, 40% of an unknown proportion of 76 people, defined as 'floating voters' (some of whom might not vote at all), 'have drifted', and, later, that 32 % (sic) said Hague would be forced out of office and another 40% said he would still be in charge after the election. Not even what they thought should happen, but what they thought would happen, on a decision that would be taken by MPs rather than the public in any case! Or, as it happened, by Hague's own decision the day after the election.

Focus groups work a little better on TV, though the Channel 4 News hype and graphics and the enthusiasm with which they presented the quite ordinary focus group and soundbite poll done by the somewhat tarnished Frank Luntz, the American pollster they brought over to show us how to do it, who seemed mostly to be replicating the work we were doing for Harold Wilson in the seventies, was a little overblown. (Frank Luntz was censured by the American Association for Public Opinion Research for cutting corners and refusing to co-operate with the enquiries into his methodology. Does Channel 4 know about this?)

Voodoo polls

Even worse than the sins of the print and broadcast media in reporting reputable polls, is the phone, fax, and now internet scams, asking people to 'vote' in phone, fax or internet 'polls' which charge up to £2 a minute, or page, to take part in a 'poll' which will then be reported, sent to No. 10 or the White House, as if anyone in either would be taken in by them.

These are the polls that come in over the fax machine which promise to be collated and sent to No. 10, relevant House of Commons' committees, on various subjects, the handling of foot and mouth disease, the monarchy, the Euro and yes, the election, which aren't worth the paper they are printed on, and only serve to line the pockets of the unscrupulous people who stoop to this sleazy way of turning a buck.

Findings trumpeted by 'The Nation's Barometer', includes that 'Teletext viewers' believe that MPs don't deserve a pay rise 99%, Parents must have the right to smack their children 95%, and The death penalty should be re-introduced 85%. They may or may not be right, but they are certainly not representative! They claim that 'over two million viewers have registered their votes on subjects from sex to Sunday shopping', concluding they don't know the impact these have made, but that their findings have 'even been used by MP John Redwood in seeking election for the Tory party leadership'. So there.

Daily it seems we are confronted, confounded and sometimes infuriated by these phone(y) polls, fax polls, phooey polls and my collective name for them, 'Voodoo Polls'.

The newspapers sometimes try to justify these on the grounds that their samples are bigger. In the early days of polling, George Gallup and his rivals, Archibald Crossley and Elmo Roper, made their reputations by correctly predicting the result of the 1936 US Presidential election using small but scientifically-selected samples when the long-established straw poll organised by the magazine *Literary Digest*, which analysed millions (sic) of postal responses but with a sample biased by its reliance of directories of telephone and car owners, called the result disastrously wrong. In just the same way today, worthless phone-in polls organised by newspapers or TV stations may get hundreds of thousands of responses but are unable to control the composition of their samples (or, quite often, to prevent people voting more than once). The tabloids love them in particular, but they are not the only culprits. The *New Statesman*, for example, has persisted in running and reporting the results of internet voodoo polls on topical political issues, and the *Daily Telegraph* asked its Conservative readers to write in to help it track the course of the Clarke/Duncan Smith leadership contest.

During the 2001 election, a phone-in poll in the *Sun* reported on the front page two days before the 2001 election put the Tories ahead by a margin of three to one![189] Meanwhile an internet "poll" by www.handbag.com had figures of Labour 47%, Conservative 16% and Liberal Democrat 14%, the remainder presumably being don't knows.[190]

The *Mail on Sunday* carried the latest results in the "survey of 18,000 chocolate lollies sold by Thorntons in the form of the leaders' heads (Hague's the bald one), and has found Blair at 46% of sales, Hague sticking (sic) at 34% and Kennedy appealing (sic) to 17%". Not bad, for once.

Of course the Thornton's poll is fairly harmless, and presumably it sells chocolate; nobody, including Thornton's, is likely to take it seriously as a reading of public opinion. But not all voodoo polls are so innocent, and these wretched things that some people describe as 'just a bit of fun' can be serious when there's a war on. Take the war in Kosovo in 1999. The first Sunday of the war there were three opinion polls published in three Sunday newspapers, carried out by three different polling organisations, asking three different question formulations about the use of British bombers in the NATO strike force, using three different sets of telephone interviewers, using three different but all legitimate sampling methods, and all coming up with the same result: 2:1 public support for the use of British airplanes to bomb Kosovo.

Just what you'd expect? Well not *Sunday Business*, who did not commission their own poll, but wrote a leader about how public opinion was against the war, based on the 84% who'd taken part in a phone-in poll on Talk Radio who opposed the war! That followed parallel pieces the day before in *The Times* and the *Guardian*, which without benefit of proper poll findings also shot from the hip, the *Times*' headline reading 'Backlash in Britain against Bombing', largely based on letters to local newspapers and interviews with local newspaper editors. *The Times* did not report to its readers on Monday the poll findings from the Sunday

---

[189] Charles Rae & Mark Bowness, "How come there's a big swing to the Tories?", *Sun*, 5 June 2001. The *Sun*'s editorial speculated "Some cynics reckon Tory HQ rigged the result. We reckon it's just that the Tory girl on the *Sun* bus had the biggest cleavage!". No doubt they know their own readers best.
[190] "Soundbites: Handbags nearly out", *Daily Telegraph*, 29 May 2001.

newspapers that had commissioned them.

Paul Routledge, writing in the *Mirror* was also taken in. 'Public opinion is divided about Britain's war in the Balkans, and may be turning against the Nato bombing. That is the message coming through from your letters to me over the last two weeks.'[191] Reminds me of Tony Benn announcing in the House of Commons during the first weeks of the Falklands War in April 1982 that 'Public opinion is swinging massively against the war', waving a sheaf of letters that had been sent to him. The following day we published a poll in the *Economist* showing that 78% of the British public supported sending the task force to the Falklands.

What is it about some journalists and politicians that lead them to set up polls as some sort of straw men, to be toppled by letters to newspapers or phone ins, no matter how often the validity of these alternatives has been tested and shown to be wildly out of line with reality?

Then there was the *Sunday Mirror* DIY poll. The *Sunday Mirror* have forsook the professionals, and mounted their own poll of "first-time voters" among an unreported number of "young people" (undefined), carried out sometime (no mention of when), somehow (no mention of how the interviews were carried out) but finding 67% answering "yes" to the blunt question "Are you going to vote at the general election?" 'In a month of Sundays'. I said at the time.

At the last election, fewer than half of young people had done so, and this time, I'd guessed 45% is a more likely turnout. (It was 39%). Further, when asked "Which single thing would you change if you were Prime Minister?", the "elimination of university tuition fees" topped the poll. I'd never have guessed it. I sometimes say that the job we do is to ask the right people, the right questions, and add up the figures correctly. The *Sunday Mirror* added up the figures correctly so far as I can tell.

---

[191] *Daily Mirror*, 10 April 1999.

And the moral of all this is – the press hypes its stories, it is in the nature of the beast. (Or, indeed, of *The Beast*).

- Rely on the text in preference to the headline, and in the tables with the actual numbers therein.
- Rely on the original report rather than the secondary reporting if possible. Secondary reporting (of which the MORI poll digest is an example, albeit we hope a good one) can only at best be a paraphrase, and accidents will happen. Use the secondary report to alert you to the poll's existence and, if you can, go back to the original.
- Remember that not every journalist knows the difference between a survey and a focus group, or what each can be used for.
- Watch the share, not the gap. It is of much greater moment to see that the Conservative share is at 30%, or 35%, when they need to get to 40% to be in the frame, than to know that Labour has a 12% or a 7% lead, which more likely than not is accounted for by a change in the share for the Liberal Democrats.
- If there is table or panel giving fuller details, consult it – you are not forced to accept the journalists' interpretation of the figures or judgement of what is most important. If full details are not available in the newspaper, you should be able to obtain them from the pollster. (For all MORI's published polls, you can normally find details on www.mori.com).
- Trust the data.

5. The Second Term

Public hopes and expectations of government

The public is in no doubt about its priorities for Labour's second term: as before, improvement in public services, but first and foremost in the National Health Service.

Table 99: Priorities for the next Government

Q. I am going to read out a number of different things the next Government could do. Please tell me which one or two, if any, of these, should be the top priorities for the next Government?

	%
Cut hospital waiting lists	69
Put more policemen on the beat	39
Reduce school class sizes	38
Keep interest rates low	16
Ban Fox Hunting	8
Enter the Single European Currency	7
Other	2
Don't know	1

Source: MORI/ *The Sun*
Base: 1,008 British 18+, 30 April–1 May 2001

There is little sympathy for the government's apparent agenda of widening private sector involvement in the provision of public services, although only a minority object to using private hospitals to treat NHS patients. Opposition to privatising state schools is greater even than that to joining the Euro, and nearly three-quarters would support returning the railways to the public sector, which suggests a rocky future for the government if it continues to fight for part-privatisation of the London Underground under the PPP scheme. It may also be worth noting that although the majority support a ban on fox hunting, it is very low on most Britons' shopping list of policies.

Table 100: Support for possible government policies

Q. *I am now going to read out a list of policies that a new Labour Government might carry out. Please tell me whether you support or oppose each.*

		Support	Oppose	Don't know	Net
Bring railways back into public ownership	%	72	19	10	+53
Have more NHS patients treated in private hospitals	%	69	25	6	+44
Require companies to give fathers paid time off work when their children are born	%	67	29	4	+38
Ban fox hunting	%	57	31	11	+26
Increase income tax to 50% for highest earners	%	57	33	9	+24
Let secondary schools select pupils who are good at certain subjects	%	45	43	12	+2
Put up to £800 of taxpayers' money into an account for every new born child. They would be able to spend this money as they like when they are 18	%	38	53	9	-15
Join the European Single Currency	%	27	58	15	-31
Allow private companies to run state schools	%	23	62	14	-39

Source: MORI/*Economist*
Base: 1,010 British 18+, 4-5 June 2001

Perhaps the public's expectations point to the real dangers in the second term. Three-quarters expect Labour to increase taxes, yet the party was re-elected convincingly. This time round, the public will surely be demanding value for its money. Three in five believe that school standards will rise, and more than half that the NHS will be improved. If it happens, all well and good. But if those expectations are dashed – in the case of the NHS, dashed again – there is an obvious risk that the public's patience will run out.

Table 101: Expectations of Labour in its second term

Q. *If a Labour Government is elected after the next General Election, do you think it will or will not .... ?*

		Will	Will not	Net
...increase taxes?	%	74	16	+58
...improve standards in schools?	%	60	29	+31
...improve the NHS?	%	55	35	+20
...give a strong voice to Britain in Europe?	%	49	37	+12
...help to improve your own standard of living?	%	38	52	-14
...keep its promises?	%	31	54	-23
...be controlled by the Trades Unions?	%	18	65	-47

Source: MORI/ *The Times*
Base: 1,013 British 18+, 29 May 2001

If it all goes wrong for Labour, that will raise two questions. In the circumstances, can Tony Blair win the referendum on the Euro? And what can we guess at this point about the future of the Tories and their likely credibility as an opposition in 2005 or 2006?

The referendum on the Euro

Perhaps the biggest challenge facing Tony Blair in his second term is the one he ducked in his first term , to hold – and win – a referendum on taking Britain into the Single European Currency. When will the referendum be? According to some newspapers' interpretations of the Prime Minister's answer to a question in the Commons[192], he has already promised it will be held in the first two years of the next Parliament. That wasn't what he said.

I was asked to review that day's Prime Minister's Question Time on BBC Radio 5 Live, so I was watching it very closely indeed. The spin from the member of the shadow cabinet I spoke to was how glum Gordon Brown looked and how shocked he looked. Not true. I looked at it again on *Newsnight*, and yet again on Breakfast TV and frankly he didn't crack a smile. He was looking like the Easter Island statue, he just sat there just as solid as he could be.

Apparently the Prime Minister still thinks they can win. In the *Financial Times*[193] the prime minister was asked whether he could persuade voters to support British membership (in the Euro) and said: "Of course, provided you mount the argument well, provided we are setting out why it is economically and politically in Britain's interest."

I don't think he can. And if he were to call it, and lose it, would make him a "lame duck" prime minister, not something T. Blair would allow.

Originally I thought that the referendum would be held in 2001, in late October or early November, in the honeymoon after this election but before the introduction of the Euro on the continent, and the six months of chaos I expect to take place with vending machines, counterfeiting, banks running out, etc.

---

[192] House of Commons *Hansard*, 7 February 2001, col 918.
[193] Brian Groom & Jonathan Guthrie, "Blair says he can win euro debate", *Financial Times*, 25 May 2001.

I said in a booklet for the Foreign Policy Centre, and then in a chapter in the Federal Trust booklet, "Britain and euroland: A collection of essays",[194] that the government would win such a referendum, narrowly, because of the lessons I learned working with the Prime Minister and the Foreign Secretary during the 1975 European referendum, when they turned around 22 people in a hundred in just six months to win it.

Yes, it happened in 1975. But in 1975 there was a united front of the political parties, all the main ones; the media, all the national daily and Sunday newspapers; the business community, the main trade unions, the City, and most of the economic pundits.

This time the Tories won't be on side, a significant portion of Labour will be sceptical, if quiet about it a large chuck of the media is opposed, many business leaders, several key trade union leaders, and a very effective Business for Sterling pressure group.

I consistently and continually hear from politicians: "What matters is how you ask the question (and so forth) in a referendum"; it does not. Referendums are not the same as opinion polls. Polls are top of mind.

Polls are, of course, a great deal more convenient, quicker, and cheaper than referendums. So what is the point of holding referendums at all, when you can take opinion polls? Painful as it is to admit it, opinion polls of course have some disadvantages. First, because they only interview a sample, they are subject to a margin of error. Although in a properly conducted poll this margin should be small, and for almost all purposes for which the polls are legitimately used such a level of accuracy is quite sufficient, they are clearly not a substitute for a democratic vote when the electorate is entitled to expect an exact result; the improbability of the wrong side winning a decision by opinion poll would not excuse the theoretical possibility.

Second, and more significantly, the opportunity for participation in a referendum is itself a part of the point of holding a referendum, which is

---

[194] Robert Worcester, "The British: Reluctant Europeans" in Stephen Haseler & Jacques Reland (eds), *Britain and Euroland: a collection of essays* (Federal Trust, 2000).

intended to confer or deny extra democratic legitimacy to a government proposal. Even if an opinion poll could be guaranteed to predict with absolute accuracy what the result of a referendum would be, it would not be a substitute for holding it, any more than it could be a substitute for holding a general election.

But most significant of all, consider what happens before a referendum. There is a full scale election campaign lasting days or weeks. Both sides have an opportunity to put their case, and the public have leisure to consider it and to make up their minds. In Britain, at least, there would be spending restrictions, regulation of the television coverage to ensure a balanced debate, and the probability that even the most biased newspapers will make some concessions towards considering the opposing point of view. Future British referendums will be overseen by the highly competent eye of the new Electoral Commission, and will be all the better for it. None of this is true when an opinion poll takes a snapshot of public opinion, even on an issue which is well established in the public mind and which many of the population hold strong views on.

With polls, the way the question is worded is vital, and it is possible to get the answer you want depending on how you phrase the question. That there is no incentive for pollsters to "get the answer you want" is often forgotten, but there you are.

Polls are ongoing, here today gone tomorrow. They are not binding. When an interviewer on behalf of a polling organisation asks you for your opinions, your attitudes or your values, your behaviour or your knowledge, it is not binding. You do not feel an obligation to think carefully and thoroughly about what it is that is being asked. It is relatively unimportant; it is not something you have thought about necessarily, you are just courteous enough to answer the questions. The media will not have covered the question matter in advance, for the most part, and the wording is vital.

I remember doing an experiment some 20 or 25 years ago when I concluded in a poll for the *Daily Express* that depending on how you asked the question, you could have support for hanging running from

52% to about 90%. 90% of the British public would say: "Yes, I am in favour of the death penalty for a convicted child murderer and rapist who kills a prison guard while escaping". They will say "Yes, I suppose in those conditions, I am in favour". Then on the other hand, it goes down to around 52% for an unpremeditated marital situation.

For example, we have asked about general attitudes to the Euro recently in three different ways: when we asked if respondents were generally in favour or against, 58% said they were opposed; when we asked how they would vote in "a referendum now", 61% said they would vote against; but when we put the question in terms of whether "Britain should keep the pound" or not, 72% thought that we should. The people are not anti-European – 66% support the aim of "being at the heart of Europe" – but they are suspicious, to say the least.

Referendums on the other hand are considered. At the end of a three or four week campaign people know what is at issue, and the people who cast their vote have thought something about it. It is not sprung on them, nor is it a surprise to them that elicits an instant response. It is on a certain day; you know when it is. It is morally binding because you have been asked by your elected government to help them decide on an issue, normally of sovereignty, and this is why I am generally opposed to referendums. But in this instance, on the Euro, I believe everybody who has a vote – and I don't – should have the opportunity to have their say, because once sovereignty is given away it will never come back. Shared sovereignty is lost sovereignty in my view.

A referendum is by definition nationally important and because of that, it is the subject of media focus, and frankly the wording is very unimportant. Because of the wording of the Italian constitution, when they had a referendum on abortion, you had to vote "No" to say "Yes". And so that was the slogan of the people who were for changing the constitution, because you had to vote no to say yes, and everybody knew exactly what was at issue and how they were voting. That is not so in an opinion poll.

So how can Tony Blair win his referendum on Europe, if fixing the wording won't help?

I don't think he can, I don't think he should try and, knowing him to be a highly cautious political strategist, I don't think he will. For if Blair does go for a snap referendum on the Euro, I believe he will lose it, and if he does, his authority is gone, and his lock on political power will be considerably damaged, possibly beyond recovery.

Table 102: Attitudes to the Euro

Q. *Which of the following best describes your own view of British participation in the single currency?*

	Aug 1996 %	Jan 1998 %	Feb 1999 %	Mar 1999 %	Jun 1999 %	Aug-Sep 1999 %	Jun 2000 %	Aug 2000 %	29 May 2001 %
I strongly support British participation	10	17	17	15	12	13	13	13	10
I am generally in favour of British participation, but could be persuaded against it if I thought it would be bad for the British economy	27	27	29	24	23	23	21	21	23
I am generally opposed to British participation, but could be persuaded in favour of it if I thought it would be good for the British economy	21	24	21	26	36	25	24	23	24
I strongly oppose British participation	33	23	24	28	23	27	33	32	36
Don't know	9	9	9	7	6	11	9	10	6
Support	37	44	46	39	35	36	34	34	33
Oppose	54	47	45	54	59	52	58	55	60
Net support	-17	-3	1	-15	-24	-16	-24	-21	-27
"Waverers"	48	51	50	50	59	48	45	44	47

Source: MORI/various

If Tony Blair wants to win endorsement in a referendum for taking Britain into the single European Currency, he is going to have to change a lot of people's minds. It is still possible, but attitudes against the Euro have hardened. There are fewer open minds than once there were; the government has lost a lot of ground to the Euro-sceptic camp, while reluctant to start its campaign in favour in case it damaged Labour's electoral prospects.

The open minds are still there. Simple "for or against" surveys are now consistently finding that the antis lead by more than two-to-one, but it is clear that many of those who would vote in a referendum have not yet made up their minds. In our fourth election survey for *The Times*, we repeated a question we have used several times in the past few years, inviting respondents not only to tell us their general support or opposition but whether they might be persuaded.

The waverers have fallen from a high of 59% two years ago to 47%.

What does this mean in terms of a referendum? If all those who say they strongly support or oppose the euro turn out to vote (which may on the evidence of the general election be far too sanguine an assumption), we already have about a 46% turnout, splitting 36:10 against. The overall turnout is unlikely to be more than 70% at best, so the Prime Minister must forge his victory among that 24% of the electorate who might be persuaded to vote, but have not yet made up their minds for certain which way it will be. Simple arithmetic tells us that it can't be done – even if all the rest of the 70% voted in favour, he would still lose. He has to win over some of those who say they have already made up their minds to vote against, or hope that in the event they don't turn out.

Of course, the country has been through all this before. As I explained in my pamphlet for the Foreign Policy Centre[195], in the six months before the 1975 referendum in which Britain voted to stay in the Common Market, Harold Wilson managed to swing opinion from being 55:45 against to a 67:33 vote in favour, a swing of 22%.

---

[195] Robert M Worcester, *How to Win the Euro Referendum: Lessons from 1975* (Foreign Policy Centre, 2000)

313

However, there is a less hopeful parallel. At the start of 1975, as well as asking their respondents how they would vote in a referendum, Gallup also asked 'If the Government negotiated new terms for Britain's membership of the Common Market and they thought it was in Britain's interest to remain a member, how would you vote then?'. This question produced a huge swing in opinion and was in fact a very close predictor of the final referendum result six months later. In the MORI Financial Services polls for Schroder Salomon Smith Barney, and occasionally for other clients, we have been asking a similar follow-up question: the 'persuasion factor' is there, but it is much smaller than in 1975, as the graph shows – generally between 3% and 5%.

Figure 21: The Euro – if the government were to urge...

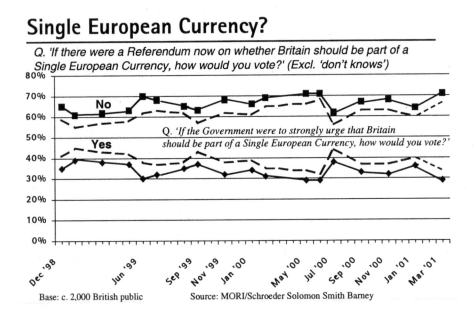

Single European Currency?

Q. 'If there were a Referendum now on whether Britain should be part of a Single European Currency, how would you vote?' (Excl. 'don't knows')

No

Yes

Q. 'If the Government were to strongly urge that Britain should be part of a Single European Currency, how would you vote?'

Base: c. 2,000 British public   Source: MORI/Schroeder Solomon Smith Barney

Nevertheless, the key factor is sure to be the degree of trust that the public has in the spokesmen putting each side of the argument, as it was in 1975. Before the petrol crisis it looked almost possible. Not now. In mid-2000 we found in a poll for the *News of the World*[196] that of the

---

[196] MORI Telephone Surveys interviewed 1,002 British adults aged 18+ on 22-23 June 2000.

likely key figures only Charles Kennedy had a positive trust rating on Europe, though both Tony Blair and Gordon Brown broke even.

Table 103: Trust in politicians on Europe

Q. And for each of the following, please tell me whether you would or would not trust them to make decisions about Britain's future role in Europe which will be in the interests of the British public?

		Trust	Not trust	Neither	Net trust
Liberal Democrat leader Charles Kennedy	%	41	31	28	+10
Prime Minister Tony Blair	%	43	44	13	-1
Chancellor Gordon Brown	%	41	42	17	-1
The European Parliament	%	34	48	18	-14
Conservative Party leader William Hague	%	32	52	15	-20
Foreign Secretary Robin Cook	%	31	53	16	-22
The European Central Bank	%	25	48	27	-23
Shadow Chancellor Michael Portillo	%	21	59	20	-38
Peter Mandelson	%	14	62	24	-48

Source: MORI/*News of the World*
Base: 1,002 British aged 18+, interviewed by telephone on 22-23 June 2000

Most people in Britain know little about the Euro (only 16% claimed to have heard of Wim Duisenberg in the same survey), and want to know more. Only a quarter believe the government has encouraged a sensible debate on the issue, while half think it is trying to hide the facts from the public, and three in five expect it to try to "bounce" the British public into agreeing to join. In these circumstances, putting the issue in emotive terms works well, and the antis are doing so.

Can Tony Blair win a referendum on the Euro within the first two years of the new Parliament? The government is not totally alone. For one thing, as a MORI survey for the Corporation of London has demonstrated, on balance the City is in favour of Britain joining the Euro. Furthermore, almost twice as many of the public thought that joining the Euro would be bad for Britain's economy as thought it would be good. If the government could win the economic argument in the public mind, it might have quite an effect. Obviously the opinions of the majority in the City may well have a bearing in this way when the time for the referendum campaign comes.

An NOP survey for *Powerhouse* during the election seems to support this: putting the proposition "if there were a referendum in a year or two, with the Government and a number of business leaders arguing strongly that Britain would be better off joining the single currency": of those expressing an opinion, 53% said they would be in favour, 47% against.[197]

But anyway, there is a lot of room for manoeuvre. In the Foreign Policy Centre pamphlet, I thought that the referendum would be in the autumn of 2001 and that they would win very narrowly indeed, something in the region of 52% to 48%. Clearly there will now not be a referendum this year, but two years down the line? Tony Blair is a terribly cautious Prime Minister. Now is this conservative, cautious Prime Minister going to call a referendum that he is not sure he will win? No way, Jose! So I think it may just be that they will find towards the end of 2002, after the introduction of the single European currency and coinage on the continent and all the chaos that will cause, that – apparent commitment or not – they can't make a decision after all. I think it more likely than not the referendum will not come in this Parliament at all, but in the Parliament yet to come. In 2005 or later the British public will be asked to agree to join the Euro and will probably do so – and, indeed, that is what the public thinks too[198], even if they don't like it.

---

[197] *Evening Standard*, 31 May 2001; The *Sun*, 31 May 2001.
[198] In a poll for grahambishop.com on 4-8 January 2001, 41% of the public thought it likely rather than unlikely that people in Britain will regularly use a single European currency and coinage by 2005, and 68% thought it likely by 2010.

Tory leadership

As we go to press, we do not know whether the Tory members have elected Ken Clarke or Iain Duncan Smith as their leader. The decision will probably make a huge difference to the future direction of the party, although at this point it looks almost inconceivable that they can win the next election under either (or under anyone else).

Table 104: Best Tory leader after Hague

Q. *If the Conservatives lose the General Election and William Hague steps down as party leader, which one of the politicians I am going to read out, if any, would you like to see lead the Conservative Party?*

	31 May-2 Jun 2001		4-5 Jun 2001	
	All	Con voters	All	Con voters
	%	%	%	%
Michael Portillo	15	22	18	29
Ann Widdecombe	12	13	10	12
Margaret Thatcher	8	11	7	11
Kenneth Clarke	17	11	15	10
John Redwood	4	8	4	4
Malcolm Rifkind	3	2	3	3
Francis Maude	2	4	1	2
Iain Duncan Smith	1	2	1	1
Liam Fox	2	3	1	1
Bill Emmott	n/a	n/a	*	*
David Davis	*	1	*	0
Other	1	2	2	4
None of these	14	6	12	6
Don't know	21	15	26	16

Source: MORI

Michael Portillo's exclusion from the Tory leadership race may have taken both his colleagues and the media by surprise, but it was following the trend of public opinion over the previous few weeks which had seen him lose much ground. Even at the time of the election, it did not seem was Michael Portillo the answer.

In two MORI surveys during the election (for the *Sunday Telegraph* and *The Economist*), when we asked the public who should take over the leadership if William Hague were to step down, Mr Portillo was the clear frontrunner among Conservative supporters, and even among the public as a whole he was neck-and-neck with Kenneth Clarke. Mr Clarke's opponent in the final ballot, Iain Duncan Smith, barely troubled the scorer; the clear choice of a third candidate appeared to be Ann Widdecombe.[199]

A week before the election, we tested[200] the public's attitudes to the then frontrunners as alternative leaders should William Hague step down. Using a series of "trial heat" questions, asking how the public would vote if one of three other possible candidates were Tory leader; Ann Widdecombe fared best, but the gap was only narrowed slightly.

Table 105: Voting under alternative Tory leaders

	Standard voting intention (i.e. Hague leader) %	If Michael Portillo were leader %	If Kenneth Clarke were leader %	If Anne Widde-combe were leader %
Conservative	27	28	28	31
Labour	50	50	50	49
Liberal Democrat	17	16	16	15
Other	6	6	6	5
Conservative lead over Labour	-23	-22	-22	-18

Source: MORI/*Sunday Telegraph*
Base: 1,010 adults 18+ interviewed on 31 May-2 June 2001

Furthermore, each of these alternative leaders while attracting some supporters from outside the party's currently diminished ranks would have lost some of the support that the Tories already had: if Mr Portillo were leader, 6% of Tories said they would switch their vote to other

---

[199] MORI surveys for the *Sunday Telegraph*, published on 3 June (MORI interviewed 1,021 British aged 18+ by telephone on 31 May-2 June 2001) and for the *Economist*, published on 8 June (MORI interviewed 1,010 British aged 18+ on 4-5 June 2001). In the latter survey, the name of Bill Emmott (the editor of the *Economist*) was included as a dummy to test for random answers.

[200] MORI survey for the *Sunday Telegraph*, published on 3 June. MORI interviewed 1,021 British aged 18+ by telephone on 31 May-2 June 2001.

parties, 6% would not vote, and 2% were undecided or refused to say. Mr Clarke would lose an alarming 11% to other parties (almost half of whom would switch to minor parties – presumably UKIP), 6% would not vote and 4% were undecided. Under Miss Widdecombe's leadership, 7% would switch, 4% would not vote and 4% would be undecided or refused to say.

After the election there was a shift of attitudes. Our poll for *The Times* at the end of June again asked the public who they thought would do the best job of leading the party, giving the five nominated leadership candidates as the options. Now it was Mr Clarke who had a commanding lead, with 32% naming him and only 17% Mr Portillo; Mr Duncan Smith (7%), Mr Ancram (6%) and Mr Davis (4%) trailed well behind, though that is only to be expected as – not being former Cabinet ministers like the other two – they are far less well-known to the man-in-the-street.

The gap was narrower, though, when we looked only at those currently supporting the Tories: in that case Mr Clarke's lead was only 29% to 25%. Similarly, when we put Kenneth Clarke and Michael Portillo in a head-to-head contest as best candidate, Mr Clarke triumphed two-to-one among the whole general public (51% to 25%), but only 49% to 39% among Tories.

This difference has two implications. The first, assuming that the paid-up Conservative members are likely to be more similar to Tory voters than to the public as a whole, is that notwithstanding Clarke's substantial lead among the public the leadership vote itself, had those been the two candidates, might have been rather less predictable. The other, though no surprise, is that Mr Clarke is the better equipped to appeal to those currently supporting other parties or no party at all.

It is interesting to note, though, that when we look at which groups of the population supported each candidate, Portillo had higher than average support among younger age groups. It is possible that though of less wide appeal to non-Conservatives at the moment, Portillo would have had a greater potential than Clarke to spread the Conservative message wider into groups where the party is weak at the moment.

But now the choice is Clarke or Duncan Smith and here it is more difficult to draw deep insights because Duncan Smith is so little known. The views of the ordinary Conservative voters may well not reflect those of the party activists, who will likely have a far clearer view of shadow cabinet members; nor is the general public's current attitude much clue as to how they will receive him if he is elected leader. Unlike Clarke, he starts with a clean slate. The same was fairly true of William Hague, and he was not a success; on the other hand Paddy Ashdown was quite as obscure when elected leader, yet eventually was an undoubted asset to his party.

Surely the shambles in the Conservative party cannot continue indefinitely. It seems highly unlikely that the Tories will win the next election under either Clarke or Duncan Smith, but it is vital that whichever wins restores some unity to the party and offers credible opposition; the British electorate will surely not tolerate the lack of a realistic alternative indefinitely. We tend to agree with Peter Kellner, "The Conservatives will not carry on as they are. They will either discover a new purpose, or fade into third place."[201]

---

[201] *Dialogue*, July 2001.

Conclusions

It's over for another four years, and for all the hoopla, nothing really happened.

Labour's 1997 landslide of a 179 majority over all other parties in the House of Commons is now 167 for the next four or five years. The Tories have added just one new MP to their 165, and regained the seat they lost to the Liberal Democrats in a by-election.

One independent Member of Parliament has replaced another. There's been a substantial reshuffle. Hague has announced his resignation. The one excitement is whether or not the Prime Minister has the bottle to call a referendum on whether or not Britain goes into the Single European Currency.

And we look forward to 5 May 2005, so those of us who find politics more fun as a spectator sport, or even as a bit player or in our case scorekeeper, will take out a new scorecard and start marking up the satisfaction figures, the economic optimism, the issues and above all the voting intentions of the Great British Public, even though we all know that there will not be any election before four years from now.

Watch for the third book in the series, to be published, by Politico's, in the Autumn of 2005. It's title? "Explaining Labour's Third Landslide".

Appendices

Appendix I: An Almost Infallible Forecasting Model
(Sweet FA Prediction model©)

Roger Mortimore

Professor Robert Mackenzie was once quoted as saying that he enjoyed election nights in the same way other people enjoyed the Cup Final. Research for the June-July 2000 edition of *British Public Opinion* newsletter suggests that there is more to this remark than meets the eye.

Allow me to present a prediction model for determining the outcomes of British general elections, which over the period since 1950 has a record to match Bob Mackenzie's swingometer. (See Table 106.) All you have to do to predict which of the major parties will have an overall majority in the Commons following the election is to note the shirt colours usually worn by the current holders (on election day) of the FA Cup.

Table 106: The Political Football

Election	Winner	FA Cup holders (year of final)	Shirt colour(s)	Correct?
2001	Lab	Liverpool (2001)	RED	Y
1997	Lab	Manchester United (1996)	RED	Y
1992	Con	Tottenham Hotspur (1991)	WHITE	Y
1987	Con	Coventry City (1987)	Sky BLUE	Y
1983	Con	Manchester United (1983)	RED	N*
1979	Con	Ipswich Town (1978)	BLUE	Y
O'74	Lab	Liverpool (1974)	RED	Y
F'74	Hung	Sunderland (1973)	RED & WHITE	Y
1970	Con	Chelsea (1970)	BLUE	Y
1966	Lab	Liverpool (1965)	RED	Y
1964	Lab	West Ham United (1964)	RED ("Claret")	Y
1959	Con	Nottingham Forest (1959)	RED	N
1955	Con	Newcastle United (1955)	Black & WHITE	Y
1951	Con	Newcastle United (1951)	Black & WHITE	Y
1950	Lab	Wolverhampton Wanderers (1949)	YELLOW ("Old Gold")	Y

* Would have been correct if Brighton & Hove Albion (BLUE) had not missed an open goal in the dying seconds of the FA Cup final, before losing the replay.

If their shirts are predominantly in the Conservative colours of blue or white, a Conservative victory will ensue; on the other hand if the predominant colour is red or yellow, Labour will be successful. (Black stripes are ignored.)

This, which I have christened the Sweet FA Prediction model, has failed only twice over the last fourteen elections; furthermore, the sensitivity of the prediction method is demonstrated by the election of February 1974, which produced the only post-election hung Parliament since the War – that election was fought when the cup holders were Sunderland, whose striped shirts are red and white in equal measure. The obvious improbability of such a pattern arising by chance gives the model a high degree of statistical significance.

Or perhaps not. The point of this *jeu d'esprit* is to demonstrate that it is possible to find an apparently statistically significant pattern in almost anything, given a sufficiently free hand. (Rather as certain scholars discovered "hidden messages" to prove that Francis Bacon wrote the plays of Shakespeare; Mgr Ronald Knox, when he set his mind to it, was able to use the same methods to "prove" that Queen Victoria wrote Tennyson's *In Memoriam*.) Of course, even this degree of freedom is not enough for some. In the 2001 election we had, as we always have, predictions aplenty by methods that cannot claim even the semblance of a track record: astrology (Jonathan Cainer in the *Mirror* on 3 April noted that "If he [Blair] does pick June 7 for the general election he will find it very inauspicious. This won't stop Labour from winning but it could well bring them a significantly reduced majority"); "voodoo" polls (prizewinner in 1997 the Tesco "Electoral Roll" poll with a predicted 13% share for the Monster Raving Loonies); "on the basis of history". (Dr David Carlton was undisputed loser of the 20 Reuter's experts in 1997, who even at the last predicted a hung Parliament because he believed history showed that a swing big enough to give Tony Blair a majority was impossible).

Of course, not all methods of prediction are so crude. The Kellner-Sanders index (based at yougov.com and reported in the *Observer* for some months before the election) had a greater degree of sophistication, based on a combination of opinion poll results and economic indicators, or so they claimed at the time. But as one of its two originators, Professor David Sanders, knows, the most elaborately tried and tested economic formulas are not necessarily proof against the anomalous behaviour of the British electorate. (In 1997 Professor Sanders, using economic formulas which had worked successfully for predicting election results in the 1980s, was Dr Carlton's nearest challenger for the Reuters wooden spoon.)

It is always possible to construct a pattern which fits the past. But unless it explains the past, in a way which still applies in the present, it will not help predict the future. The initial test of any model must be its inherent plausibility as a causal explanation, and this is a test that relies on judgment, not mathematics; if this is forgotten, "statistically significant" becomes a meaningless, perhaps dangerously misleading, term. Nor is "track record", as such, anything more than a perceptional delusion. Is the Sweet FA model more plausible now that it has been proved right once since I first published it?

But then perhaps it is. The 2000 FA Cup winners were Chelsea, who play in blue. If the election had been held on 3 May, as was generally predicted, Chelsea would still have been the cup-holders, and the model predicts that the Conservatives would have won. However, the election was not held on 3 May, but instead on 7 June; in the interim, another cup final was held and the FA Cup was now held by Liverpool (who are nicknamed the Reds for the obvious reason). So was it really Foot and Mouth that caused the election postponement? Or are Tony Blair and his football-loving entourage perhaps a little superstitious?

Appendix II: Reflections on the Comments by our Critics

Robert Worcester

Memorandum to:

John Curtice ("Getting it all wrong on the night", *Independent,* 12 June 2001)
Alan Travis (" Poll scars", *Guardian*, 13 June 2001)
Malcolm Dickson ("Hindsight gives clearer view of muddled picture from the polls", *The Herald*, 9 June 2001)
Stephen Glover ("Don't believe what you read in the newspapers: the opinion polls did not get the election right", *Spectator*, 16 June 2001).

cc. **Nick Cohen** ("The mystic Megs polish their crystal balls", *New Statesman*, 14 May 2001).

From: Robert Worcester

Subject: Personal Reflections on the Comments by our Critics

Remember next time, gentlemen:

1. Polls never 'predict', except on the eve of the election day when they all change their methodology to try to meet the unreasonable expectations of the media to provide a 'forecast', something the late George Gallup always refused to do. See my articles in April and May in *Parliamentary Monitor* in case you say this is 20/20 hindsight, which you know so well. True, sometimes pollsters do, but pollsters aren't polls.

2. Even then, as we know from polls conducted after people have voted, c. 8% of people change their mind on the final day (i.e., after the fieldwork for the final polls is completed)

3. The Association of Professional Opinion Polling Organisations published the final polls' results by each of the major pollsters the

afternoon of 8 June for the world to judge which pollster had what result, against the actual election result on 7 June. This has been the practice for several elections, so that the actual figures can be examined, not what some journalists imagine they saw published or broadcast or made up. The system that is used was originally designed by Professor Richard Rose of Strathclyde University over 20 years ago.

4. APOPO congratulated ICM for the most accurate forecast according to the Rose method, although ICM is not a member of APOPO.

5. The APOPO announcement pointed out that NOP's last poll before election day was carried out a week before, and could not be considered a forecast by any reasonable criterion except those used by the poll pickers.

6. For over two decades I have urged journalists and analysts to ignore the 'gap' and instead watch the share for each party, and especially in the past three elections, the Tory share, but we have no control over what anyone except our direct clients say about our polls. Often over the past few years newspapers' readers and broadcasters' listeners and viewers have been misled to think that because the Labour lead over the Tories was reduced that the Tories were doing better, when instead, inspection would have showed that it was an improved share for the Liberal Democrats at the expense of Labour, with the Tories' share remaining constant. Travis at least does focus, correctly, on the share, not the gap in the graphic, if not in the text of his critique.

7. Averaging the poll findings over the course of the election and comparing it to the final result to show how unreliable a 'forecast' it was is just silly, exposing the statistical ignorance and political naivety of the writer.

8. In virtually every election for thirty years, an 'underdog' effect has been seen, with the party in the lead doing less well than the final polls as some people see that they can vote for another party than the one in the lead without jeopardising the overall result, or indeed, as

in 1997 and 2001, to decide not to vote at all. The larger the lead going into election day, the greater I suspect there will be a tendency for an underdog effect.

9. Weighting by past voting would have made the MORI 'forecast' poll worse, not better, in every election in which we've been doing public polling starting in 1979, up to 1992; arguably, since then it would have improved it.

10. The exit polls, mentioned in the penultimate paragraph of Curtice's 12 paragraph article, were astonishingly accurate; they are however, not 'completely different creatures from opinion polls' as his final paragraph states. They do have the advantage of focusing on the people that have actually voted, and so do not have to estimate their final figures based on people's intentions to vote, which are subject to change as people change their minds, i.e., their intention to vote (which isn't 'lying to pollsters' as is sometimes alleged). Their results should lay to rest the argument that there is an army of 'shy Tories' out there, refusing to answer pollsters' questions.

11. No one seems to recall at least in print that in 1997 63% of the British people said they expected Labour to put up their taxes, and yet gave them their landslide victory, despite my reminding listeners this on a score or more of radio and television interviews and including it in numerous articles.

12. Alan Travis, the *Guardian*'s usual poll writer, calls for urgent reforms. We are very open to change, and constantly re-evaluate our methods. Our objective is to perform a difficult task as effectively as possible. At the same time, I'd like to see some humility on the part of the journalists who pick at the polls (other than those their paper publishes, of course) and give further thought to the lessons that should have been learned long ago about the way polls are reported. Polls are a marriage of the art of asking questions and the science of sampling, and the laws of sampling means that 19 times out of 20 the share, NOT the gap, will be within a plus or minus three percent

sampling tolerance, and every election since the war, save 1992, the polls on the eve of poll were within this band, including in 2001.

13. Malcolm Dickson also uses the gap, rather than share, and makes the elementary error of talking about the polls 'at a UK level', when we all poll only in Britain, not Northern Ireland.

14. It is curious that the ICM/Strathclyde 'Variometer' disappeared so quickly from their web site the day after the election, after underestimating the 1997 election outcome by 37 seats, and forecast their close share estimate to a Labour majority of 98 instead of the 167 majority Labour actually got on the night. Everything else remained on their web sites.

15. Nick Cohen gets the wooden spoon for being the worst commentator on polls, clearly exposing his ignorance of research methodology and unwilling to learn, dismissive of pollsters' attention to detail, prone to use lurid ('quackery', 'sly') language, quick to carp and unwilling to listen to explanation of the limitations of any sampling or statistical exercise, and knocking over straw men. One treasured comment from his article: "Yet even at 10 p.m. on election night…various Dimblebys on various networks will announce the conclusions of the exit polls collected by their minions at considerable expense. These polls will be discussed as if they are somehow on a par with real results from real constituencies." Yes Nick, they are, and no doubt you will in some future article avow that the exit polls were 'wrong again' for each exit poll *only* being within 10 seats of the final tally.

16. Cohen's win of the 2001 British general election wooden spoon for the worst article on the polls is only challenged by Stephen Glover's use of tabloid doorstep tactics to put words into my mouth, suggesting that I characterise my reaction to the final polls as 'satisfied'; I replied when he rang and asked me if I was satisfied, 'No, critical', but the words I used at the time did not appear in his article. Instead, having decided he wished to portray me as complacent, quoted selectively from newspapers' headlines quoting

poll leads to show us up, and then suggested that to complain that journalists concentrate too much on the gap between parties is perhaps a little disingenuous. 'Pollsters allow their data to be portrayed in a certain way', he adds. Stephen, since when do mere journalists, much less pollsters, decide what headlines say?

17. Glover also misses the point when he avows that 'Not one opinion poll among the many during the election campaign put Labour's lead as low as the nine points it achieved on the night. That's right. Not one poll." This is hardly surprising, as the Tories started the election in a hole, and kept digging week after week, talking about first taxation, then asylum seekers, then the Euro, and didn't click with the public until they hit on frightening the public with talk of meltdown themselves, otherwise described as 'Labour landslide'. As to 'never get the pollsters to concede fault', we do more often, and more openly, than most journalists. As he says, prophets go on prophesying even when their prophecies come unstuck. As I have so often said, polls don't 'predict', but some pollsters do, and I am one of them. On the Tuesday before the election at the KPMG non-executive directors' breakfast, I predicted a Labour majority of 166, splitting my guess between 165 and 167. The result was 167. How did Stephen Glover do? Not so well.

18. John Curtice's 'Getting it all wrong on the night' completely ignores the most obvious reason why the final pre-election day polls overestimated Labour's share, which I forecast in my article in *Parliamentary Monitor* in April before the election began. In that article I warned that "Old Labour" lags, who certainly voted for a Labour government in 1997 (and think they didn't get one) wouldn't be so keen to vote for another Blair landslide in 2001, and they didn't. But as most of them were in safe Labour seats, that didn't affect the outcome in seats, but certainly did in numbers of voters (turnout) and shares. Also, Curtice implies that telephone polls have an advantage over face to face surveys, but this does not explain why the personal interviewing did so well by comparison with the other telephone polls, or why for four years they have been so stable along side telephone polls. Nor does he cover the advantages that face to

329

face polls have, in the use of being able to show electors in each constituency the names and parties of the candidates standing in that constituency, once nominations close (the much commented on 'change of methodology' MORI stood accused of, and cheerfully acknowledged, pointing out that it was just the same in 1997.)

Oh well, there's always a next time. However, no doubt these same guys will be harping on the same themes four years from now, and no matter the final polls, will find something to pick at.

Index

Adam Smith Institute, 34
advertisements, political, 166, 170-72
age
    and political identification, 130-2
    voting behaviour by, 200-202, 205-208
agenda setting, 101-2
agricultural constituencies, 209-15
American Presidential election (2000), 191, 274, 280, 282-84
Ancram, Michael, 319
animal welfare
    as election issue, 30, 31, 101, 228
    fox hunting, 128-29, 213, 305-306
apathy, 179-80
Archer, Jeffrey (Lord), 63
Ashcroft, Lord (Michael), 62
Ashdown, Paddy, 108, 225, 227, 320
ASL (Audience Selection), 253
Assinder, Nick, 40
Association of Professional Opinion Polling Organisations (APOPO), 284, 325-26
astrology, 323
    asylum seekers
    as election issue, 29-30, 82-83, 84, 101, 228
    Conservative campaigning on, 71, 82-83, 93-95, 329
Atkinson, Simon, xvi, 61
Attlee, Clement, 19, 233, 234
Ayr
    by-election (to Scottish Parliament), 65, 105
    constituency polls in (2001), 296
'baby bonds', 129-30, 306
Bacon, Francis, 323
Baines, Paul, 10, 80
Baker, Kenneth, 287
Baldwin, Stanley, 50
Baldwin, Tom, 143, 164
Banks Hoggins O'Shea FCB, 299
Barnett formula, 229
BBC, xii, 292
    BBC News Online, 40, 176, 240, 242-43
    ICM election day poll for, 280-81
    neutrality of reporting, 148
    Newsnight, 240, 308
    NOP exit poll for, xiii, 280, 284
    On The Record, 211
    Radio 5 Live, 240, 308
    reporting of polls, 240, 284

    Today programme, 183, 188
BBC History Magazine, 233
belief in God, 218
Bell, Martin, 213
Benn, Tony, 303
Bennett, Rosemary, 164, 299
Bermondsey by-election (1983), 245
best party on key issues, 28-31
best Prime Minister, 41, 71, 226-27
best team of leaders, 77-78
betting on elections, 233, 235-38
Biberian, M., 270
'Black Wednesday', 25, 51, 96
Blackman, Oonagh, 164-65
Blair, Cherie, 12, 220
Blair, Leo, political impact of birth, 11-12
Blair, Tony
    and religion, 220
    chocolate heads of, 302
    compared with Hague, 41, 57, 71-72, 74-75, 138-39, 151, 226-27
    considered honest and principled, 120-21
    decision on election date, 215-17, 324
    Gordon Brown as leadership rival, 28
    handling of petrol crisis, 52
    leader image attributes, 21-22, 75
    leader image overall rating, 21-22, 138-39
    like him/like his policies, 20-21, 74
    newspaper coverage of, 163
    no commitment on Euro referendum date, 308, 316
    number wanting to watch him on TV, 151
    opinions of business leaders, 72
    panic over image and Gould memos, 36-45
    positive effect on party fortunes, 17-23
    promise not to increase income tax, 96
    satisfaction ratings as Prime Minister, 11-12, 18-20, 39, 53, 60
    support for Dome, 104
    trust on Europe, 315
    and *passim*
Blunkett, David, 18, 119
bookmakers, 217, 233, 235-38
Boon, Martin, xiii
boring, whether the election was, xiv, 141-45, 166-67
Boulton, Adam, 287
Boycott, Rosie, 160

Bradley, Peter, 210
Braintree, 88
British Council, 89
British Election Panel Study, 271
British Election Study surveys, 96, 117, 239-42, 243, 246, 254
British Institute of Public Opinion, 233
British Journal of Political Science, 270
British Medical Association, MORI surveys for, 33-34, 119-20
'Britishness', 88-95
broadcasts, party election, 94, 144-45, 148-49, 166-67, 170, 173
Brock, George, xvii
Brogan, Benedict, 164
Brown, Gordon, 17, 18, 52, 231, 308
    as leadership rival to Blair, 28
    attitudes of business leaders, 72
    compared to Michael Portillo, 72
    perceived lack of trustworthiness, 57,58
    press coverage of, 163
    public recognition of, 67
    record as Chancellor and its significance, 23-31, 53, 72
    spending announcements after petrol crisis, 54-55
    trust on Europe, 315
Brown, Michael, 214
Brunson, Michael, 280
BSE ('Mad Cow Disease'), 104, 216
budgets, public satisfaction with, 26-27
Burke, Edmund, 158
Burkholder, Richard, 237
Bush, President George, 119
Bush, President George W, xvii, 274, 275, 282, 283
Business for Sterling, 309
Butler, David, 117, 189, 233, 291
Cainer, Jonathan, 323
Callaghan, James, 19, 23, 38, 43, 48, 52
campaign, election
    campaigning by parties, 166-72
    Liberal Democrat gain in support during, 221-29
    media coverage of, 149-65
    most effective party, 222
    public interest in campaign, 142-9
    switching of voter support during, 13-14, 142
Campbell, Alastair, 64
Canavan, Dennis, 45
candidates
    perceived quality of, 11
    satisfaction with information about, 150-51
canvassing, 166-70

canvass returns, 287
Carlton TV, 213
Carlton, David, 323
CBS, 283
Chamberlain, Neville, 234
Channel 4
    Channel 4 News focus groups, 300
    ICM poll for, 241
    NOP poll for, 44, 56
    see also Powerhouse
Chappell, Brian, 234
Chartered Institute of Marketing, 171
Cheadle, 88
christianity, 218-20
Christmas, Linda, 163
Church of England, 219-20
Churchill, Sir Winston, 233-35
churning of votes, 13
City University Graduate School of Journalism, 163
civic duty as reason for voting, 111
Clarke, Harold, 240
Clarke, Kenneth, 18, 61, 62, 301
    leadership election (2001), 317-20
    would have been better leader, 2
Clarke, Percy, 299
class
    and political identification, 130-32
    and voting behaviour, 195-98, 200-202
class sizes in schools, 32-34, 305
Clause Four of Labour Party constitution, 196
Clifton, Andy, 237
Clinton, President William J., 50
CNN, 283
Coe, Sebastian (Lord), 63
Cohen, Nick, 236, 237, 325, 328
Coleman, Stephen, 175-78
Commission for Racial Equality, 82
Commission on the Future of Multi-Ethnic Britain, 89
compulsory voting, 190, 193
Conservative Party
    avowed disbelief of polls, xi-xiii, 1, 65, 234-35, 258, 269
    canvass returns, 288
    Central Office, 61, 62-64, 287, 288
    divisions on Europe, etc., 68-71
    electoral record (1997-2001), 64-67
    expected consequences of Tory win, 99-100
    fundraising, 62
    ideological divisions analysed, 126
    image, 76-81
    judged over 20th Century, 76

leadership election (2001), 317-20
leadership election rules, 63
members' 'referendum' on Euro policy, 69
party staff, 62-4
perceived attitude of newspapers, 161
private polls, 66, 287-88
readiness for government, perceived, 41, 76-81
record of previous Tory governments a liability, 102-106
search for election winning issues, 82-106 and *passim*
Consignia, 188
constituencies, public knowledge of names, 122
constituency polls, 295-97
constitution, as election issue, 29-30, 228
consumer confidence, 23-26
control freakery, 45-51
Cook, Robin, 18, 315
Corporation of London, 315
Coughlin, Con, xvii
crime,
    as election issue, 39
    government record on, 34-35, 39, 82-83
Crossley, Archibald, 301
Curtice, John, 236, 237, 246, 263, 271, 292, 293, 325, 327, 329, 330
D'Ancona, Matthew, xvii
Dacre, Nigel, xvii
Daily Express, 63, 133-34, 153-65, 254
    MORI surveys for, 310
    NOP surveys for, 63, 198, 221, 290
Daily Mail, 133-34, 153-65, 245, 258
    MORI surveys for, 261
Daily Mirror. See Mirror
Daily Record, 155, 159, 161
    Scottish Opinion polls for, 244, 295-7
Daily Star, 134, 153-61
Daily Telegraph, 34, 89, 94, 133-34, 153-65, 246, 258, 268, 302
    Gallup surveys for, 52, 68, 72, 85, 103, 106, 221, 259, 264, 275
    reporting of polls, 297-8
    use of voodoo polling, 301
Dale, Iain, xi
date of election, 215-17, 243
David, Peter, xvii
Davies, Ron, 46
Davis, David, 18, 317, 319
decisions, time of, 14
defence, as election issue, 29, 30, 101, 228
delivery on promises, Labour failure, 31-35
demographic break down of voting, 5

Desmond, Richard, 160-61
devolution, 30, 31, 35, 49, 228-31
Diana, Princess of Wales, death of, 19, 32
Dickson, Malcolm, 325, 328
digital TV, voting by, 191
disengagement, political, 116-22
Disraeli, Benjamin, 286
divided parties, 2, 57, 69-70, 79, 84, 126
Dixville Notch, 283
Dobbie, Peter, xvii
Dobson, Frank, 46-47, 65, 230
Dome, Millennium, xi, 2, 36, 51, 53, 104, 126, 262
Dorset Mid and Poole North, 88
Dorset South, 88, 213
Dudley North, 210
Duisenberg, Wim, 315
Duncan Smith, Iain, 183, 301, 317-20
Duncan, Emma, xvii
Durant, Henry, 234
East Yorkshire, 94
Eastham, Paul, 164, 165
Eastwood, 296
Ecclestone, Bernie, 58
Echo Research, 152- 65
Economic and Social Research Council (ESRC), 240
Economic Optimism Index, 23-26
Economist, The, xvii
    MORI surveys for, 24, 28, 30, 41, 90, 97, 127, 129, 132, 133, 180, 207, 222, 223, 241, 246, 247, 303, 306, 318
economy, managing the
    as election issue, 17, 24, 25, 26, 28, 30, 31, 101, 228, 315
    political significance of, 23-31
Eddisbury by-election (1999), 65, 268
E-Democracy Programme (Hansard Society), 175
Eden, Anthony, 19
Edinburgh Pentlands, 296
education
    and devolution, 228-29
    as election issue, 26, 28-31, 101-102, 207
    class sizes in schools, 32-34, 305
    expecations for second term, 306-307
    government record on, 32-35
    importance to public, 82-83, 84
    leader most in tune with public, 41
    public knowledge of policies, 106
    private companies running state schools, 128-29, 306
    Section 28, 105, 219
    selection in schools, 119, 129, 306

spending on, 97
unrest among teachers, January 2000, 36
effectiveness of campaigns, 222
Electoral Commission, xiii, xvii, 109, 111, 112, 114, 115, 144, 146, 147, 149, 151, 152, 156, 168, 170, 171, 173, 183, 185, 187, 188, 190, 192, 194, 212, 226, 310
electoral register, 20, 36, 109-10, 193-94, 217
electoral system, 180-81
electronic voting, 191
Emmott, Bill, xvii, 317, 318
environment, as election issue, 29
Epictetus, 6
epolitix.com, xiv, xvi, 290
Essex, University of, 240
Ethnicity, voting by, 5
Europe
    British self-identification as European, 91
    business attitudes to Single Currency, 316
    Conservative choice as election issue, 81-8, 329
    Conservative divisions over, 2, 68-71, 84-85, 128, 130
    expectations of government in second term, 307
    importance as election issue, 29-30, 101-102, 228
    leader most in tune with public, 41
    leaving EU "extremist", 85-86
    public attitudes to EU, 85-86, 92
    proposal for Rapid Reaction Force, 85
    single currency, 86-87, 106, 129, 305, 308-16
European Central Bank, 315
European Commission
    consumer confidence index, 24
    Eurobarometer surveys, 90, 148, 297
European Democratic Group, MORI survey for, 85
European elections (1999), 9, 40, 46-47, 64-66, 69, 84, 87, 114, 135, 182
    opinion polls during, 268, 278
European Parliament, 315
Evening Standard, 159, 237
    ICM surveys for, 34, 47, 104, 231, 244, 246, 247
    IDA London Monitor survey, 72
    MORI surveys for, 13
    NOP surveys for, 103
Exchange Rate Mechanism, European, 25, 51, 96
exit polls, xii-xiii, 280-85, 327, 328
    in the USA, 282
    NOP/BBC exit poll (1997), xiv
expectations of Labour in second term, 305-307
expectations of parties if elected, 76-77
Falconer, Lord (Charles), 36

Falklands War, 303
farming constituencies, 209-15
Federal Trust, 309
fickleness of public opinion, 13-15
Field, Henry, 234
Financial Times, 24, 36, 134, 153-65, 233, 299, 308
first time voters, 205
floating voters, 10, 15, 70, 142, 169-70, 220, 300
focus groups, xii, 63, 68, 72, 152, 286, 304
    Labour party private polling, 37-44
    media reporting of, 298-300
Foot and Mouth Disease, 24, 26, 82, 102, 104, 168, 184, 209, 211, 213, 214-17, 324
Foot, Michael, 43, 227
football, 90, 163
    "Sweet FA" prediction model, 322-24
    World Cup matches and elections, 15
foregone conclusion, election was, 179-80
Foreign Policy Centre, 309, 313, 316
fox hunting, 128-29, 213, 305-306
Fox, Liam, 317
fraud, electoral
    risk of with new voting systems, 193
Freedom of Information Act, 36
Galloway & Upper Nithsdale, 212
Gallup, xi, 237
    accuracy of final polls, 246-47
    fieldwork for British Election Study, 239, 240
    poll methodology, 239, 249, 253-35, 257-59, 262-64, 268-69, 275-77
    polling in 1930s and 1940s, 233, 234, 235
    polls in US elections, 240
    reporting of June 2000 survey, 297-98
    results of surveys by, 19, 58, 59, 68, 72, 85, 103, 106, 198, 314
    voting intention polls, 52, 221, 241, 284
Gallup, Dr George, 234, 255, 301, 325
gender gap in voting behaviour, 199-204
Getty, John Paul, 62
GfK, 24
Glover, Stephen, 246, 325, 328, 329
GMTV, 240
Goldsmith, Sir James, 172, 245
Goldsmiths College, 237
Goldwater, Barry, 54, 269
Gore, Albert, 274, 275, 282, 283
Gould, Philip, 49, 50, 152
    leaked memos, 2, 36-45
'government by opinion poll', 49-50
GQ, 64
grahambishop.com, 316
Granada TV, 121, 122

Great Reform Act (1832), 286
Greater London Authority, 228, 230-31
Greenwich by-election (1987), 65
grey power, 205-208
Grice, Andrew, 164
Groom, Brian, 164-65, 308
Guardian, xvii, 36, 75, 133-34, 153-65, 180, 203, 287, 302
    ICM surveys for, 45, 84, 87, 94, 98, 106, 221, 237, 241, 246-47, 258, 259, 264, 273
    reporting of polls, 278, 293, 325, 327
    variometer, 292-94
Guildford, 88
habit as a reason for voting, 111-12
Hague, Ffion, 64
Hague, William
    attitudes of business leaders, 72
    "Billy Bandwagon", 53
    chocolate heads of, 302
    claim to have drunk 14 pints in a day, 64, 262
    compared with Blair, 41, 57, 71, 74, 138-39, 151, 226-27
    considered honest and principled, 120-21
    "foreign land" speech, 89, 94
    image as leader, 39, 71-75
    leader image, overall rating, 128-29
    like him/like his policies, 73
    newspaper coverage, 163
    number wanting to watch him on TV, 151
    personal image, 67-68
    readiness to be Prime Minister, 41, 71-75
    satisfaction ratings as Tory leader, 70
    trust on Europe, 315
    and *passim*
Hall, Nicola, 175
Halliwell, Geri, 154
Hansard Society, 175-78
Hardie, James Keir, 196
Hardy, James, 164-65
Harman, Harriet, 203
Harris Poll (US), 218, 242, 244, 274
Harris Research, 172, 253, 267, 269
Harrow East, 210
Hartlepool, 245
Haseler, Stephen, 309
Hatfield rail crash, 103
health care, *see* National Health Service.
Heath, Edward, 15
Herald, The, 295, 325
    System Three polls for, 229, 244, 295
Hereford, 88
Hertsmere, 299

Hewitt, Patricia, 196
Hexham, 217
Himmelweit, Hilde, 270
Hinduja affair, 58
Holborow, Jonathan, 63
Hollick, Lord (Clive), 160
Holmes, Sherlock, 64
honeymoon period, 19-20, 32
Hornchurch, 210
House Magazine, 66, 238
House of Lords, 35, 46, 48, 49
housing tenure, voting by, 5
housing, as election issue, 5, 28-30, 101, 228
Hoy, Craig, xvi
HTV, 244
Hughes, David, 164, 165
Hughes, Simon, 245
ICM, xi, xiii, 297, 298
    accuracy of final polls, 246-47, 326
    constituency polls, 295-96
    election day poll for the BBC, 280
    internet polls, 242, 243
    poll methodology, 239, 253, 257-59, 262-65, 267-78, 293-94
    private pollsters for Conservative Party, 287
    results of surveys by, 46, 47, 84, 86, 87, 93, 98, 104, 105, 106, 183, 184, 226, 229, 231, 237
    variometer, 292-94, 328
    voting intention in Scotland, 244
    voting intention polls, 45, 221, 241
IG Index, xi, 237
image, importance of, 7-13
immigration, 82-83, 88-95, 101
    importance to voters, 28-30, 83, 101, 228
importance of who wins, 135-36
Independent, The, 36, 134, 153-65, 214, 239, 263, 325
    Rasmussen polls for, 239, 241, 246, 247
Independent on Sunday, 134, 156-61, 245
inflation, 32-33
information, political
    importance of, 145-47
    sources of, 147-49
Institute for Citizenship, 189
Institute of Directors, 108, 238
interest in politics, 122-24
interest in the election campaign, 141-49
interest rates, 32-33, 305
internet, xiv, 173-78
    as source of political information, 147, 166
    BBC News Online, 40, 176, 240, 242-43
    epolitix.com, xvi

MORI website (www.mori.com), xv, 54, 184, 253
poll details on newspaper websites, 239, 273, 275, 292
polling by, 242-44, 300
tactical voting websites, 226
voting by, 192
issues
important in deciding vote, 28-31, 84, 101-102
most important facing Britain, 82-83
issues, best party on, 28-31
reasons voters ignore them, 9
ITN, xii, xvii, 284
MORI exit poll for, 280-82
ITV, perceived neutrality of reporting, 148
Jay, Patrick, xi
Jenkins, Roy, 227
Jennifer's Ear, War of, 102
Johnson, President Lyndon B., 269
Jones, George, 163-64, 298
Jordan, 154
Joseph Rowntree Reform Trust, 122
jury trial, 35
Kavanagh, Trevor, xvii, 164-65
Kellner, Peter, 2, 66, 237, 270, 320, 323
Kennedy, Charles, 18, 41, 44, 71, 108, 163, 225, 226
chocolate heads of, 302
predicted to lose his seat, 295
trust on Europe, 315
Kennedy, President John F., 270
Kettering, 88
key issues, best party on, 28
King, Anthony, 19, 278
Kinnock, Neil, 43, 96, 138, 139, 196
Kirby, Ian, xvii
Knox, Mgr Ronald, 323
Kosovo, 302
KPMG, 2, 238, 329
Kuttner, Stuart, xvii
Labour Party
candidate selection for London Mayor, 46
control freakery, 45-51
Gould memos on private polls, 36-45
image of, 77-81
panic over public image, 35-51
perceived attitude of newspapers, 161-62
private polls, 286-7
and passim
Ladbrokes, 237
Lancaster & Wyre, 88

late decisions by voters, xiii, 14, 142, 223, 248, 278-79
law and order
as election issue, 26, 28-31, 39, 44, 71, 101, 207, 228
fast-track punishment for young offenders, 32-33
leader most in tune with public, 41
See also crime.
leader image, 8, 10-11
Blair's image, 21-22, 38-40
combined ratings of Blair and Hague very poor, 138-39
Hague's image, 71-75
perceptual map of, 75
relative importance to public of attributes, 21, 23
leaders
dominance of election media coverage, 151, 163
importance to voters, 7
number wanting to watch them on TV, 151
satisfaction with information about, 151
leaders, team of, 77-81
leaflets through the door
as source of political information, 147
number delivered and received, 166-70
letters to voters from party leaders, 166
Letwin, Oliver, 64
Leverhulme, 1st Viscount, 172
Liberal, self-description of political values, 126-34
Liberal Democrats, 221-27
MORI private poll for, 288
tend to slip in polls between elections, 269
and passim
Literary Digest, 301
Little, Alison, 164
Livingstone, Ken, 36, 46-47, 104, 230- 31
Lloyd George, David, 227
local campaigning, 166-70
local elections, 40, 65, 67, 114, 135, 182, 191
Local Government Act. See Section 28
Local Government Association, 191
London
election of Mayor, 2, 35, 40, 46-49, 63, 65, 72, 217, 228, 231, 247
impact of devolution, 228-30
polls in, 244
London Assembly, Greater
elections to (2000), 40, 65
London News Network, MORI survey for, 231
London Underground, 103-104, 230-31, 305
Long, Chris, xvii

Los Angeles Times, 282
Loughborough University Communications
    Research Centre, 151
Ludlow, 212
Luntz, Frank, 300
MacArthur, Brian, xvii, 152, 154
Mackenzie, Robert, 322
Macleod, Iain, 189
Maguire, Kevin, 62, 164
Mail on Sunday, xvii, 133-34, 152, 156-62, 302
    MORI surveys for, 28, 39, 41, 43, 45, 56, 57,
        58, 59, 60, 82, 85, 95, 97, 215, 218, 261
Major, John, 15, 19, 25, 42, 57, 59, 67, 69, 70, 73,
    77, 102, 136, 138, 139, 227, 327
Mandelson, Peter, 58, 60, 87, 165, 245, 299, 315
manifestos
    Labour launch receives little coverage, 154
    public attitudes to, 140
    public recognition of policies, 106
marginal seats
    Conservative failure to make ground in after
        petrol crisis, 53-55
    fall in turnout less in, 181-86
    polls in, 53-55, 184-85, 243, 281, 295, 299
    rurality of, 210-11, 216
    targeting electors in, 7-9, 168-69
Market Research Society enquiry into the polls
    (1992-4), 254, 264
Market Research Wales, 230, 244
Marplan, 253
Martin, Tony, 82
Mattinson, Deborah, 203
Maude, Francis, 287, 317
Mayor of London, election of, xvi, 40, 46-49, 63
McSmith, Andy, 164
media. *See* newspapers, television, radio
Michael, Alun, 46
'Michigan' Question, 116-17
middle class. *See* class
Millar, Stuart, xvii
Millennium Dome. *See* Dome
Mirror, The, 65, 133-34, 143, 153-65, 303, 323
mobile phones, 176
Monmouth, 88
Moran, Lord, 235
Morgan, Rhodri, 46
MORI
    accuracy of final polls, 246-47
    campaign polls, 241
    Economic Optimism Index (EOI), 24-26
    exit polls for ITN, xii-xiii, 280-82, 327, 328
    political team, xvi

poll methodology, 239, 249-55, 257-79
Tory lead in voting intention polls, September
    2000, 51
    website (www.mori.com), xv, 54, 184, 253
    and *passim*
MORI Excellence Model, 76, 136, 137
MORI Scotland, 219
MORI Technology Tracker, 173
MORI Telephone Surveys, xvi, 17, 28, 39, 45, 56,
    58, 67, 103, 120, 171, 216, 222, 314
Morris, Dick, 50
Mortimore, Roger, xv, xvi, 54, 61, 184
MOSAIC geo-demographic marketing class-
    ification, 211
MPs
    public knowledge of names, 121-22
    public satisfaction with, 120-21
    satisfaction with, 226
Murphy, Joe, xvii, 286
National Health Service, 102
    and devolution, 228-29
    as election issue, 26
    expected improvement in second term, 306-307
    government record on, 32-35
    hospital waiting lists, 32-35, 305
    importance to public, 29-31, 82-83, 98, 101-102,
        207, 216
    leader most in tune with public, 41
    spending on, 96-98
    use of private hospitals, 129-30, 305-306
    winter crisis 1999-2000, 35
national identity, 89-91
NATO, 85, 302
NBC, 283
New Labour
    attraction to middle classes, 131, 197
    self-description of political values, 126-34
New Statesman, 217, 237, 325
    use of voodoo polling, 301
Newman, Cathy, 164
Newport, Frank, 275
News Chronicle, 233-35
News of the World, xi, xvii, 133, 152, 156-61
    ICM surveys for, 243
    MORI surveys for, 51, 52, 208, 261, 314-15
Newsnight, 240, 308
newspaper coverage
    content of, 150-52
    direction and negativity of, 152-65
    political influence of, 158-61
    public satisfaction with scale of, 150
newspaper readership

and political identification, 133-4
    voting by, 158-60
newspapers
    as source of political information, 147-49
    items of most interest to readers, 162-63
    reporting of opinion polls, 289
NOP, xi
    Bermondsey by-election poll (1983), 245
    exit poll for the BBC, xiii, 280, 284
    poll methodology, 239, 253-55, 259, 271, 275-
        76
    private polls for Labour Party, 286-87
    results of surveys by, xiv, 34, 58, 59, 63, 72, 87,
        98, 99, 103, 151, 198, 207, 229, 243, 316
    Tory lead in voting intention poll, (September
        2000), 43-44, 51-52, 56
    voting intention in Wales, 244
    voting intention polls, 221, 241, 246, 290, 326
Norfolk North, 88
Norfolk North West, 212
Norris, Steven, 65
Northampton South, 88
Northern Ireland, as election issue, 29-31, 101, 228
O'Flynn, Patrick, 164-65
O'Grady, John, 245
Observer, The, 133-34, 152, 156-61, 236-37, 323
    ICM polls for, 86, 226, 241
'Old Labour', 17, 108, 181, 329
    self-description of political values, 126-34
older voters, 205-208
On The Record, 211
on-the-spot fines, 39
'One-Nation' Tories, self description of political
    values, 126-34
Opinion Dynamics/Fox News survey (US), 218
opinion polls
    "adjusted" polls, 268, 271-73, 293-94
    accuracy since 1945, 247-48
    ad hoc polls and regular polls compared, 261
    calculation of figures, 249-53
    campaign polls (2001), 241
    companies polling nationally in 2001, 239-42
    constituency polls, 295-97
    distinguishing voters from non-voters, 273-78
    early history in Britain, 233-35
    effect on voting behaviour, 179
    face-to-face and telephone interviewing, 254-55,
        258-62, 330
    final polls (2001), 246-48
    'government by opinion poll', 49-50
    inaccuracy, reasons for, 249, 266, 273-79
    internet polls, 242-44

interviewing in street, 254
    late swing, 248, 278-79
    media reporting of, 58-59, 289-304, 325-30
    methodology, 249-79
    non-national polls, 244-45, 295-97
    number of, 152
    private polls for political parties, 38-39, 66-67,
        195, 286-88
    prompted voting intention, 263-68
    quasi-random sampling, 254, 257-62
    question order, 253-54
    question wording, 250-1, 263-8, 310
    quota samples, 28, 45, 94, 141, 249, 255, 257-62
    reported past vote, 269-72
    sampling, basic theory of, 255-57
    seat projections from voting polls, 290-5
    underdog effect, 179-80, 248, 278-9, 326-27
    was pre-election lead misleading?, 186
    weighting, 251-2, 279
    weighting by reported past vote, 268, 271-73,
        279, 293-94, 327
Opinion Research Business, 218
"out of touch" - image of leaders, 20, 22, 39, 71,
    213-14
Owen, David, 253
Parkinson, Cecil (Lord), 299
Parliamentary Monitor, 35, 44, 325, 329
Parris, Matthew, 50
Party Election Broadcasts. See broadcasts
party identification, 116-17, 126-34
party image, 8, 69-70, 76-81
    combined overall rating of Labour and Tories,
        139-40
    importance to voters, 7, 10-11
    perceptual map of, 80
Pascoe-Watson, George, 164, 165
patriotism, 22-23, 39, 88-95
pensions
    75p rise, 203, 208
    as election issue, 30, 31, 83, 101, 207, 228
Perth, 296-97
petrol crisis, xi, 20, 42, 43, 51-57, 78, 97, 103, 125,
    203, 208, 209, 211, 314
Phillips, Trevor, 89
phone-in polls, 300-303
Pickett, John, xvii
Pimlott, Ben, 237
Pinto-Duschinsky, Michael, 189
Pirie, Madsen, 34
Platell, Amanda, 62, 64
'playing the race card', 88-89, 93-94
Poison Index, 156-57, 163-65

policemen on the beat, 305
policies
    importance to voters, 7-11
    party with best, 77-78
    public knowledge of, 106
    public priorities, 305
    public's overall assessment of parties', 81
    satisfaction with information about, 151
    See also issues.
political triangle model, 7-10, 140
    illustration, 8
    trends, 10
polling cards, 109, 187
polling stations, abolition of, 192
popular leadership index, 74
Portillo, Michael, 18, 62-63, 72, 77, 163, 287, 315, 317-20
postal strike, 167
postal voting, 108, 167, 187-90, 217
posters on billboards, 166, 170-72
Powell, General Colin, xvii
Powerhouse (Channel 4), 240, 280
    NOP surveys for, 34, 58, 59, 103, 290, 316
prediction of election result
    by means other than opinion polls, 233-38
    by polls - *see* opinion polls
    by Robert Worcester, xi, 2-3, 237-38
Prescott, John, 18, 67, 154, 163, 231
    punches a protester, 155
Prime Minister, most capable, 41, 71, 226-27
Prime Ministers, satisfaction ratings of, 19
private polls for political parties, 38-39, 66-67, 195, 286-88
privatisation, 305
    railways, 103, 128-29
private sector provision of public services
    in state schools, 128-29, 306
    NHS patients in private hospitals, 129-30, 305-306
Pro-Euro Conservative Party, 69, 237
promises, parties trusted to keep, 79, 307
promises, whether government had kept, 17, 31-33, 39, 81, 96, 97, 102, 108, 119
proportional representation, 46, 67, 87, 129, 180-81, 291
proxy votes, 188
Public Perspective, 218
Public Private Partnership, 103-104, 231, 305
public spending, 23
public transport
    and devolution, 228-31
    as election issue, 28-30, 35, 101

government record, 34-35
importance to public, 83
London Underground, 103-104, 230-31, 305
railway safety, 103
renationalising the railways, 129
qualitative research. *See* focus groups
Queen Elizabeth II, H.M., 20
Queensland tactic, 278
race
    effect of Tory asylum policies, 94-95
    race relations, 82, 94-95
    voting by, 5, 94
radio
    as source of political information, 147-49
    content of coverage, 151
    Radio Broadcasting Authority, 284
Railtrack, 103
railways
    renationalisation of, 103, 128-29
    safety, 103
Rallings, Colin, xvii, 66, 188
random digit dialling, 239, 243, 257
Rapid Reaction Force, European, 85
Rasmussen Research, 239-40, 246, 247, 275
Reader's Digest, xvii, 93
reasons for voting, 111-113
Red Pepper, 2, 108, 238
Redwood, John, 301, 317
Rees-Mogg, William (Lord), 210, 221
referendum on the Euro, 57, 70, 84, 178, 307, 308-16, 321
Referendum Party, 87, 172, 250, 287
referendums not the same as opinion polls, 309
registration to vote, 20, 36, 109-10, 193-94, 217
Reland, Jacques, 309
religion, 218-20
Representation of the People Act (2000), 284
results of election, 3
Reuters, 236, 323
Riddell, Peter, xvii, 164, 209, 251, 267, 277, 289
Rifkind, Sir Malcolm, 296, 317
right to vote, perceived importance, 111-13
right wing, Conservatives too, 198
Road to the Manifesto, The (1996), 3-33
Roberts, Yvonne, 203
Roman Catholicism, 219-20
Romsey by-election (2000), 40, 65, 66, 225
Roper Center, 218
Roper, Elmo, 301
Rose, Richard, 247, 326
Routledge, Paul, 164, 165, 303
Roxburgh, Selkirk & Peebles by-election (1965), 65

Royal Family, 20, 89
Royal Mail, 168
Runnymede Trust, 89
rural constituencies, 209-15
safe seats, low turnout in, 181-86
Saga Magazine, xvii
salience of issues, *see* issues.
Sanders, David, 25, 240, 324
Saunders, Michael, xvii
Scargill, Arthur, 245
school, Labour campaign launch in, 50-51
schools. *See also* education
Schroder Salomon Smith Barney, xvii, 314
Scotland
    devolution, 228-30
    identification with Britain, 89-90
    image abroad, 89
    polls in, 244, 295-97
Scotland on Sunday, 295-96
Scotsman, The
    ICM polls for, 46, 105, 229, 244
Scottish Opinion Ltd, 244, 295-96
Scottish Parliament, 35, 45, 47, 64, 105, 228, 229,
    230
    elections to, 67
seat projections from voting polls, 290-5
Section 2(a). See Section 28
Section 28, 105, 106, 219
Seddon, Mark, 237
Select Committees, 51
self-selecting polls, 300
sex
    and political self-dentification, 130-32
    voting behaviour by, 199-204
Shakespeare, William, 323
share prices, 24
    manipulation by false rumours of polls, 285
Sharpe, Graham, 237
Sheffield Hillsborough, 210
Shrimsley, Robert, 164, 165
'shy Tories', xii-xiii, 267, 268-73, 277-79, 293-94,
    327
single European currency. *See* Europe
Sky News, 287, 322
sleaze, 17, 57-60, 66
Smith, John, 196
Smith, Nicole, xvii
social class. *See* class
social democrat, self-description of political values,
    126-34
Social Democratic Party (SDP), 253
Socioconsult, 91, 93

Socio-Political Activism, vi, 117, 118
Somerton & Frome, 88
Spears, Britney, 154
Spectator, 237, 325
spending, public, 23, 54, 55, 56, 96, 97, 98, 99, 172,
    229, 310
spin doctors, xii, 6, 15, 48, 50, 51, 52
Spink, Bob, 183
'spiral of silence', *see* 'shy Tories'
Steel, David, 227, 253
Stevens, John, 237
Stewart, Marianne, 240
Stirling, 296, 297
stock market, 24
    manipulation by false rumours of polls, 285
Stockdale, J., 270
Stokes, Donald, 117
Stothard, Peter, xvii
straw polls, 301
Straw, Jack, 18, 89
Sullivan, Colleen, 275
Summerskill, Edith, 234
Sun, The, xvii, 37, 52, 133-34, 153-65
    MORI surveys for, 17, 18, 67, 120, 186, 216,
        221, 305
    phone-in polls, 301, 302
Sunday Business, 134, 157, 302
Sunday Express, 156-62
Sunday Herald, 219
Sunday Mail, 159
Sunday Mirror, 134, 152, 156-61, 303
Sunday People, 134, 156-61
    NOP surveys for, 207
Sunday Post, 159
Sunday Telegraph, xvii, 133, 152, 156-62, 271, 286
    MORI surveys for, 32, 33, 34, 35, 41, 73, 74,
        99, 101, 146-47, 149, 179, 203, 207, 216,
        222, 223, 225, 318
Sunday Times, 51, 133-34, 156-61, 270, 287
    MORI surveys for, 249
    NOP surveys for, 72, 87, 98, 99, 151, 243, 246
supermarkets, voting in, 191
switching and churning, 13
    trends 1979-2001, 14
System Three, 229, 244, 295
tactical voting, 65, 177, 222, 225, 226, 266, 294
Talk Radio, 302
targeting of campaign activities, 9, 167, 168
Tatchell, Peter, 245
Tatton, 213
tax, 23, 32, 33, 34, 81, 96, 97, 98, 99, 102, 128,
    129, 306

as election issue, 30, 83, 84, 101, 207, 228
Conservative policy on, 64, 95-100
effect on result of 1992 and 1997 elections, xii, 96, 327
further increases expected, 306-307
importance as election issue, 29
perceived increases under Labour, 32-33, 95
petrol tax, 51-556
Tayside North, 296
team of leaders, 77-81
telephone canvassing, 166, 168, 216
telephone, voting by, 191
television
as source of political information, 147-49
coverage, content of, 151
television licences, free to over 75s, 207
Tesco, 323
Thatcher, Margaret, 42, 68, 95, 138, 139, 195, 202, 206, 317
Thatcherites, self-description of political values, 126-34
Thornton's, 302
Thrasher, Michael, 66, 188
time of decision, xiii, 14, 142, 223, 248
Times, The, xvii, 2, 36, 44, 50, 133, 143, 153-65, 209, 210, 221, 302
MORI surveys for, xi, xii, xvii, 5, 10, 11, 12, 22, 26, 30, 33, 36, 39, 40, 41, 51, 53, 55, 59, 60, 62, 69, 73, 74, 76, 77, 78, 79, 82, 83, 96, 99, 119, 120, 121, 124, 125, 136, 137, 139, 144, 151, 161, 182, 186, 188, 208, 215, 222, 223, 228, 239, 241, 243, 247, 251, 252, 254, 258, 259, 260, 261, 262, 264, 289, 291, 307, 313, 319
reporting of polls, 251, 253, 267, 289
Today programme, 183, 188
Torbay, 75
Townend, John, 82, 94
Toynbee, Polly, 180
trade unions, 307
as election issue, 30, 101, 228
members, voting by, 5
transport. *See* public transport
Travis, Alan, 45, 278, 293, 325, 326, 327
trial by jury, 35
Tribune, 237
trustworthiness, 57, 63, 119-21
truth, trusting to tell the, 119-20
turnout
at European elections in 1999, 66
by marginality of seat, 183
decisions not to vote made during campaign, 13
effect of devolution, 228
importance of voting, perceived, 113-16
in London Mayoral election, 48
non-voters predominantly Labour, 181-86
prediction from opinion polls, 124-26, 274-78
reasons for low turnout, 107-94
reasons for voting, 111-13
TV coverage
public satisfaction with scale of, 150
Twisk, Russell, xvii
UKIP, 13, 87-88, 250, 252, 287, 319
underdog effect, 179-80, 248, 278-9, 326-27
unemployment
as election issue, 26, 30, 31, 83, 101, 228
of young people, government record on, 32-33
uniform swing, 291
values
political self-identification, 126-34
importance to voters, 7
'variometer' (ICM/*Guardian*), 292-94
Vaz, Keith, 58
veracity, 119-20
video cassettes as campaigning tool, 172
volatility of public opinion, 13-15
difference between men and women, 203
voodoo polls, iii, 243, 244, 300-303, 323
Voter News Service (VNS), 282
voting, *see* turnout.
voting, alternative modes of, 190-93
Wales
devolution, 230
identification with Britain, 89-90
image abroad, 89
voting intention polls in, 244
see also Welsh Assembly.
Wales on Sunday, 230
Walker, Kirsty, 164
Waller, Robert, xv, xvii, 267
Walters, Simon, xvii
Warren, Robert, xvii
Watford, 210
Watson, Roland, 63, 164
Watt, Nicholas, 75, 164, 165
Waugh, Paul, 163, 164
weather, effect on voting, 265
Webster, Philip, xvii, 44, 164
Welsh Assembly, 35, 46, 47, 64, 228
elections to, 67, 181
West Fulham by-election (1938), 234
Western Mail, 230, 244
Weston-super-Mare, 88
Wheeler, Stuart, xi, 62

Whelan, Charlie, 217
White, Michael, 45, 163, 164
Whiteley, Paul, 240
why people vote, 111
Widdecombe, Ann, 18, 77, 317-19
Wilby, Peter, 237
William Hill, 237
Wilson, Harold, 15, 19, 28, 38, 43, 195, 206, 300, 313
Winning, Cardinal Thomas, 219
winter fuel payments for pensioners, 207
Winter of Discontent, 52
women
    political identification of, 130-32
    voting behaviour of, 199
Women's Institute, Blair speech to, 2, 43
Worcester, Robert M.
    as Labour private pollster 1969-88, 7
    not Labour's private pollster any more, 287
    predictions for 2001 election, xi, 2-3, 108, 237-38
word of mouth campagning, 136
working class. *See* class
World Cup, 15
Wybrow, Robert, 19
"You paid the taxes", 34, 96-97
yougov, 243, 323
young offenders, government record on, 32-33
Younger, Sam, xvii
Zinoviev Letter, 158